Rural-Urban Migration in China

This book attempts to document and analyse the complicated role new media play in the adaptation and integration of China's new generation of migrant workers.

By analysing the interviews and observations of more than 500 migrant workers under the age of 25 between 2010 and 2015, the author tries to understand how new media shape the experiences of this significant group of people at different stages of their lives. This study profiles the daily life of this new generation of migrant workers and examines the intricate connections between media and the reconstruction of migrant workers' identity, as well as their urban life adaptation and social inclusion. Not only is their interaction with new media a key factor in decisions to migrate to the city in the first place, but it continues to play a crucial role in how their outlook on life, sense of identity, lifestyle, personal relationships, and aspirations change as they navigate their new environment.

These findings reveal the impact of new media on China's accelerating urbanization and modernization. This book will be of interest to students and scholars of contemporary China studies, and those who are interested in the urbanization of China in general.

Dr Zheng Xin is Professor at the School of Journalism and Communication, Nanjing University, China. He has researched extensively in the fields of communication sociology, rural communication studies, youth culture, and applied communication. He has published more than 50 articles, and received a number of awards, including China's Ministry of Education's New Century Distinguished Scholar Award.

China Perspectives

The *China Perspectives* series focuses on translating and publishing works by leading Chinese scholars, writing about both global topics and China-related themes. It covers Humanities & Social Sciences, Education, Media and Psychology, as well as many interdisciplinary themes.

This is the first time any of these books have been published in English for international readers. The series aims to put forward a Chinese perspective, give insights into cutting-edge academic thinking in China, and inspire researchers globally.

To submit proposals, please contact the Taylor & Francis Publisher for the China Publishing Programme, Lian Sun (Lian.Sun@informa.com)

Titles in media communication currently include:

Communication and Community in the New Media Age
Wang Bin

Cultural Expression and Subjectivity of Chinese Peasants
Sha Yao

The Nanjing Massacre and the Making of Mediated Trauma
Hongtao LI and Shunming HUANG

Environmental Risk Communication in China
Actors, Issues, and Governance
Jia Dai, Fanxu Zeng

Documentaries and China's National Image
Chen Yi

Rural-Urban Migration in China
The Impact of New Media
Zheng Xin

For more information, please visit www.routledge.com/China-Perspectives/book-series/CPH

Rural-Urban Migration in China

The Impact of New Media

Zheng Xin

Routledge
Taylor & Francis Group

LONDON AND NEW YORK

Sponsored by the Chinese Fund for the Humanities and Social Sciences (No. 19WXWB001).

First published in English 2023
by Routledge
4 Park Square, Milton Park, Abingdon, Oxon OX14 4RN

and by Routledge
605 Third Avenue, New York, NY 10158

Routledge is an imprint of the Taylor & Francis Group, an informa business

English Version by permission of Social Sciences Academic Press (China)

British Library Cataloguing-in-Publication Data
A catalogue record for this book is available from the British Library

Library of Congress Cataloging-in-Publication Data
Names: Zheng, Xin, 1973– author.
Title: Rural-Urban Migration in China : the Impact of New Media / Zheng Xin.
Other titles: Jin cheng. English
Description: 1 Edition. | New York, NY : Routledge, 2023. | Series: China perspectives | Includes bibliographical references and index.
Identifiers: LCCN 2022038689 (print) | LCCN 2022038690 (ebook) | ISBN 9781032430850 (hardback) | ISBN 9781032431307 (paperback) | ISBN 9781003365785 (ebook)
Subjects: LCSH: Rural-urban migration—China. | Migrant labor—China. | Social integration—China. | Social media—China—Influence.
Classification: LCC HB2114.A3 Z47951413 2023 (print) | LCC HB2114. A3 (ebook) | DDC 307.2/40951—dc23/eng/20220815
LC record available at https://lccn.loc.gov/2022038689
LC ebook record available at https://lccn.loc.gov/2022038690

ISBN: 978-1-032-43085-0 (hbk)
ISBN: 978-1-032-43130-7 (pbk)
ISBN: 978-1-003-36578-5 (ebk)

DOI: 10.4324/9781003365785

Typeset in Times New Roman
by Apex CoVantage, LLC

Contents

1 Introduction: Exploratory Communication Studies on How the New Generation of Migrant Workers Adapts to Urban Life   1

2 Media Mirror Image: The New Generation of Rural Migrant Workers' Imaginary City Life   16

3 My Mediatized "Looking-glass Self": Identity Construction Among the New Generation of Rural Migrant Workers   53

4 Media-driven Planning for Life Among the New Generation of Rural Migrant Workers   85

5 Escaping Isolated Islands: Interpersonal Communication of the New Generation of Migrant Workers   119

6 "Opening the Lock and Scaling the Wall": Information Literacy Among the New Generation of Migrant Workers   146

7 The Media as Capital: Continuing Education Among the New Generation of Migrant Workers   174

8 Media Support: Professional Adaptation Among the New Generation of Migrant Workers   203

9 Media Experience: The Leisure Life of the New Generation of Migrant Workers   231

10 Blending in With City Lives Through Consumption   257

vi *Contents*

11 Ruptures and Bridges: Cultural Identity Among
     Rural Migrant Workers   286

      References   321
      Index   329

1 Introduction

Exploratory Communication Studies on How the New Generation of Migrant Workers Adapts to Urban Life

Since the launch of the Chinese economic reform in 1978, people living in the countryside have been leaving their hometowns in search of work in cities, resulting in the emergence of a new population known as "migrant workers" in China. As older migrant workers pass their prime, a new generation now makes up the largest share of China's urban labour force.

In contrast to their older counterparts that engaged in gradual circular migration, this generation of off-farm workers are bound to migrate to cities from the moment they are born. They follow in their parents' footsteps with the high expectation of improving their lives. To this end, they are swept up in the fast-paced transformation of the Chinese society, becoming a mere statistic in the country's ever-growing urban population. The formation and development of this phenomenon in which young people move from rural areas to cities are inextricably linked with the historical backdrop against which it takes place.

China has undergone extensive transformation since the mid-1990s. Being part of that era, these migrant workers have been deeply influenced by the political, economic, and social changes in the country.

One of the major changes that influenced new-generation migrant workers is the gradual disappearance of the rural-urban dichotomy. Since the establishment of the People's Republic of China, the government has adopted a household registration system that has strictly separated rural and urban populations. This system has divided the entire population into two fundamental groups, namely rural and urban households. As a result of this division, people with different household registration status received different welfare benefits. Therefore, this household registration system and its corresponding measures formed the institutional basis of a rural-urban dichotomy in terms of social welfare distribution. The strict dichotomy largely impeded off-farm workers from freely moving between countryside and cities.

However, the original dichotomy in the country has started to transform into a trichotomy in which migrant workers emerge as a vital force in contemporary Chinese society (Li, 2004), particularly since the start of the 21st century. To better understand the social and historical background, the series of social structure changes that have occurred in China since the 1990s has to be considered. One of the most crucial changes witnessed in terms of social structure is the breaking

DOI: 10.4324/9781003365785-1

down of the rural-urban dichotomy (Sun, 2003), providing a new generation of migrant workers with the freedom of moving between cities and countryside.

Another remarkable change is the advancement of a market economy and foreign trade in China, which created numerous jobs and living opportunities for migrant workers in cities. Ever since the end of the 1990s, China has achieved several socioeconomic goals that attract global attention. An increase in the opening up of markets, internationalization, promotion of economic reforms, and expansion of foreign trade has enabled the government to provide job opportunities to migrant workers through a market-oriented system. Particularly, the cheap labour, state-of-the-art infrastructures, and enormous consumption potential of the coastal regions of eastern China have turned the country into an ideal destination for global companies to relocate their manufacturing base. Consequently, a new generation of migrant workers has set out to live and work in cities, as the market demand of those workers has witnessed a gradual increase.

Finally, the Chinese government has put forward favourable policies to ensure that migrant workers can live a better-off life in major cities. The increasing emphasis placed on their welfare and benefits has substantially improved their living conditions in urban areas, thus offering them greater freedom and development opportunities. To this end, the General Office of the State Council promulgated a No. 1 Central Document (hereafter referred to as "the Document") in 2003. In 2004, the Document recognized that migrant workers constituted an essential part of the Chinese manufacturing workers and in turn requested that local governments improve their employment conditions. In 2006, the State Council proposed the "Opinions on Solving Problems Related to Migrant Workers", which presented a strategy to solve problems encountered by migrant workers as part of building socialism with Chinese characteristics. In the second half of 2008, a national policy tailored for the endowment social insurance of migrant workers came into effect. In 2010, the Document released by the State Council, titled "Proposals on Strengthening the Efforts of Coordinative Urban-Rural Development and Further Consolidating the Basis of Agricultural and Rural Development", used the term "new-generation migrant worker" for the first time. This document requested that specific measures be implemented to solve problems related to new-generation migrant workers. The aforementioned progressive policy reforms highlight the emphasis placed by the central government on migrant workers, particularly of the new generation, as expressed by the mobilization of policy for the improvement of their living conditions and development in cities.

Although the Chinese society has held an open and inclusive attitude as aforementioned, giving migrant workers better chances to live and develop a career in cities, they are still faced with countless impediments as an underprivileged group. The said policy reforms may not provide those workers with a definite chance to better adapt to and integrate into urban life. Compared with their counterparts growing up in urban areas, these groups of workers are hindered by disadvantages including low education levels, low incomes, less employee benefits and welfare, and insufficient social safeguards. The loopholes in the current social policies have had a hindering effect on their individual development and adaptation to city life. Moreover, the increasing level of labour market saturation and discrimination among some urban residents remains unsolved. Therefore, there is still a long way to go to break the rural-urban dichotomy and provide a fair chance for those workers to work and live as their urban counterparts.

Taken together, helping new-generation migrant workers to adapt to and integrate into urban life is an issue to be resolved. These problems will determine the country's future social transformation. In this regard, the Chinese academia and society have placed their focus on investigating the social role, lifestyle, values, and sociopsychological changes experienced by this group and providing tools for them to better adapt to city life and urban society.

1. How Migrant Workers Adapt in an Urban Environment: A Hot Issue of Great Social Concern

When adapting to urban life and blending in this new environment, migrant workers must continuously adjust and change their working patterns, social interactions, and other sociopsychological aspects of life after their arrival. The *Sociology Dictionary* defines adaptation behaviours as "behaviours adopted by an individual to adapt to a social environment" (Wang, 1988). Through socialization, individuals understand their rights and duties in society. Therefore, they develop the knowledge, skills, values, and personalities that meet social standards, enabling them to behave in a way conforming to social standards during social interactions and when taking actions. By contrast, those who cannot favourably adapt to a social environment may be confused. Accordingly, migrant workers' adaptation to city life can be defined by their continuing socialization in a new urban environment.

Various theories have been proposed and extensive research has been conducted in Western countries on the adaptation problems of migrants and mobile population in general. In classic urban sociology, the problem of adaptation to city life among migrants was identified a long time ago. For example, Park addressed cultural maintenance and assimilation among foreign migrants after they enter cities. Mendras conducted research on the end of small-scale peasant economy and urbanization of farmers. Wirth and Gans analysed urbanism and urban life. Thomas and Znaniecki explored the survival resources of Polish migrants in US cities. Goldscheider discussed the adaptation process of migrants in cities in developing countries. Urban anthropologists have focused on the adaptability to urban life of farmers from the countryside, particularly those of minorities. For example, Mangi et al. studied illegal structures and the so-called outlander regions and slums in Africa. Anderson and Little observed voluntary associations founded by farmers with the aim of adapting to urban life. Despite the differences between migrants in said studies and Chinese migrant workers discussed herein, those findings contribute to the research on Chinese migrant workers' urban life adaptation.

The adaptation to city life among migrant workers has long been a popular research topic in disciplines such as sociology, demographics, and economics, and numerous exceptional insights have been provided. Li (1996), Zhou (1998), and Jiang (2003) focused on defining the process undertaken when passing from a traditional, rural, and isolated lifestyle to a modern, urban, and opened one among the workers who moved from the countryside to cities as well as the acquisition of modernity characteristics. Zhu (2002) and Wang and Zhang (2004) argued that urbanization, resocialization, and even assimilation are crucial elements for migrant workers to become urban residents. The researchers proposed three aspects associated with urban life adaptation of migrant workers, namely the economic, social, and psychological aspects. Wang (2006), Chen (2007), and Xu (2007c) meticulously investigated the circumstances under which migrant workers cannot actually blend into urban life, resulting in incomplete socialization. Migrant workers in cities have also been defined as "double outlanders" in that that these workers, drifting from rural to urban borders, encounter situations of semi-urbanization, illusory urbanization, and alienated settlement.

Focusing on social interactions and conflicts, Li (1995), Wang (2001), Pan (2007a), Guo and Chu (2004), and Zhou, M. (2004) identified problems associated with rural-urban integration and urban life adaptation using concepts of social conflict, social identity, social exclusion, social distance, and cultural adaptation. Furthermore, Qu (2001), Li (2003), and Fu (2006) used analytical frameworks of social network, social capital, and lifeworld to examine the adaptability to urban life of the new generation of migrant workers. Other relevant studies have described and analysed the current impediments, content, safeguards, trends, and measures of urban life adaptation among Chinese migrant workers from systemic, economic, legal, and political aspects. In brief, the aforementioned studies have laid a solid theoretical and empirical foundation for contemporary research on the urban life adaptation of new-generation migrant workers.

However, previous studies have mostly focused on sociological analysis, whereas the journalism and communication perspectives have been ignored. These studies have also largely overlooked the effect of media and communication on migrant workers' adaptation to city life.

In recent years, media technology has seen rapid advances, improving the access to media in China. In cities, information from various sources such as television, newspapers, magazines, and the Internet can be accessed by individuals of any social status anytime and anywhere, which is closely aligned with urban lifestyles. Migrant workers also live in this environment providing highly advanced media communications. Notably, the external world presented by mass media is substantially different from the rural world where those workers originally come from. Consequently, the information transmitted by mass media is likely to exert a strong effect on the workers. This inevitably influences their urban experiences and cognition, thus triggering changes in their thinking mode and values, accelerating socialization, and helping these individuals adapt to urban life (Xu, 2007c). Considering the great penetration and influence of modern mass media, the relationship between Chinese migrant workers at the urbanization stage and mass media is undoubtedly an important topic in communication studies.

In the research field of journalism and communication, existing research on migrant workers in China mainly focuses on the following aspects.

First, researchers have conducted textual analysis on images of migrant workers represented by news media. Chen (2004) performed a text analysis on news reports depicting migrant workers with unpaid wages. Li and Qiao (2005) studied the social conditions of migrant workers as reported by the media. Li (2006) conducted a narrative analysis of related news reports in contemporary urban newspapers. Wang (2007) also reviewed reports depicting the image of migrant workers in *People's Daily*, a mainstream party-run newspaper.

Second, research has drawn attention and criticized media's discrimination and bias against migrant workers. Xu (2008) argued that the bias and indifference to migrant workers as shown in news reports reflect the existing discrimination among different social groups. Huang (2009) indicated that media tend to demonize migrant workers in news reports. Such demonization implies a discourse of violence, revealing of the power asymmetry between city residents and rural migrant workers. Xu et al. (2009) also examined migrant workers' experiences in a mass media environment and the deeper reasons for the difficulties that they have encountered.

Third, scholars have performed surveys on the media exposure and media literacy of migrant workers from rural areas. By conducting a questionnaire survey, Tao (2003) examined the media exposure of migrant workers in the Xuhui District of Shanghai City. Tang (2005) profiled migrant workers' media exposure in Nanjing and six surrounding cities. Liang and Wang (2007) and Li (2009) published empirical studies on the media use and media information access among migrant workers in Changsha, capital city of Hunan province, and several districts of Beijing.

Fourth, research has focused on the power of discourse and freedom of media expression among underprivileged groups. Using the "Suicide Show" phenomenon of migrant workers in China as an example, Wei (2004) discussed the relationship between mass media and migrant workers' right to speak. Taking into account social stratification, Duan (2004) investigated the right to control and use media among an underprivileged group of migrant workers. Li (2005) conducted an empirical study on the relationship between news media and underprivileged groups in pre-existing communication studies in Western countries. Zhou, H. (2004) and Yang (2005) examined migrant workers' discourse on self-interest and their relationship with the media.

Fifth, the influence of mass media on the belief system and socialization of migrant workers has been discussed. Tao (2004) conducted an empirical survey on migrant workers' beliefs and intuitions on consumption, defences of rights, marriage, and Shanghai residency status. Wang (2004) assessed the effects of mass media on optimizing migrant workers' living conditions during their urbanization process. A discussion on the continuing socialization of migrant workers guided by mass media was also performed from the perspective of communication studies (Yang & Xie, 2008). However, the findings of studies on this aspect are considerably limited.

In addition, scholars have analysed the communication phenomenon and effect on rural-urban migration of workers from the perspective of interpersonal communication. Studies on such basis have supplemented research on the relationship between mass media and migrant workers' adaptation to city life.

Although journalism and communication scholars have already done fruitful research on Chinese migrant workers or even topics related to the *Three Rural Issues* (i.e., agriculture, rural areas, and farmers), past studies are overwhelmingly focusing on theoretical analysis, detailed descriptions and the discussions of countermeasures. The empirical studies and studies proposing innovative concepts and theories are still large gaps to fill.

After reviewing research on migrant workers' adaptation to city life in all disciplines over the last two decades, we detected a certain absence of communication studies. In the mid-1990s, this critical social phenomenon caused scholarly attention in other disciplines, whereas communications studies did not investigate this topic until 2003, the year when studies on migrant workers became trendy under the guidance of national policies. The absence of communication studies at an earlier stage resulted in a weak basis in this line of research. Moreover, in the next decade, the research scope of related communication studies was limited to general areas defined by mass media. Specifically, most studies only relied on image construction in media texts, and few of them discussed specific communication patterns and social reality, consequently limiting the research scope. That is, the depth and width of communication studies are insufficient compared with those in other disciplines. This problem remains today and has not been adequately solved.

Notably, the majority of studies have been focusing on the functions of news reports, yet relatively few have investigated the effect of mass media on modernity and urbanization process of migrant workers (Zheng, 2011b). Regarding the research content, the focus is on the communication patterns of mass media and media has been considered as an inseparable research subject. This viewpoint has considerably limited research subjects to concrete forms of medium. Consequently, relevant studies have yet to incorporate a broad communication environment or various communication constituents in the process of migrant workers' adaptation to city life.

2. Focusing on Media: Understanding the Urban Life Experiences of Migrant Workers From a Communication Perspective

Migrant workers' adaptation to city life does not only mark human migration from rural to urban areas but also represents cultural migration in the sense of modernization as well as the transformation process from traditional to modern values, psychological patterns, and behavioural patterns (Zhu, 2002). Exhibiting great differences in aspects such as living environment, cultural literary, and expectation of urban life with their parents, this generation of migrant workers have developed distinct off-farm employment motivations, intentions of urban residency, levels of active adaptation to city life, as well as communication opportunities and skills with city residents. Improved knowledge base, mobility, awareness of modern civilization, and the concept of protecting their own rights all help them better adapt to urban life and accelerate the integration process.

Therefore, when exploring their adaptation to city life, excessive attention does not need to be paid to macroeconomic structural and institutional factors. Rather, migrant workers' capacity or, as rational human beings, establishing their living environment and sense-making should not be downplayed. Similarly, there is no need to overemphasize migrant workers' dependence on and linear relationship with urban civilization, modernity, and urban dwellers (as a reference group). The essential effects of field factors, including off-farm workers' rural life memories, urban life experiences and current situations, and public opinions, merit scholarly attention. Moreover, negative factors such as the dichotomy-generated conflicts, disputes between rural and urban dwellers, and social stereotypes that impede migrant workers from engaging in urbanization should not be exaggerated. By exaggerating said factors and aspects, we might neglect the frequent contact between migrant workers and urban environments (including the media environment) and their positive interactions as well as novel socialization powers conducive to the modernization of those workers, such as their awareness of urban life and capital acquisition in this information era. Because of the rapid advancement of mass media and improvement of communication channels, the motivations of media use, media consumption capacity, information acquisition channels, and media literacy among the new generation of migrant workers begins to change. Emerging media, including the Internet and mobile phones, have inarguably changed the values of migrant workers, such as their perceptions, modernity formulation, urbanization, continuing socialization, and identity. Compared with other factors affecting their adaptation to city life, the mass media are expected to play an increasingly important role.

Numerous factors affect the adaptation to city life of migrant workers. However, previous studies have been confined to the mere discussion of mass media and tend to overlook the far-reaching influence of media in a broader spectrum. Therefore, this study intends to, based on the premise that the systematic variable is controlled for, consider "media" as a variable and examine the effects of media on migrant workers' socialization, urbanization, and modernization.

Therefore, communication studies on city life adaptation of new-generation migrant workers should not be limited to the virtual world represented in media text analysis and conventional mass media. Instead, they should turn to observing the real world and regard media as a critical power that can change and reshape a society. We must acknowledge that adaptation to city life is an inclusive concept involving multiple factors, aspects, and variables. It is necessary to conduct studies from a systemic perspective considering all-inclusive elements. Researchers should also identify and compare the effects of media by observing urban adaptation indicators before and after migrant workers enter cities and portraying the process of adaptation to city life and urban survival of new-generation migrant workers (Zheng, 2011b).

To begin with, studies measuring indicators that are closely related to adaptation to city life of new-generation migrant workers should be conducted.

Specifically, studies comparing the effects of indicators before and after migrant workers enter cities should be reviewed. These indicators include their expectation, identity, rural life memories, urban life experiences, intention of urban residency, and sense of identity and belonging to a city. Moreover, researchers should keep an eye on the economic, social, and cultural aspects and explore the effects of mass media on migrant workers' use of and satisfaction towards information services, power of discourse, social networking and cultural capital, modernity growth, and urbanism acquisition, along with elements of adaptation to city life (from a superficial to a deep level) such as their working patterns, lifestyles, and values. Media environments associated with the adaptation to city life of new-generation migrant workers also merit investigation. In particular, studies on the ecology of media to which migrant workers are frequently exposed (e.g., support of media environments for adaptation to city life and communication problems caused by different types of media) should be taken into consideration. Furthermore, approaches to migrant workers' adaptation to city life should be verified. From the sociological perspective and based on relevant indicators of adaptation to city life and specific media ecology, studies should conduct a scenario analysis on the daily activities, living spaces, and survival approaches of new-generation migrant workers according to their sex, education level, occupation, place of origin, and background during the processes of successful and unsuccessful adaptation. Therefore, the image, life, workplace, and approaches to adaptation to city life of younger migrant workers should be clearly presented (Fu & Jiang, 2007).

Scholars have proposed that a perspective of pragmatic sociology can yield novel empirical evidence, through which new theories can be developed. Specifically, pragmatic sociology emphasizes the stance, vision, and experience of research participants and the identification of empirical evidence. By focusing on the historical and factual implications derived from the daily life and behaviour of typical actors, researchers avoid neglecting the agency of and action strategies made by typical members of the society. In other words, future studies should focus on lively migrant workers who actually exist instead of abstracting their images presented through demographic statistics. Adaptation to city life does not symbolize a process with clear boundaries but a dynamic and continuous flow that is mainly defined by the life experiences of people. During adaptation to city life, life experiences per se can most genuinely reflect social facts. Therefore, going back to experiences and facts is necessary. Researchers should understand and analyse migrant workers' (actors') daily life and the connotation and meaning of their work and strive to identify interactions between migrant workers, as individuals, and structural and institutional factors. By observing individuals' living experiences and logic of practice, scholars can grasp those individuals' attributes, social processes, and social facts.

When studying the adaptation to city life of new-generation migrant workers, we should not only emphasize the outcomes or their static status at a specific time point but also consider such adaptation as a dynamic process. This process involves interactions of the government, media, social organizations, urban dwellers, and new-generation migrant workers, as well as the construction of factors affecting the relationship between mass media and new-generation migrant workers. This demonstrates the agency, practicability, and sense-making capacity of all participants involved. Therefore, only by adopting the perspective of pragmatic sociology can researchers accurately observe the movement, employment conditions, and life of new-generation migrant workers. This will also help transform the originally abstract images into their logic of practice, hence providing greater insight in this field of study.

To sum up, studies on migrant workers' urban adaption conducted from the communication perspective should (1) regard their daily media use and living practice as empirical research topics; (2) detach themselves from paradigms of structural, action, and institutional theories; (3) use sociological imagination and rhetoric to understand the modernity establishment and logic of survival among the migrant workers; and (4) explore the dynamic and interactive mutual deconstruction and reconstruction of media and new-generation migrant workers.

Because mass media has greatly influenced human modernity through its popularity and extensive development, studying the adaptation to city life of new-generation migrant workers from the communication perspective is required. Inkeles and Smith (1992) once indicated in a famous statement that mass media provide information on multiple aspects of modern life to human beings, open a door for humans to create new concepts, present new behaviour patterns, inspire diverse discussions and opinions, and stimulate and strengthen expectations of education mobility. All of these elements can lead to a greater modernity in those who are willing to accept external effects (Inkeles & Smith, 1992). In the past two decades, media environments in the country have undergone extreme changes. As a result, the motivation of media utilization, consumption capacity, information acquisition channel, and media literacy of these younger migrants have also been altered. Living in a media environment where information transmission technology is highly developed, these workers are inevitably influenced on multiple aspects such as their values, identity, modernity formulation, urbanization, and socialization. Thus, media has become a deciding factor affecting the urban adaption of these young migrant workers.

As such, a communication perspective is unique not only because it helps depict the group image in a media-constructed virtual world but also because it helps rediscover the essential role of media as a strong force that stimulates the socialization and modernity of migrant workers. This phenomenon is witnessed in the context where new-generation migrant workers are frequently exposed to media information and positively interact with the media. Such perspective also reveals the effects of media on migrant workers during the urbanization and modernization process. The significance of such studies lies in two main aspects. First, they provide practical guidance to recognize and solve major problems in terms of urban adaption of new-generation migrant workers in the country's urbanization phase. These studies, by confirming the relationship between media and migrant workers' adaption to urban life, can determine the effects of media on these workers' identity, cultural adaptation, and social blending. The subsequent findings can thus provide valuable reference for "allowing new-generation migrant workers to better blend in cities and enabling urban dwellers to better accept these migrant workers", as set by the Chinese government. Second, empirical research centring adaptation to city life of migrants and media use effects on underprivileged groups, by turning their focus on the daily life practices of these individuals, can help expand the area of communication studies on Chinese migrant workers. Furthermore, these studies contribute to the improvement and development of research methods and theories in rural communication studies in China.

3. Qualitative Research: Depicting the Daily Lives of the New Generation of Migrant Workers

Current studies on the new generation of migrant workers mostly collected data from questionnaire surveys, content analysis, or text analysis. These methods are susceptible to oversimplification. In particular, the abstract images of migrant workers described through demographic statistics are likely to lose sight of their stance and vision, or underestimate the essence of empirical evidence. Adaptation to city life does not symbolize a process with clear boundaries but a dynamic and continuous flow that is mainly defined by the life experiences of these people (Fu & Jiang, 2007). During their adaptation to urban life, life experiences per se can most genuinely reflect social facts. As such, qualitative research facilitates the meticulous observation of these workers' migration, employment, and life. Only by transforming the originally abstract images of off-farm workers into real characters who act according to the logic of practice, can scholars overcome limitations of existing research and broaden and deepen the research scope.

Qualitative research refers to a comprehensive exploration of adaptation to city life of the new generation of migrant workers using various data collection methods under naturalistic circumstances (Chen, 2002). Such research requires researchers and participants to interact in order to enlighten interpretive understanding of participants' adaptation behaviours and relevant meaning construction. A specific method commonly used is the process-event analysis (Sun, 2000), which considers the adaptation of new-generation migrant workers as a dynamic process. By performing a panel study on the dynamics of those workers' adaptation to urban life, researchers can experience the real urban life as well as the mentality of migrant workers through active participation. Therefore, researchers can observe the practical patterns of interactions between media and migrant workers and gain a fresh insight into the comprehensive situation of such interactions.

The aforementioned panel study refers to a follow-up investigation on the entire linear or circular process when new-generation migrant workers leave their hometowns, enter cities, and either reside in those cities or return to their hometowns. This investigation provides an understanding and record of each spatial change and positive or negative subtle changes in indicators during urban life adaptation until notable changes are observed. These indicators include the survival strategies, lifestyle, concepts, identity, social capital, social networks, rural memories, urban experiences, cultural activities, and social relationships of those workers. The effect of media on these changes can also be measured.

The participants included in this study are the new generation of migrant workers. However, scholars are divided on how to define the term "new-generation migrant workers". Wang (2003) first proposed this concept in 2001 and stated later in 2003 that the term had two layers of meanings. Firstly, it refers to individuals from rural areas aged 25 or younger that migrated to cities to seek jobs or business opportunities in the 1990s. This group of off-farm workers exhibits evident differences in terms of social experience compared with their counterparts of the previous generation. Secondly, these younger migrant workers have a higher education level and less experience in farming compared with their senior counterparts, implying a fundamental change in the motivation for leaving their home (Wang, 2003). Herein, we defined the new generation of migrant workers based on their age. Given that Wang proposed this definition more than ten years ago, the early generation of migrant workers is now over 30 years old and are entering middle age. The present study selected participants who were born between the early 1980s (the oldest new-generation migrant workers) and after 1995 (the youngest group of migrant workers). In other words, we selected migrant workers with a rural household registration status who were born after the 1980s (aged 16–36 years) and went to cities to find a job in the 1990s.

As aforementioned, this qualitative research attempted to rigorously observe the migration, employment, and life of the new-generation migrant workers and transform their originally abstract images to real characters of migrant workers by collecting and analysing empirical data (Chen, 2002). We chose this approach mainly because of its applicability to this study. By overcoming drawbacks such as excessive levels of abstraction and quantification among existing studies, this study aimed to depict the actual life and work of migrant workers as well as the logic of practice with which they act in specific contexts. To study their daily life experiences, questionnaire surveys and statistics may not draw a comprehensive picture of the participants and can easily overlook hidden logic (Fu & Jiang, 2007) that cannot be detected without detailed observation. Conversely, a qualitative research design has enabled us to obtain empirical materials that cannot be collected through quantitative methods. These materials comprehensively depict migrant workers' urban life experiences, and interactions with the participants also help us grasp a deeper understanding of the situation and process of urban life adaptation.

Indeed, qualitative research is similar to a broad umbrella comprising numerous branches. In this study, a detailed description of new-generation migrant workers, and of their self-experience and realities was a requisite for understanding their actual life practice. To achieve this goal, the research team conducted interviews because interview results tend to reveal deeper and more abundant perceptions of the participants. An interview is an activity in which a researcher asks questions to and has a conversation with an interviewee. It creates a research-oriented verbal conversation, during which the researcher collects (or constructs) first-hand data from the interviewee. Through an interview, the researcher is able to understand the interviewee's thoughts, including their values, feelings, behaviours, life experiences, and the relevant life incidents they have heard or witnessed, and their interpretation of these incidents. Therefore, a broad and comprehensive image of participants can be represented, allowing researchers to profoundly and meticulously describe an incident from multiple perspectives (Chen, 2002).

During the five-year research period, the researchers conducted field surveys on multiple occasions among participants in Nanjing, Changzhou, Suzhou, Shanghai, Hangzhou, Wenzhou, Yangzhou, and Nantong. During the process of empirical data collection, semi-structured in-depth interview and nonparticipant observation methods were adopted. In a semi-structured interview, researchers normally propose a rough interview outline and ask questions to interviewees according to their research design. However, this outline only serves as a reminder on content to be discussed during an interview. Researchers also actually encourage interviewees to raise questions and flexibly adjust the interview content based on some specific situation (Chen, 2002).

The migrant workers the researchers reached out to for an interview mostly worked in the service industry. Interviewees from the service industry work in open spaces (e.g., shopping malls, restaurants, bubble tea shops, hair salons, and nail salons), allowing the researchers to approach them by purchasing products or services from them. The researchers interviewed the participants by chatting with them at work or during a break. Such an approach is efficient and simple. The advancement of the service sector in urban areas has attracted a great number of young workers from the countryside, thus becoming a major choice for new-generation migrant workers. More importantly, migrant workers in the service sector exhibit more vivid characteristics and stronger demands of urban life adaption compared with their counterparts in construction and processing industries. Due to the openness of their life spaces and workplaces, migrant workers in the service sector are closely aligned with urban life and constantly interact with urban dwellers. Their cognitive beliefs, attitudes, behaviour, and sociopsychological status are profoundly influenced by the entire urban environment, including the media environment that affects their adaptation to urban life. By contrast, because of their isolated life spaces and workplaces, workers from industries such as construction are only involved in physical movement during their rural-to-urban migration. That is, urban society exerts relatively little influence on their lifestyle. It was also difficult for us to observe and describe the influence of media on their adaptation to urban life. Therefore, participants working in the service sector were more suitable for this study.

In addition to the data collected from the aforementioned places, we gathered data through some other supplementary approaches. For example, migrant workers tend to live in the same neighbourhoods. Therefore, we visited their neighbourhoods to interview target participants. Unlike their older counterparts, new-generation migrant workers are more often exposed to new media and frequently use communication tools such as instant messaging applications (e.g., Tencent QQ) and social networking services (e.g., Weibo and WeChat). Moreover, they tend to form groups of friends on the Internet, hence another effective approach to search for interviewees.

The research team has built amiable relationships and engaged in long-term and frequent interactions with the interviewees, thus accomplishing a panel study on the dynamics of urban life adaptation to the greatest extent. Although the researchers could not fully engage with the migrant workers because of their identity and unique working and living environments, they could, by being outsiders, conduct nonparticipant observations on the migrant workers' daily life behaviours and manners. Therefore, objective data (e.g., clothes, behaviours, habits, working status, and leisure activities) were collected, serving as a supplement for research analysis.

The research team interviewed and observed more than 500 migrant workers between 2010 and 2015, from which the recorded data formed the primary empirical reference of this study. By processing and analysing the collected first-hand data, this study profiles the daily life of the new generation of migrant workers and examines the complicated connections between media and the reconstruction of migrant workers' identity as well as their urban life adaptation and social inclusion.

References

Chen, F. (2007). From isolation to adaptation: The culture transition of migrant workers in Chinese cities. *Journal of East China University of Science and Technology (Social Science Edition)*, *3*, 84–87.

Chen, H. (2004). Research on the relation between mass media and social marginal groups: A case analysis of news on wage arrears for migrant workers. *Journalistic University*, *4*, 6–10.

Chen, X. (2002). *Qualitative research in social sciences*. Educational Science Publishing House, 169, 171.

Duan, J. (2004). The division of social classes and the manipulation and use of media in China. *Journal of Xiamen University (Social Science Edition)*, *1*, 44–51.

Fu, P. (2006). Urban adaptability of young migrant workers: A perspective of sociology of practice. *Society*, *2*.

Fu, P., & Jiang, L. (2007). Limitations and breakthroughs in studies of migrant workers' integration into city life. *The World of Survey and Research*, *6*, 14–17.

Guo, X., & Chu, H. (2004). Rural to urban: An empirical study of social distance between migrant workers and urban residents. *Jianghai Academic Journal*, *3*, 91–98.

Huang, D. (2009). Demonizing and reproduction of power relations: A content analysis on news coverage of migrant workers. *Northwest Population Journal*, *3*, 35–40.

Inkeles, A., & Smith, D. (1992). *Becoming modern: Individual change in six developing countries*. China Renmin University Press.

Jiang, L. (2003). Urbanity & the adaptability of rural-to-migrant workers. *Social Science Research*, *5*.

Li, H. (2003). Strength of relationships & virtual community: A new perspective on rural migrant workers' research. In P. Li (Ed.), *An economical & sociological study of Chinese migrant workers*. Social Sciences Academic Press.

Li, H. (2009). *Rural communication and urban-rural integration: An empirical study of Beijing natives and rural migrant workers*. Social Sciences Academic Press.

Li, H., & Qiao, T. (2005). Stigmatization and labelling: The media image of migrant workers. *21st Century*, *7*.

Li, P. (1996). The social network and social status of migrant workers in China. *Sociological Research*, *4*, 42–52.

Li, Q. (1995). Emotions of rural-to-urban workers and social conflicts. *Sociological Research, 4*, 63–67.

Li, Q. (2004). *Rural-to-urban migrant workers and social stratification in China.* Social Sciences Academic Press.

Li, Y. (2005). News media and "the underprivileged" in western communication studies: A literature review. *Journalism & Communication, 2*, 48–55.

Li, Y. (2006). Portraying a heterogenous group of people: A narrative analysis of news coverage on "PIL" in China's urban newspapers. *Journalism & Communication, 13*(2), 2–14.

Liang, Y., & Wang, S. (2007). Migrant workers' access to public health information. *China National Conditions and Strength, 3*, 43–44.

Pan, Z. (2007a). Social exclusion and predicament of future development: An empirical study of migrant workers in China. *Zhejiang Social Science, 2*, 96–103.

Qu, J. (2001). Strength of relationships in real life: The life trajectory of rural migrants in Chinese cities. In L. Ke & Hanlin Li (Eds.), *Off-farm migrants in large Chinese cities.* Central Compilation & Translation Press.

Sun, L. (2000). Process-event analysis and the state-farmer relations in contemporary China. In *Tsinghua sociology review* (Special ed.). Lujiang Publishing House.

Sun, L. (2003). *Cleavage: The Chinese society since 1990s.* Social Sciences Academic Press.

Tang, X. (2005). *Mass media and rural-to-urban migrant workers*, PhD. Thesis. Nanjing Normal University.

Tao, J. (2003). Media exposure of rural migrant workers: A case study of Xuhui District in Shanghai. *Journalistic University, 4.*

Tao, J. (2004). A study on the influence of mass media on migrant workers' perceptions. *Journalism & Communication, 11*(2), 10–15.

Wang, C. (2001). The social recognition and integration of a new generation of rural migrants in China. *Sociological Research, 3.*

Wang, C. (2003). Social mobility and the change of social status of migrant workers. *Journal of Jiangsu Administration Institute, 4*, 51–56.

Wang, C. (2006). Watch out for rural migrant workers' "belief in fatalism". *Chinese Cadres Tribune, 5*, 1.

Wang, F. (2007). The relationship between mass media & migrant workers: A case study of People's Daily's coverage of rural migrant workers. *Research on Development, 1*, 45–48.

Wang, K. (Ed.). (1988). *Sociology dictionary.* Shandong People's Press, p. 352.

Wang, X. (2004). Mass media and the urbanization of rural migrants. *Journal of Wuhan University of Technology (Social Science Edition), 4*, 467–470.

Wang, Y., & Zhang, D. (2004). Re-socialization of migrant workers in the urbanization process. *Journal of China Agricultural University (Social Sciences Edition), 1*, 9–13.

Wei, S. (2004). Mass media and the discourse power of farmers: The case of rural migrant workers' suicidal jumping from high-rise Building. *Journalism & Communication, 2*, 16–20.

Xu, C. (2007c). Will the new arrivals settle down? A study on the adaptability of a new generation of migrant workers in Chinese cities. *South China Population, 4*(22), 52–59.

Xu, X. (2008). On media prejudice and discrimination in news coverage of rural migrant workers. *Journal of International Communication, 2*, 40–43.

Xu, X., Ren, M., & Wu, M. (2009). The media representation of rural migrant workers: Realities and causes. *Modern Communication-Journal of Communication University of China, 4*, 39–41.

Yang, D. (2005). Communication and the articulation of migrant workers' rights and interests. *Contemporary Communications*, *6*, 3.

Yang, S., & Xie, X. (2008). How does mass media guide the socialization of migrant workers? *Southeast Communication*, *9*, 35–37.

Zheng, X. (2011b). On the new generation of peasant workers' adaptation to city life: From the perspective of communication. *Nanjing Journal of Social Sciences*, *3*, 71–77.

Zhou, H. (2004). The media discourse of Chinese farmers and their access to mass media. *Press Circles*, *3*, 46–47.

Zhou, M. (2004). The culture adaptability and personal identification of retained young migrant workers in Chinese cities. *Society*, *5*, 4–11.

Zhou, X. (1998). The impact of migration and rural experience on the modality of off-farm workers in Chinese cities: A comparative study on two local communities in Beijing and Wenzhou City, Zhejiang Province. *Sociological Research*, *5*, 14.

Zhu, L. (2002). On the adaptability of rural-to-urban migrant workers. *Jianghai Academic Journal*, *6*, 82–88+206.

2 Media Mirror Image

The New Generation of Rural Migrant Workers' Imaginary City Life

The new generation of rural migrant workers grew up during China's reforms and opening up to the outside world. They differ from the older generation of rural migrant workers in that they have higher and different expectations regarding their work and their lives. The older generation of rural migrant workers invariably were "passing travellers" in the cities. They hoped to obtain wealth from the city which could not be gained living in rural areas, and thus enjoy a better life in the village. Other than this, they had no further expectations of life in the city. However, the new generation of rural migrant workers is different. The gradual enrichment of their material lives has caused the level of their needs to evolve from labouring on the edge of subsistence into a developmental mode. The advancement of mass media and telecommunications technology, along with higher levels of education, have enabled them to form pluralistic values and open-minded new ways of thinking, spurring their attraction to urban culture and the urban way of life.

The clash of the urban dream with the harsh realities of life in the city urgently demands that we pay greater attention to the inner world of the new generation of rural migrant workers. In fact, prior to coming to the city, this new generation of rural migrant workers imagined different scenarios of urban life. After entering the city, such imagined scenarios did not come to an end but rather continued to transform and extend themselves into richer and more variegated forms. Imagination is cognition formed when the brain combines and processes external information. Research on what the new generation of rural migrant workers imagine urban life to be is an ideal entry point for exploring the inner feelings and life-world of this group.

1. Before Entering the City: Formation of Imagined Urban Scenarios While Living in a Rural Environment

During the years since China's reforms and opening up to the world, rural China has been filled with attraction for and imaginings of urban life. This especially holds true for the new generation of rural migrant workers who basically have no experience doing farm work and whose understanding and love of the land is far less than that of their parents. Living in the village, they are subject to the

DOI: 10.4324/9781003365785-2

expectations of their parents and the opinions of their community who hope that they "get a university education, change the fate of their rural existence and truly become urban residents". Although most of them find it impossible to walk this road, the desire to "go to the city" has taken root in their hearts. As they grow up, the culture and knowledge they learn in school and on television, which take up most of their time outside of class, fill them at every turn with images of urban life. Today, many people from rural villages go to cities to work, while the parents, relatives and friends of the new generation of rural migrant workers are themselves working in urban areas. This phenomenon enables the new generation of rural migrant workers to form rich and colourful imagined scenarios of urban life before they go to the city.

1.1 City Life: The Proliferation of Mass Media

Mass media and the proliferation of urban images are interconnected in thousands of ways. The impression and cognitive awareness people have of urban life is invariably based on information distributed by the media. Compared with the past, today's rural residents are more concerned about and have a greater understanding of urban living, while the majority of village dwellers are curious about life in the city and exhibit an awareness of and desire for better living conditions. They have greater sensitivity towards and care more about better conditions offered by the environment outside the village (Gao & Zheng, 2013). Due to the geographic distance between and separation of urban and rural areas, the new generation of rural migrant workers often depends on television, radio broadcasts, newspapers, and other media to define their perceptions of the city.

> I remember when I was very young the telephone pole at the entrance to our village had a large loudspeaker on it, which would broadcast the news every morning. The male and female announcers would take turns saying "China National Radio", and would then begin to broadcast the news in succession. I couldn't understand most of the content and it seemed as if they were speaking of events in a world which was very far away. Before my family bought a television, we also used a radio. My grandfather and grandmother would listen to Chinese opera. I liked to listen to songs, and especially liked to listen to Mao Amin (a Chinese singer). I and my companions in the village often talked about Mao Amin. Once they told me that Mao Amin lived in Beijing, that she looked like a beautiful woman from the realm of the immortals, and that she would never die. I really believed this, and longed to go to Beijing to also become an immortal beauty. At the time, I truly never imagined that I would go to live in a city, although it wasn't Beijing.
>
> (Dan Hong, female, from Liyang, Jiangsu)

Prior to her family purchasing a television set, Dan Hong, born in 1983, always understood the outside world through the radio. She believed that cities were beautiful and mysterious and that China's capital, Beijing, was an even more marvellous place. Being able to go to live in the city was her constant dream. Naturally, many more members of the new generation of rural migrant workers have grown up constantly surrounded by television, and the influence of television on their imagined scenarios of city life has been tremendous.

Xiaojuan, who is 28 years old, set up a small food stand in the vicinity of a certain institution of higher learning in Nanjing. She has lived in the city for close to ten years, and her memories of life in the village seem very remote and distant. Xiaojuan comes from a village in Zhijin, Guizhou. She also has a younger brother and a younger sister. In addition to doing farm work, her parents also have a vegetable stand in the town and work very hard all year long. They have no time to supervise the education of their three children. As a result, outside of class, Xiaojuan would frankly spend a lot of time watching television, and television became the best companion for her and her siblings.

> I love to watch television. When I was young, I would watch cartoons. After I grew up, I loved to watch television dramas. My younger sister and I liked to watch love stories. My younger brother liked to watch stories about chivalrous martial arts masters. We often argued over the television about who got to watch which program. Our parents did not allow us to constantly watch television every day and made us spend our time at home studying and doing homework. This was impossible. Television was much more interesting than reading books. I still remember immediately turning off the television and running to open up a book when I heard my mother and father's footsteps as they returned home. That was many years ago.
>
> (Xiaojuan, female, from Zhijin, Guizhou)

The experience of Xiaojuan and her siblings is quite typical. Even if parents in rural villages do not go out to work, they don't pay as much attention to the education and upbringing of their children as do parents in urban areas. They labour all day long and have little time to pay attention to their children, other than making sure that they are well fed and warmly dressed. This holds even more true for the new generation of rural migrant workers who were once children left behind in the villages by their parents who went to other places to work. As children, the new generation of rural migrant workers, outside of schoolwork, had television as their companion. They spent their free time watching television and absorbed everything the television taught them about city life. The television fan Xiaojuan, before coming to the city, saw many shows featuring teenage idols, which for the most part were filmed in cities. After watching such shows over a long period of time, Xiaojuan formed her impressions of the city.

The intimate connection between television and the village life of the new generation of rural migrant workers before entering urban areas can be seen from this example. Television, through its rich, variegated images and abundance of information, has shown them successive features of urban life. Dongdong, a young man of 20 from Ziyang in Sichuan, has led a rough life. Not long after he was born, his mother argued with his father and subsequently killed herself by drinking pesticide. When his father remarried, little Dongdong's stepmother refused to accept him, so from an early age he lived with his paternal grandparents in their native village. His father and stepmother were always away from home working in Guangdong, and seldom returned to the village to see him. Dongdong's grandparents were illiterate and never asked Dongdong about his studies. Dongdong muddled through his time at the primary school at the village. Other than playing unrestrainedly with his young companions, Dongdong's greatest love was watching television. Dongdong, in his loneliness, would often sit on a small bench in front of his family's 14-inch black and white television and spend most of the day watching TV. He would watch his favourite television program, *Journey to the West*, over and over again. He also enjoyed watching martial arts dramas. For a time, his love for television got him into trouble with his grandfather, because Dongdong wanted to go to Shaolin Temple to learn martial arts and become a master martial artist to fight for justice. Because his father was always working in the city, Dongdong paid close attention to everything he saw on television related to urban life.

> Children in cities really lead happy lives. Their parents don't have to leave home to find work. Every day, after they finish school, they go home to be with their parents. There are public parks, amusement parks, science and technology museums, and zoos in cities. From an early age, they can visit these places to have fun. Affluent families take their children on trips overseas. If I could lead such a life, I would be overjoyed. In my native village, I have never eaten anything from Kentucky Fried Chicken or McDonald's; however, I often see their television commercials, hamburgers with layer upon layer, which look very delicious. My father and my stepmother have had another baby, my little brother. I wonder if their lives in Guangdong are like what I see on television?
>
> (Dongdong, male, from Ziyang, Sichuan)

Dongdong, lacking parental love since childhood, paid close attention to the life of children living in the city. Many children in his village had parents who worked in the city and found it difficult to return home, even at the end of the year. Accordingly, Dongdong felt that these children were about the same as he was. Only those children living in the city were happy. They not only lived with their parents but also enjoyed a modern life with material comforts. In Dongdong's eyes, economic conditions for families in cities were better. They could enjoy good things to eat and drink and their lives were filled with warmth, in stark contrast to his deprived, impoverished family situation.

The new generation of rural migrant workers living in the world of the village comprehend the outside world and urban living through the window of television. They obtain indirect cognition of the city through news broadcasts, film and television, variety entertainment programs, advertisements, and so on, whereby they unconsciously absorb impressions of urban lifestyles, infrastructure, economic development, urban fashions, habits, customs, and leisure activities.

Accordingly, mass media continuously delivers information on the city to the villages, causing the new generation of rural migrant workers to imagine all kinds of scenarios about urban life. Although the specific content of their respective imaginings about urban life may vary according to differences in family situation, personality, personal experience, and use of media, they are attracted to the city's well-developed facilities, prosperous economy, and modern lifestyle. Naturally, certain members of the new generation of rural migrant workers "hear about" and "see" from the mass media the gap between urban and rural life and the difficulties faced by persons from rural areas who live in the city, which colours their attraction for the city with unavoidable concerns for the situation they will face after they move to an urban area.

1.2 The Seductive Urban Identity: Guidance by Interpersonal Communication

Unlike the indirect, gradual influence of mass media, the impact of interpersonal communication is direct and apparent. First-hand information on the city obtained through interpersonal communication may arouse even deeper imaginings among the new generation of rural migrant workers. This is especially true regarding family members, friends, and neighbours returning from working in the city, who present a natural example for the new generation of rural migrant workers who have not yet entered urban life.

Twenty-five-year-old Yuehong has nine years of work experience. After graduating from junior high school at the age of 16, she came to Hangzhou to live with her maternal second uncle and help him sell breakfast foods at his takeout restaurant.

> My maternal second uncle and maternal second aunt came to Hangzhou in the 1990s to prepare and sell breakfast foods. At that time, I was still studying in primary school. My maternal second uncle also brought his two children to Hangzhou to attend school. Every year during Spring Festival the whole family would return and everyone crowded around them to ask about their life. I heard my maternal uncle say that Hangzhou was a very wealthy city, and that you could often find coins on the street, which were of no interest to local people who weren't willing to take the time to bend over and pick them up, because to scavenge such small change from the street would cause a loss of face. When I heard this, I felt very excited and decided to go to Hangzhou to get rich by scavenging coins. Everyone says that "Heaven is above, and Suzhou and Hangzhou are here below". At the time, I felt that Hangzhou was heaven.
>
> (Yuehong, female, from Luohe, Henan)

After she realized her dream of coming to Hangzhou, Yuehong discovered that the ground was not covered with "coins" and that local people who saw money lying on the ground were keen to pick it up. Although the breakfast food business made money, it was extremely hard work. She had to get up at 3 am to make dough, mix stuffing, and prepare dumplings. Customers would come to buy food beginning at around 7 am and she would be continuously busy until well past 11 am. Yuehong, who had just graduated from junior high school, found this life unbearable. She gave up her plan of also opening a breakfast shop in the future, and ended up working at a clothing factory in Xiasha District in Hangzhou. After two years, she couldn't stand the boredom of working in a factory, and found a job working as a service staff at a hotel. When she spoke about her experiences over these past several years, Yuehong said she really regretted not pursuing further studies after graduating from junior high school; after living in the city for nine years, she had nothing to show for it.

> I have many older male and female cousins who went elsewhere to work and there are many children from our village who did the same. After a year or so, when they returned home, all of them had changed a lot! They had dyed their hair blond, wore high heels, and had fashionable clothes. Most of them also had mobile phones. During Spring Festival when they returned home, I would always hang around them, hoping to hear something about life in the city. There were so many things in the city that were fun! They went to the KTV to sing, and they went to the ice-skating rink to learn how to ice skate. My older female cousin had also learned how to dance! I really envied them. I also wanted to quickly start living the city life, so as soon as I graduated, I went to help my maternal second uncle.
>
> (Yuehong, female, from Luohe, Henan)

To a greater or lesser degree, rural residents who have experienced life in the city have adopted the habits of city dwellers, which can be seen from their out-ward appearance and attire. When such residents return home, this creates shock among the new generation of rural migrant workers who have never lived in the city and believe that they will also undergo such changes after living in the city. In fact, the relevant research indicates that neither the older nor the new genera-tion of rural migrant workers are able to find what most people consider to be "decent" jobs when they go to the city and also fail to enjoy the same benefits and remuneration as urban dwellers. On the other hand, rural migrant workers returning to their villages are even more keen on sharing the colourful side of their experiences in the city and consciously or unconsciously overlook the reality of being cruelly left behind in an urban environment.

For example, Yuehong, in her conversations with her peers who had returned home, saw the fashionable and bright side of "city dwellers" and thus had an even greater yearning to go live the city life.

Xiao Dai from Mingxi in Fujian works at a manicure and nail shop in Nanjing. With her tall figure and beautiful demeanour, people always imagine that she is a genuine city girl. In fact, in Xiao Dai's birthplace, people hold the very traditional view of favouring men over women. She is the third daughter in her family, and, in order to avoid family planning penalties, was sent by her parents to be raised by her maternal grandparents. Xiao Dai finally returned to her home at the age of 12 when she enrolled in junior high school. Her exceptional childhood experience caused Xiao Dai to be very envious of girls raised in the city. She hopes that her parents will show concern for her, and that she will not become the most unwanted, most disregarded person in her family.

> My older sister said that many of her college classmates were girls from the cities who were the only children in their families spoiled and cherished by their parents. In our village, it's not like that. If a woman doesn't give birth to a son, she doesn't give up trying. In a family like mine with an excess of daughters, my parents can't take care of me. I must go to the city. If I remain in the village, I will have no hope and can only get married and have children. My older sister said that it's different in the city. In Beijing and Shanghai, there are many women who are over 30 years old and still unmarried, because they want to pursue their careers. Although I didn't pass the college entrance exam, I will not live the life of those village women. I want to go to the city to struggle, and ultimately, I will make something of myself.
>
> (Xiao Dai, female, from Mingxi, Fujian)

Xiao Dai continuously took offense at her experience as a child raised away from home. In her eyes, the city was a paradise where men and women enjoyed equality, a place where girls could feel proud and satisfied with themselves. For Xiao Dai, the city was attractive not only because it was prosperous, wealthy, and colourful. Of greater significance was that the city offered many possible choices for each individual to define the trajectory of their lives. She was terrified of the monotonous existence offered by life in the village. She believed that the city was a place of diversity, that only by living in the city would she be able to achieve her personal goals. Junwen from Anhui also held the same beliefs.

Before he had reached the age of 19, Junwen had gone to Huzhou to help out at the supermarket opened by his father's male cousin, who was well known in his native place as a "capable person". Before he had turned 40, he had already acquired two residential properties and a large supermarket in Huzhou. This cousin of his father was a typical example of someone who had started from nothing. He had many brothers and sisters, which put a strain on family finances. He took his wife and one child from the village to seek their fortune in the world. Because he and his wife had little education, they started out working from a small stand. Over the course of ten years, they went from Hangzhou to Cixi, Ningbo, and other cities, and finally were able to make a stable life for themselves in Huzhou. Junwen had always been in awe of his father's cousin. After he graduated from junior high school, he chose not to go with his older brother to work in Hangzhou, but found a job at his father's cousin's supermarket.

> My father's cousin is the most successful person I know. He has bought two homes in Huzhou and owns a BMW. My father's cousin and his wife have also transferred the household registry of their two sons to Huzhou. It seems

like his son is studying at a private school where the tuition is very expensive. Before I went to help him at his supermarket, I often heard my parents talk about him. He and his family now enjoy a better life than most people in the city! The supermarket has hired many workers and my father's cousin and his wife manage the business. They very rarely return to their home village, and often take their children on trips to Sanya during Spring Festival. I feel that people should be like my father's cousin, who through his own hard work enabled his family to lead a good life and become true city dwellers.

(Junwen, male, from Mengcheng, Anhui)

Junwen has worked at his father's cousin's supermarket for two years, where the wage is not much higher than that paid by a factory. When business is good, he is often so exhausted that it feels like his body is going to collapse. He also enjoys having a good time. When he has time off, he often goes out with his co-workers to dance and hang out at bars. Nonetheless, he always keeps in mind why at the start he made the choice to come work here.

Previous research shows that the older generation of rural migrant workers came to the city for the first time when they are 30 years of age or older, at which time most of them were married and had children. They had an intense desire to make money in the city to support their family's needs. They didn't have much feeling or imagination when it came to the city, and inevitably regarded the city as a place to "pan for gold" (Guo & Zhang, 2016). On the other hand, most members of the new generation of rural migrant workers are around 15 or 16 years old when they first come to the city, and the significance which the city holds for them goes far beyond merely "making money", because in the city they hope to live a life different from that of the village. They want to "fulfil their personal dreams" and "achieve the status of an urbanite". This is their deepest aspiration for their lives in the city.

1.3 Anxiety Over Going to the City Through Various Communication Channels

Before coming to the city, the majority of the generation of new rural migrant workers have rather positive expectations of what the city will be like. "I never gave it too much thought, at any rate, I want to experience the world while I'm still young." "I feel excited about going to the city, life in my home village has no meaning." Unlike the older generation, the new generation of rural migrant workers are more often than not 17 or 18 years old when they first go to the city, and their youthful exuberance makes them exceptionally fearless. Naturally, a small number among the new generation of rural migrant workers feels differing degrees of anxiety when they think about going to live in the city. Through various communication channels, they have more or less come to understand the side of city life which people find frightening or unfriendly.

Zhenzhen is a young woman born in 1990 from Congjiang, Guizhou. She is very shy in front of strangers and often speaks in very simple, short sentences when answering questions raised during an interview. However, after being around her for a long time, we find that she is very sensitive and harbours deep feelings. Zhenzhen, at the age of 15, came to live in Nanjing where she first worked at several factories. Currently, she works as a service staff at a hotel. Zhenzhen comes from a very poor county which is mountainous, with little arable land and no auxiliary industry. One can imagine how little income villagers there earn.

Her family's poverty and her early dropping out of school have caused Zhenzhen to feel extremely inferior to others. She is attracted to the prosperity of the city, but at the same time this attraction is always accompanied by her anxiety about city life. Over a long period of time spent watching television, she became aware of many things which caused her to feel anxious.

> Living in the city is quite different from living in the mountains. The persons on television all speak *Putonghua*, while I can't speak it at all. During my school years, my teachers also didn't speak *Putonghua*. If I speak Congjiang dialect, people will definitely laugh at me and will not be able to understand me, which really worries me. People in cities wear fashionable clothes which we can't buy in our mountain village. There was a television show called "Nanny" which talks about a country girl who goes to the city to work as a nanny, who is looked down upon by those city people who feel that she is unrefined and knows nothing. Accordingly, it's not easy for people from the villages to go live their lives in the city. I really want to go to the city; however, I am not up to standard and am afraid people will ridicule me.
>
> (Zhenzhen, female, from Congjiang, Guizhou)

When describing what she imagined prior to going to the city, Zhenzhen repeatedly said that "she feared being ridiculed". Her understanding of the differences between city life and rural life from the images she saw on television caused her to imagine various scenarios in which "she would be ridiculed". Before going to Nanjing, she made a special trip to the local town to buy the Rejoice shampoo to take with her, because "the shampoo commercials often appear on television, and most people who live in the city probably like to use this brand". Zhenzhen's seemingly ludicrous action actually reflects her fear of not being able to fit into city life.

Xiaojie from Mengcheng, Anhui, drives a freight truck in Nanjing, and once studied at Mengcheng's best senior high school – Mengcheng First Middle School. Xiaojie once dreamed of going to college and worked hard at his studies, beginning from primary school. After taking his middle school entrance examination, he successfully enrolled at Mengcheng First Middle School. Just when his whole family believed that he was definitely on his way to college, excessive pressure from his studies caused him to suffer long-term insomnia and neurasthenia, and he abandoned his studies without even taking the national college entrance examination. After he left school, his neurasthenia went away without requiring treatment. He then came to Nanjing with his father to work in transportation/shipping, thus using an alternative method to achieve his "city dream".

My eagerness to go the city, for the most part, was due to the stimulus I received from watching television, because I envied the lifestyle of white-collar workers who appeared on television. My father drives a freight truck in all kinds of weather, wind and rain, doesn't eat well, and doesn't sleep well. His waist and spine have been damaged by excessive sitting. However, year in and year out, he doesn't make much money. But those white-collar workers dress in clean and beautiful attire and have easy jobs which also pay well. I want to attend university to become a white-collar worker. I don't want to work as arduously as my father. Ha! If we villagers can attend university and work in the city, we can get better jobs; otherwise, we can only work as labourers.

(Xiaojie, male, from Mengcheng, Anhui)

Seeing his father work so hard as a freight truck driver to make ends meet, Xiaojie doesn't want to walk the same road. In his mind, only by enrolling in university and entering the city will he be able to live a fairly respectable life as a city dweller. Yinan, from Longgang, Anhui, shares the same thoughts as Xiaojie.

Twenty-six-year-old Yinan and her husband set up a stand at a vegetable market to sell vegetables. The reason she is named Yinan is because she is the second daughter in her family. When she was born, her parents had really hoped she would be a boy. After their disappointment, her mother repeatedly became pregnant and after aborting the births of three female infants finally gave birth to Yinan's younger brother. Yinan always felt that she had no status in her family and developed an introverted personality. When she was just beginning primary school, her parents took her younger brother to Hangzhou to set up a vendor's stand, leaving Yinan and her elder sister to attend school in their home village, where they often lived with their paternal grandparents. Yinan always wanted to make something of herself by attending university, quite unlike the other children in her village, who hoped to go to the city to work after graduating from junior middle school.

My parents sell vegetables in Hangzhou, work very hard, and don't get enough sleep, because they always get up at midnight to make purchases (of vegetables). They only return home for several days during Spring Festival. I often ask them what Hangzhou is like. My mother says that she really doesn't want to go Hangzhou: she gets really car sick. Every time she rides in a car, she feels really bad, as if she was extremely ill. There are many wealthy people in Hangzhou who live in beautifully decorated houses. However, the rented dwelling in which my parents live is very rundown. Father told me that I must study hard so that I can attend university and become a true urbanite, so that I won't have to live like them, getting up early and working late into the night to earn money. . . . I really made an effort, but I am not so clever. Finally, I was unable to continue my studies, so I got married, and here I am selling vegetables.

(Yinan, female, from Longgang, Anhui)

After learning how difficult it was for their family members to struggle to survive in the city, Xiaojie and Yinan decided not to live as "urban migrant workers". In their minds, the city would not provide rural migrant workers with a fair and satisfying life, while urban dwellers were not only wealthy but also cold and cunning. In fact, this does not mean that Xiaojie and Yinan rejected the city, but rather that they were not confident in their status as villagers, and yearned to enter city life equipped with better resources and equal social status. In reality, this expresses an even deeper yearning for the city.

To sum up, the vast majority of the new generation of rural migrant workers prior to going to live in the city have not personally experienced urban life. As they see it, the city and urban dwellers are heterogeneous, quite different from their rural experience. We can borrow the concept of "others" to analyse their imaginings about the city. In the eyes of the new generation of rural migrant workers, the city is "that other world" quite different from the rural village. Under the joint influence of mass media and interpersonal communication, they have imagined scenarios of city life at multiple levels. It may be said that under the influence of the media, the new generation of rural migrant workers entering the city has formed its own imagined scenarios of the city. Naturally, regardless of the content or type of imagined scenario, such scenarios, to a greater or lesser degree, contain fantasy and biases, and in varying degrees are at odds with objective reality. However, the new generation of rural migrant workers will naturally believe that the city is the way they have imagined it to be. After entering the city, this type of imagined scenario is unavoidably struck down and undergoes changes.

2. Confronting Reality: Changes in Imagined Scenarios of Urban Life Which Occur After Initially Arriving in the City

The move from the village to the city, with respect to the new generation of rural migrant workers, does not merely entail a change of living space but more significantly entails a tremendous change of lifestyle. They have left their place of birth, their parents and family, and a familiar living environment in their race to the city to begin a new life which is completely different from their past. Their way of living and ideas and concepts are totally different from those of the older generation of rural migrant workers; nonetheless, in the same way as those who preceded them, prior to entering the city they have never experienced urban life and have not made the necessary preparations for the transformation of their roles in society. In fact, the level of satisfaction regarding city life among the new generation of rural migrant workers is lower than that of the older generation. During the initial period after their arrival in the city, they are faced with even more circumstances to which they cannot adapt. This is not because urban conditions for rural migrant workers have worsened but rather due to rising expectations among the new generation of rural migrant workers with respect to city life, which far exceed the expectations of the older generation of rural migrant workers (Li & Li, 2014). Members of the new generation of rural migrant workers who have just arrived in the city are confronted with unanticipated challenges to their psychological well-being and daily living activities. As a result, imagined scenarios of urban life which they formed prior to coming to the city undergo drastic changes.

2.1 Psychological Gap Experienced Upon Initially Arriving in the City

Once members of the new generation of rural migrant workers enter the city, the city, or "others", is no longer a distant reality. They begin to personally experience city life. Members of the new generation of rural migrant workers are inevitably filled with excitement and curiosity when they initially arrive in the city. They know that their lives will undergo tremendous changes. They have left the familiar environment of their villages to begin their new lives in unfamiliar cities. They also feel uneasy because they have no way of determining whether the city will resemble what they imagined it would be like and have no way of predicting what kind of persons and events they will encounter.

Bing Yao from Mengcheng, Anhui, is a truck driver who works with his uncle-in-law transporting goods all over the country. Born in 1988, he has driven a truck for almost ten years. He has driven all over the Yangtze River Delta region, the Pearl River region, and China's Southwest. During recent years, many people have bought large trucks to transport goods, because it is said that a person who transports goods makes much more money than an ordinary labourer. After Bing Yao graduated from junior middle school, he came to work with his uncle-in-law on his truck, helping out with shipping goods while learning how to drive. His parents hoped that after he earned a lot of money, he would be able to buy a truck. Bing Yao really likes driving a truck. He feels that his peers who leave home to work are always stuck in one place, while he can travel all over.

> As soon as I graduated, I went to work for my uncle-in-law on his truck to help out. I still remember the first time I worked on his truck, transporting goods from Nanjing to Kunming. I didn't even have time to take a look around Nanjing and just got on the truck and left to drive several days and nights continuously on the freeway. I felt very bored on the truck and also didn't know what to talk about with my uncle-in-law, so I began to feel homesick. I missed my bed, my mother's cooking, and my buddies whom I went to school with and played with. I thought about giving up, but I was too embarrassed to return home when I had just ventured out into the world to start work.
>
> (Bing Yao, male, from Mengcheng, Anhui)

Bing Yao's special type of work has caused him to continuously live on the periphery of the city. Occasionally, when he has nothing to ship or is too tired, he and his uncle-in-law will stay in a hotel in the city for a short rest. He really wants to go out to play in the city; however, the prospect of going out fills him with an unexplainable fear.

> When I first came to the city, I didn't know anyone. My uncle-in-law is getting on in years and only likes to stay indoors and sleep, so there was no one to take me out to play. I would just walk around the neighbourhood. I didn't know the bus routes and I didn't speak *Putonghua* very well, so I didn't dare to go to places far away. Before I came, I thought that everything in the city was good. After coming to the city, I also felt afraid. Isn't that strange?
>
> (Bing Yao, male, from Mengcheng, Anhui)

Members of the new generation of rural migrant workers who have just entered the city face an unexpected new environment which often causes them to feel confused and at a loss, and many of them experience homesickness. Although the city is prosperous and thriving, everything familiar to them in the village gives them a sense of security. They come to the city with wonderful imaginings. However, city life when they initially arrive inevitably is filled with many disappointments. Accordingly, members of the new generation of rural migrant workers often experience a tremendous psychological gap between their fantasized scenarios and reality.

Twenty-nine-year-old Xiao Shi comes from Xi'an and has lived in Nanjing for over ten years. He currently works as a hairstylist at one of the Huazai hair salons. As early as 2004, when he had just turned 17, after graduating from a vocational institute, he was sent to work as an electric welder at a factory in the Shiqiu District of Nanjing. Although he had come at a very tender age to work in Nanjing, a thousand kilometres from his home, Xiao Shi recalls that he didn't feel afraid and, on the contrary, yearned to make something of himself in the outside world.

> I had heard of Nanjing when I was young, including the Yangtze River Bridge and the Nanjing Massacre Memorial Museum. I had read about them in my textbook at school. At the time, when I learned that my school was going to send me to Nanjing, I felt very excited. I felt that such a large city would be very interesting. However, after I came to Nanjing, I then realized that working as a labourer in a factory was really boring. I never intended to study electrical welding. My parents said that I could earn money as an electrical welder and enrolled me at the school. To my great regret, the factory where we worked was fundamentally a closed management operation. We ate and lived at the factory and basically had no contact with the outside world. We had very little time off, and I was also unfamiliar with Nanjing and seldom went out to enjoy myself. Although I earned a good income as an electrical welder, I was bored stiff and felt that I didn't enjoy the same freedom and peace of mind I had living at home in the village. Moreover, when I first arrived in Nanjing, I wasn't used to the weather here, because it was too humid, while the weather in Xi'an was very dry. I had never imagined what it was really like. I originally thought that coming to Nanjing would be

like fortuitously falling into a pot of honey. In fact, it was the same as being locked up in prison.

(Xiao Shi, male, from Xi'an Shaanxi)

Like so many other labourers, Xiao Shi first worked at a factory after coming to the city. The work environment at a factory is rather closed, and the content of the work is for the most part monotonous. As ordinary labourers, they are firmly tied to the production line and live redundant lives. Although the persons they come into contact with are basically also rural migrant workers who have come to the city to work, the interpersonal relationships and survival mechanisms in the factory are manifestly different from those in rural society. Many of the new generation of rural migrant workers have also been bullied and exploited. After leaving the familiar life in their villages, they don't know how to protect their rights. When they first arrive in the city, everything which they experience is in sharp contrast with their imagined scenarios of urban life before coming to the city. This makes them realize that although city life is full of vibrancy and colour, living in the city is no simple matter.

Although members of the new generation of rural migrant workers experience a transfer of social space when they enter the city, they are unable to change the habits of their rural lifestyle in a short period of time. Xiao Sun, a young woman of 23 from Fuyang, Anhui, describes her exasperation with regard to boarding the subway when she first arrived in Shanghai.

I was most unaccustomed to boarding public buses and subways. I really couldn't tell the difference between north, south, east, and west. Back home, we don't have buses and subways. We always ride a bicycle or motorcycle when we go out. Especially with regard to the subway, there are so many lines, and after a long time I still couldn't figure them out. I enjoy excitement, and when I first came to Shanghai I planned to go to Happy Valley to have some fun. However, as of today, I still haven't gone there, because I don't know how to ride the subway and can't figure out how to go. (We suggested to her that she take the subway and ask for directions along the way, that she would eventually find her destination. However, Xiao Sun shook her head in rejection of our proposal and decided that it wasn't safe.) You meet all kinds of people in the city, and if I ask people directions, I'll sound like a country bumpkin. People in the city will definitely look down on me.

(Xiao Sun, female, from Fuyang, Anhui)

In fact, many people among the new generation of rural migrant workers really admire the city's highly developed public transportation prior to entering the city. However, when they actually have a chance to use it, this complex, strange system causes them to feel helpless, and they require time to get used to it.

After they leave the village and enter the city, members of the new generation of rural migrant workers are able to personally experience the city first-hand. Although when they are growing up, they have unlimited imagined scenarios of city life, they have very little knowledge of how they will actually live after they arrive in the city. This is especially true for persons who work in factories, who work intensely at tasks which are simple and redundant and lead modularized lives. Young people who are brimming with vitality and dreams are unable to tolerate this. Not to mention that they have just arrived in an urban environment, have not yet formed their circle of friends and feel that everything about the city is strange. They inevitably feel isolated and helpless. This holds true even among members of the new generation of rural migrant workers who are somewhat psychologically prepared. For instance, take Zhenzhen, whose experience was discussed earlier. After she arrived in Nanjing her worries became real. Her heavy Guizhou accent and outdated attire made her feel inferior when she faced her fashionably dressed peers at the factory, not to mention when she interacted with city dwellers. To a certain degree, negative imaginings about urban life are reinforced among the new generation of rural migrant workers after they enter the city, while they also face psychological difficulties.

2.2 The Harsh Reality of Migrants' Lives

Although they yearn for the city life, members of the new generation of rural migrant workers still unavoidably encounter huge psychological gaps when first entering the city. Journeying far away from their homes for the first time gives them a taste of loneliness. The new generation of rural migrant workers has discovered that coming to the city does not mean that they can live an urban life. Their survival situation in the city is completely different from what they imagined city life to be like. They enter into an alternative lifestyle which doesn't resemble that of urban dwellers and also doesn't resemble that of people in a rural village. Whether it be survival conditions, consumption capacity, or cultural taste, they cannot compare with urban dwellers. At the same time, they have also separated themselves from their original mode of living in the village. In this narrow spectrum of survival conditions, their imaginings about city life also undergo further change.

A head of hair has grown a bit and has been dyed blonde, a set of clothing looks fashionable but is modestly priced, you chatter with friends whom you know well but remain tart and taciturn in the presence of strangers. When you encounter Xiao Zhao on the street in Nanjing at a certain restaurant, that's the way he is. Xiao Zhao entered the workforce without graduating from high school, because, as he puts it, his grades were not good, and he felt it was meaningless to continue his studies. Xiao Zhao comes from Huai'an in Jiangsu province and is the only child in his family. His parents run a fresh fruit stand in his hometown. His family is rather well-off. They built a two-story home at the time that Xiao Zhao left home to work in the city. Even though his parents have repeatedly opposed his decision, Xiao Zhao would still rather go it alone and find his fortune in Nanjing. He hopes to live the life of an urban dweller. However, he is highly disappointed with the environment of the dormitory provided by the restaurant.

When I first came to Nanjing, my employer provided food and lodgings and paid me 2000 yuan per month. My work was exhausting, but what could I do? My lodgings were extremely rundown, with just a large bed in the room, nothing else. my colleague and I put our belongings in a pile on the floor. The window had no drapes, so we covered it with newspaper. The place was not as comfortable as my lodgings back home. I believed I was living in possibly the most rundown building in Gulou District. In the past I just believed that people in the city led better lives than people in the village. Now I see that's not always the case.

(Xiao Zhao, male, from Huai'an, Jiangsu)

Gulou District is in the centre of Nanjing, with many tall buildings, and has a prosperous look. However, although Xiao Zhao lived in the midst of this, he was unable to enjoy a modern comfortable environment. He wanted to rent a room for himself with slightly better conditions, but the price of housing in the surrounding area was shockingly high. He couldn't afford such high rent on a monthly salary of 2000 yuan. His awful lodgings put a blight on his life. He felt that city conditions were really unfair, especially for outsiders from rural villages. Indeed, the cost of living in the city posed a great challenge. The urban lifestyle which the new generation of rural migrant workers yearns for inevitably requires a certain level of economic power to sustain it. This is obviously quite difficult for such workers just entering the workforce who are earning a low income.

Cui Ping, who is 25 years old, has lived in Shanghai for many years. When she first left home, she worked as a teacher at a private nursery school, earning a monthly salary of 1200 yuan. Cui Ping is a lady who loves fashion. The abundance of merchandise in Shanghai made her head spin. She would often spend her whole salary before the month had ended. Although she would often live beyond her means, she couldn't resist the impulse to buy clothes. The poor quality of the clothes sold at the market back home disgusted her. She was attracted by the clothes sold at the mall, which were superior quality and the latest style. However, as Cui Ping recalls she was very unhappy the first time she went shopping at the mall.

When I went shopping at the mall with a friend of mine from back home, we saw a skirt for 400 yuan. I felt that wasn't a problem: I could make the sales person a counter offer of 150 yuan. Ultimately, the sales girl rolled her eyes and said, "Can you negotiate prices in a shopping mall? That's ridiculous." Then she began to talk with her colleague in Shanghainese. Although I couldn't understand what they were saying, I knew that they were definitely ridiculing me. Then I realized that items sold at a shopping mall were sold at the prices marked on them, which was different from items sold back home. Ai! To tell you the truth, I had never gone shopping at a mall before I came to Shanghai, so I made a fool of myself. In Shanghai, everything is expensive. You set your heart on something, but you can't afford to buy it. I feel it's quite unbearable.

(Cui Ping, female, from Lingbi, Anhui)

Cui Ping who had come to Shanghai to live finally realized that she had to pay a price for beauty. Workers like her who earn such low wages cannot possibly spend money at the same standard as urban dwellers. Cui Ping's encounter at the mall actually also reflects the differences between urban and rural culture often encountered by the new generation of rural migrant workers when they enter the city.

Xiao Bai who works in a barbecued meat restaurant in Taizhou has lived in the city for three years. Xiao Bai, from Zhuzhou, Hunan, is outgoing, enthusiastic, and optimistic. After arriving in Taizhou, Xiao Bai has continuously worked at this restaurant. She is very familiar with how to provide good service to customers and now works as the head waitress three years after coming to the city. Recalling the time when she had first come to the city, she remembers that working at the restaurant was quite demanding, especially for a girl like her who knew nothing about the city or society.

> When I had just arrived in the city, I saw a young mother with her child who was very cute. I just wanted to pat him on the head. I had just finished saying, "Come here, shake my hand", when his mother said, "Ai! Can't do that, there are germs." At that moment, I had held out my hand, but I pulled it back. I felt very distressed. Did she dislike me? Ai! I really don't understand people in the city. Sometimes they are really terrible.
>
> (Xiao Bai, female, from Zhuzhou, Hunan)

Xiao Bai at the time really couldn't understand why this had happened. Why had her enthusiasm been met with coldness? When she was living in the village, she loved children, and often hugged or even kissed other people's children. Their parents never objected. Later her co-workers told her that the customers didn't necessarily dislike her. It was just that city dwellers were rather particular, and didn't let people randomly touch their children. If she took notice of this in the future, everything would be okay. Although she had been given this explanation, Xiao Bai, who had just come to the city for the first time, still felt deeply hurt. She suddenly felt that the city was not as attractive as she had imagined it to be. At the very least, relationships between people in the city could not begin to compare to those in the village. Especially with regard to the new generation of rural migrant workers working in the service industry, due to their extensive contact with the outside world, when they first enter the workforce, they often encounter conflicting urban and rural viewpoints. This causes them to realize that the city is not merely a material venue but also contains much hidden soft culture with which they must become familiar.

The difficulties encountered in the city by the new generation of rural migrant workers may be analysed in terms of culture shock occurring in cross-cultural exchanges. Culture shock refers to the anxiety and confusion people feel when they leave their familiar surroundings and encounter a foreign cultural environment (Jiang, 2007). The culture shock experienced by persons facing a completely new cultural environment causes them to be at a loss as to how to cope. Although the situation for the new generation of rural migrant workers who come from the village to the city is different from that of Chinese who go to live in a foreign country, there are similarities in the situations which they face, both of which demand that they adapt to a completely unfamiliar environment, comply with a new code of conduct, and interact with people from a different cultural background than their own. Before entering the city, members of the new generation of rural migrant workers believe that they have a good understanding of the city. However, after entering urban life, they discover that they are unfamiliar with many aspects of the city. Although the modern lifestyle which they yearned stands before their eyes, members of the new generation of rural migrant workers are forced to deal with horrible living conditions, exorbitant prices, and a vastly different cultural ambience. The realities of urban life have cruelly transformed the scenarios they imagined prior to coming to the city.

2.3 The Unavoidable Differences Between Urban and Rural Identities

Given the slow progress of modernization in China's rural villages, this process of modernization, from facilities to people, lags behind that of the cities. After China's opening up and reform, large numbers of rural migrant workers streamed into the cities to work. Due to the backwardness of rural villages and the huge differences between rural residents and urban residents, rural migrant workers in the cities have encountered varying degrees of discrimination. The new generation of rural migrant workers has an even greater desire to integrate into urban life. Accordingly, when they suffer discrimination, they experience even greater emotional and psychological distress.

Twenty-two-year-old Xiaowei, who comes from Shangqiu, Henan province, currently works as an assistant at a beauty shop in Shanghai. Xiaowei was brought to Shanghai by a friend, so her first job was at this beauty shop. She is looked after by her sisters from her hometown and everything has gone smoothly. However, it has taken her quite some time to transition from being a student to getting used to her role as a shampoo assistant in a beauty shop. Xiaowei was rather introverted in school and usually would read her textbook and do her classwork in silence. After she came to work at the beauty shop in Shanghai, the boss asked her to take the initiative to enthusiastically interact with customers, and to become skilled at promoting the sale of various items to customers at the beauty shop.

> I remember when I first came here, on one occasion I carelessly spilled shampoo paste on a customer's clothing. The customer became extremely angry and said that their clothing was exceptionally expensive and could not come into contact with water. Although I apologized profusely, the customer would not let the matter rest. Finally, I was reprimanded for quite some time by my boss and a deduction was made from my wages (as punishment). I felt really hurt. How could Shanghainese people behave like this? It was quite obvious that they were taking advantage of me because I was an outsider, someone

who wasn't from Shanghai. That evening I lay sleepless for a long time on my bed and decided to tell the boss on the following day that I was quitting.

(Xiaowei, female, from Shangqiu, Henan)

After being comforted by her sisters from her hometown, she decided to keep her job and struggle on. Everyone told her that at the beginning it was unavoidable that she would have a rough time, but as time passed, she would adapt and things would get better. These encounters made Xiaowei realize that there was a great difference between the real Shanghai and how she had imagined life in Shanghai would be.

My overall impression of Shanghai was not very good. It wasn't that Shanghai was a bad city, the main issue was that Shanghainese were not friendly, and showed obvious prejudice in their treatment of outsiders. I rather disliked the local Shanghainese. In the past, I thought that they would be very cultured and cultivated. However, they feel that we village folks are different from them, that we have a lower social status.

(Xiaowei, female, from Shangqiu, Henan)

Members of the new generation of rural migrant workers imagine that city dwellers usually are "highly cultured", "fashionably dressed", "well-paid and flush with cash", prior to entering the city. On the other hand, they underestimate the relationships and differences between themselves and urban dwellers, which causes a considerable number of migrant workers to feel that local people are unfriendly or even prejudiced towards them. They clearly realize the difference in status, that they and city dwellers are in two disparate groups. Even though they have migrated from rural villages to live in the city, city dwellers will not naturally accept them as fellow members of the urban class. Members of the new generation of rural migrant workers fervently hope to achieve the citizen identity of urban dweller, and thus truly become a part of city life. However, they very quickly discover that they are faced with numerous difficulties.

Tongtong, who is from a certain village in Baicheng, Jilin, has been fond of playing from an early age and never applied herself to her studies. Her elder sister, who is six years older than her, is famous in her village as an outstanding student, who easily achieves the highest test score in her class. Tongtong's parents often admonished her to emulate her elder sister, to study hard so that she could enter a good university and live in the city in the future. Tongtong always disagreed with her parents' exhortations. She vaguely believed that no matter how hard she tried, it would be impossible for her to achieve the same academic results as her sister. Accordingly, she didn't apply herself to her studies. Tongtong believes that book learning is not the only available path in life. She believes that by working hard she will also be able to stay in the city and become a genuine urbanite.

After graduating from a polytechnic middle school, Tongtong came to Wuxi to live with her elder sister. At that time, her elder sister had already graduated from a famous university and was working as an administrator at a German multinational company. Tongtong, who had just arrived in Wuxi, was overflowing with confidence. She believed that as long as she made an effort, she could be just as successful as her sister. Tongtong very quickly found a job as a cashier at a bakery, with a less than ideal income, which was several times less than what her sister was earning. Although they were living in the same city, Tongtong felt that she and her sister lived in two different worlds. Her sister had already achieved urban status, while she still had quite a distance to cover to be able to achieve the same.

> Ever since she was young, my sister loved to study. She always criticized me for not applying myself. I didn't care. A life of study was not the only road a person could take. As a result, there is a huge difference between us, and we have less and less to talk about. I have no understanding of the affairs of her company, a multinational, I just feel that it's really outstanding. Sometimes, when my sister entertains her classmates and friends at home, she invites me to join them. Everyone is very friendly towards me. I love to listen to them talk; however, I have nothing to contribute to their conversation.
>
> (Tongtong, female, from Baicheng, Jilin)

Tongtong had been very proud and confident prior to going to the city. However, when she compared her colleagues' life trajectories with her elder sister's, she quickly realized how difficult it was for rural migrant workers to make a life for themselves in the city. She really wanted to struggle to make a life for herself, but at the moment was unable to find a way to go about doing it. Tongtong was quite fearful that her life trajectory would be like that of her colleagues, working for years in the city, but still remaining on the periphery of urban life. When members of the new generation of rural migrant workers first go to the city, whether they encounter prejudice or experience the differences between urban and rural identities, they develop a clearer perception of how they have been labelled as persons from a rural background. They realize how difficult it is to truly integrate into urban life. The new generation of rural migrant workers entering the city are different from the preceding generation of rural migrant workers. The new generation of rural migrant workers seeks progress and development and wants to achieve a real transition from rural to urban identity. This is not only a spatial transition but more importantly involves a change of status. Accordingly, after they encounter the cold reality of urban life, they feel at a loss and their uncertainty with regard to the direction their lives should take becomes even more intense.

The new generation of rural migrant workers come to the city with beautiful dreams of how their lives will be and unlimited yearning for new lives. They expect that city life will be more comfortable, more colourful, and filled with more opportunities for development than rural life. However, the transition necessarily involves going through pain, and adapting to a different environment, a heterogenous group of people, and a different cultural milieu has a huge impact on such migrants. Of greater significance is the inferior position which China's rural areas have consistently occupied in comparison to the cities. When compared to the cities, rural villages are "backward", "provincial", and "insipid". These are labels which are often used to describe rural residents who live in villages (Zhang, 2011). Members of the new generation of rural migrant workers make a transition from a weak culture to a powerful culture. Although urban and rural environments and lifestyles are vastly different, and the life experiences and standards of conduct of rural residents and urban dwellers are different, people who go to the city are intangibly requested and expected to conform to all aspects of city life, which makes them feel even more helpless.

It is impossible to equate imagination with reality. Arduous and monotonous work, the high cost of living, the difference in status, and a completely unfamiliar cultural environment cause members of the new generation of rural migrant workers to drastically revise their imaginings about the city. Before entering the city, they "saw" the prosperity of the city, "witnessed" its modern lifestyle, and further "perceived" the allure of urban identity through the lens of the media. After coming to the city, they discovered that "modernity" and "prosperity" had little or no connection to their own lives. In fact, imagined scenarios of a wealthy city only serve to magnify the difficulties that the new generation of rural migrant workers encounters when initially coming to the city, and their imagined scenarios then shift towards another extreme. Naturally, notwithstanding the many psychological and survival difficulties members of the new generation of rural migrant workers encounter when they first come to the city, very few of them return to their hometowns on account of such tribulations, because in their minds the village no longer provides a spiritual refuge to which they can retreat. They continue to maintain the urban struggle and to increase their awareness of the city over the long course of their city life.

3. Pursuing the Dream: Reconstructing Imagined Urban Scenarios Over the Course of Adapting to Life in the City

In spite of the significant gap between real city life and what they had imagined it to be, members of the new generation of rural migrant workers generally will not easily abandon the city, and choose to continue to struggle on. After being shaken by the "shock" they encounter when they first move to the city, they begin to slowly explore how to adapt to their new life and how to better improve themselves. Throughout this process, they experience the city as they live their life and also utilize media tools to obtain information on the city: these two activities jointly form the source of a new round of imagined urban scenarios constructed by members of the new generation of rural migrant workers.

3.1 Emulation and Following-up Under the Guidance of Modernity in Urban Interactions

In China's villages, great importance is placed on blood ties and kinship. Members of the new generation of rural migrant workers who initially come to the city are basically all "interrelated", coming to the city on the heels of their family members, friends, and neighbours. Where they live when they first enter the city and their first job are all highly connected to the people who brought them to the city. Sometimes, a whole family may be found working at the same factory, all of whom have found their jobs through relatives and friends who work there (Huang et al., 2008). When asked why they don't enter the city on their own, many of the new generation of rural migrant workers reply, "If I did so, my family would worry about me", "I don't know a lot about the city, how can I go to the city with no one to show me the way?" "I can't find work on my own. I don't know how to go about finding it." Given this background, when they first go to the city, members of the new generation of rural migrant workers mostly interact with their relatives, fellow villagers, and colleagues who are there, who will also tell newcomers about their urban experiences and viewpoints on living in the city. However, with the passage of time, newcomers will gradually break away from this initial social circle, which primarily is based on blood relations and family members, and begin to increase their interaction with other people living in the city.

Ayong, from Suqian, Jiangsu, is only 20 years old. Although he has lived in Nanjing for only two years, he has already changed jobs once and is now planning to change jobs again. Like many other rural migrant workers who have just come to the city, Ayong first worked as an ordinary labourer at a factory. After working there for half a year, he went to work as a waiter at a restaurant. He has now grown tired of taking orders and serving food every day. He says he wants to work as a hairstylist. This idea originated from his close contact with several hairstylists at a hairdresser in his neighbourhood. These several young men have lived in Nanjing longer than Ayong, earn comfortable incomes, and lead very urban lifestyles. Ayong is quite envious of them.

> I don't want to talk about my first job. It's quite meaningless, and I couldn't continue working there. The job I have now is somewhat better than my first one; at least it's not mechanical and repetitive. However, it's also very tiring and has no future. Am I supposed to serve people at a restaurant for the rest of my life? I've made a decision to become a hairstylist. There are so many handsome guys at the hairdresser, such a beautiful sight. They make themselves up beautifully every day and often change their hairstyles. They also dress stylishly. Those of us who work at restaurants can't compare to them. Our wages aren't as high as theirs. I plan to first work at the hairdresser as an apprentice and slowly move up the ranks. Ultimately, I may possibly open my own hairdresser shop.
>
> (Ayong, male, from Suqian, Jiangsu)

A profession is fundamental to the new generation of rural migrant workers who want to put down roots and make a life for themselves in the city, and is an important standard for evaluating their living conditions. Accordingly, after provisionally settling down in the city, many people make plans to find a better job. During his interaction with the hairstylists, Ayong felt that their profession had a better future than his job. They lived lives which more resembled true urbanites. Therefore, his hopes were set on changing his job.

Actually, urban interpersonal communication has a direct impact on charting the course of the new generation of rural migrant workers. This type of guiding force is not only embodied in a person's profession but is also embodied in many aspects of a person's life. For example, clothing and accessories in the minds of the new generation of rural migrant workers are very important. Prior to coming to the city, they are under the impression that most city dwellers dress "fashionably" and "expensively" and "look like people on television". After coming to the city and interacting with city dwellers, this mental image starts to solidify.

Xiao Huang, who is 25 years old, is the owner of a store which sells hardware and daily-use items. He and his parents have run this store in Chuansha, Shanghai, for many years. Because, I, the author of this book, often go to purchase various daily-use items at their store, I know his family very well. On one occasion, Xiao Huang angrily told me that he wanted to leave his parents. Every time he bought name brand clothing and shoes, his parents became upset with him and accused him of spending money recklessly. He couldn't stand this type of living where his freedom to spend money was restricted.

> Actually, what I buy isn't expensive! Most of my clothing is Meters/Bonwe, and for shoes I like Michael Jordan and Tebu, which at the most are three or four hundred yuan. My parents don't pay attention to what brands local people wear, Nike or Adidas, which sell for seven to eight hundred yuan a pair. We have lived in Shanghai for such a long time: however, my parents still keep their village mentality. They buy clothing for less than one hundred yuan from street vendors. You have to kill me first to make me wear such clothes! I have many local buddies here who wear top quality clothing, so I can't dress too poorly.
>
> (Xiao Huang, male, from Putian, Fujian)

Indeed, Xiao Huang, who has lived in Shanghai for seven years, looks no different from an urbanite. However, his parents still retain the simple ways of country folk. There are quite a few members of the new generation of rural migrant workers who are like Xiao Huang, who crave brand name clothing after entering the city. This holds especially true for that group among the new generation of rural migrant workers who have lived in the city for a long time and have had extensive contact with city dwellers. Based on their imaginings about urban identity, they unconsciously emulate how urbanites dress, and to a certain degree dress even more "fashionably" than city dwellers.

Compared with other issues, the problem of "accommodations" is an issue which plagues the new generation of rural migrant workers. Compared to local residents, rural migrant workers' housing conditions are usually worse, with a great difference between conditions for migrant workers and conditions for local residents, in terms of per capita living space and housing infrastructure (such as water, electricity, television, electric fan, air conditioning, private toilet facilities, etc.) (Wan, 2010). However, unlike the preceding generation of rural migrant workers who only wanted to improve their living conditions back home, and were unwilling to use too much of their income on immediate consumption in the city, the new generation of urban migrant workers is more inclined to strive to improve their current living conditions in the city, to live under better conditions, or even own their own home. This has become the goal pursued by many members of the new generation of rural migrant workers.

Jingjing, born in 1991, is already the mother of a year and a half old boy. She and her husband currently live in a small town in Yuhang District, Hangzhou. Her husband works in a factory, and she is a full-time mother who stays at home taking care of their child. Since the three of them came from their home in Anhui to work in Hangzhou, they have changed residences many times. When they first came, her husband didn't have a job, so they lived with her parents (her mother and father work at local jobs). After one month, they felt that this arrangement wasn't convenient, and they moved to a house across from her parents' home. The rented room where they lived had no kitchen, so they always went to her parents' home to eat. Later, due to certain conflicts with her sister-in-law, Jingjing moved to their current home, where they pay monthly rent of 200 yuan.

Jingjing usually takes her child to play at the nearby apartment complex, and gets along well with other parents caring for their children in this community. During her interaction with them, Jingjing gradually started to think about buying a home.

> People in the city care a lot about their children. I have gone to the homes of several parents with whom I am close. Their children all have a dedicated play area. I feel that those of us who are migrants have very poor living conditions, which is unfair to our children. I must buy a home; if I want to live like city people do, a house is a necessity. If I live in a place like this, when my son attends school and brings his classmates to our home to visit, I will feel embarrassed.
>
> (Jingjing, female, from Mengcheng, Anhui)

Jingjing, who has many years of experience living in the city, early on gave up striving to eat and dress the same as city people. She has begun to yearn to become a true urban resident, and her ticket to urban residence status is to have a home of her own. It can definitely be said that owning a house will not, as Jingjing imagines, solve all her problems. However, after she owns her own home, her imaginings about city life will not cease.

Interpersonal communication in an urban space is the most real form of communication. Most of the new generation of rural migrant workers use work ties and local ties as mediums to develop social relationship networks. During their interactions in the city, they observe differences in work and lifestyle between themselves and those with whom they interact. They hope to attain a better life for themselves by emulating and following the example set by the urbanites. Naturally, compared to the preceding generation of rural migrant workers, the new generation of rural migrant workers has a stronger sense of autonomy. Although they emulate city dwellers, they are also searching for a way of life they can call their own.

3.2 Debugging the Imagination: Changing the Way Traditional Media Influences

In the village, television as the representative mass media exerts an extremely important influence on the new generation of rural migrant workers as they grow up. Through the window of the media, they understand the outside world and construct their imaginings about the city largely under the influence of the media. Prior to coming to the city, members of the new generation of rural migrant workers have not personally experienced urban life. When they attempt to imagine what the city is actually like, their minds draw a blank. Thus, television and other media broadcasts whose main content revolves around city life tend to fill the vacuum they have with regard to information on and understanding of the city. It may be said that the relationship between members of the new generation of urban migrant workers in rural society and the media is in line with the Magic Bullet Theory since they widely accept information provided by the media (Fang, 2001). After entering the city, the reality confronting their imagination causes them to become even more autonomous, and they selectively use television and other traditional media.

Nana, who is 23 years old, is from Yancheng, Jiangsu, and works as a waitress at a coffee shop in Hangzhou. She has lived in the city for five years, and early on learned how to go online. She has gone through two or three mobile phones, but still maintains the habit of watching television. The coffee shop is not the same as a restaurant where it gets hectic at meal times while during other times workers can take a break. In fact, there is an intermittent flow of customers who come to the shop. After a day's work, Nana often feels so tired that her legs ache. The dormitory where she lives is provided by her boss, an apartment with one living room and three bedrooms, occupied by over ten girls. Although the living room is very small, the good thing is that it has a sofa and television.

> After work I turn on the television, slouch down on the sofa, eat a snack, and surf the TV channels for a program I like to watch. This is the happiest time of day for me. I like to watch Hunan TV's variety shows on the Mango Channel. Wang Han and He Jiong are my favourites (among television program hosts). They are intelligent and humorous. I am their loyal fan. I also like to follow TV drama series, the ones about love in the city. I just watch them for fun. There is no way I would believe them, as I once did. People on television may possibly really exist, but we don't live in the same world. I watch television to relax and feel happy. After coming to Hangzhou, I also watched local television programs, to learn something about life here.
>
> (Nana, female, from Yancheng, Jiangsu)

Nana's thoughts represent the change in feeling that occurs among quite a few members of the new generation of rural migrant workers when they watch television. After coming to the city, the "city" is no long a distant image portrayed in the media. Some members of the new generation of rural migrant workers, after living in the city, undergo a great change in media literacy compared to the time when they lived in the village and begin to independently evaluate the information broadcast by the media.

Ying Hong, who has worked at a machine factory in Ningbo for more than ten years, is a young man who really enjoys watching television. From childhood, he has spent a lot of his time watching television. After coming to the city, Ying Hong continued to maintain his habit of watching television. He lived in the factory dormitory, and because he was introverted, shied away from interacting with others. Usually, during his leisure time, he would often lie in bed at the dormitory and watch television. However, Ying Hong confessed that his selection of programs had undergone a significant change.

> In the past, I liked to watch television series, and liked Kung Fu dramas and dramas about the city the best. I really enjoyed the fighting and killing portrayed in Kung Fu dramas, while stories about city life were romantic and beautiful. Now my taste has changed. I feel that watching television series is really a waste of time, because they are randomly written and sometimes too farfetched. Now I enjoy watching documentaries, mysteries, and programs on the military, science, and human culture. I don't have an educational background, so I can learn quite a lot from watching documentaries. In this way, when I talk with other people, I can show that I am a knowledgeable person.
> (Ying Hong, male, from Bijie, Guizhou)

Ying Hong's attitude represents a change that has occurred among quite a few members of the new generation of rural migrant workers in their use of mass media. They are no longer passive, a "target" which can be hit at one shot. Their experiences living in the city have enabled them to perceive that television and other mass media do not possess such objectivity. They have begun to autonomously use media and to understand information presented by the media based on their cognitive framework. Ying Hong, who has lived in Ningbo for over ten years, has a completely new perception of television and the city.

> It's not that television is very fake; it has some real content and it also has some false content. You can't believe all of it. After living here for a long time, I feel that Ningbo is also like this. You can earn money here, and life is also more interesting than back home. However, people here discriminate against outsiders, and it's true that they look down on people from the countryside.
> (Ying Hong, male, from Bijie, Guizhou)

After living in the city for a long time, members of the new generation of rural migrant workers such as Nana and Ying Hong can differentiate between various types of information on television and other mass media. By doing so, they recover a more objective image of the city, which is not the same as the beautiful image of the city they initially imagined, and is not as terrible as what they perceived when they first came to the city. They have also begun to realize that they can use the media to improve themselves. In the preceding text, we mentioned Xiao Zhang who works at a certain auto repair shop in Nanjing, who came to understand the city by reading the newspaper every day, to become more knowledgeable. After Xiao Zhang left the factory where he worked in Jiangning, Nanjing, he found work through a friend from back home at an auto repair shop in the city, where he usually washed cars for customers. The workload was not continuous and he had many intermittent breaks. Xiao Zhang's boss loved to read the newspaper. Their shop had subscribed to four or five newspapers and when Xiao Zhang had free time, he loved to read them.

> In the past I hated reading. Ha ha, otherwise I would not have performed so poorly in school. Sometimes, I have a lot of free time here, and the newspapers are piled up over there, so I read them. After some time, I began to feel that reading the newspaper was very interesting. I learned about a lot of things, and was able to hold a conversation with others. I enjoy reading the *Jinling Evening News* most, because since I live in Nanjing, I should learn more about this city.
>
> How can I put this . . . at the time when I first arrived here, I was bullied at the factory, and felt that Nanjing was really an awful place. Naturally, I don't feel this way now. Every place has both good people and bad people. It was unavoidable that I would be taken advantage of when I first came here. In fact, this happened because I was too naive and didn't know how to talk to people. Now I wash cars every day and sometimes can really hold a good conversation with the car owners. Perhaps this is because I read a lot of newspapers.
>
> (Xiao Zhang, male, from Fengbu, Anhui)

Although his current salary is not ideal, and his work doesn't have much of a future, Xiao Zhang is now able to speak more candidly than when he was at the factory. He feels that the city has always been what it is, what's crucial is how you perceive the city. In brief, the new generation of rural migrant workers have undergone a tremendous change in how they use traditional media. The media has truly become a tool for them to obtain information and improve themselves. Heightened media acumen has enabled them to more objectively view information in the media. Now the city in their eyes has become a multisided entity, and they have gradually adapted to the life they are living. How to better improve themselves has become the new subject of their urban dream.

3.3 *Searching for a Breakthrough: Multiple Functions in the Use of New Media*

Television as representative of traditional media is indispensable to the new generation of rural migrant workers, while new media, primarily, the Internet and smartphones, have developed rapidly during recent years. The rate at which broad audiences, especially young people, are using new media is steadily increasing. Such audiences are progressively coming under the sway of new media, and the new generation of rural migrant workers is no exception. A scholarly survey of members of the new generation of rural migrant workers living in the Shanghai area discovered that the current percentage of netizens among members of the new generation of rural migrant workers living in Shanghai is 75.4 percent, while 96.4 percent of them own mobile phones, both figures being higher than the percentage among them who rely on traditional media. When comparing the popularity of new media among the new generation of rural migrant workers in Shanghai with other social groups, it was discovered that, firstly, whether it be the use of the Internet or mobile phones, the rate of popularization of new media among the new generation of rural migrant workers was higher than the average rate for Shanghai residents and the public nationwide. The new generation of rural migrant workers constitutes a group in society which actively uses new media. Secondly, even when compared to the youth group in Shanghai, the percentage of the new generation of rural migrant workers who own mobile phones does not lag behind (Zhou & Lv, 2011). From this it can be seen that use of new media is quite popular among the new generation of rural migrant workers. Due to a relative deficiency of economic and social resources, the new generation of rural migrant workers is extremely active in its use of new media. The new media assists members of the new generation of rural migrant workers to transcend the bounds of their inherent living scenarios, to change their urban dreams, or to stimulate them to create new dreams.

Wei Dong who comes from Quanjiao, Anhui, is 26 years old and works at a factory in Nanjing. Although he is young, he is already an experienced netizen. He frankly says that the Internet and his mobile phone are the best prescription for his monotonous life.

> My enjoyment of the Internet has come in phases. Initially, I enjoyed watching martial arts TV series, playing video games, and listening to music. Now, I prefer to watch the news and browse chat forums. When I work during the day, I always stay tuned to QQ. QQ News often has pop-up information. However, in the factory we are not permitted to play with our mobile phones, so in the evening I go back to my lodgings and log on again to get the details.
>
> (Wei Dong, male, from Quanjiao, Anhui)

When Wei Dong was living back home, he would often watch CCTV's news broadcast with his parents. But he lost interest in watching it after he started to log on to the Internet. He says,

> There are all kinds of opinions on the Internet. It is no longer just one voice speaking. I feel that the information I previously received was too monotonous. My Internet friends have all kinds of opinions and talk about everything.
>
> (Wei Dong, male, from Quanjiao, Anhui)

Life at the factory is repetitive and monotonous, while the Internet provides workers like Wei Dong with a new channel for understanding the city. By using new media, what they see and hear is a perspective which is different from that of traditional media and their own personal experience. Through the Internet, they meet friends outside their immediate social circle and experience the clash of diverse information and viewpoints. This clash assaults the stereotypical impressions which they have always clung to. As they learn to view the city and their own living environment from different perspectives, their values also silently undergo a change.

A Yi, born in 1986, is a senior hairstylist at a Shanghai hairdresser named T-JS. He earns a very decent salary and dresses in the latest fashions. No one could possibly imagine that he comes from a remote village in Hunan. A Yi has lived in Shanghai for over ten years, and has always worked as a hairstylist. Working his way up from minor apprentice to senior hairstylist, he has undergone a tremendous change. He loves electronic products, and owns a notebook, iPad, and mobile phone.

> The computers provided for customer use by T-JS stores are all Apple, which demonstrates the stores' good taste. At the store I have become accustomed to using an Apple computer so my own notebook, iPad, and mobile phone are all Apple. Their speed is fast; they never get jammed and they are very enjoyable to use. When I go online, I do just about what everyone else does. I watch television, read the news, and browse some hairstyling websites and groups. I usually use my mobile phone more, and when I have nothing to do, I log onto Weibo and my circle of friends. Every time I style a customer's hair, if she agrees, I will take a picture as a memento, and if I have done a really good job, I will share the picture on my circle of friends and Qzone, which helps to advertise my work. I also like to use the Momo software application, because I can meet a lot of people. I once had a girlfriend whom I had met on Momo. She was attending a vocational school in Shanghai and was still a student.
>
> (A Yi, male, from Xiangxi, Hunan)

A Yi has had many girlfriends, but none of them turned out to be that special soul mate. He doesn't pay much attention to his parents' urging him to get married.

> My parents are old fashioned in their thinking. No matter how much they push me, I won't listen to them. I don't want to get married and have a child: it's too tiring and too much trouble. I want to live free and easy and don't want to step into the grave of marriage.
>
> (A Yi, male, from Xiangxi, Hunan)

After living in Shanghai for a long time, A Yi has ideas about marriage and family which are quite different from those of people in his village back home in Hunan. For him, getting married and having a child is no longer something which must be done based on age, but rather has become an event determined by fate. A Yi now has vague memories of how life was for him in Shanghai when he came here over ten years ago, and found himself unable to answer the interviewer's questions, such as, "Were you accustomed to living here when you first arrived?" and "What was your impression of Shanghai before you came here?"

During the interview, A Yi gave the impression that he was very confident in himself and very satisfied with life. His values and lifestyle had become highly urbanized. This was perhaps because he did not plan to start a family. A Yi showed no concern about the issues of purchasing a house and carrying out household registration. In his eyes, the city was a place where he could enjoy a modern life, and identity was unimportant.

The emergence of WeChat commerce on smartphones has also provided quite a few members of the new generation of rural migrant workers with the opportunity to build their own businesses. A girl named Jiaojiao, who is 24 years old, has been engaged in WeChat commerce for over one year. Jiaojiao is from Haimen, Jiangsu, and has worked in Hangzhou since she was 17 years old. She first worked in a clothing factory and then in a restaurant. Finally, she worked as a sales person at a bakery. It was at this time that she met her boyfriend who was working at the same shop as a baker. And with the help of her boyfriend's elder sister, she began to do WeChat commerce, selling a skin care product called "Wuhai Weiyan".

Jiaojiao's WeChat nickname is "Meidani", and the photo placed in her WeChat circle of friends portrays her as an exceptionally beautiful girl, in a style reminiscent of the self-portraits of various Internet stars. In order to promote her products, she often makes an appearance and posts a talk online, sharing her feelings about using the product among her WeChat circle of friends, supplemented by photos. In addition to selling product, Jiaojiao also often posts certain artistic, romantic quotes, accompanied by her own indolent, beautiful self-portraits. From her appearance, we can't discover any stereotypical impressions we may have of the new generation of rural migrant workers. Her entire WeChat circle of friends is filled with fashion, the avant-garde, and artistry.

> During the time when I first came to the factory to make clothing, I was very unsophisticated. However, I slowly learned and slowly began to change. Especially when I began to sell "Wuhai Weiyan", I realized that if I didn't make myself look beautiful no one would believe that the product I was selling had any benefit. They would say, "If your product is so good, why hasn't it improved the quality of your skin?" If my business grows, I will no longer work as a salesperson at the bakery and will fully devote myself to selling product on WeChat.
>
> (Jiaojiao, female, from Haimen, Jiangsu)

Jiaojiao plans to marry her boyfriend after a year. Her boyfriend also plans to open his own bakery. After they marry, they will continue to struggle to live in

Hangzhou. When she speaks of her feelings about Hangzhou, Jiaojiao has a very indifferent attitude.

> In Hangzhou, or for that matter anywhere, if you want to lead a stable life in the city, you must work hard to earn money. There are also many local people from Hangzhou who are very poor. Outsiders are not necessarily worse off than they are.
>
> (Jiaojiao, female, from Haimen, Jiangsu)

From the preceding cases we can see that members of the new generation of rural migrant workers are not much different from urban youth in their use of new media. The new media provides the new generation of rural migrant workers with another window on understanding the city, to perceive the city from another angle. Xiaowen, a young man of 26 from Huangshan, Anhui, describes his feelings about logging on to the Internet as follows:

> The Internet has a lot of fast-breaking news on problems in the city, news about smog, pollution, and others. There are also good things about living in the countryside. The environment is good and the food is healthy. However, we have no choice. We must earn money in the city. Once you have money, you can live in a good house and drive a good car. Nothing else is important.
>
> (Xiao Wen, male, from Huangshan, Anhui)

It may be said that the new media provides them with a plethora of diverse information, and has also gradually become a tool for their personal development. Members of the new generation of rural migrant workers have broadened their field of vision in their use of new media. They no longer blindly worship everything about the city. On the contrary, they view the city from a more objective, more reasonable perspective. Identity is an unnegotiable obstacle in the urban lives of members of the new generation of rural migrant workers. When they first arrive in the city, they feel anxiety and even despair when they realize how difficult it is to obtain urban identity. However, under the influence of new media broadcasts which "challenge tradition and authority", they no longer blindly seek acceptance from the system and urban residents. On the contrary, they begin to imagine how they can obtain a better life in the city in their own ways.

In a nutshell, the gap that members of the new generation of rural migrant workers encounter between their imaginings about the city and the realities of city life after they come to the city is unavoidable. However, they don't remain immersed in a state of bewilderment, and don't abandon the city to return to their rural homes. They begin to make an effort to adapt to their new lives. They continuously discover new problems, find disparities, and attempt to integrate themselves into the cities where they are living. Throughout this process, the new generation of rural migrant workers has even more frequent contact with the media. Their urban dreams also undergo reconstruction. Naturally, the scenarios in this new round of urban dreams are vastly different from the scenarios they imagined prior to coming to the city. Members of the new generation of rural migrant workers no longer merely entertain dreams about what attracts them to city life and urban identity, but further consider how to close the distance between where they are now and the life and status they want to achieve.

4. Phased-in Adaptation: Media Constructs of Urban Dreams and Their Dynamic Change

The city holds a special meaning for rural migrant workers. The city is not their original home, but is a place where they can ideally find a better life. This is especially true for members of the new generation of rural migrant workers. Although they are from farming families and come from villages, the environment in which they have grown up is completely different from that of their parents. They have an even stronger yearning for the city. From living in a village to initially coming to the city, and then living in the city, during this spatial migration, members of the new generation of rural migrant workers experience a transformation of their roles and huge changes in their lives. As a result, their inner feelings are also inevitably transformed and enriched. The media and the reality of their lives provide members of the new generation of rural migrant workers with all types of information on the city. In their minds, they further refine the means by which they ultimately achieve their urban dreams.

In the clash between media constructs and real life, the urban dreams of members of the new generation of rural migrant workers pass through a series of changes from "formation" to "transformation" and ultimately "reconstruction". However, this does not represent the end of their dreams. On the contrary, their urban dreams continue to evolve. Unlike their parents, members of the new generation of rural migrant workers have a strong desire to integrate into city life. To achieve this, they continue to actively adapt to all aspects of the city, while their urban dreams stimulate their attraction to the city and also exert a dynamic effect on their adaptation to city life.

In his book *Understanding Media*, Marshall McLuhan (2000) postulates that "media is an extension of the human body". He believes that media is an extension or expansion of human sensory abilities (McLuhan, 2000). Indeed, from the first print media to today's mobile terminals, humankind has become progressively dependent on the media for obtaining information in order to understand the outside world. In his seminal work *Public Opinion*, Walter Lippman states that media is a mechanism which serves to reconstitute our environment. The "pseudo-environment" shown in the media is not a "mirror" representation of the objective environment, but is a "secondary environment" which is not the same as the environment per se. Accordingly, our cognition of many objects inevitably originates from media constructs.

The media has also developed on the heels of urbanization and modernization, because the media is intimately and inseparably connected with the city. The relevant research indicates that most information and content in the media is related to the city. However, serious consideration should be given to the quantity and quality of programs related to rural life. Whether it is traditional media such as radio, television, newspapers and magazines, or new media such as the Internet and mobile phones, all of them merely revolve around the city and city dwellers. This is due to the progressive marketization of Chinese media, under which most types of media assume sole responsibility for their profits and losses. In order to survive and obtain greater space for development in the increasingly intense and ruthless media market, they must learn how to pursue and maintain market share and profits. They must learn how to keep a close watch on those who control social capital, while advertisers need to attract consumers to purchase merchandise. Accordingly, the attention paid by consumers inevitably lies at the core of competition among the media. According to Western economic theory, market demand equals population plus purchasing power plus purchasing intent. In order to earn sizeable advertising revenue, media outlets will naturally focus more on the city, where there is high residential population density, and purchasing power is stronger than that of rural areas. In addition, looking at the autonomous development of mass media, the convenience of urban transportation, and the advanced state of communications, it can be seen how the collection and production of urban news and other types of information on urban life are quicker and easier than in a rural environment. Accordingly, in terms of propagation cost, urban residents are ideal targets for sales and marketing. Therefore, it is not difficult for us to see that the mass media's scope of activity, content focus, and customers targeted by its services are defined by urban factors (Jing & Yang, 2008). The media is an important means by which people obtain information and is also inseparable from the city. Accordingly, the media is a key factor in building the urban dreams of the new generation of rural migrant workers. From the rural village to the city, the relationship between the city and members of the new generation of rural migrant workers undergoes a transformation from "distant view" to "personal experience". Throughout this process of dynamic transformation, the media provides the new generation of rural migrant workers with a window for understanding the city, and is also a necessary tool in their daily lives. Whether in the village or in the city, members of the new generation of rural migrant workers obtain large amounts of information on the city by using the media. They then form their urban dreams after mentally processing this information.

The population in China's rural areas is sparse, with residential points distributed throughout environments where agricultural production occurs and farming households live together in villages. Generally speaking, villages contain several thousand or several hundred people and the social environment is rather simple. Farming households have rather small social circles. A social interaction mechanism comprised of persons with whom one is familiar makes rural villages unable to generate their own media. This situation is compounded by the monotony of leisure activities in rural villages. Rural residents spend a great deal of their leisure time on television, radio broadcasts, and other such mass media. Most members of the new generation of rural migrant workers are still in school when they are living in rural villages, and, compared to children of the same age who live in cities, rarely attend extracurricular courses or classes which interest them. The television inevitably is their constant companion weekend after weekend, holiday after holiday. After the mass media has inundated them over a long period of time with "information on the city", members of the new generation of rural migrant workers have a "mental picture of the city" imbedded in their imaginations. Nonetheless, this picture may vary from person to person, and images of the city may be different in each person's mind. In the broadcast environment of the village, use of the media by members of the new generation of rural migrant workers is one-dimensional. Their dearth of real-life experience makes it impossible for them to differentiate whether information is high or low quality, true or false, and they are highly dependent on the media in their formation of imaginings about the city. In addition to mass media, interpersonal communication also provides an important source of what members of the new generation of rural migrant workers imagine about the city. This type of "reporting" on the city is highly personal and subjective. Nonetheless, for the most part, they take such word-of-mouth information on the city at face value.

Actually, in mass media and interpersonal communication, information on the city is not completely positive. Some of it is negative. For example, "City people are prejudiced against rural migrant workers", "It's not easy for rural migrant workers to make a living in the city", and so on. If you carefully analyse the "ugliness" of the city, you will discover that members of the new generation of rural migrant workers are concerned with negative assessments which are primarily related to status as "country folk". Within this lies the hidden implication that "as long as you make an effort and struggle, you can obtain urban status and solve your problems". Accordingly, prior to entering the city, imaginings about the city held by members of the new generation of rural migrant workers are generally rich with emotive colour. Lacking extensive experience with regard to city life, they equate the city with what they imagine it to be based on the limited information they possess.

When members of the new generation of rural migrant workers leave the rural society with which they are familiar and come to a strange environment to begin a new life, their previous imaginings about the city suffer an impact. The prosperity and splendour of the city excites them. However, the arduous work, meagre income, high prices, and complicated interpersonal relationships make them feel the disparity between what they imagined and what they experience in real life. They encounter a dilemma which plagues them psychologically and in their day to day living. A huge reality hits them in the face, and their imaginings about the city undergo a tremendous change. Actually, the transformation of their imagined scenarios after they come to the city is not due to the complete falseness of what they imagined before coming to the city, but is due to the difference which exists between a "distant view" and "personal experience". In the same way, imagined scenarios aroused by real-life experiences cannot be equated with reality. The distress they feel in adjusting to the "shift" in their lives causes those have just come to the city to tend to magnify the difficulties they encounter, which results in their imagined scenarios moving towards another extreme.

With the passage of time, members of the new generation of rural migrant workers gradually become accustomed to their current lives. The media occupies an important position in their lives in the city. Since the time that Gutenberg, the inventor of moveable type printing in the West, invented the first printing press, media has undergone rapid development, with the continuous emergence of new forms of media. Human beings increasingly rely on the media for their perception of the world. It can be said that, other than through real-life experience, we understand many things, especially things about which we have no knowledge, through media constructs (Yin, 2014). Urban dwellers still need the media to form their perceptions of everything about the city, and there is a significant element of imagination in such "understanding". By comparison, members of the new generation of rural migrant workers, who have over 10 to 20 years' experience living in rural villages, have an even greater need to rely on the media for their understanding of the city. Constrained by the limitations of their jobs, social circles, and other such factors, the scope of their personal experience of city life is inevitably narrow and restricted.

In the city, members of the new generation of rural migrant workers come into contact with the Internet and quickly acquire their own mobile phones. The new media, using attributes different from traditional media, opens a portal for them to obtain information. Together with interpersonal communication in their living environment, the channels by which members of the new generation of rural migrant workers obtain information are far more numerous than those in their rural villages. The emergence of multiple modes of communication, together with their personal experience of the city in real life, enables them to learn to make distinctions in their acceptance of information. Communication is no longer one-dimensional but results from the interaction of information in the media and real life. At this time, their city dreams become imbued with even more ideal images. Members of the new generation of rural migrant workers no longer define the city in terms of black or white. The content of this new round of city dreams focuses on self-advancement and obtaining identity as an urbanite. Although members of the new generation of rural migrant workers prior to coming to the city also have the desire to "find opportunities for personal development" and "become a real urbanite", and thereby realize such dreams, their dreams at that time are ultimately nebulous and don't contain specific details. After coming to the city, members of the new generation of rural migrant workers begin to develop concrete expectations with regard to their personal development in terms of how they imagine their jobs, their appearance, their education, and so on. They still yearn to "obtain status as an urbanite and integrate themselves into city life". However, at the same time, they are also aware of the special nature of their own group. Accordingly, they hope to attain more realistic objectives through their own efforts.

In summary of the preceding, mass media, through news broadcasts, television dramas about city life, variety shows, commercial advertising, films portraying images of the city, and interpersonal communication through personal interaction, potential influences and other modes, jointly define the city dreams of the new generation of rural migrant workers. There are two causes driving the ongoing transformation of the city dreams of the new generation of rural migrant workers: firstly, members of the new generation of rural migrant workers, when leaving the village and coming to the city and afterwards during their lives in the city, are faced with a living environment undergoing constant changes, and modes of media which they can come into contact with are also being transformed in accordance with such changes. Secondly, after gaining more experience living in the city, members of the new generation of rural migrant workers experience a tremendous change in the context of how they use media, pay attention to media content, and understand media information. Throughout this process, prior to coming to the city, the media is the key factor in constructing their city dreams. During the short transition period, real-life experience is the key factor. During the long process of adapting to city life, the media and real-life experience jointly come into play. Under the concepts defined in this book, the city itself may be considered to be a type of "media". Accordingly, the city experience also defines the dream. It can be confirmed that the city dream of the new generation of rural migrant workers is a dynamic, changing process, which after undergoing "formation", "transformation", and "reconstructing" will also undergo changes in their lives going forward. Naturally, the city dreams of the new generation of rural migrant workers are complicated and are not merely positive, realistic, and dynamic. They are also negative, illusory, and pessimistic. We have not sedulously differentiated them, because the type of dream is not important. What is significant is that the dreams themselves deeply reflect the relationship between the new generation of rural migrant workers and the city, thus forming the driving force which motivates them to forge ahead.

Hence, members of the new generation of rural migrant workers have created their city dreams under the construct of the media. They put forth a real effort under the guidance of these dreams. In the clash between their city dreams and reality, such dreams may be achieved or revised. Afterwards, the new generation of rural migrant workers may create new dreams for life in the city during the course of their lives. As they continuously strive to achieve their dreams, they reach a point where they adapt to the city in "phases". So-called phased-in adaptation to the city differs from complete adaptation to the city: in a closed loop in which city dreams undergo change, members of the new generation of rural migrant workers fail to resolve all their problems. Their life in the city is still faced with many challenges and they are still quite far from obtaining urban resident identity. However, when compared to their condition when they first came to the city, when they were at a loss as to what to do, members of the new generation of rural migrant workers who have achieved "phased-in" adaptation have attained some degree of provisional stability in their lives and in their mental outlook.

We may anticipate that the dreams of the members of the new generation of rural migrant workers will continue to undergo changes in the future, and that they will also attain new levels of "phased-in" adaptation. The internal composition of the new generation of rural migrant workers is not uniform. In terms of individuals, their urban dreams and the means by which they adapt to urban life are also not completely the same. The processes and outcomes described earlier are merely an overall trend. Accordingly, under the influence of their urban dreams, members of the new generation of rural migrant workers will achieve level after level of "phased-in" adaptation. Their adaptation to the city may generally be expressed as an "upward spiral". The process under which they adapt to the city may have twists and turns and may sometimes regress. However, the overall trend is still upward.

References

Fang, X. (2001). An investigation and analysis on the use of mass media in rural areas of Jiangsu province. *Journalism & Communication Review*, *1*, 125–132+267+274–275.

Gao, M., & Zheng, X. (2013). City imagination and identity identification of rural residents: Evidence from Jiangsu. *Chongqing Social Sciences*, *4*, 43–49.

Guo, L., & Zhang, X. (2016). Modernity conflict and bridging between urban and rural cultures from the perspective of migrant workers. *Gansu Social Sciences*, *1*, 165–168.

Huang, H., Ma, Q., & Liu, D. (2008). Migrant workers' adaptation to cities and its influence on their social cognition. *Journal of Southwest University*, *34*(6), 148–152.

Jiang, L. (2007). Cross-cultural communication: Culture shock and how to deal with it. *Sino-US English Teaching*, *3*, 61–65.

Jing, E., & Yang, L. (2008). *An analysis of the problems of metropolis image constructed by mass media*. Communication Studies and China. Fudan University Forum.

Li, Q., & Li, L. (2014). Peasant workers' modernity and urban adaptation from the perspective of cultural inclusion. *Nankai Journal (Philosophy Literature and Social Science Edition)*, *3*, 129–139.

McLuhan, M. (2000). *Understanding media: The extensions of man* (D. He, Trans.). The Commercial Press, p. 58.

Wan, T. (2010). Housing levels and housing consumption of the new generation of migrant workers – A comparative analysis based on intergenerational perspective. *China Youth Study*, *5*, 47–51.

Yin, X. (2014). Media constructed "city space": A discussion from the perspective of communication study. *Journal of Hangzhou Normal University (Social Sciences Edition)*, *36*(2), 118–124.

Zhang, C. (2011). Modernity and marginalization: A discussion on the characteristics, problems and outlets of the new generation of migrant workers. *Academic Journal of Zhongzhou*, *3*, 98–102.

Zhou, B., & Lv, S. (2011). An empirical study on the use and evaluation of new media of the new generation of migrant workers in Shanghai. *Journalistic University*, *2*, 145–150.

3 My Mediatized "Looking-glass Self"

Identity Construction Among the New Generation of Rural Migrant Workers

Rural migrant workers are a group which has emerged and received widespread attention amid the transformation of Chinese society. However, for a period of time, this attention was largely focused on the embarrassment they felt regarding their identity. The duality and mutual opposition of government policies for urban and rural areas has placed rural migrant workers in the position of being neither farmers in the traditional sense nor modern industrial workers. They fall into a group stranded between these two. In terms of profession, they no longer depend on agriculture for their livelihood. Large numbers of rural migrant workers in the city work in manufacturing and service industries. Living in the city year-round has caused them to progressively increase their interaction with urban groups. Having been involved in industrialization and consumption of consumer goods, their emotional ties to rural areas have also gradually undergone a change. Under the restrictions imposed by dual household registration systems for urban and rural residents, although rural migrant workers are the driving force powering urban growth, and have made an outstanding contribution to China's economic and social development, nonetheless, they cannot attain equal status with urban dwellers in their enjoyment of the city's social and cultural resources and basic welfare benefits. Cultural and institutional "enclosures" affect how they live and what they experience in an urban environment. Many of them are unable to achieve a sense of belonging in the city. Born in rural areas and working in the city, they are always wandering on the perimeters of these two social venues.

The new generation of rural migrant workers is different from their predecessors. Although the older generation of rural migrant workers were also anxious and bewildered over their self-identity, nonetheless, they had certain emotional ties to their rural origins. This enabled them to enjoy more space in which to manoeuvre when facing issues related to their identity. Even if they failed to integrate themselves into city life, they at least had another option, which was to return to the village. Conversely, the new generation of rural migrant workers does not have such an option. Compared to the preceding generation, they have less historical baggage. Since they have had little contact with agricultural production activities, they don't have many emotional ties to the rural village. Moreover, the emergence of globalization and consumerism has caused them to strongly identify with and yearn for the city. What is confusing is that they embody a mixture of both rural

DOI: 10.4324/9781003365785-3

and urban attributes. Confronted by the gap between ideals and reality, their self-identity becomes an apparent problem.

1. "My Original Self": Position and Awareness of Identity in Rural Life

As an emerging group of migrant workers in the city, the new generation of rural migrant workers are the same as the older generation of rural migrant workers, in that they also spent their childhoods in the countryside. The difference between them is that the universal implementation of nine-year compulsory education in China has allowed the new generation of rural migrant workers to have received more years of formal education than members of the older generation. As a result, they have had limited participation in agricultural production activities. Studying and playing comprised the totality of their lives in the village. Growing up in this environment, their peer group has become the most predominant "significant others" during their socialization. In addition, members of the older generation, such as parents and teachers, have also played important roles in their lives as they grew up. These significant others have served as mirrors in their perception or evaluation of individuals and have affected how they perceive their own identities. Harry Stack Sullivan, the American psychoanalyst, believed that significant others influence an individual's sense of happiness to generate an ego system which forms a part of a person's identity (Hsu, 2001). It is worth noting that the relationship between an individual and a significant other may be real or may also be imaginary. Various types of media proliferate modern society and serve as significant others in structuring an individual's imaginary interpersonal relationships. This is because when individuals interact and converse with all types of media, they interpret media content to satisfy certain personal needs. Moreover, media content is structured by people in the media. Accordingly, their dialogue is with persons behind the media, or with persons who are embodied in or structure the media (Fang, 2012). As a generation which has grown up during the growth of the Internet, the new generation of rural migrant workers' contact with the new media may be seen as a type of simulated social communication process. This process also plays a significant role in an individual's understanding and recognition of their self-identity. By exploring, sensing, and understanding the role played in their own self-evaluation by these significant others (their peer group, the older generation), and the new media, the new generation of rural migrant workers has begun to comprehend and recognize the gradual formation of their own self-identity.

1.1 Persons With Playmates: Acceptance and Attraction in Communication Among Peers

In the transformation of a traditional society into a modern society, the importance of peer groups has notably increased. In traditional society, the older generation held authority, and inculcated the younger generation with various ideas about the world. They set the appropriate standard for social behaviour for the younger generation. In ancient China, under an almost stagnant "hyper-stable structure", the experience, skills, and knowledge of their ancestors passed down by the older generation was sufficient to handle various changes in society. The older generation provided a model for the younger generation to emulate. However, the constant state of change inherent in all aspects of modern society has broken the authority of the older generation, as young people learn new things and their adaptability to new changes exceeds that of the older generation. Accordingly, we have abandoned the "pre-figurative age" and have entered into a completely new "post-figurative age". "Cultural feedback" has become the social norm, and the importance of one's peer group has markedly increased. The peer group in the village which the new generation of rural migrant workers knew before coming to the city has become the significant other in their growth process. This peer group's evaluation of its own self-image affects the new generation of rural migrant workers' cognition and evaluation of its own self-identity.

Xiao Cheng, whose family lives in Sihong, Suqian, Jiangsu, works as a cook at a small restaurant in Nanjing. During our interview, Xiao Cheng, who is already 27 years old, spoke freely. However, he said that in the past he was very shy and gradually became gregarious and outgoing only after coming to the city. He is the only child in his family and was doted on by his paternal grandparents. When he attended school, due to his introverted personality, he indulged in video games, had poor grades, and was always the subject of rebuke. Even though many of his classmates were unwilling to get along with him, he never lacked playmates. By playing video games, he was able to find pals who shared his aspirations.

> At that time, I loved to play video games, the ones on computers. My grades suffered and my teacher always reprimanded me. There were many things I just couldn't seem to learn. Perhaps this was due to my excessive indulgence in video games, so my grades didn't go up. Everyone likes someone who makes good grades. My classmates shunned me, so I just played video games. The group of people I played video games with were fond of playing and they also didn't have good grades. Their families also didn't care. I play video games really well, games where you pay by dropping a coin into a slot, and games online. I was good at all of them. However, I really had no confidence in my academic abilities. I fell behind my classmates many times, and was unable to learn.
>
> (Xiao Cheng, male, from Suqian, Jiangsu)

Xiao Shi, who also comes from Suqian, at the age of 26 was the mother of two children. Xiao Shi, who looks no more than 20-something, is a cashier at a fast-food restaurant. Her husband works as a clamshell shovel operator at a company in Lishui District, Nanjing. Because she has children, she always feels that she doesn't have enough money to spend. When she reminisces about her life in the village, she fondly remembers the time she spent in school and the great happiness she felt playing with her classmates. She had an outgoing personality and enjoyed talking with them. She would also often watch television with them. It can be seen from her communication with her peer group that she was someone who did not lack playmates. Since she loved to watch television and didn't earn good grades at school, she felt that study held no benefit for her, and left home with her friends from the village to go to work.

> No one back home subscribes to such things as newspapers. At the time, I really liked watching television. I was very fond of it. I especially liked the Chinese drama "Princess Pearl", also known as Huan Chu Ko Ko (Huan Zhu Ge Ge). We watched it every day, and sometimes would skip our meals. My grades were not good, and the teacher didn't pay any attention to me. I liked to talk to people in class and couldn't understand the curriculum. I wasn't good at English or mathematics. When I tried to study them, I got a headache. Around the second year of junior middle school, I dropped out. I couldn't just stay at home and play all the time. When I left home to work. I played all winter vacation. I felt bored, so I went to Zhenjiang. At that time, we really had fun playing, didn't go back to school and had bad grades. Some of us stayed home and some like me went out to work.
>
> (Xiao Shi, female, from Suqian, Jiangsu)

Many of the new generation of rural migrant workers said that during their school years, they had poor grades, because they did not have close communications with their classmates who performed well in school. Actually, in the macro-environment of the rural village, where there is widespread deficiency in the overall quality of rural education, students such as those who perform poorly in school comprise the vast majority. Accordingly, even though they are not held in high esteem by students who excel in their studies, they never lack playmates and the size of their social circle is often much greater than that of students who do well in school. Notwithstanding such factors as individual personality, how an individual handles matters, and differences in individual status within a peer group, in general, most migrant workers by and large are accepted and recognized by their surrounding peers.

1.2 People Who Are Cared For: Intergenerational Protection, Love, and Concern

In his book published in the 1940s, *Under the Ancestors' Shadow: Chinese Culture and Personality*, the Chinese-American anthropologist, Francis L. K. Hsu analysed the culture and personalities of people living in traditional Chinese society. He pointed out that under the organized lifestyle of the extended family, the relationship between parents and children formed the core of family life. This relationship originated from innumerable ancestors and was linked to the uninterrupted continuity of succeeding generations of children and grandchildren in future generations. People lived under the shadow of their ancestors (Hsu, 2001). Up until the present time, in rural villages, it is an indisputable fact that the nuclear family occupied the mainstream position in society. Although intimate relations in people's private lives have undergone a series of adjustments, family life still has quite a distance to go before it shifts from a "parent-child axis" to a "husband-wife axis". Compounded by the "one child policy" promoted for many years in China, children, especially those with no siblings, occupy the core position in the nuclear family. Even taking into consideration that a considerable number of the new generation of rural migrant workers are children who were left behind and did not grow up with any substantial care from their parents, nonetheless, most of them are still cherished by their parents as "their beloved children". Every word their parents speak and every action their parents take have an effect on how members of the new generation of rural migrant workers feel about and evaluate themselves.

Xiao Ling, born in 1984, is from Youyu County, Shuozhou City, Shanxi province. At the age of 19, she failed to pass the college entrance examination and was not admitted to university. Having two younger sisters, parents who were ordinary factory workers, and a family which was not well off, she abandoned further study. In 2003, she came to Shanxi's provincial capital, Taiyuan, to work. Having neither a good educational background nor a social network, she had no choice but to begin working at the lowest paying jobs. At that time, she spoke with a strong regional accent, dressed very simply, and was unaccustomed to urban life. She also had no friends, felt very lonely, and was looked down upon by others. Being far away from her parents, performing arduous work, and leading a lonely life, she really missed her home and her family.

A young female apprentice earns half the money that a full-fledged worker makes, only ¥ 500 per month. One has to survive on one's own. Since I couldn't afford to rent housing, I lived in the workers' dormitory. Because the place where I lived was rather remote, I had to prepare to leave for work every day at the crack of dawn and would finally arrive home from work at 7 or 8 pm. If I worked the night shift or worked overtime, I would arrive home even later. The district where I lived was not very safe. At night when I came home alone, I felt very afraid. I also ate very simply and ate very little meat. In this type of environment, I really missed home. Once, the television at a store was broadcasting a song which had the word "mama" in its lyrics. When I heard this song, I cried out "mama" and then my face was covered with tears. In the beginning, I would go home every one or two months, by long distance bus, which took two or three hours before I arrived home. Inevitably, I could only stay at home for one night. I would frequently write letters to my family, often writing about how I felt and the environment I lived in. I would ask them about how they were doing and about my classmates back home.

(Xiao Ling, female, from Shuozhou, Shanxi)

Xiao Yu, who is almost 18 years old, comes from Zigong, Sichuan. Before attending high school, he directly went to learn how to be a chef. Currently, he works as a chef at a large hotel on Puyuan Road, Pukou District, Nanjing. He begins work every morning at 8 am and is usually busy until around 11 pm. He has very few days off and is busiest on weekends. Xiao Yu has been in Nanjing for almost one year, and during the time he has worked has never returned home. He has never gone back during Spring Festival. He now earns monthly wages of ¥3,800. Xiao Yu is approximately 165 centimetres tall and very well built. His skin is dark and there is a scar on his eyebrows from an injury. His hands have many scars and old calluses. He has an outgoing, straightforward personality.

> In the village, I didn't attend kindergarten but went straight to preschool, studying with my cousin who is one year older than me. I performed better in school than he did, which made me feel very proud of myself. During elementary school, my grades were always very good. However, when I started junior middle school, I didn't study very hard. I feel that perhaps I was really going through puberty. I was adamantly against my parents and my teachers trying to control me. I especially disliked my parents always complaining to me about my behaviour. I was extremely rebellious and loved to play. I angered my mother to the limit. Looking back, I now feel that I really didn't behave sensibly. All day long I only thought about playing basketball, fooling around and wasting time. Now I really regret that I didn't apply myself to my studies. I threw away so much valuable time.
>
> (Xiao Yu, male, from Zigong, Sichuan)

Prior to formally going to the city as migrant workers, most members of the new generation of rural migrant workers have attended school to receive an education for a varying number of years. During their time at school, they met various teachers who were their "significant others" during their puberty. In the Chinese tradition, teachers have always played a role similar to fathers', referred to in the saying "a teacher for one day and a father for all one's life". In ancient times, the ranking together of "heaven, earth, ruler, parents, and teacher" prominently demonstrated the importance of this role. The relationship between students and teachers actually may be considered to be the same as the relationship between parents and children. The love and concern of a teacher for their students can enable a person to clearly recognize their own position in life, and even enable delinquent or lost children to rediscover themselves.

Xiao Liu, who is 23 years old, comes from Weifang, Shandong province, and now works as a machine operator at a certain garment factory in Yantai. She dropped out of school after graduating from junior middle school and left home to work in the city. She has worked for approximately three years. She spent a long time working in the factory as an apprentice and now has finally become a "master" worker who can train "apprentices". She has trained over several score apprentices, however, none of them have stayed at the factory for long. She feels that they are unable to bear hardship. She was once a "poor student" in the eyes of her teachers and classmates, rebellious and wild. Afterwards, with encouragement and help from her teachers, she changed into a completely new person, and her demeanour became coy and gentle. She also began to act sensibly and to behave well, which really astounded them.

> Life indeed gives people many challenges, to let people learn more. I really miss my teacher Ms Qu. Sometimes, I will send her a brief message. When I look back on the time I was in school and with my former teachers, she was the best. She was very good to me. I don't want to talk about what I was like in the past. Now, I have completely changed! Do you know why I made such a big change? It was because of her that I changed. In the past, my parents worried about what would become of me when I grew up. They were very anxious and never imagined that I would become who I am today. My transformation occurred due to the efforts of my teacher Ms Qu. She has a very special place in my heart, and I often think of her. No matter what, I will work hard to do my job well, so that my parents won't have to worry about me.
>
> (Xiao Liu, female, from Weifang, Shandong)

Naturally, quite a few persons among the new generation of rural migrant workers said that their teachers "only cared about those students with good grades and didn't pay any attention to us", and that "some teachers themselves were not up to standard", etc. School organizations usually pinned their hopes on children "who studied well" and looked down on individuals who didn't get good grades as "persons who failed to make something good of themselves", even to the point of discriminating against them or labelling them. Many people among the new generation of rural migrant workers had become weary of studying before they became migrant workers. However, generally speaking, their teachers were different from the bosses they encountered after entering society. Even if their teaching methods were not correct, teachers still showed love and concern for these young people. It was just that many of them in the rebellion of their puberty didn't necessarily perceive or correctly understand the criticism they received from their teachers.

Xiao Qiu, born in 1993, from Hefei, Anhui province, currently works in the lobby of a club on Xuanwu Avenue in Nanjing. Although he is the son in his family, his parents like his elder sister better, perhaps because she was more well behaved, made better grades, and easily entered university. He, on the other hand, wasn't a good student and was also mischievous. Because he disliked studying, he dropped out of school. His family felt that it was useless for him to continue his education, so he left home to work. Now when he recalls how his teachers criticized him during his school days, he finally realizes the profound meaning of what his teachers said at that time.

> Because at the time I was truly very stupid, couldn't continue my studies, and didn't apply myself at school, I played all the time and thoughtlessly wasted my time. Afterwards, I also felt that this was meaningless. At that time, on one occasion, our class monitor said something and I argued with him. He said to me, "A student like you is wasting time studying." I replied, "Okay,

then I don't want to study. Studying is not good." At school, my teachers didn't like me. However, at that time at my age, that was the way I was. Teachers discriminated against you and really looked down on you. I said to myself, I can't stay in school, so I will discontinue my studies. Actually, people like me who don't study, who stop studying at an early age, who drop out of school early to go to work, several years later regret what they have done. If you don't study, you don't have enough knowledge. If you don't have much schooling, when you go out to work, you can't find a good work environment. You can only do some jobs which other people are unwilling to do.

(Xiao Qiu, male, from Hefei, Anhui)

Both parents at home and teachers at school, as members of the older generation, have spoken and acted out of love and concern for the new generation of rural migrant workers. Their behaviour in this regard has influenced how the new-generation migrant workers understand themselves. Even if misunderstandings arise at the time, as circumstances change with the passage of the years, they are able to re-evaluate what they have experienced.

1.3 People Who Take Command of Their Lives: Arousal and Affirmation Through Exposure to the Media

The popularity of various media in rural areas varies widely, restricted by economic development and standards of education of residents in those areas. Generally speaking, television and radio broadcasts are most popular, while few people read newspapers and magazines. Over the past several years, widespread use of smartphones and other types of digital media, has greatly optimized the media environment in rural villages. The new generation of rural migrant workers was born at an optimal time, when the Internet was experiencing monumental growth in an era of unprecedented developments, when the existence of the new media in their daily lives was as natural as the air they breathed. Compared to their passive contact with mass media, the new media involved a process of dynamic, self-determined acceptance. In their contact with and use of new media, such as social chatting and games, they had the power to selectively explore a world as yet unknown to them, to continuously deepen their understanding of themselves. The arousal and acknowledgement of the media as a "significant other" has served as an important source in playing out their awareness of their self-identities.

Xiao Cheng, from Suqian, Suzhou, who was mentioned earlier, often got into fights at school, and, as a result, was disliked by his teachers, who often felt that he would adversely influence his classmates. His family only exhorted him to excel at his studies and didn't show much concern for him. He often had no one to talk to, and no one to play with. After coming into contact with computer games, it was as if he had discovered something new and refreshing in his life. Because his grades were falling, his teachers and his parents always criticized him. He felt very frustrated at that time and felt that only games could redeem him. The characters in the Internet games became an embodiment of himself. This other self always succeeded, and was the master of the game room. Other players who wanted to mount an attack had to necessarily receive his permission. When other young classmates of his who had never known him personally learned that he excelled at computer games, they admiringly asked him to help them score, and to obtain equipment. The sense of achievement Xiao Cheng felt in the world of computer games entered his real life, and enabled him to compensate for his feelings of inferiority.

> I loved playing computer games. At that time, I always played and my grades suffered. However, I had nothing else to do. We had a computer at home, so after class I would play a game. Sometimes my family would give me pocket money and I would go to the Internet bar to play online games. Now, when I recall what I did, I realize that I was really thoughtless. However, at that time, I felt that playing online games was really fun. They made me feel satisfied. Now, I don't play anymore. I feel that in the past I wasted all my time. Now, playing computer games has no meaning for me.
>
> (Xiao Cheng, male, from Suqian, Jiangsu)

Xiao Li from Shuyang County, Suqian City, in Jiangsu province, currently works as a cashier at a convenience shop in a university cafeteria. She doesn't find her work difficult. Before coming to the city, she had continuously attended school in Shuyang. Many of her classmates around her in school had already begun to use mobile phones. Xiao Li, whose family didn't have much money, primarily relied on newspapers and television as sources of information. She would listen with great interest to broadcast content often viewed by others as dull. Xiao Li was an obedient child at home. Sensible and clever, she seldomly made unreasonable demands of her parents. Xiao Li's parents were usually busy at work. To alleviate their daughter's loneliness, they would often bring newspapers home for her to read and Xiao Li would always read them with great interest. Unlike her classmates, Xiao Li, whose family was not affluent, did not start using a mobile phone at an early age, and usually did not go to Internet bars or game arcades. Her primary form of entertainment was listening to radio broadcasts and watching television. She said that the radio was her favourite tool for receiving information. A continuous stream of various types of information became the primary channel by which she learned more about another world different from the environment in which she lived.

> At that time, I was still attending junior middle school, and didn't have a mobile phone or a computer. There were many things reported on the radio. It was as if I had another eye. When I was alone, I would listen to the radio. I felt as if someone was having a conversation with me. I really liked to listen to the radio, and would chat with my classmates about songs and events the radio broadcasted. They said I was a bit old-fashioned. However, some songs they had never heard before.
>
> (Xiao Li, female, from Suqian, Jiangsu)

Contact with and use of media differs conspicuously by gender. If we say that male members of the new generation of rural migrant workers are addicted to various types of games, female members are especially fond of short stories and television dramas. Xiao Cheng and Xiao Li's behaviour is a snapshot of how the new generation of rural migrant workers uses the media before coming to the city. Outside of their usual study at school, due to the extreme dearth and monotony of information available in rural village society, the media has become something to which they are closely attached. Members of the new generation of rural migrant workers learn through the media information, which is different from what is taught in rural village schools. They establish new circles of communication while surfing various Internet venues and chatting on the Internet to attain a sense of achievement which cannot be obtained in real life. Although the world of the Internet is simulated, the sense of achievement and admiration from others which it generates extends into real life, causing members of the new generation of rural migrant workers to feel surprise and satisfaction. They then begin to develop their abilities in other areas. These abilities are a powerful driving force in re-establishing their self-confidence: the dissemination of information and establishment of mediated platforms play a conspicuous role in this process.

During the interviews, certain members of the new generation of rural migrant workers said they didn't really like their "past identity" in rural village life, while others couldn't articulate whether they liked or disliked their "previous selves". Some persons said that although in the past they were not sensible and aware of things, nonetheless, they had very happy lives. Generally speaking, members of the new generation of rural migrant workers prior to coming to the city have nebulous notions of their self-identity: their companions among their peers and their lives with their parents determine their role and mission in life. Many among this new generation are not clear about what they want. They are stopped from furthering their educations by poor grades, and leaving home to work is a road which they have no choice but to take. Under these circumstances, members of the new generation of rural migrant workers may speculate that their work after going to the city may change their current rural village identity, that they will have freedom, earn money, support their families, and will not become dependent on others. Many of them cannot clearly say whether they are satisfied with rural life, and whether the decision to go to the city was of their own free will. When they make the decision to leave the village, they struggle inside themselves. Faced with an impending new existence, they feel both excitement and anxiety. Many among this new generation start the journey to a life of working in the city under the guidance of their families and friends.

2. Encountering the City: Anxiety and Confusion Over Self-identity in the Initial Period After Coming to the City

Even if such "significant others" as the village, peer groups, one's parents' generation, and various types of media which exist in a limited number help members of the new generation of rural migrant workers to form an awareness of their self-identity, this identity still remains vague and easily changeable, while the vast space of the city seems to provide various possibilities for exploring oneself.

Accordingly, members of the new generation of rural migrant workers consciously or unconsciously are filled with a yearning for the city. In their imaginations of "a more colourful life in the outside world", they enter the city, to have their first "encounter at close quarters" with this new urban space. A huge gap exists between working and living in the city and life in rural society.

The workplace becomes the most important space in which the new generation of rural migrant workers engages in resocialization. A huge transformation also occurs in the "significant others" who help them become aware of their identities. Work-related groups within an enterprise; urban resident groups met through work, residence, and personal interests; and urban media systems, which are much more developed than media systems in rural society, become the most important sources in forming an "urban identity".

When people change their physical space, this is not only accompanied by a change in specific, material, directly experienced factors such as residential environment, work opportunities, and way of life but also by a change in deeper, more abstract issues, which include a series of questions related to individual and group identity such as "Who was I in the past and who am I now?" and "Who do other people believe that I am?" (Qin, 2005). This shift of space from rural village to city is not only a population shift of geographical significance but is also a cultural migration of psychological significance. Within this shift there exists a tension between the adoption of urban culture and the abandonment of rural culture. Even if they have through various channels come to understand certain aspects of urban culture, nonetheless, during the initial phase when members of the new generation of rural migrant workers come to the city, they are still "outsiders" who are foreign to urban culture. The clash between urban and rural culture causes them to experience unprecedented anxiety and confusion over their self-identity. Their initial experience after coming to the city is accordingly also filled with hardship and suffering.

2.1 Becoming a Person "Who Is Out of Touch": Atomized Survival in Communication Within an Organization

In a rural environment, most members of the new generation of rural migrant workers can receive protection and love from their parents. However, after coming to the city, they are far away, out of sight of their parents. Although to a certain degree they have obtained freedom, for example, many persons expressed that "My parents can no longer control me", nonetheless, when adapting to difficulties, they also are bereft of a shoulder they can lean on. At home, members of the new generation of rural migrant workers are the undisputed, deserving centre of attention, whose parents, whether they are working at home on the farm or working outside as labourers, organize their lives around matters concerning their children's future marriages and careers. However, when these rural migrant workers go to work, they become insignificant solitary members of socialized mass production. The fast-paced life of the city makes employee turnover a common occurrence of everyday life. Every individual is merely a cog in the machine. For members of the new generation of rural migrant workers who have not received higher education and who lack human capital, this set of circumstances is even more cruel. The assembly line mode of an enterprise, compounded by rapid turnover of employees, makes it difficult for communication within an organization to achieve stability.

Xiao Yu at the age of 17 came to Nanjing to work, and has now lived in Nanjing for almost 17 years. He comes from Xuzhou and originally worked at a hotel near the Hongshan Forest Zoo. Afterwards, he worked at several small restaurants before coming to the Chinese restaurant where he now works. He works as a chef in the kitchen and gets along well with his co-workers. On weekends, he goes out with them to sing and have a meal. Sometimes, he gets together with friends from his hometown. When speaking about how he felt when he first came to Nanjing, he recalls that during that time he was very lonely and had a hard time coping with the situation.

> At that time, I had just arrived, having been brought to Nanjing by an older buddy of mine. My first job involved butchering fish and the like and sometimes I would prepare accompanying dishes. At that time, my life was really very difficult. I didn't know any of the people who lived with me at the place I rented. Many of my colleagues were local people from Nanjing. When they spoke in their dialect, I couldn't understand what they said. I still had to do my work. After all, this place wasn't home.
>
> (Xiao Yu, male, from Xuzhou, Jiangsu)

There is a huge difference between working at a location far from home and working in one's home area. A local group's feelings of superiority will cause it to divide a group of workers originally working at the same organization into "us" and "them", with circles drawn around communication within a business organization. There are no trustworthy people with whom one can communicate inside the organization. In the city, simplification of the structure of the ontology of self and the monotony of life content causes rural migrants to experience atomization in their lives.

Xiao Zhang, 20 years of age, is from Suzhou, Jiangsu. After graduating from technical school, he worked in Suzhou and Wuxi, starting from odd jobs such as unloading merchandise and wiping burrs off the surface of work pieces. He is currently working in the machine industry in Hefei as the operator of a digitally controlled lathe. His experience rushing around between jobs in these three cities has provoked him to give a lot of thought to his work and has enabled him to develop a very deep understanding of relationships among co-workers. According to his view, it is very difficult to develop stable friendships within organizations.

> Here in Hefei, there is nothing out of the ordinary. I have become more intelligent, that's all. Basically, nothing exceptional has happened. People here

are very easy to get along with, there's nothing to it. However, when I first enter an unfamiliar environment, I won't treat people as friends. Objectively speaking, the relationship between co-workers is not the same as the relationship between personal friends. When co-workers work together, they sometimes cooperate and sometimes compete with each other, especially when this involves promotions and salary increases and other such matters related to personal benefits. Some people become good friends with their co-workers and share a lot of private feelings with them, especially their feelings of dissatisfaction towards the enterprise and towards their superiors. However, the other person will ultimate report this to their superiors. Some people are promoted based on their actual abilities. However, those who originally were their good friends may believe that they did something behind their backs to get promoted and feel betrayed. Such good friends then disclose the other person's private matters to others, in order to get revenge. Society and school are quite different.

(Xiao Zhang, male, from Suzhou, Jiangsu)

In a nutshell, members of the new generation of rural migrant workers after coming to the city mostly experience communication between formal roles within an organization based on work relations. Every individual according to their assigned role takes appropriate action. There is a lack of further emotional communication among such individuals. And the rather high turnover rate among members of the new generation of rural migrant workers places extreme limitations on the formation of stable interpersonal relations. Accordingly, inside an organization, to the extent that people eat together, live together, and play together, these are mostly relationships among replaceable companions, in which people only fulfil the need for mutual companionship, and do not represent communication at a deep spiritual level. This state of atomized survival causes migrant workers within an organization to resemble people who are isolated from each other and who are out of touch with one another.

2.2 Becoming a Marginalized Person: Discrimination and Isolation in Communication Between Urban and Rural Groups

The French sociologist Gabriel Tarde, in his book *The Law of Imitation*, posits the concept of "social distance" (Tarde, 2008). He uses this concept to emphasize the objective differences between different groups, as a sign of class differences among them. Parker stresses that social distance describes a mental state which causes us to consciously realize the differences and isolation between ourselves and groups which we are unable to fully understand (Xu. 2007b).

What members of the new generation of rural migrant workers feel when they first come to the city is precisely the social distance between themselves and urban groups. In their minds they have a strong desire to integrate into urban groups. However, urban groups, through education, knowledge, cultural tastes, language, and behaviour, differentiate themselves from the new generation of rural migrant workers, who must undergo a process of identification to achieve urban social identity. This causes members of the new generation of rural migrant workers to feel that urban groups discriminate against them.

After coming to the city, members of the new generation of rural migrant workers, separated from a rural environment begin to experience a change in how they organize into communities. Their colleagues and customers are the main subjects with whom they communicate when they are at work. The small communities where they live are their primary places of rest. Their landlords are the most important urban residents whom they must face. Many members of the new generation of rural migrant workers expressed that their interaction with their landlords has not been pleasant. Xiao He from Suqian has a rather upbeat personality with a sunny disposition and comes from a family of modest means. Although he has been swindled in the past prior to entering the labour force, he takes this experience as a lesson which he paid for with cash. Although he has classmates and friends from the local area, when he encounters difficulties, he tries to find a solution on his own. Xiao He learned of certain employment opportunities through his classmates and friends. Although he sometimes plays computer games with them, drinks with them, and even sometimes buys the same style of clothing as them, he seldom contacts them in his daily life. Sometimes, when he can't understand what local people are saying to each other, he becomes anxious. However, this does not interfere with his effort to adapt to life's inevitable ups and downs.

> My landlord never griped to me about anything, but sometimes talked a bit too much. When I first came, I wasn't able to say a lot. She sometimes said that we used too much water and electricity, at which point I gave her a little extra money; it's not that I didn't give it to her. She raised the rent and said she wouldn't rent to us. Originally, I rented the place together with a friend of mine, which was arranged by the shop (where we worked). Afterwards, I moved out and rented a space with a bed. Now, everything is fine.
>
> (Xiao He, male, from Suqian, Jiangsu)

Many members of the new generation of rural migrant workers when they come to the city are cheated by employment agents, are owed wages by employers, and are bullied. Their initial experiences in the city are definitely not very pleasant. The term "urban resident" seems to be synonymous with "fraudulent" and "untrustworthy". When faced with insurmountable problems, most members of the new generation of rural migrant workers give up. They believe that "the boss is always like that". They don't seek assistance from organizations in the community where their work unit is located or from social organizations in the city. Many members of the new generation of rural migrant workers after being cheated on the job are unwilling to seek help from community groups or organizations in the city. They feel that they themselves "don't have sufficient power" to deal with the outside world. "Where can I go to retrieve this money? Why would they (urban community organizations) show concern for us?"

"I also don't know where they (such organizations) can be found." "If worse comes to worst, I will quit my job." Such statements reflect commonly held feelings among rural migrant workers. In the subconscious minds of members of the new generation of rural migrant workers, organizational commitments in the communities where they live are considered to be weak. These rural migrant workers who lack a sense of security still maintain employer-employee relationships; nonetheless, the urge to quit their jobs is very strong. It may be said that getting paid is their most direct and most inflexible demand. In their work, organizational commitments which they perceive to be weak cause members of the new generation of rural migrant workers to have little faith in community organizations. Xiao Yu and Xiao Shi, who were mentioned in the preceding text, have had experience interacting with community groups.

> We are living in other people's territory and don't know where to find community groups. I have never heard of them before. Where can I find them? You also mentioned to me that there are groups dedicated to helping us. We don't know if this is true or false. If by any chance these groups intend to cheat us out of our money, it's best just to leave things alone. If we encounter problems and seek their help, they won't necessarily assist us. People here who run shops all know each other.
>
> (Xiao Yu, male, from Xuzhou, Jiangsu)

> Afterwards, I went to work in Liuhe, Nanjing. They owed me wages. However, at that time I was already living with my current husband. We had a friend at work who at that time was also owed wages. He went to the Yuhuatai community office. After filing a law suit which dragged on for a while, he received compensation. We asked this friend from work how to institute legal proceedings. He told me and we went to the community office as well. The people there were very kind. That factory boss was known for owing workers' wages. Everyone knew about him. They helped us recover our wages. After that, my husband and I left. At that time, after I met him, I was able to deal with problems and was not afraid; after all, he was a man.
>
> (Xiao Shi, female, from Suqian, Jiangsu)

Following a change of living environment, family ties and local ties which members of the new generation of rural migrant workers originally had in the village undergo a shift in time and space and begin to undergo a transformation. A series of strategies and actions involving various social cultural resources are used in real life in the city (Pan, 2007b). This causes them to fail to obtain a sense of belonging when they compare themselves to groups of urban locals. Social structures formed after urban groups undergo consolidation make rural migrant workers, who come from a different social background, feel that such groups are very difficult to enter.

Social boundary constructs demarcate the differences between the new generation of rural migrant workers and urban groups. Categorized social behaviour and information transmitted through symbolic language and intent convey the stereotypes which local groups have of members of the new generation of rural migrant workers. Although their professional relationships at work give them an opportunity to come into contact with urban groups, when rural migrant workers first come to the city, they feel cold and disconnected, at a distance from urbanites.

Their mistrust of organizational commitments at work continues to inform their perception of urban communities. Harbouring their own suspicions coupled with their mistrust of organizations, many members of the new generation of rural migrant workers are unable to directly confront problems they encounter in the city. They have been saddled with an image of the preceding generation of rural migrant workers which was solidified during their urban sojourn, and are thus more easily bullied and challenged by local urban groups.

Overall, because most of the groups they encounter at work and in daily life are local urban groups, members of the new generation of rural migrant workers feel distant and unfamiliar when interacting with them. The long-term feeling that they have been stripped of their social rights and lack representation causes self-doubt, giving rise to mental impulses which prompt them to solidify their perceptions of themselves as people living on the margin of urban society.

2.3 Becoming the Underprivileged: Media Representation and Reproduction of Stereotypes

Identity is related to the understanding of the question "Who am I?" in the epistemological sense by a meaning-making subject, and is also related to the politics of difference which defines how different groups are reproduced in various cultural discourses. Identity is a means for understanding the crux of contemporary cultural phenomena (Chang, 2015). As a marginalized group in the city, the new generation of rural migrant workers is not the core audience of media organizations. Compared to urban residents, its image in the media, to a considerable degree, has been hidden. The inferior position of its social vulnerability as represented by the media becomes "media vulnerability". Even if members of the new generation of rural migrant workers appear in the media, they are portrayed to the public as being poor, pitiable, culturally deprived, and of a lowly nature. Over many years and months of diffusion and dissemination, these negative labels have become public stereotypes of rural migrant workers. Faced with the mass media's top-down power in information distribution, members of the new generation of rural migrant workers hold mental reservations about such sensational coverage. However, because they cannot obtain the power to hold discourse in the media, they have no choice but to let others paint a picture of who they are and embellish their image as a group.

When talking with interviewees we mentioned the term "new generation of rural migrant workers", a term with which they said they were unfamiliar. The information they came into contact with usually described their group as "labourers". They were apathetic towards and had filtered information on their own group. In one aspect, this reflects the disapprobation of the new generation of rural migrant workers of reports in urban mass media and also illustrates how urban media has failed to deeply understand this group and harbours a strong bias when reporting on it. The new generation of rural migrant workers has formed a solidified perception: although it is continuously transforming itself in the urban setting, urban society barely acknowledges its existence. The media's portrayal of "migrants" to the city is an obstruction to the new generation of rural migrant workers on the road to becoming aware of its social identity and even affects recognition of its own self-identity.

> I seldomly watch the news. Every time I play with my mobile phone, I take a look at news with headlines which really grab people's attention. I see very little news on those of us who are migrant workers. According to my impression such news doesn't seem to exist. I watch a lot of television and movies, especially famous Hollywood movies. They have a lot of roles but I only remember the leading actors and actresses. The leading roles are usually played by handsome men and beautiful women, which has nothing to do with us migrant workers.
>
> (Xiao Jin, female, from Hubei)

> I basically don't read the newspaper. National events have nothing to do with us small folks. If the news is about rural migrant workers, it also doesn't interest me, because most of it is fake, and always talks about how we should feel concern for rural migrant workers, feel concern for this and that; it's all just talk.
>
> (Liu Zi, male, from Jiangxi)

> The media is also like that. What they report about the lowly nature of rural migrant workers is also a fact. Definitely some rural migrant workers use foul language and don't behave properly. As long as I do what is right, that's what counts.
>
> (Xiao Li, female, from Sichuan)

On the one hand the absence of media coverage of rural migrant workers reminds them of the fact that they are a marginal audience, that they are different from the mainstream audience of urban residents. On the other hand, rural migrant workers as a group appear in the media in sensational news stories. Given this unfair treatment, they understand that their right to hold media discourse is minimal, that they can't be discussed as equals of urban residents. Surrounded and bombarded by mass media, they have become the weak, deprived of their right to hold discourse.

3. "The Person I Am Now": Restoring and Reconstructing Identity in Urban Life

With the passage of time after they come to the city, members of the new generation of rural migrant workers increase contact with the groups around them. In an urban space which is relatively modernized with a wide variety of media, as they gradually become familiar with the city, their feelings of discomfort gradually subside. The formation of new circles of social relationships impels members of the new generation of rural migrant workers to slowly begin to relax their psychological lines of defence. As the fear caused by feelings of mystery and uncertainty when they first entered the city gradually disappears, they begin to build their self-confidence based on their understanding of and adaptation to the city. The diversity of media and heterogenous groups of people open the door to a new world for the new generation of rural migrant workers. They learn new types of behaviour in their dealings with different groups of people; in their discussions with colleagues, they learn all kinds of information about the city. Their initial feeling of distance from others is diminished by numerous and varied social interchanges. At the same time, their ability to utilize various media resources is gradually strengthened, and their enhanced media literacy helps them to selectively screen information. Based on its understanding of the responses of surrounding groups, the new generation of rural migrant workers gradually achieves the restoration and reconstruction of its identity in the city.

3.1 Searching for Their Place in Society: Transformation of Awareness in Urban Survival

After members of the new generation of rural migrant workers have lived in the city for a length of time, they begin to learn to adjust to the rules governing life in the city, predicated on determining their own positions in society. In terms of existing human capital, social capital, and cultural capital, there is still a significant gap between them and true urbanites. However, if they return to the village, after having been saturated by urban living for so many years, they will find it difficult to accept traditional rural life and customs. Accordingly, most members of the new generation of rural migrant workers position themselves as persons who are drifting, waiting for the right opportunity. "Drifting" describes their position as persons who are unable to fully integrate themselves into urban life and who also cannot go back to surviving in the village. "Waiting for the right opportunity" reveals that they will not abandon any opportunity to integrate into city life. During our interviews, we often heard many people say "I lack the opportunity", or "When I have the opportunity, I want to do a little business". These statements reflect their change of awareness as persons surviving in the city. The city need not adapt to them, rather, they must take the initiative to adapt to the city.

Xiao Wang, who comes from Yunnan, is 26 years old. Before coming to Hangzhou to work, he stayed in Shaoxing for a period of time. The boss at the factory where he originally worked cheated him, so he came to Hangzhou to work. Although life as a labourer was hard, Xiao Wang believed that this was merely a necessary phase in his life experience. Xiao Wang stated that his former experience working as a salesperson at the factory enabled him to accumulate much experience in dealing with people. He told me, the author, that he left Shaoxing to find a job he would enjoy, where he would also be accepted by others. Xiao Wang exudes the conviction that members of the new generation of rural migrant workers will not merely take difficulties encountered in life as burdens but will convert them into valuable spiritual assets to further advance their adaptation to city life.

The transformation of Xiao Wang's awareness after coming to the city, is a process experienced by many members of the new generation of rural migrant workers. They don't care about the physical hardships they endure as a direct result of living in the city. They begin to simplify their life objectives. In the tolerant environment of the city, their self-confidence begins to grow significantly. They reflect on their urban life experience to adjust their mental outlook. They further adapt themselves to developments and changes in the city by making adjustments throughout their ongoing social behaviours. At this time, standards which are internalized in their urban lives begin to form the foundation of their new identity. Although the fast pace of living in the city affords the members of the new generation of rural migrant workers little time to reflect on whether they can integrate themselves into city life, or change the city, subtle transformations in reference objects cause them to be driven in their city lives to unconsciously take actions beneficial to improving their current status. Most people "don't think too much" and feel that "to live a contented life is sufficient".

Xiao Lu who works at another beauty shop in Hangzhou, is also 26 years old and comes from Guizhou. He is very adept at learning from others. He works at two jobs. In addition to earning money from handing out flyers, he can also earn extra commission on new customers he recruits to come to his shop. At the present time, his income is not high, nonetheless, he believes that performing well at his work will help him in his future life. He believes that a professional attitude is extremely important. Only by correctly understanding one's position can one survive and make a living in the city.

> Working in society, you should not feel that you are insignificant. You must feel that you are important. You must have a good attitude. Those of us in this profession must have a good attitude. If we don't have a good attitude, we won't be able to pass out many flyers in one day. If you just stand there and complain, it's not good. During the first several days when I came here, I was like that. However, I then saw *Tiny Times* on television in which the writer of the story says: "Don't complain about any profession, because every profession has stood the test of time. Every profession exists for a reason." The writer also said, "A man's mind grows when he feels wronged". Accordingly, if you are somewhat looked down upon in your line of work, you must learn from this experience. Therefore, we must have an optimistic attitude at our present job. If the first day doesn't go right, try again the second day. You will ultimately find opportunity, right?
>
> (Xiao Lu, male, from Guizhou)

Regarding their future plans in the city, many of the new generation of rural migrant workers said that they would "take things one step at a time". This means that they are very flexible in their cognition. On the one hand, they don't want to abandon the hope of integrating into city life. On the other hand, given that they lack a clear grasp of the situation, maintaining present circumstances may be their best plan. Xiao Liu, one of the new-generation migrant workers, comes from Fuyang, Anhui province, and is barely 18 years old. He works as a chef in the back kitchen of a restaurant on the shores of West Lake, and often works for as long as 12 hours a day. Hangzhou, with its beautiful scenery, captured his heart. He says although now life is rather difficult, he is committed to trying his best to stay in this city.

> I don't want to make comparisons. I left home to work, to earn my wages on this job. There is no way I can make comparisons. I don't feel that my life is hard. I live very simply. Sometimes, I play poker or stroll around the streets with my colleagues. I really want to stay in Hangzhou. I feel that as long as I believe in myself, I will definitely make a place for myself here. Every day when we take a rest we go out to play together. I lead a very simple life and don't feel tired. If I think about too many things, there's no way I can accomplish them, so it's not necessary to give them any thought. I take things one step at a time.
>
> (Xiao Liu, male, from Fuyang, Anhui)

Xiao Liu's attitude towards life reflects the self-awareness of the new generation of rural migrant workers. As one of the main forces driving the construction of the city, they realize that urbanites view the work which they perform as very low level and very arduous. However, this does not cause them to negate the substantial contribution they make to the city. They have begun to correctly recognize the changes they themselves experience, and their attitudes towards surrounding groups are also changing. They have increased their tolerance of themselves and of the city. From the preceding cases, it can be seen that the powerful clash of culture and environment when facing city groups, spurs the new generation of rural migrant workers, with nowhere to retreat, to begin to adjust its attitude in its cognition of urban society. Members of the new generation of migrant workers have begun to make an effort to adjust themselves to adapt to a new environment, to continuously absorb elements of their work which are beneficial to their self-advancement, and have begun to clarify their life objectives and plans.

3.2 Negotiating Continuously for a New Self-identity: Emotional Adjustment in Interpersonal Communications

As outsiders who deluge the city, members of the new generation of rural migrant workers encounter difficulties to a greater or lesser degree when communicating with urban residents who have lived in the city for over ten years or for several decades. When I, the author, asked members of the new generation of rural migrant workers whom I interviewed to grade groups of people in the city where they lived, most of them gave a grade of 60 or 70, while some of them only gave a grade of 50 (100 being the highest score). Urban society and culture are greatly accepted among most of the new generation of rural migrant workers; however, they often feel pressure in their communications with urban groups. This does mean that they reject contact with urban groups. In order to better integrate themselves into urban life, they actively use various media to expand their social circles in the city, starting with their contacts among the group of people from their native place. They continue to break out of this inner circle by expanding outwards beyond it. As they increase their opportunities to contact urban residents, they continuously negotiate their own identity, and readjust their feelings towards others.

Xiao Cai, 28 years old, comes from Nantong, Jiangsu province, and works with her husband in Yutang, Changzhou. As a supermarket cashier, her monthly income is ¥1500. Her husband has opened a construction materials store, and his income is now much more than when he first came to Changzhou. When recalling her struggles when she first came to Changzhou in 2007, she sobbed and sighed repeatedly.

> During the first year, business was not good at all and we operated at a loss. Afterwards, our life became very hard. I felt that it was very difficult and couldn't bear it. My husband told me, "If you want to go back home, go home by yourself. I'm not going back." He felt that since we had come here, if we didn't make a life for ourselves here, we would really lose face if we returned home. Even if we lived as beggars, we had to stay here. We had to make money here before going back. Afterwards, my husband felt he could no longer stay at home waiting for an opportunity. So, he visited neighbouring construction sites and furniture factories to sell his merchandise. Gradually, we had more business. Although we didn't know anyone here, still we had to eat and couldn't just wait for something to happen. Doing business here, how could we not interact with other people? At this point, we have quite a few frequent customers. However, when we hear of construction work anywhere, we immediately go there to see if there is a business opportunity for us.
>
> (Xiao Cai, female, from Nantong, Jiangsu)

Xiao Cai's husband, as a member of the new generation of rural migrant workers, used himself as an intermediary in the city to work hard to dispel their identity as "outsiders", an identity originally entrenched in the minds of local groups. Drawing on their perseverance stemming from rural social traditions, they dispelled certain long-term misconceptions which had existed between rural and urban sociocultural systems. They achieved success in their work and also won approval as a new urban group. In their work, certain members of the new generation of rural migrant workers utilize their outstanding work performance, excellent communication skills, and proficient use of media to cultivate clients who highly trust them. They even successfully extend certain work relationships into offline circles of friends in their lives. Good personal relationships with customers enable members of the new generation of rural migrant workers to gain a wealth of value-added happiness, which opens up their circles of urban communication.

Xiao Cai's husband is representative of members of the new generation of rural migrant workers who have worked hard to break down misunderstandings between urban and rural society. They actively accept information they receive in the city and based on outstanding personal qualities nurtured by their rural social experience, such as "simplicity and dependability", dispel from within suspicions held by certain urban groups concerning their rural identity. They also successfully form new information circles and communication circles in the city. People in their group closely connect the work in their lives with the media. Their outstanding ability to communicate with others and their use of mass media enable them to lead relatively unhindered lives in the city and to enjoy smooth sailing in their endeavours.

Many new-generation rural migrant workers have also discovered that not all urban residents are the deceitful and dishonest persons they had imagined them to be. Many of them communicate with rural migrant workers in an unbiased, even-minded way. This causes the new-generation rural migrant workers to continuously revise their cognition of urban residents and enables them to clearly realize that migrant worker is just one quality in their diverse group. Other than this identity, each individual may be defined in other dimensions. Accordingly, by negotiating their own identity, they continuously deepen their self-identity. For example, Xiao Shi, from Suqian, Jiangsu province, who was mentioned in the preceding text, has had this experience.

> These women are local people, some of whom look down on me. But I am not afraid of them. All of us are workers. Local people and outsiders are all the same. I have worked here for quite some time. I feel that people (local people) are not bad; they don't create difficulties for us. Sometimes in the evening we encounter customers who have had too much to drink and such. They will also greet us and never refuse to pay their bill. I really like my current job.
>
> (Xiao Shi, female, from Suqian, Jiangsu)

From the preceding cases, we can see that after coming to the city, members of the new generation of migrant workers begin to become highly efficient and professionalized in their production modes and in their lifestyles. The structural environment of the modern city also provides a strong impetus for them to change their behaviour. The modern city, different from rural society, enables the new generation of rural migrant workers to expand their living space and communication space. Pulled along by these factors, members of the new generation of rural migrant workers experience a transformation of their behaviour, life styles, and values. They continuously enhance their social characteristics, and after becoming deeply involved in urban life, are gradually accepted by local groups. In their daily interactions they sense gradual changes in the attitudes of these groups. They also dynamically form their own self-identity. They re-socialise their own behaviour, which ultimately influences their awareness of their new identity.

3.3 Attempting to Speak Out: Behaviours Empowered by the New Media

In modern society, the media has become an important domain in which marginalized groups can represent themselves. Mass media, characterized by its one-way communication, cannot be fully utilized by the new generation of rural migrant workers. The rise of new media has resulted in a profound adjustment of the relationship involving both producers and recipients of information. The new generation of rural migrant workers has evolved from a "receiver" of information into a group which both "receives and communicates". As a generation which has grown up with the Internet, it has begun to attempt to utilize new media to speak out, in an effort to create a comprehensive picture of the new generation of rural migrant workers.

This primarily involves the adoption of technology used to communicate information to become closer to true urbanites. The mobile phone as a representative of new media is an attractive feature of the city's modern life. Major symbolic differences exist with respect to having or not having a mobile phone, and whether it's good or poor quality. The developed new media environment of the city gives individuals an intangible sense of exclusion. Speech, behaviour, and actions among urbanites with respect to the value judgments of this group in its adoption of information communication technology makes their sense of exclusion more specific and intense. Xiao Mao, from Zhenjiang, Jiangsu province, after graduating from a vocational middle school, was introduced by an aunt with a few connections to work at a toll station in Changzhou. After performing well on the job, she was assigned to Nanjing. She has often changed her mobile phones, from clamshell phones to bar phones, from feature phones to smartphones, always closely following trends. She now uses an HTC mobile phone. She expressed her intense dissatisfaction with the discrimination she has encountered from urbanites.

> Urbanites look down on us and feel that we are persons from small county towns who have never seen the world. Some of them even believe that we need people to teach us how to use mobile phones and computers. In fact, they basically don't understand that we started from the era of using knock-off cell phones and smuggled cell phones, and then Nokia and Lenovo, up to the present where we use Samsung, HTC, Sony, and iPhone. In fact, early on, times had changed. They (those urbanites) are no more advanced than we are.
>
> (Xiao Mao, female, from Zhenjiang, Jiangsu)

She said she had obtained a cell phone using her own earnings and that she really enjoyed using it. Furthermore, it was a brand of cell phone that she could display with confidence, without fearing ridicule from others. In an imaginary way, consumption helps members of the new generation of rural migrant workers to break through the symbolic boundary which exists between them and city dwellers. At the very least, in her adoption of new media technology, Mao Mao avoided the feeling of discrimination originating from urban society. Regardless

of whether discrimination is tangible or intangible, members of the new generation of rural migrant workers urgently need objective symbols which can demonstrate their status, to legitimize who they are. Mobile phones, as representative of
new media terminal equipment, function as explicit material symbols which play
an important role in expressing the self-identity of the new generation of rural
migrant workers. At the very least, they can show that they have integrated into
city life in their adoption of information technology. Through their possessions,
by consumption of material symbols of the new media, they convey to the outside
world their yearning for emotional acceptance from others. They pursue a sense
of psychological satisfaction to compensate for the emotional divide they feel
between themselves and others.

In addition, society has saddled the new generation of migrant workers with
many biased views of who they are, which on the platform of the Internet are
strengthened and conversely also deconstructed. Notwithstanding that many
members of the new generation of migrant workers say they seldom watch
news reports on migrant workers, and rarely participate in related discussions,
they mostly keep their feelings about urban society to themselves. In their use
of new media, they have been lurkers who shun discussions and remain silent
on the Internet. However, this does not mean that they do not have a voice and
are merely onlookers who are isolated in the new media. In their efforts to
integrate into urban life, they subconsciously emulate the behaviour of local
groups in the city, and strive to gain entry to urban groups. Members of the new
generation of rural migrant workers will also redefine their own group image.
Through equitable dialogue and communication, they enable others to gain
a greater understanding of rural migrant workers and thus better understand
themselves.

Xiao Wu, a young man from Guizhou, born in 1985, has loved the Internet
since childhood. He worked at a Foxconn factory for several years and once
held the position of supervisor, in charge of 70 or 80 people. However, he
couldn't adjust to the flexible work system of working back-to-back shifts,
so he left the factory and worked for a time in real estate sales. Income in
the sales industry was unstable, and he was required to deceive home buyers,
which went against his conscience. Unable to do this, he took a job working in
website construction and production. He himself remains a silent participant on
the Internet, but he admitted that many people actively participate in changing
stereotypes, in the process of redefining the image of the new generation of
rural migrant workers.

> When I go online, I only read the news and seldom participate in discussions
> because it's too bothersome to type. People in some discussion groups say
> bad things about us migrant workers, saying that we are this or that, saying
> that we have no manners and are filthy when we take public buses. Some of
> my friends on the Internet exchange angry words with them. In fact, we don't
> all fit their description of us. Some people may indeed not pay attention to
> their personal image. However, most of us will not engage in such unseemly

behaviour in public places. Quite a few people give their thumbs up in such discussions.

(Xiao Wu, male, from Anshun, Guizhou)

The new generation of rural migrant workers also strives through image modification to narrow the visual gap between themselves and urbanites. Xiao Luo, born in 1996, comes from Huanggang in Hubei. At the age of 15 he left home to work and has worked at several raw materials processing plants. At the time he was young and wanted to go out and play. He now works as a bartender at a hotel, where the work is stable but wages are not high. He has a girlfriend, and realizes that there are many things which they must talk over together. He has always dreamed of opening a tea shop. He is now taking steps towards opening his own business. He is a very handsome person, but doesn't believe that a man's charm comes from his good looks. He believes that a man's sense of responsibility and initiative are extremely important. Utilizing the platform of the new media, he has successfully promoted his own image, and has fought to give rural migrant workers a good name. Actually, they also have a fashionable, trendy side.

Many people on the Internet scornfully say that we rural migrant workers are "smart" or outlandish. Every group has some abnormal people. Most of us have normal appearances. With respect to the clothes we wear and how we dress up, we are not much different from people in the city. Some time ago I participated in an event of what makes a man charming. I frequently play on WeChat and I follow a public account called "xxTong" set up in my hometown. It held an event called "WeChat Male Idol". Every session it would introduce male idols, most of whom came from the city. My friends and colleagues often say that I'm very handsome, that I look like the Hong Kong movie star Luo Zhixiang and that many girls like me. So I went to participate in the event. They asked me what the most important qualities of a male idol were. I have always believed that a male idol should come off as handsome, play in a cool way, and shoulder responsibility. That's what I told them. They also asked me what I would like to say to my future self. I answered them, "Remember how I struggled, and my nonchalant attitude towards life".

(Xiao Luo, male, from Huanggang, Hubei)

Although the social reality is that Internet platforms still contain stereotypes of rural migrant workers, the new generation of rural migrant workers' impulse to progressively rewrite their own image as time goes on provides the most direct driving force for self-empowerment. In step with the ongoing advancement of media literacy, they actively use the new media to empower themselves, to attempt to speak out on Internet platforms, to actively show the real conditions they themselves experience as rural migrant workers, in order to enhance understanding between themselves and the outside world. During this process, even if their image is still inhibited by habits of prejudice, they are able to achieve slight improvements.

4. My Mediatized "Looking-glass Self": Moving From "Rural Self" Towards "Urban Self"

During the process of moving from rural culture to urban culture, the new generation of rural migrant workers, as immigrants in a fluid culture, have issues of self-identity which really stand out and are conspicuous in their adaptation to the city. How they perceive themselves, define themselves, and reconstruct their own identities are worthy of in-depth exploration by social scientists, including those in the field of communication studies.

The American sociologist Charles Horton Cooley once postulated that "People are mirrors who reflect each other", to describe the social attributes of people's self-identities. His "looking-glass self" has become a classic concept in describing social interaction. He pointed out that self-cognition has three key components: the image we imagine ourselves to have in others' eyes, how we imagine others judge us based on this image, and certain feelings about our self-identity, such as pride or humiliation (Cooley, 1989). In plain language, "looking-glass self" primarily resolves three issues: Who I am in the minds of others, how others see me, and how I see how others see me. From this perspective, we can view the formation of a mediatized "looking-glass self" as a communication process in which the individual and others engage in communications. During this process, the role played by "significant others" is actually similar to that of the media. As Cooley sees it, initial interpersonal interaction within groups is extremely important in the formation of "looking-glass self". People naturally are an important medium. In addition, we should also not overlook media organizations such as newspapers, magazines, radio, television, and the Internet. All things which assist in the formation of one's self-consciousness may be considered to be "others". In conjunction with the new generation of migrant workers' utilization of communication practices in the formation of their identity, we are putting forth the concept of mediatized "looking-glass self" to point out the important role played by the media as a significant variable in forming their identity.

4.1 Mediatized Self-awareness: Obtaining Self-identity in the Mirror Image of Media

As multifaceted, interactive others who are "significant others", peer groups in a person's rural village experience, persons in one's parents' generation, or industry-related groups encountered after going to the city, urban residents, and mass media all affect the self-consciousness of the new generation of rural migrant workers by continuously exporting information on identity. This may be considered to be an information communication process. The role of "significant others" is like media which sends out information. This includes interpersonal media, mass media, and the new media, which are just like mirrors. Members of the new generation of rural migrant workers receive positive or negative information through these channels and begin to understand their own identities. They begin to consider the question of *Who Am I*, a fundamental issue in identity construction.

Interpersonal media are an important means of communication for the new generation of rural migrant workers before coming to the city and play a very important role in forming their rural "identity". Significant others in the real world, companions in the virtual world: these actual or simulated worlds are like a mirror which reflects images of members of the new generation of rural migrant workers in their rural lives. In the eyes of their parents and teachers, they are identified as "the younger generation" and "students". In the eyes of members of their own generation, they are viewed as "brothers" and "classmates". In the games they play and the short stories they read, their identities become that of persons who are masters of their own interests and who have the ability to explore.

Clearly, in the traditional sense, even if their academic performance does not always meet expectations, members of the new generation of rural migrant workers have been protected and loved by their parents and do not lack companions to play with in their real lives. In addition, their young companions of the same age have introduced them to the world of the Internet. In this virtual world, people who play well are "heroes". In the roles they play in Internet games, they search for the sense of identity which is missing in their lives. In a virtual world where "all are important regardless of their origin", they search for a false sense of equality. Sometimes, in the short stories they read, they are able to find life experiences similar to their own, for example, dissatisfaction with real life. They find reflections of themselves in the details of short stories. When the protagonist in a short story achieves happiness at the end, they also secretly wish for a turning point in their real lives. Notwithstanding class divisions among them, to a certain degree, they are still waiting to be treated with respect as equals.

After coming to the city, members of the new generation of rural migrant workers begin to have multifaceted interactions with various groups of people in the city, and they increase the means by which they communicate. Through a series of activities involving industry-related groups, urban residents, and information communicated by mass media, they discover a society which is completely different from a rural environment. Under the reflection of the urban media, members of the new generation of rural migrant workers perceive how their "rural self" fails to blend in with urban life. They receive new information on themselves through various channels in the city, and gradually discover the differences between themselves and urban groups. In their minds, they begin to doubt the image of identity passed on to them by the village. In the social communication contexts of internal communication in industry organizations, interpersonal communication with urbanites, and contact with mass media, members of the new generation of rural migrant workers gradually form their views on self-identity and social status. They digest and reorganize the information they have received in two specific media environments, the village and the city, to go beyond the two phases of self-identity they respectively experienced when they initially came to the city and mid-way during their lives in the city. In the city they form a new awareness of their own identity, filled with anxiety and uneasiness. Members of the new generation of migrant workers, when encountering the onslaught of information from the media and when colliding with others in interpersonal communications, face unprecedented confusion in determining their own identities.

Whether they are understanding and accepting their identity in a rural media environment, or feeling confusion and anxiety over their identity in an urban media system, images of identity which they derive are inextricably linked to information on identity extracted from the media. Accordingly, this is a process of mediatized cognition.

4.2 Mediatized Modification of Self-image: Identity Reconstruction Under the Guidance of the Media

In everyday life, a social cultural system is like a big net which binds people in a certain historical or cultural context. In order to establish identity relationships with the world and with others, to integrate into the surrounding environment, people as "selves" must form a set of corresponding cultural coding processes to gradually modify their own original coding process, to establish their individual roles in current environments. And conscious or unconscious modification of self-image is necessary to an individual in their role of obtaining collective, self, social, and other types of approval. Image modification plays a role in handling complicated matters with ease in this process and is at the heart of social cognition. As an essential component of social interaction, image modification is continuously carried on in communication with others, and occurs based on how other people react to and evaluate oneself. An individual, after understanding other people's ideas, through a series of "ornamentation" measures, influences the image other persons form of himself or herself. During this process, they often attempt to control how other people perceive them, which results in the creation of a new "looking-glass self". The media as an important source of information in the lives of members of the new generation of rural migrant workers, exerts a definite influence on how they form roles for themselves in the cognitive process of adapting to urban society. In addition to solidifying a group's images, the media also will be affected by the imperceptible influence of these images in its production of information.

To obtain a certain desired image, during the process of interacting with multiple significant others, the new generation of rural migrant workers utilizes various media to adopt a policy involving a series of "enhancements" (modification, concealment, ornamentation), to influence its image in the eyes of urban groups. Influenced by information in urban media, members of the new generation of rural migrant workers begin to embellish their own image; adjust the rhythm of village life; and interact with urban colleagues, home owners, and heads of households in their communities. After a period of adaptation, they will follow the rhythm of the city in their lives and recreational activities. In their daily living habits, the new generation of rural migrant workers is not very different from urban groups. Through acquiring information, they modify those elements of their cultural coding process which do not conform to an urban environment. They begin to utilize reshaped cultural codes and interaction with urban groups, to gradually form their new "selves". And as urban groups gradually get used to them, members of the new generation of rural migrant workers have completed the modification of their identity.

As they become enlightened by what they learn from the media, members of the new generation of rural migrant workers discover the differences existing between themselves and urbanites. While seeking to actively embrace urban standards, they also complete their own re-socialized transformations. In this process of conflict, adjustment, and modification of self-identity, the media's primary role is in comparing social behaviour. At this time the media primarily serves to reflect and modify the self, and "enhancement" behaviour during this phase appears all the more evident. After gradually adapting to the rhythm of the city, the new generation of rural migrant workers through various media begins to understand information on the city, begins to compare itself to urban groups, and begins to revise its identity. With the diversification of channels by which information is communicated, members of the new generation of rural migrant workers develop a cognition of their own identity. Their implicit attitudes are automatically activated when encountering information stimuli from the outside world. These certain attitudes, coupled with their unconscious behaviour accumulated from past experiences and existing attitudes, will affect their cognition of social objects (urban groups, urban media, social organizations) and subjective objects (their own identity), their emotional orientation, and their behavioural responses.

From this it can be seen that the media plays a definite role in the process of promoting the modification of the cognition of identity until it is ultimately reshaped by the new generation of rural migrant workers after coming to the city. Under circumstances in which the "self" of the village fails to receive approval from society and from oneself, the new generation of rural migrant workers conceals personal deficiencies in real life through interpersonal communication with persons of their same generation or through the creation of self-images in the virtual world, in an attempt to embellish their self-image in another way. In this process, the media is like a tool which the new generation of rural migrant workers uses to arm its new identity. This armed component is precisely what gains approval as being vastly different from traditional standards of measurement in rural society. Approval generated by this component can greatly add to their sense of self-respect and also foreshadow their renewed contact with the media after they come to the city. And at this time, the media plays a role in the creation of a new "self" and in arming the real "self".

4.3 Mediatized Identification: Recognition of Self-identity With Affluent Media Choices

Mediatized identification refers to the process of self-identity and social status established by members of the new generation of rural migrant workers in their interpersonal interactions, community experiences, organizational experiences, and other specific media environments. In the two specific environments of the village and the city, they digest and reorganize various types of information provided by the media and experience a shift in the orientation of their self-identity and their identification in two phases. In these two phases, the continuation of new "selves" and contact with and exchange of information involving members of the new generation of rural migrant workers is primarily completed through the media. After employing various types of media, they unearth information on a different side of themselves, with the prospect of integrating themselves into the social field where they are situated over the long term. Moreover, the effects of the social organization and interpersonal communication which have become integrated into the details of the lives and work of members of rural migrant workers in a rapidly developing information society also gradually take on mediated characteristics.

At the same time that the media is transmitting its views and acknowledgement of this group, the new generation of migrant workers is also giving feedback to urban groups with information on undergoing changes of its identity in the city. In this process of transitioning from passive to active transmission of information, certain members of the new generation of rural migrant workers discover that they themselves have undergone dynamic changes in adaptation accomplished through the media which challenge inherent images of them held by urban groups and members of their own generation. They gradually rewrite the definition and content of the term "rural migrant worker", to break down regionalism in urban society and invisible boundaries lurking in social prejudices. Accordingly, they establish standards for cognition of self-identity and further develop an awareness of their own identity in the city. This group of people, after remoulding cognition of their identity, gradually achieves integration into city life. They complete the recognition of their new identity through a strategy of embellishment through the media. However, certain members of the new generation of rural migrant workers are also unable to use information they obtain from the media to accurately determine the orientation of their social identity. Such persons are uncertain about whether they will be able to continue to survive in the city and integrate into city life.

Undeniably, as society is gradually shaped by the media, various groups and social organizations are caught up in this process. Identity shaped by the media emphasizes giving urban media networks diversified social cognition through the inclusivity of the media, to further enable the coexistence of multiple identities. Members of the new generation of rural migrant workers develop a specific understanding of what their identity is in the city by contrasting their own or the group's image in the media. After the group achieves self-awareness, it evaluates the image of itself which exists in the media, internalizes information on the image of its identity, remoulds it, and then express this dual identity which exists internally and is expressed externally. Mediatized identification, which exists in the new generation of rural migrant workers, helps to generate an image awareness and self-identity. This identity is also conveyed to urban groups and the media organizations. This identity originates from the mediatized identity of the new generation of rural migrant workers after re-socialization, and is no longer a single stereotype; on the contrary it is multifaceted and vibrant.

Generally speaking, mediatized identification exerts a significant effect in the formation of old and new identities of the new generation of rural migrant workers. This effect is induced by information in the media, specifically through information communication, permeating the entire process experienced by rural migrant workers before and after coming to the city, including their future social orientation and urban identity. Moreover, it has a significant impact on their integration into city life. Although the media is merely one relatively inconspicuous factor in the whole process of identification, this factor exerts a penetrative effect. Or perhaps the new generation of rural migrant workers has not taken the effect of various forms of media to heart. Nonetheless, various forms of media continue to exert an effect on their identity in their everyday lives and at work.

Accordingly, during the process of resolving difficulties encountered by the new generation of rural migrant workers in forming their identity, we should not overlook the role played by the media. We encourage mass media and new media to objectively and truthfully report the diverse aspects of rural migrant workers. We call on urban residents to at the very least respect and understand the group of rural migrant workers that lives with them in the same city. We also recommend that various enterprises enhance their corporate culture, to create a platform for rural migrant workers to live well and improve their lives. Only in this way will the new generation of rural migrant workers be able to accurately orientate and affirm its self-image.

Notably, even if members of the new generation of rural migrant workers as an active group have the ability to create their own world in which to live and the ability to construct meaning, for a long time after coming to the city, they continuously utilize interpersonal communications and the new media to communicate and implement image modification, to achieve the restoration and reconstruction of their identity. On the other hand, it must be said that the identity of the new generation of rural migrant workers is formed through interaction with "significant others" such as co-workers, urban residents, mass media, and other such multi-faceted subjects, and is also constructed by external forces such as economic and industry structures, and the household registration system with its dual opposition between rural and urban registration. To a very large degree, the identity crisis encountered by the new generation of rural migrant workers during the period after they enter the city hinges on a fundamental adjustment and loosening of restrictions which the system forces on them as persons identified as rural migrant workers. The government has the responsibility to give rural migrant workers fair treatment as citizens, to enable them to progressively enjoy the rights which they should have as urban residents, and resolve the issue of their identity. Only in this way can the transformation of the new generation of rural migrant workers into urban residents continue to progress.

References

Chang, J. (2015). Nostalgia with a pioneering stance: A study of the identity of Chinese internet culture producers. *Journal of International Communication, 37*(5), 106–124.

Cooley, C. H. (1989). *On self and social organization* (F. Bao & Y. Wang, Trans.). Huaxia Publishing House.

Fang, Y. (2012). An analysis of medialized interpersonal relationship. *Journal of International Communication, 34*(7), 52–57.

Hsu, L. K. (2001). *Under the ancestors' shadow* (F. Wang & L. Xu, Trans.). Taipei Nantian Bookstore.

Pan, Z. (2007b). Social classification and group symbolic boundaries – The case of migrant workers' social classification. *Society, 4*, 48–67+206.

Qin, M. (2005). A study on the construction of emigration identity. *Zhejiang Social Sciences, 1*, 88–94.

Tarde, G. (2008). *Laws of imitation* (D. He, Trans.). China Renmin University Press.

Xu, C. (2007b). The social mentality of the new generation of migrant workers in urban life. *Science of Social Psychology, 10*, 57–59.

4 Media-driven Planning for Life Among the New Generation of Rural Migrant Workers

As a proactive expression, a life plan reflects the desire of the new generation of rural migrant workers to live actively and seek upward mobility. A life plan infuses confidence and courage in the new generation of rural migrant workers' vision of future development and inspires them to continuously strive to work for a better tomorrow. A life plan also determines their goals and aspirations in urban life, guiding and propelling each individual as they create their life in the city. From before coming to the city to after coming to the city, from the time when they initially arrive in the city to the time when they have lived in the city for a certain period, the life plan of the new generation of migrant workers undergoes changes, or is overturned and reconstructed. Individual factors, the influence of others, environmental effects, government policy orientation, and urban events and experiences, all have an impact on their life plans. Accordingly, with respect to members of the new generation of rural migrant workers who lack sufficient experience, this is destined to be a process in which they feel lost and continuously search for solutions.

1. Evolution in a State of Flux: Temporal and Spatial Transformation and Questions About the Future

As a special group in urban society, the new generation of urban migrant workers follows in the footsteps of the preceding generation, once again moving along a trajectory from the village to the city. Although most of them were born and grew up in villages, they have a natural apathy towards the land. Their detachment from the land, which they have felt since birth, causes them to lack the deep, strong ties to the village felt by the older generation. Accordingly, they find the prospect of leaving the village and the land to go to a prosperous, vibrant city to be fresh and stimulating. In fact, most members of the new generation of rural migrant workers have for various reasons discontinued their academic studies, and choosing to leave home to work has become their most normal choice and course of action. Filled with unlimited anticipation of a beautiful life in the city, they enter a social environment which is completely different from the village, and, filled with hope, begin a new life. Through the passage of time, they grow and mature mentally and physically. The change of time and space causes them to personally experience

DOI: 10.4324/9781003365785-4

the reality and cruelty of urban life, and their initial aspirations are dealt a heavy blow. Their beautiful urban dreams are broken. They begin to have doubts about the future, and start to think even more deeply about the meaning of their lives. As they mature mentally and accumulate more economic and social capital, their life plans also gradually evolve from a nebulous to a clear state of being.

1.1 From Anticipation to Reality: The Shattered Urban Image

China's traditional society is rooted in the local village. Farmers have deep feelings for the villages in which they have lived for generations, and for the land on which they depend for their survival. Having strong ties to the village is a prominent characteristic of the older generation of rural migrant workers. They are naturally and indivisibly connected to the land. This sentimental attachment is the primary obstacle which consistently prevents them from being able to truly integrate into the city. The new generation of rural migrant workers is clearly different. During recent years, given the continuous decrease of income derived from farming operations as a percentage of farmers' total income, the improvement of basic infrastructure in the village, and an increase in the mechanization of agriculture, the labour force has greatly been liberated from its bonds to the land. Although most members of the new generation of rural migrant workers grew up in the village, they have spent a very limited amount of time or even no time engaged in agricultural production activities. Accordingly, they have no emotional ties to the land, even to the point that they have a strong desire to disengage themselves from the restrictions placed on them by a rustic and land-bound life.

Contrary to being emotionally tied to the land, members of the new generation of rural migrant workers have an exceptional yearning for the city. Following an increase in rural living standards and an improvement in basic infrastructure, the role of the media has been extended to every corner of village life. Whether it be mass media's presentation of beautiful images of prosperous cities or descriptions of modern urban life given by persons returning to the village, such information potentially fires the imaginations of members of the new generation of rural migrant workers with unlimited scenarios of urban life. Lacking experience in the outside world, members of the new generation of rural migrant workers perceive the city as a place which is modern and fashionable, filled with enchantment, where opportunities abound and dreams can be made real. Accordingly, they always carry beautiful visualizations of urban life with them when they come to the city, hoping that they can change their destiny and achieve a new social status.

Xiao Liu, a girl from Zhuzhou, Hunan, left home to go to work at the age of 18 after she graduated from high school. Filled with hope, she came to Taizhou, Zhejiang, and has lived there for three years. She currently works at a hairdressing salon. When she spoke of her understanding and thoughts about urban life prior to coming to the city, she said:

> At that time, I believed that Taizhou would be a rather large city and would definitely be much bigger than my hometown. So, I thought that it might be

more prosperous, that the city would be very beautiful, that it might have more opportunities. At that time, I really wanted to go to Taizhou. I felt that I would learn about even more things. That I would no longer remain living in ignorance in a small county town. I felt very happy. At the time, I hoped to have a better job and a better life in the city.

(Xiao Liu, female, from Zhuzhou, Hunan)

And Xiao Tan, who also works in the hairstyling industry, also expressed the same thoughts. He is 25 years old, comes from Hubei, and has struggled to make a living in Nanjing for the past six years, solely depending on his own efforts to make a life for himself in the city. Recently, he was promoted from assistant to full-fledged hairstylist. During our conversation, we could feel that he was positive and highly motivated. When we spoke of his thoughts about Nanjing prior to coming there, he recalled:

Prior to coming here, I didn't know much about this place, and got most of my information from television or newspaper reports. I knew it had many tall buildings, many people, many beautiful things, and was very prosperous. At the time, I was young and really wanted to go to Nanjing. I thought that when I arrived in the city, I would be able to come into contact with so many things. This made me feel very excited.

(Xiao Tan, male, from Hubei)

Actually, during interviews, many interviewees expressed similar thoughts, especially towards large internationalized cities such as Shanghai and Beijing. Prior to going to the city, they greatly admired and yearned for an urban life, hoping that they could make a life for themselves in such a thriving environment. "Push-pull-theory" can be used here to analyse the spatial migration and yearning of the new generation of rural migrant workers. It is an important theory utilized in conducting research on mobile populations and migrants. This theory views population movement as the outcome of the effect of forces moving in two different directions. One force impels the movement of populations, while another force impedes it, resulting in a push and pull effect (Chen, 2010). With respect to the new generation of rural migrant workers, the dilapidated, backward conditions and the monotonous, dull life of rural villages push them to move to urban centres to seek better opportunities, better incomes, and more fresh, interesting phenomena offered by the city. Such factors collectively form the pulling force of the city. Under the combined effect of the aforementioned two forces, the new generation of rural migrant workers is naturally filled with yearning for urban life, and hopes to migrate from the village to the city.

However, after they actually come to the city, members of the new generation of rural migrant workers face a reality which is not as beautiful as they had imagined. The high cost of living, complex issues which obstruct household registration, discrimination by urban dwellers, loss of social security, and the narrow range of their interpersonal interactions cause the beautiful yearnings which they originally cherished to be abruptly shattered. The cruelty of their actual circumstances leaves them no choice but to silently accept the hardships and cramped conditions of urban living. In their struggle to survive day after day, they lose the dreams and aspirations they once had and become members of an underprivileged class living on the periphery of urban society.

Xiao Li is a young female labourer who works at a restaurant in Nanjing. She has just turned 21. She is fair-complexioned and beautiful, and always has a sweet smile on her face. After she graduated from vocational middle school, she was directly assigned to a garment processing factory in Wenzhou. Afterwards, she felt the work was too arduous, left her job, and came to Nanjing, where she works as a waitress at a restaurant. When we spoke about her life after leaving the village to come to the city, her facial expression conspicuously showed that she felt uncomfortable recalling her past experiences.

> I worked there (in Wenzhou) for about two years. The work was really too arduous, too exhausting. I spent all day in the workshop, making clothes nonstop. Moreover, we were responsible for processing Septwolves brand clothing and Lilanz brand suits, both of which were high-end clothing lines with very strict requirements. If we didn't perform our work well, we would have to redo it.
>
> (Xiao Li, female, from Hefei, Anhui)

Xiao Sun, a young girl from Northeast China, once worked at a beauty salon in Beijing. She now works as a manicurist at a manicure shop in Shanghai. She is 26 years old and has worked away from home for many years, following her boyfriend from place to place. She has an upbeat personality. When speaking about how she now feels about Shanghai, she said:

> Shanghai is very prosperous and you can see many people here. However, goods here are very expensive and the life here is not good. I feel I can't really enjoy myself here. Rent is very high, so I can't buy many of the things I want to buy. I feel that Shanghainese are also rather fussy and discriminate against outsiders. The pace of living is also too fast and rather stressful. At any rate, life here isn't as good as I imagined it would be.
>
> (Xiao Sun, female, from Northeast China)

As persons who belong to a passionate, youthful generation, members of the new generation of rural migrant workers in the midst of rapid social change, long to change their socioeconomic status, to transform their traditional role as "farmers who toil arduously in the fields facing the ground with their backs to the sky". Accordingly, they are filled with a yearning to come to the city. However, reality is always cruel and the city has more faces than just its prosperous side. For members of the new generation of rural migrant workers who lack capital, the difficulty of surviving and improving their lives in the city is all the more real. This gap also affects their psychological cognition, causing them to change the future life plans they had made for themselves prior to entering the city and to create new life plans in the midst of their personal urban activities.

1.2 From Ignorance to Maturity: Real Life Experience

Based on the earliest definition of the new generation of rural migrant workers put forth by Wang Chunguang, members of this generation are persons who were born after 1980, who are under 25 years old, and who are members of a group which left home to work and do business in the 1990s (Wang, 2003). However, as research grows, human socialization has proven to be an ongoing process of development over time, and the new generation of rural migrant workers has also proven to be a self-renewing, dynamically developing group, in which members born after 1990 have also grown up. Accordingly, the current scope of the new generation of rural migrant workers should be appropriately expanded to include persons born in the 1980s and 1990s, groups of youth which have successively left the village to come to the cities from the end of the 1990s until the present time. Furthermore, our interview data also indicates that such members of the new generation of rural migrant workers primarily stopped attending school for various reasons after graduating from junior high school, senior high school, or vocational school. Most of them left home when they were 16 to 18 years old, bearing the weight of their future responsibilities on their young shoulders. At that time, they were still young, and as yet physically and emotionally immature, with nebulous and idealized visions of the future. However, spatial transformation and the trials of time expose them to the cruelty of urban life, and their mental awareness grows. Life's major events leave them with indelible impressions, causing them to change their plans for living.

Xiao Wu, who decided to discontinue his education at the age of 16 because he failed his senior high school entrance examination, is from southeastern Guizhou and now works as a small-time labourer repairing electric motors in Taizhou, Zhejiang. Prior to taking his senior high school entrance examination, his only dream was to attend the high school of his choice. However, his failure to successfully pass the senior high school entrance examination shattered his dream and caused him to lose hope. As a result, he chose to go with his father to Taizhou, where he didn't plan to stay long. He never imagined that in the blink of an eye he would stay there six years.

> When I first arrived in Taizhou, the precinct station police came in the middle of the night to check my temporary residence certificate (which is now called a residence certificate). I felt they were extremely inhumane in the way they handled matters. I then realized that I was an outsider. I later came to understand that children from other localities who attended school there were not treated the same as local children. They had separate schools for locals and for outsiders. Local people could attend public schools while outsiders had to attend private schools. This caused me to feel such discrimination even more deeply.
>
> (Xiao Wu, male, from Guizhou)

And when Xiao Liu, the girl from Zhuzhou, Hunan, who was mentioned earlier, talked about such things when working in Taizhou, she also felt wronged:

> When I first came here, when I first began working, I could only work as an assistant, washing customers' hair. Once when shampooing a customer's hair, I carelessly spilled shampoo paste on their clothes. That customer became very angry and said that her clothing was very expensive and could not be exposed to liquids, etc. My profuse apologies were useless. Finally, my boss reprimanded me for quite some time and deducted money from my wages. At the time I felt extremely unhappy, that I had no money and no social status which resulted in my being bullied. I then made up my mind to become a boss in the future.
>
> (Xiao Liu, female, from Zhuzhou, Hunan)

Actually, the distance and discrimination existing in urban society poses serious obstacles to members of the new generation of rural migrant workers in their attempt to smoothly integrate into the city, especially with respect to the lack of understanding which naturally exists between them and urbanites. Such factors exert a great influence on their state of mind and their willingness to integrate. Much sociological research has been conducted from the perspective of social distance and social discrimination, such as using factor analysis to measure social distances. It has been discovered that the relationship between the new generation of rural migrant workers and urbanites is one in which they are "spiritually isolated from one another while sharing the same geographical space" (Shi, 2010). Research on current survival conditions of the new generation of rural migrant workers from the perspective of social discrimination has concluded that the new generation of rural migrant workers encounter discrimination in numerous areas of society in their integration into the city, including social networks, dual labour markets, and urban social systems (Pan, 2007a). This distance and discrimination are reflected in numerous contacts between urbanites and the new generation of rural migrant workers, in which urbanites primarily play the role of consumers and members of the new generation of migrant workers are service providers. A latent gap in social status exists in the transaction and service activities between them, in which urbanites unconsciously feel a sense of superiority and contempt, easily causing members of the new generation of migrant workers to feel provoked and hurt. Xiao Li, mentioned earlier in the chapter, is a young girl working at a restaurant in Nanjing. When she spoke about her urban experience, she said:

> Sometimes you will encounter rather intractable customers, We usually have a lot of customers and are quite busy. Some customers will push us to expedite their orders, and others will say that our restaurant's staff don't have a good service attitude. Actually, we are very busy. Once a customer waited half an hour for an order which was still not ready. Later, when I went to the kitchen to get the dish and brought it to the table, the customer grabbed it. However, this dish had actually been ordered by people in another of our

private rooms. I said, "This is not your order". He then very angrily said, "We've been waiting half an hour for our order. I don't care whose dish it is. Anyway, we want to eat." There was nothing I could do. I could only tell the people in the other private room, "Something went wrong with your order of fish. Please wait a while." I felt I was at loss, and didn't know whether to laugh or cry. The customer who grabbed the dish was really unreasonable.

(Xiao Li, female, from Hefei, Anhui)

Xiao Tan, who works at one of the Langtao hairstyling salons in Nanjing, often encounters various types of customers. After working for many years, he has learned to carefully observe the language and expressions of his customers, and to determine in a short time what they like, so that he can entertain them to the greatest extent possible.

Once I encountered a young girl who came to our salon to have her hair permed. She just sat there without saying anything. No matter what I said to her, she basically ignored me. At first, I thought she felt annoyed, so I just stood there and didn't say anything. Afterwards, when I had finished perming her hair, she silently shed tears, which made me feel awkward for a moment. After asking her what was wrong, I found out that she had quarrelled with her boyfriend and in her anger had decided to change her hairstyle. I could do nothing but to amuse her by standing there and telling silly jokes to make her laugh. Sometimes I encounter customers who purposely give me a hard time, who often vent their pent-up feelings on me. Sometimes they even insult me with extremely rude language. Although we say that the customer is God, they don't give me even the most basic respect. Sometimes, I really feel humiliated, but I have nowhere to release my feelings.

(Xiao Tan, male, from Hubei)

Over time, as members of the new generation of rural migrant workers live life in the city, their original naïve and nebulous feelings gradually mature. Certain experiences which stand out cause them to grow. Xiao Wang comes from Taigu, Shanxi, and currently works as a service staff at a bar in Taiyuan. She believes that the person she is today and the person she was when she first came to the city are two completely different people.

When I first came here, I just wanted to play, to make money. Now that I have experienced various things, I have become more mature. I want to buy a home in Taiyuan and settle down. Before, I tended to trust people. When I saw a girl on the street with a sign saying that she had lost all her money and needed car fare to get back home, I would give her money. Later, several steps down the road, after also seeing another girl who had a sign saying that she needed money for car fare, I didn't believe such stories ever again.

(Xiao Wang, female, from Taigu, Shanxi)

Filled with youthful dreams, they want to come to the city. However, various experiences in real life cause members of the new generation of rural migrant workers to grow and mature as they undergo hardship. The estrangement which exists between them and urban dwellers causes them to feel even more alienated and their minds begin to evolve from uncertainty to maturity. The urban experience, while rich and variegated, also runs cold and hot at a personal level. Such important life experiences have a great impact on their plans for living and transform their ideas about the future.

1.3 From Obscurity to Clarity: A Change of Thinking With Regard to Belonging

Members of the new generation of rural migrant workers leave their places of birth not only for economic reasons but, more importantly, because they want to see the world, and find a new way of life. Migrating from the rural village to the city is the principal means by which they obtain a new social status. There is a conspicuous difference between them and the first generation of rural migrant workers with regard to their thoughts on where they belong in the future, which also illustrates the differences in attitude between these two generations of rural migrant workers with respect to their sense of belonging. Most members of the older generation of rural migrant workers clearly understood that they were merely transient guests in the city, that they came from the village and would return to the village. Their sentimental attachment to the land formed a knot in their hearts which could never be untied. Accordingly, most of them considered making a living and earning money to be their primary objectives. Initially and ultimately, the city was a place where they resided temporarily. The land and the village remained the places which shaped their dreams throughout their lives. It can be said that the older generation of rural migrant workers fundamentally had no interest or ambition to integrate into the city and forever lived on the periphery of urban life.

Members of the new generation of rural migrant workers gradually obscured and even left behind their impressions of rural culture. They found it difficult to accept the dilapidation, poverty, and slow pace of life in the village, and gradually became accustomed to the prosperity and fast pace of urban life. They longed to find a place where they could put down roots and grow in some corner of the city. Accordingly, they didn't have the older generation's strong desire to return to their rural homes. As a youthful group, as they experienced urban life, they continued to explore and consider the question of returning to the village in the future versus remaining in the city. They embarked on their lives in the city with great confidence. However, the reality they experienced caused them to realize that living was not easy and they quickly matured under life's pressures. During this growth process, their ideas about where they belonged in the future and their plans for life shed their obscurity and became clarified.

Xiao Chen, a young man from Liu He, Nanjing (Liu He was formerly an outlying semirural district which has now been incorporated into Nanjing) came to the city of Nanjing five years ago. He now works as the senior hairstylist at a hair salon on Hankou Road near Nanjing University. At the age of 26 he looks quite fashionable and has his hair cut in the latest style. He also fluently speaks Nanjing dialect. Prior to coming to Nanjing, he had no clear objectives, not to mention any plan for his life. He also had no idea what he would do in Nanjing.

> After I arrived in Nanjing, I played around for a while. Then, because I had an interest in hairstyling, I began to work at a hair salon. I was promoted several times, and am now the senior hairstylist at this salon,
>
> (Xiao Chen, male, from Liuhe District, Nanjing)

he said with great satisfaction. Compared to the past, he now has a clear plan for himself.

> My present goal is to open my own hair salon in Nanjing and then purchase a home here. I estimate that I probably need two to three years to accomplish this. As far as my personal life is concerned, I want to marry my current girl-friend and have my own home in Nanjing. The only problem is that housing prices in Nanjing are too high. If they could come down just a little bit, that would be even better.
>
> (Xiao Chen, male, from Liuhe District, Nanjing)

Compared to the older generation of rural migrant workers, the new generation of rural migrant workers is more intensely proactive with respect to its choices for the future. Its motivation for leaving the village involves both economy and survival. Its identification with an institutional identity is weakening, and its rural identity has been endowed with even greater social meaning. Members of the new generation of rural migrant workers feel more impelled to urbanize, and have begun to actively identify with urban society. They also want to remain in the city through their own efforts, which indicates their intense desire to integrate into urban society. Accordingly, even if their life in the city is filled with the unknown, they still search to find the direction of their future development through their own hard work, and continue to struggle to put down roots in the city. Xiao Zhang is an ordinary service staff working at the Daxinggong branch of Haidilao Res-taurant in Nanjing. He has just turned 20 and hasn't lived in Nanjing for a long time. With his crewcut and slight build, he appears to be exceptionally smart and capable. He is from Suqian, Jiangsu, and graduated from a vocational school in Shandong, where he studied automotive repair. He wanted to come to Nanjing to find a suitable job, because he felt that Nanjing was prosperous and offered more job opportunities. However, he had never imagined that the work situation would be so bad. He attempted to find work at many places but was unsuccess-ful. Although he has encountered many setbacks, he now has a clear vision of his plans for the future.

> My current plan for the future is to first find a job. I still hope to work at a 4S automotive shop. I believe my prospects for the future are quite good.

> My next step, my ideal, is to open my own shop, such as an automotive decoration shop or auto maintenance shop. However, this takes time. I must first save enough money to do this. I just can't open it at the drop of a hat.
>
> (Xiao Zhang, male, from Suqian, Jiangsu)

Although they have seen their dreams of the city shattered and have led a difficult life, it can be seen that members of the new generation of rural migrant workers possess a confidence and courage unique to youth, which propels them to continuously fight for the future. Prior to entering the city, their visions of the future primarily were idealized and imagined scenarios which were often nebulous and abstract. After coming to the city, they had profound experiences which taught them about life. As their thoughts grew deeper, they gradually abandoned certain overly ambitious aspirations and realized the importance of having a plan for their own future and began to realistically draft their plan for life. They also began to fight hard and struggle to achieve their plan.

Xiao Hu, a young man of 25 from Sichuan, currently works as a hairstylist. His parents also work in Shanghai. After abandoning his studies during his second year of senior high school, he came to Shanghai to work. At that time, he didn't know what he would do, but he knew that he really couldn't continue his studies. He wanted to leave his village to experience the world. He also came to Shanghai because his parents were working there. Now, he has a very clear idea about his plan for life.

> My short-term goal is to find a job at another high-calibre hairstyling salon. My long-term goal is to open my own salon. I have lived in Shanghai for many years. During my first two years, I worked at various jobs. I worked as a service staff at a hotel, and as a worker doing odd jobs at a factory, etc. Ultimately, I discovered that if I wanted to lead a stable life and make something of myself in this city, I needed to have a special skill. That was why I studied hairstyling.
>
> (Xiao Hu, male, from Sichuan)

Xiao Shan, who is 22 years old, is a bartender and cashier at Ellen's Bar, next to a university in Nanjing. He comes from a village near Yancheng, Jiangsu. After graduating from senior high school, he left his village to see the world. He spent six months in Suzhou and Changzhou working at jobs in factories. However, he felt such jobs were monotonous and arduous. At the bar he can come into contact with various types of people and the environment is good, so he chose to work at a bar.

> In the future, I want to continue working at a bar. I want to open my own bar, because bars make a lot of profit and you only need several hundred thousand yuan to open a bar. I am now working here, but later I want to work at a larger, standard bar to learn how to mix different types of drinks. After

I become familiar with all the different aspects of the business, and I have enough money, I will open my own bar.

(Xiao Shan, male, from Yancheng, Jiangsu)

Coming from the village to the city, the change of continuum causes the youthful members of the new generation of rural migrant workers to taste the hardship and difficulty of fighting to live in the city, which also causes them to begin to have doubts about the future and to think about their plans for life. The city of their dreams remains an imagined scenario. Living at the bottom, on the fringe of society, they inevitably must undergo stressful situations in real life in order to mature, and then begin to design and create their own lives. Although they have encountered many setbacks, they have not lost the confidence and courage to pursue their future. A progressively clear picture of their lives slowly appears before their eyes, and they move forward with determination, step by step.

At this time, members of the new generation of migrant workers not only experience changes in their jobs, salaries and status, but more importantly undergo a transformation of their lives and destinies. At this time, their lives are filled with vigour and vitality as they come to the city with beautiful fantasies in their hearts, which nonetheless are deeply impacted by the inexorable reality of city life. Their instincts and strong proactivity as youth support them as they slowly navigate the complexities of urban society and move forward. Honed by the challenges in life, their self-identity and cognition of the future becomes more mature and clearer. During this process, their plans for life undergo continual change, guiding and propelling their life experience in the city.

2. Seeking Direction in the Midst of Confusion: Life Planning in an Urban Environment

Compared to rural society with its limited access to information, deficient infrastructure, and slow pace of life, the urban environment offers various types of highly developed media, with massive amounts of information covering every aspect of society, highly frequent communications and a fast paced, intense lifestyle. Members of the new generation of rural migrant workers who are new arrivals in the city are definitely overwhelmed by the hustle and bustle, prosperity and colour of an urban environment: various styles of television programs which appear in succession, outdoor LED screen displays, mobile digital television on buses and subways, large outdoor advertising billboards, various types of videos and images give them an unending stream of visual shocks. Internet coverage in every corner of the city, and various types of handheld intelligent mobile equipment used by urban residents, open the door for them to enter the virtual world of the Internet. Beautifully attired, stylishly dressed urban youth live and interact with them in the same place on a daily basis, providing them with samples of behaviour to be referenced in their interaction with other people. From first entering the city to becoming familiar with the city, members of the new generation of rural migrant workers witness the gradual evolution of their future from one of nebulosity to one of clarity. Throughout this confusing process, various types of media in the city also transform their life plans.

2.1   Ongoing Expansion of Modernity: Positive Orientation of Mass Media

The city is saturated with all types of mass media. And the daily lives of the new generation of rural migrant workers are inextricably linked to mass media. An endless stream of urban pop dramas on various themes, all manner and variegated forms of television programs, and information from all over provided in news reports are media content to which the new generation of rural migrant workers living in the city is repeatedly exposed. And all types of information in the media which are related to planning one's lifestyle exert a subtle influence on transforming this generation's views of the future. Members of the new generation of rural migrant workers are also saturated with guidance from mass media.

The transfer of members of the new generation of rural migrant workers from rural villages to cities follows an extension of individual modernity and an unlocking of information. Throughout this process, the trajectory of the older generation of rural migrant workers has been unable to satisfy the expectations of the new generation of rural migrant workers with respect to the future. Furthermore, they are unable to benefit from the experiences of their parent's generation. Accordingly, mass media greatly satisfies their need for information and provides them with guidance on choosing the lives they want to lead.

Let's take the example of Xiao Chen, the young man from Liuhe District, Nanjing, mentioned earlier, who really enjoys watching television, and who talks incessantly when various television series are mentioned. He has currently been promoted to the rank of senior hairstylist, and is usually busy at work until almost 10 or 11 o'clock at night. Although the place where he lives doesn't have a television set, he has a modest amount of savings, and has bought the latest iPad mini. Usually, after work, he goes online and uses PPS software to watch television drama series or watches them directly on a Samsung smartphone. Usually, when there aren't many customers, he will contentedly watch them directly at the hair salon. He speaks with great familiarity about television series with themes centred on the real lives of youth, such as *Struggle, Beijing Love Story, Dwelling Narrowness, Beijing Youth,* and *Chinese Bare-bones Marriage,*[1] and very disapprovingly believes that if one has not watched any of these popular dramas, one will be out of step with the times.

> I know that television is make-believe. However, I really like watching these kinds of programs, because the people in them are about the same age as me and we share the same feelings. For example, the drama series *Struggle* has really inspired me. People should make their way in the world while they are still young. You can't go wrong if you work hard and will definitely be rewarded for your efforts. Although I don't have a father as good as Lu Tao's,[2] I can emulate Huazi[3] and depend on my own intense efforts to make

a better life for myself. *Dwelling Narrowness* and *Chinese Bare-bones Marriage* also very realistic. I feel that in the future I cannot let my girlfriend lead a deprived life. I must give her a life of material comfort, and work hard for our future life together.

(Xiao Chen, male, from Liuhe, Nanjing)

Xiao Chen's QQ name is "Work hard for the future! Work hard! Work harder! Our happiness is not far off!" which expresses his confidence and courageous attitude towards the future.

In addition to being influenced by television drama series with themes on youthful ambition and the realities of life, in recent years, the new generation of rural migrant workers has begun to take note of popular television programs on starting a business and finding a job. Such programs not only inspire their thoughts but also broaden their paths for future development. The preceding text mentioned that Xiao Zhang, a young man working at Haidilao hotpot in Nanjing, was keenly interested in this topic, and enthusiastically spoke about a series of shows which he felt were interesting.

I really like to watch Tianjin Satellite Television's program "You're All I Have". Looking for work, I feel that this approach to finding a job is really novel. On one episode, wasn't there a student looking for work, who had returned to China after studying overseas in France, but couldn't bear being cross-examined for a job and fainted on stage? I feel that such a person is really too fake, too unreal. It was clear that the school where they studied overseas was about the same as a vocational school, and yet after returning to China they tried to deceive people about their educational background. What a loss of face! Accordingly, I believe that when looking for a job in the future, I definitely must have real ability and a solid background. Otherwise, I won't be able to survive.

(Xiao Zhang, male, from Suqian, Jiangsu)

However, Xiao Zhang only sought to get some inspiration from such programs on job searches, and could not summon the courage to use such channels to seek opportunities for himself. From this it can be seen that there is still room for development with regard to the subjective initiative of the new generation of rural migrant workers. They will reflect on the relevant content found in mass media, but not to the extent of using mass media to seek avenues of personal future development.

In addition, information from mass media has also expanded the field of vision of the new generation of rural migrant workers to enable them to develop a new awareness and new objectives for their future. Xiao Fen, from Yancheng City, Suzhou, didn't continue her studies after graduating from junior middle school. She is bashful and felt that since she had not studied hard and passed her examinations, it would be better if she learned a practical skill. Now she helps out at a steamed dumpling restaurant opened by her family. She later plans to go to vocational school to study cooking. Xiao Fen has been an enthusiastic fan of television since she was young. She said because there is a television at the restaurant, she enjoys working hard at the restaurant to help out, and watches television while stuffing and wrapping dumplings and helping to serve dishes to customers. She even watches television commercials. She is extremely fond of television dramas and movies. Being introverted, she gets all types of information from television. When she watches different types of lifestyles portrayed on television, she also yearns to live the life of her dreams in the future.

> I really want to be a chef. I often see those famous chefs on television. The beautiful dishes they make are enticing I have always been very attracted to the culture of Chinese cuisine. I have also made an effort to learn about it. I believe that if I can learn cooking and become a chef, it should be a profession which pays well. Of course, I realize that this is a very difficult job, that I actually won't become a great chef. If I can cook dishes at a school's canteen, that will also be good, or after I earn some money, I can convert the dumpling store to a small restaurant. If I can gradually expand it, that will be good. Other than cooking, I also want to learn cosmetology. When I see how people on television wear cosmetics, I always feel it's quite amazing. In the blink of an eye, you can transform an ordinary-looking person into a dazzling superstar.
>
> (Xiao Fen, female, from Yancheng, Jiangsu)

Quite a bit of useful information provided by mass media also provides guidance to members of the new generation of rural migrant workers in their professional pursuits, to help them better plan their careers. Xiao Liang, who is 23 years old and comes from Zhaoqing, Guangdong, works in HR (human resources administration) at an enterprise in Guangzhou. When it comes to mass media, she mostly reads the newspaper. When reading the newspaper, she focuses on "local news". "Occasionally, I will read about national events or read a short article." She believes that reading the newspaper is helpful to her work.

> For example, I am now working in the human resources field. On many occasions, I can read about local conditions affecting human resources during recent years, and certain human resource policies promulgated by the national government with respect to the current situation. This provides me with a certain amount of guidance and assistance when I undertake human resource planning for the company.
>
> (Xiao Liang, female, from Zhaoqing, Guangdong)

The effect of mass media on rural migrant workers with respect to their urban adaptation and social inclusion has always been an important topic worthy of research in the field of communications. Previous research has discovered that mass media has generally exerted a weak influence on the thinking of rural migrant workers, but to a certain degree has guided them in special areas such as consumption behaviours and safeguarding their rights and interests. The effect of mass media primarily has not served to "change" old ways of thinking, but rather to "form" new ways of thinking (Tao, 2004). Mass media has played an important role in guiding the ongoing socialization of rural migrant workers, which with respect to the new generation of rural migrant workers is externally expressed in how it affects the way they plan their lives. Mass media content plays an active role in guiding how members of the new generation of rural migrant workers conceive the future, and also provides guidance with respect to their jobs and lives. During this process, mass media enhances members of the new generation of rural migrant workers with respect to expanding their attributes as individuals in a modern society and broadening their horizons, to enable them to pursue a more modern, more expansive vision of the future.

2.2 Upgrading Tools: Inspired by New Media

Compared to the older generation of rural migrant workers, members of the new generation of rural migrant workers, who are living in the information age, are clearly different in their use of media tools. They have stronger contacts with the new media and a greater tendency to identify with urban youth. Most of them have mobile phones and Internet connections. A survey conducted in 2011 discovered that 75.4 percent of members of the new generation of rural migrant workers living in Shanghai were netizens and 96 percent of them owned mobile phones, a much higher percentage of usage than that of traditional media (Zhou & Lv, 2011). It may be said that mobile phones and the Internet are highly popular among the new generation of rural migrant workers, and they have become active users of new media. The new media as a new tool for communication satisfies the need of the new generation of rural migrant workers to maintain interpersonal and emotional relationships, reconcile loneliness, indulge in amusement and recreation, and even safeguard legal rights and interests, thus becoming a vital part of their daily lives.

Accordingly, the new media has played a significant role in influencing and changing the life plans of members of the new generation of rural migrant workers. Traditional mass media cannot compare with the new media in terms of information compatibility, timeliness, interaction, and novelty. The new media, especially the Internet, provides people with a wide variety of channels for online exchange and communication, such as online forums, QQ groups, WeChat groups, and so on. The new generation of rural migrant workers, by using these tools, has learned the latest information on professional developments. Such information provides guidance in career planning and development to rural migrant workers, which further benefits the enhancement of an individual's future development. Xiao Liang, who works in the HR department of an enterprise, as mentioned in the preceding text, believes that the Internet is extremely helpful in her current work and professional development and also enables her to continue on her career path in HR with greater resolution.

The forums I browse are mostly forums for HR professionals, so they provide a certain amount of guidance in assisting my daily work. The content of these forums enable me to accumulate even more professional knowledge so that I can prepare for a better future in my development.

(Xiao Liang, female, from Zhaoqing, Guangdong)

Xiao Yu from Lianyungang, Jiangsu province, is the eldest son in a family of four persons. Born in 1990, after graduating from senior middle school, he gave up his studies and went to work after failing to pass the entrance exam for the university of his dreams. He currently works at his maternal uncle's crystal shop in Nanjing. His life is rather stable. He has an upbeat, outgoing personality and really enjoys engaging in conversation. He spoke with great interest about electronic products and the Internet. The crystal sales shop where he works has opened an online store to satisfy the demand for the sale of certain types of crystal, and he is responsible for the online store business. Accordingly, he must display products online, contact customers, strive to obtain good ratings for the online store, and contact delivery and after-sales services. After he came into contact with and learned about this type of online operation, he found it to be extremely interesting and discovered that online business had unlimited charm. Possessing outstanding business acumen, he began to use QQ and other communications tools to make friends and build a customer base. He also uses QQ to maintain contact with existing customers. He uses the Internet to compare the advantages and disadvantages of his online store versus others. He also uses it to reach an agreement on prices with other online store owners and to enrich the types of sales of crystal products. He believes that e-commerce has great potential for further development and says that he plans to continue to explore this line of business.

At this time, the new media has created a platform for information exchange for the new generation of rural migrant workers. In this virtual space, they can enjoy communicating, find inspiration, discover their own interests, be inspired to develop their careers, begin to use new media tools to help them in their work, expand their businesses, and set the direction of their future development.

The new media also inevitably gathers the latest, most detailed information on enterprises from all over the world. In this exchange and clash of information, people will come up with many original, creative ideas and concepts. In its use of new media, the new generation of rural migrant workers is easily influenced by this, which gives rise to certain ideas related to self-development, resulting in further emulation of others in planning one's own future. Xiao Li from Anhui province, who was mentioned earlier in this text, is similar to many girls in their twenties who like to be pretty and wear new clothes. After coming to the city, she discovered that she could buy fashionable, beautiful, affordably priced new clothing online. As a young woman who loved beauty, she felt as excited as if she had discovered a new world. From that time on, she would often purchase items on Taobao and other websites. When speaking of her plans for the future, she said:

In the future after I earn enough money, I definitely will open my own shop. It is highly possible that I will open a clothing store. All women love to buy clothes. If I open my own store, I won't have to worry about not having clothes to wear. I can open a brick-and-mortar store and then open an online store on Taobao. Anyway, I often use Taobao. In the future, I will probably have a brick-and-mortar store in conjunction with a Taobao store.

(Xiao Li, female, from Hefei, Anhui)

It's not difficult to see that Xiao Li's way of thinking has been gradually formed by her ongoing use of the Internet to purchase items, and the new media has made a significant contribution to this process.

Naturally, the new media has played a vitally important role in expanding the scope of social connection and enhancing the social networks of the new generation of rural migrant workers. Xiao Li from Shuozhou, Shanxi province, has been working in the provincial capital of Taiyuan since 2003. When she was 19 years old, she failed to pass the national college entrance examination.

Since she came from an economically deprived background, she abandoned the option of studying further to prepare to retake the examination, and came to Taiyuan to work. She first worked as a cashier at a shop. In the past she had only paid attention to television and other traditional media. But after starting work, she began to use her mobile phone with greater frequency. She gradually became accustomed to using her mobile phone to chat with co-workers and friends. Later, smartphones with Internet apps became popular and her co-worker helped her install QQ software on her mobile phone. She applied for a QQ account. It was exceptionally convenient to use QQ software to contact co-workers and friends. QQ also enabled her to meet many strangers online. These Internet friends were both male and female and came from different age groups, and different regions and professions. She would often talk about different topics with friends on the Internet. With girls of her own age, she would talk about romance, fashion, and delicious food. With young people like her who were living and working at locations away from home, she would talk about their work experience, interpersonal relationships, and how they missed their homes. And on the advice of a friend she met on the Internet, she decided to attend vocational classes for adults to enhance her academic standing. She has now completed her adult vocational education, which has greatly improved her work opportunities and living conditions.

Although traditional mass media influences the attitudes and thoughts of rural migrant workers, and plays an important role in guiding their ongoing socialization, the new media plays an even greater role which cannot be overlooked in the socialization of the new generation of rural migrant workers. Some scholars investigating the use of new media have discovered in their research that the new media has become a tool for rural migrant workers to build business relationship networks in places away from their native homes and has assisted rural migrant workers to break through the restrictions of time and space to engage in exchange and the transmission of social capital. They believe that in a society where change is occurring through the compression of time and space, rural migrant workers, in the individual choices they actively make to enter modern society, use the new media as a tool to construct their modernization as a group (Tian, 2012). For members of the new generation of rural migrant workers, the reality of urban life is not as beautiful as they had imagined it to be. Their earliest imaginings about the city have been proven wrong by the realities of the world, and the new media has opened a window for them. They can get together and interact in virtual space, to completely experience the marvellous world of the Internet and make more friends. This communication process gives them a certain inspiration for their future and for their lives, to pave a new road for their development in the city.

2.3 Opportunities for Interaction: Positive References in Interpersonal Communication

Classic communication theory tells us that mass communications primarily facilitate the "flow of information", while the "flow of concepts" and the "flow of influences" inevitably generate an effect through interpersonal communication. Interpersonal communication is an activity which involves the communication of information between individuals, and is also the most important means of communication for rural migrant workers after they come to the city (Xu, 2007a). Through interpersonal communication they express their adaptation with respect to basic survival, culture, concepts, behaviour and roles, social interaction, and so on (Chen, 2007). With respect to the new generation of rural migrant workers' values, mode of thinking, cultural spirit, and the resulting transformation of behavioural patterns, interpersonal communication is a vitally important factor. Members of the new generation of rural migrant workers experience tremendous changes in their lives when they abandon life in the village and begin living in an urban area, while rebuilding the behaviour and content inherent in interpersonal communication. Various modern ideas and concepts in their ongoing interaction with urban dwellers deeply affect each individual among these rural migrant workers (Tao, 2010). Thus, it may be said that interpersonal communication is the most important medium and tool by which the new generation of rural migrant workers obtains survival resources and opportunities for development, and is an important channel through which they smoothly assimilate into city life.

Planning for life is a lifetime concept which inevitably is profoundly affected by exchanges and discussions in the course of interpersonal communication. Compared with mass communications, interpersonal communication involves much more interaction, exchange, and initiative. Developments and changes in the thoughts and concepts of the new generation of rural migrant workers are closely connected to interpersonal communication. In general, the new generation of rural migrant workers currently exhibits dualistic pluralism in its interpersonal communication networks. Generally speaking, interpersonal communication networks of members of the new generation of rural migrant workers are characterized by dualistic pluralism. The circle of their interpersonal relations has broken through the boundary of rural migrant workers in the group, and has also broken out of the older generation's "inherent" interpersonal communication networks which were simply based on ties to the land and familial relationships. New interpersonal communications networks place greater emphasis on relationships among colleagues, classmates, and friends in "acquired" relationships, to enable communications network enrichment and diversification (Tao, 2010). Such diversified interpersonal communication networks also provide greater possibilities and assistance to members of the new generation of rural migrant workers by influencing and transforming their plans for the future.

In the city, interpersonal communication provides members of the new generation of rural migrant workers with an opportunity for interaction. They are also inclined to use urbanites of their own generation as a reference group, and to obtain inspiration to broaden their scope of vision when interacting and communicating with them, to recognize a different way of life. This type of interaction can also motivate the new generation of rural migrant workers to move forward and assist them to obtain broader and more far-reaching expectations. Xiao Chen, mentioned earlier in the text, who works at a hair salon near a university in Nanjing, has customers who for the most part are students at the university. These university students are the same age as Xiao Chen, being around 20 years old, and share certain ideas in common with him. However, because they are in higher education, they have a relatively deeper sense of confidence in their future development and plans for life, as university students who are filled with self-assuredness regarding their future. Xiao Chen, in his frequent communication with these customers at the hair salon, is also unconsciously affected by them and is motivated by the information they divulge in their conversations, which causes him to think about his plans for life.

> Many customers come to the salon, most of them being students from the university nearby, with more women than men among the salon's clientele. I will often chat with them as I do their hair. Sometimes I ask them what kind of work they do, and what they want to do in the future. I feel like they are very ambitious: they all want to go abroad and live in a bigger city, or go to work for a multinational or a very strong company. Sometimes, I feel that there is some distance between us, because we come from different backgrounds and naturally will lead different lives in the future.
>
> (Xiao Chen, male, from Liuhe, Nanjing)

His communication with university students has, to a greater or lesser degree, influenced his thinking. He has begun to recognize that the more one learns, the farther one will be able to go in life to lead a good life in the city. Accordingly, in 2011 he went to Guangzhou to participate in a training seminar on luxury (hair care) items. After undergoing half a year's study, he seems to have more self-confidence.

> Although this training was very expensive, nonetheless I feel that it definitely is useful. I am now a senior hairstylist. If I continue to learn more and save my money, I will be able to open my own hair salon.
>
> (Xiao Chen, male, from Liuhe, Nanjing)

He said this filled with hope.

The most important result of interpersonal communication is the construction of social networks for the new generation of rural migrant workers to assist them in accumulating social capital. The social interactions of the new generation of rural migrant workers in the city have broken down the former isolation experienced by the older generation of rural migrant workers, to gradually form a wealth of multifaceted interpersonal communication networks providing greater opportunities for self-development. Mr Chen, who is from Hanjiang, Yangzhou city, is already 25 years old, works at an engineering enterprise in Yangzhou, and earns a mere two to three thousand yuan in monthly wages. He is quite envious of the foreman at the construction site and has said that he wants to find a higher paying job.

"If I said that I don't want to free myself from my current circumstances, that would be completely untrue." The phrase "free myself from my current circumstances" indicates that he is dissatisfied with his current work, that he is "forced" to live such an existence and therefore needs "to free himself" of it. His current job was introduced to him by an acquaintance. He believes that if he wants to "free himself", he must primarily depend on someone he knows, that he must rely on his network of interpersonal relationships.

Xiao Ge, who belongs to the group of persons who have "drifted northward" to seek their fortune in Beijing, comes from Jilin province and has enjoyed singing since childhood. Eight years ago, his friend told him that Beijing's pedestrian underpasses were often peopled by many itinerant singers who performed there. Accordingly, he put his guitar on his back and hit the road to travel alone to Beijing, where he made a living by performing in a pedestrian underpass near Muxiyuan. Later, through a friend's introduction, he began to sing in the evenings as the resident singer at a bar. During this time, he was discovered by someone who worked at a record company. Although ultimately nothing resulted from this, his reputation spread, which served to enhance his stature in the neighbouring district. Throughout this process, his interpersonal communications played a huge role, to propel him forward step by step in the direction of his dreams.

In addition, the exchange and communication of information in interpersonal communication exerts an influence on members of the new generation of rural migrant workers with respect to their plans for starting a business. Xiao Tian, who works at the same hair salon as Xiao Chen mentioned earlier in this book, comes from Anhui province and at the age of 28 has begun to secretly make plans for leaving his job, because he has heard that a certain district in Nanjing plans to demolish buildings at a certain location and construct a new business district in their place. He believes that this will definitely be a new commercial centre and, in the future, will develop into a prosperous area. Therefore, having saved up a certain amount of funds in savings, he is planning to utilize the opportunity presented by this new commercial centre to secure a relatively small store front to open his business. The communication of such new government policy information through interpersonal channels is precisely what serves to change the future lives of members of the new generation of rural migrant workers.

From this it can be seen that interpersonal communications networks have a significant influence on the modernization of rural migrant workers and on their individual development. Coming to the city to work, leaving behind the traditional society of the rural village, and integrating into a broader urban society entails an expansion and overturning of simple interpersonal relationships. The more extensive interpersonal communication networks are, the greater the possibility for mutual conflict and influence among points of view held by people (Tao & Xu, 2012). The range of interpersonal interactions involving the new generation of rural migrant workers is expanding day after day. The composition of the members of such interpersonal networks is also becoming more diverse and complex. Members of the new generation of rural migrant workers have the opportunity to come into contact with even more concepts and ways of thinking. In the midst of this clash of ideas, their thoughts about and plans for their future lives are significantly affected.

In a nutshell, mass media, new media, and interpersonal communications are the three substantive means of communication which exert a major influence on the life plans of the new generation of rural migrant workers. Mass media enable the new generation of rural migrant workers to form new perspectives on life, to guide them in their ongoing socialization, and expand their modernization as individuals. New media, as a communication tool more frequently used by the new generation of rural migrant workers, creates a virtual space for them to interact and communicate while also promoting the progress of their social inclusion. The richness and diversity of interpersonal communications expands their networks of social relationship to provide more opportunities for changing their current conditions and achieving self-development. For the new generation of rural migrant workers searching for direction in the midst of confusion, the media has evolved into a dominion which influences their future choices and development.

3. Accumulation and Restructuring of Spiritual Capital Under the Influence of the Media

Labour in human society includes physical labour and mental labour. Material labour creates the material world upon which human beings depend to survive, while mental labour is of a free nature and creates spiritual wealth (Hamilton et al., 2009). Material labour determines mental labour; mental labour in turn also affects material labour. Spiritual capital refers to spiritual energy which proactively promotes material labour. It may be said that spiritual capital is the medium which connects economy, culture, and social life. Spiritual capital is different from material capital and human capital, in that spiritual capital is an intangible capital centred on values. It is an organization's or an individual's scientific knowledge, feelings, beliefs, moral sentiments, and so on, dynamic influences and forces which are generated during the course of material labour (Wang, 2011). The life plans of the new generation of rural migrant workers are an external expression of spiritual capital. Their imaginings of the future during the course of living in the city and under the influence of the media are dispelled, reconstructed, and built up over time to become the force which propels their struggle to move forward and thus transform the status of their integration into urban life.

The media plays an important role in this process of gradual advancement. Members of the new generation of migrant workers flooding into the city have seen their urban dreams shattered and have tasted life's realities. This has resulted in a transformation of their plans for living. Their pursuit of value in life is not merely limited to ontological values with respect to being able to put down roots in the city. They have begun to awaken to social values with respect to obtaining social prestige and reputation through individual efforts. Mass media, new media, and interpersonal communications have exerted a positive effect on transforming their plans for living. The media plays a vital role in the course of their lives. This spiritual capital also undergoes reconstruction and ongoing accumulation to exist as an interactive relationship shaping their integration into the city, continuously transforming how members of the new generation of rural migrant workers perceive themselves and their future lives.

3.1 Awakening of Consciousness: Life Planning in Constructing a Foundation Based on Urban Values

Although the new generation of rural migrant workers left the village long ago to begin living in the city, its values still remain rooted in village society. Since childhood, it has been infused with a system of traditional values from the village. Although its ties to the land are much weaker than those of the older generation, the new generation of rural migrant workers still cherishes memories of their native soil. No matter where members of the new generation of rural migrant workers go, they clearly understand that they are children who originate from the village, forever rooted in rural life. Accordingly, to a certain degree, they are still influenced by the system of traditional values from the village.

As rural folk, their pursuit of lofty objectives colours the details of their everyday lives. Such pursuit gives meaning to their lives. And their traditional rural values spring from a deeply rooted tradition of carrying on the family legacy and bringing honour to one's ancestors. Nonetheless, with the spread of the modernity of the West to the rural village, such traditional concepts have been declared to be mistaken and have been replaced by the hedonism and consumerism of real life as the main trend. However, after their desire to consume has been aroused, they find that they have insufficient money to fulfil such desire and accordingly lose their faith in life and their reasons for enduring such difficult living conditions, whereupon they feel rootless (Yang, 2010).

On this basis, scholars have postulated the concept of "ontological values" among farmers and believe that all behaviour among farmers is governed by a value base. They believe that unprecedented changes are occurring among values held by the current generation of Chinese farmers. Their value base is now undergoing a transformation from ontological values to social values. So-called ontological values primarily refer to an individual's feelings and thoughts about their own life, the dialogue between an individual and their inner world, the basis of how they define their place in life. The basis of how farmers define their place in life is predicated on the next generation continuing the family lineage, continuing the meaning of the finite lifespan of an individual by giving birth to children and grandchildren. On the other hand, social values primarily refer to the feelings of an individual with respect to how he or she is evaluated by another person, referring to a person's behavioural significance generated through interpersonal communications, the social prestige and reputation obtained by individual efforts, subject to a person's complying with a system of consensus held by the majority of persons in a society (He, 2007).

With respect to the new generation of rural migrant workers, this value base has undergone spatial displacement. Influenced by their memories of the village, in an urban environment they subconsciously continue this value base. And this value base is the only belief to which they can cling as they drift in the city, so that they do not reach a point where they feel rootless. The ontological values which define the meaning of life in the city for the new generation of rural migrant workers continue to survive in the city through an individual's struggle and continue the finite life of an individual through the procreation of the next generation. In the same way, their social values embody the hope that through personal effort they can win respect and recognition from others in a complex and changing urban society, as outsiders coming to a completely new social environment, to obtain prestige and a good name in society, and realize their individual dreams. Currently, the value base of the new generation of rural migrant workers in the city is undergoing a transformation from ontological values to social values.

In the preceding text we mentioned Xiao Zhang from Suqian, Jiangsu, who after graduating from vocational school, repeatedly encountered difficulties in finding a job and could for the present time only work as a service staff at Haidilao restaurant. At 20 years of age, he was clearly dissatisfied with his current living circumstances. Although he was able to feed and clothe himself, this fell far short of his ambitions.

> Actually, I am very idealistic. Before, when I was in school, I thought about a lot of things. Of course, I wanted to become a successful person. My dream was to open my own automotive maintenance and repair shop, to become my own boss and make a lot of money. At the very least, I would not have to wait upon others and serve them (tea and water). I want to lead a very respectable life and get respect from others. Not like the way things are now, where I sometimes encounter customers who are unreasonable and order us around. However, I realize that it is impossible for a person to immediately achieve success at a young age, so I must continue to work hard to be successful.
>
> (Xiao Zhang, male, Suqian, Jiangsu)

In the same way, Xiao Tan, who works at Langtao hair salon in Nanjing, when speaking about the different types of customers he often encountered at work and what he had experienced, also believed that ranking differences which currently exist at the salon caused him to feel extremely humiliated, to feel that he was not respected, which made him want to get away from this type of life as soon as possible.

> Apparent differences in rank gradually emerged at the salon. At times, a hair-stylist would unavoidably put on airs and order us around. However, when I considered how everyone had gradually achieved their current position through their own efforts, I was able to understand this. Now, I want to rid myself of my current status as early as possible through my own efforts. Afterwards, when I become a hairstylist, I naturally will not have to take orders from anyone.
>
> (Xiao Tan, male, from Hubei)

Ontological values and social values are intimately related. Ontological values possess fundamental meanings which regulate and guide social values, to enable persons to pursue social values in an orderly, temperate context. Certain ontological values are matched with corresponding social values. At times, social values will be elevated to the level of transcendent pursuits (Yang, 2010). Life plans of (members of) the new generation of rural migrant workers to a certain degree serve to construct their value base in the city. They implement their plans for the future to achieve their desired objectives and materialize value requirements as they understand them. The process of achieving this plan serves to express their own inner values. This value base gives them a foundation which supports them in their urban lives, strengthens their convictions and gives them the courage to struggle.

One interviewee, Xiao Qiu, comes from Anhui. At 20 years of age, he works as a service staff in the front lobby of a hotel nearby Xuzhuang Software Park in Qixia District, Nanjing. Although he quit school at a young age during his second year of junior middle school, he has a wealth of social experience. He previously helped out in the kitchen at a hotel in Beijing. Afterwards, he worked in the front lobby of a high-level private club. Although he now still works as a service staff, at his youthful age he is clearly not satisfied with his present circumstances. In his blueprint for the future, he constantly pursues the objective of starting his own business in Nanjing. His current job interests him, because he believes that it will enable him to accumulate experience and develop personal networks in preparation for his opening of a restaurant and hotel in the future. He describes his plan for the future as follows:

> I hope to open my own hotel, and make every effort to achieve high standards in its operation. I want to equip my hotel with the best Internet network system, and install a multitude of televisions which broadcast programs all the time. I want to place electronic editions of newspapers or electronic readers throughout the hotel, to conveniently meet the lifestyle requirements of modern urban residents, which will attract even more customers. I also want to aggressively promote my business on the Internet, because at the present time, one's reputation on the Internet is very important and you must

establish a good name for yourself. You must also comprehensively promote your business through advertisements placed on street side television screens.

(Xiao Qiu, male, from Anhui)

It can be seen that he has exceptionally detailed plans for the future and the driving force behind such plans is his desire to establish a successful business in the city, to obtain a value base founded on respect and recognition from society. Driven by such social values, he will meet his own value requirements step by step based on his life plan.

Members of the new generation of rural migrant workers, through their plans for living, construct their own value bases for the city, using these as incentives to struggle hard for the future. Compared to the older generation of rural migrant workers, who, while making a place for themselves in the city, continued to keep their ontological values of passing on their legacy to succeeding generations, the consciousness of the new generation of rural migrant workers has begun to be awakened, and their pursuit of self-fulfilment has shifted towards social values which involve making an individual effort to obtain social prestige and a good reputation. This transformation provides them with beliefs and motivation to support them in their ongoing struggle to realize their dreams.

3.2 Change of Trajectory: The Appearance of Turning Points in a Person's Life

In sociology studies, the life course theory is often used to explore intense social changes which conspicuously affect an individual's life and development. According to the American sociologist Glen H. Elder, this so-called life course refers to the different roles continuously played by individuals which are dictated by society and events. The order of such roles or events is arranged according to the age of the individual (Bao, 2005).

The life course theory is a new perspective in sociological research and has primarily been used in research on immigrant issues. The immortal work *The Polish Peasant in Europe and America*, by the American sociologist, Thomas and Znaniecki (2000), an important representative of the Chicago School, takes the lead by using methodology based on life histories, life records, and contextual definitions to research social changes and the life trajectories of immigrants. The tide of migration among China's rural migrant workers may be seen as a form of internal immigration. The new generation of rural migrant workers differs from the older generation of rural migrant workers who went back and forth between the village and the city, in that the new generation of rural migrant workers is a new generation of migrants who have moved from the village to take up permanent residence in the city. With the introduction and popularity of the life course theory in China during recent years, many scholars have applied it to research on the life courses of rural migrant workers. However, most research only focuses on the effect of specific events and roles in the life course of an individual, and overlooks the role of the media, this important social variable, in influencing and changing the roles played by individuals in their life destinies.

The life courses of the new generation of rural migrant workers may be divided into three phases: rural dwellers – rural migrant workers – urban dwellers. This trajectory also includes their life plans from the time before they come to the city to the time after they have come. The media has an effect on their life plans, while such plans will determine the trajectory of their future development. In this context, in the life courses of the new generation of rural migrant workers, the turning point in their lives will occur under the influence of the media, causing them to change their destinies and rewrite their lives.

The concept of "living in a certain time and space" is a principle found in life course theory which emphasizes that an individual born in a certain year (birth cohort effect) belongs to a group of individuals of his/her same age and to the locale at which he/she is born (geographical effect), which basically connects a person to a certain historical force (He, 2011). Chinese society is currently in the midst of a phase of development in which dramatic changes are occurring. Such intense social changes are closely connected to the life course of each individual.

Such historical phases have driven the tide of rural migrant workers entering the cities to work. And the new generation of rural migrant workers born in villages, have become a group of people endowed by this era with a unique destiny. Actually, the flow of the new generation of rural migrant workers from the village into the city, their change of domicile, and their leaving their parents to live independent lives, are all important turning points in their life histories, as the times push them forward in a society driven by accelerated modernization and urbanization, freeing them from their destiny as farmers originally bound to the land all their lives. As such, the media has thoroughly penetrated this process. This extends to depictions of thriving, modern urban life in various media in the village, and verbal renditions of city life in interpersonal communications with persons returning to the village from the city, which significantly spur the desire of members of the new generation of rural migrant workers to experience urban living and to change their own destinies. From this point on, the media affects the personal life plans of members of the new generation of rural migrant workers living in the cities and plays an important role in the course of their lives.

In the research paradigm on life course theory, another core principle emphasizes individual initiative. People inevitably advance the course of their lives through planning and choices made in the context of a definite social organizational system. Choices made by individuals, in addition to being influenced by how circumstances are defined, are also influenced by their individual experience and personal characteristics (Li et al., 1999).

In this text, we previously mentioned interviewees as examples. We mentioned Xiao Chen from Liuhe, Nanjing, who enjoyed watching television shows on youthful ambition. Such film and television programs also inspired him regarding the realities of life and what was to come, filling him with courage to fight for his future. And Xiao Zhang, who worked as service staff at Haidilao, was also inspired by programs on searching for a job, which caused him to reflect on what issues he should consider on his road to self-development. Xiao Fen, from Yancheng, Jiangsu, was influenced by a famous chef she saw on television in her decision to become an accomplished chef in the future.

After coming to the city, Xiao Li, who works at a restaurant near a university in Nanjing, being exposed to and using the Internet to make purchases, came up with the idea to open a brick-and-mortar clothing store in the future which would be combined with an online store on Taobao. All of the preceding are examples of psychological turning points in people's lives. Ideas inspire action. Changes in ideas which affect personal plans determine the road a person takes in their future development and the occurrence of series of events consistent with their objectives.

And the media plays a vital role in this process. The media provides motivation and support for the life plans of the new generation of rural migrant workers, expanding their horizons to enable them to realize a new awareness of the future. This allows them to enhance their proactivity, enabling them to exercise autonomy, and advance on life's path according to plan as they determine the course of their future lives.

Research on life course theory also emphasizes "interconnected living". Generally speaking, people inevitably live in social relationships composed of their families, relatives, and friends. An individual, through certain social relationships, becomes integrated into certain groups. Only in this way can an individual obtain support from society and shoulder certain social obligations. Social relationships are media which transmit social feelings (Li et al., 1999).

Xiao Li from Shuozhou, Shanxi, works in the provincial capital of Taiyuan. Having only a high school education, she enrolled at a vocational school. This was a major turning point in her life. It goes without saying that furthering her education had a positive effect on her future and personal development. And her choice was influenced by the media. She met many new friends through QQ and often talked about different topics with different friends on the Internet. Acting on an Internet friend's advice, she decided to attend vocational school to enhance her educational background.

Xiao Chen, who works at a hair salon near a university, by frequently talking with university students, came to realize the importance of study to personal development. Accordingly, in 2011 he went to Guangzhou to participate in a training course on luxury products, to enhance his own professional abilities. This had a significant effect on his future development.

In addition to the preceding, even more members of the new generation of rural migrant workers find work through personal introductions after coming to the city. This enables them to survive and put down roots in the city. Xiao Ge, due to encouragement from his friends, came to Beijing to survive as a singer, and through his friend's introduction became the singer-in-residence at a bar, after which he was noticed by a record company. In these series of events, interpersonal communications played an undeniable role. Thus, it may be said that media plays a hugely important role in bringing about a turning point in the life courses of members of the new generation of rural migrant workers.

During the life courses of members of the new generation of rural migrant workers, in their transition from rural dwellers to rural migrant workers to further becoming urban residents, the media, as an important social variable, plays a role which cannot be overlooked in influencing and changing individuals' destinies. Media, specifically comprised of mass media, new media, and interpersonal communications, first guides members of the new generation of migrant workers in their journey from the village to the city, and then further influences their life plans. The media shapes turning points in their concepts and minds, to influence series of related events which occur during the future course of their lives. In this context, the media facilitates the occurrence of turning points in the life courses of members of the new generation of rural migrant workers, thus changing the trajectories of their lives.

3.3 Capital Restructuring: Two-way Interaction Between Life Planning and Social Inclusion

The renown German founder of a school of history Frederich List, in his *Outlines of American Political Economy*, pioneered the use of the term "mental or spiritual capital", defining mental capital as the mental and physical energy which a person innately possesses, obtained from their social and political environment (List, 1983).

The mind or the spirit exists in different states of being and constituent elements. For spiritual elements to become mental or spiritual capital, they must conform to what is required of them to become positive and concentrated. Only active and positive spiritual energy can function to propel social history forward as most capital does and can thus become spiritual capital. Spiritual capital is also a concentrated expression of spiritual energy (Li, 2006).

If understood in this context, the life plans of the new generation of rural migrant workers may be said to be an external expression of spiritual capital which reflects their dynamic mental attitude in aspiring to better their lives, their confidence and courage in pursuing their future development, and their determination and perseverance to struggle to survive in the city. Spiritual capital's function in guiding and predetermining action is not only expressed in its ability to give purpose to action but, moreover, in its ability to accurately provide objectives to be achieved (Li, 2006).

Moreover, the life plans of members of the new generation of rural migrant workers precisely have such an effect, in that they enhance their proactivity and stimulate their unremitting efforts to build their futures. Their life plans determine their objectives and pursuits while living in the city, guiding and propelling them to advance according to plan in achieving their dreams.

Such spiritual capital is restructured under the influence of the media after the new generation of rural migrant workers enters the city, and, in its implementation, is constantly accumulated as their life plans undergo transformation, propelling the implementation of uninterrupted development, to exert a significant effect on their inclusion into urban life. This process of restructuring and accumulation progresses gradually by degrees. Initially, members of the new generation of rural migrant workers enter the city, experience the realities of urban life, and then, under the influence of the media, change their life plans. Their value bases also shift towards social values. Their previous spiritual capital is also restructured during this process and continues to accumulate as their life plans are gradually clarified and improved. Such spiritual capital in the bi-directional interaction of urban integration also influences how members of the new generation of rural migrant workers perceive themselves and their future.

Xiao Cheng, who is 21 years old and comes from Xuzhou, Jiangsu, currently works at a store in Suzhou where he is learning automotive decoration. His personal life plan is to open his own store and create his own space. He really likes this profession and is fully confident that he will succeed in his endeavours.

> I have full confidence in this industry! Business is very good at the store where I work. Currently, people who own automobiles pay more and more attention to their car's interior decoration. Although a car can be driven as soon as it is purchased, since a person has spent so much money on purchasing an automobile, they naturally want to stand out as stylish in the eyes of others, so that they enjoy more "face". Therefore, automotive decoration is naturally a must. I can say without exaggerating that nowadays cars play the same role as a man's face. An automobile's interior decoration can express the taste and class of its owner. When I buy a car, I will also assiduously decorate it.
>
> (Xiao Cheng, male, from Xuzhou, Jiangsu)

Although his work is very tiring, he is nonetheless optimistic and feels that he has adapted well to it. "The work is definitely arduous. In the beginning I really felt that it was very troublesome. Luckily, I have a strong ability to adapt."

Living alone, struggling to survive in an unfamiliar city, he unavoidably feels lonely. However, as a frequent user of media and as a person who has excellent interpersonal relationships, he feels that his life is not bad. He often uses his mobile phone QQ to check on how his friends have been doing lately, express his opinions, and talk with others. He also places great importance on getting along well with his colleagues at the store. He is honest with others, is highly trustworthy, and very diligent in his work. All of his senior colleagues really like him. When he encounters something he doesn't know how to do, he will politely and humbly ask others for instruction, who are more than willing to help him. He is the only employee at the store who is not a local person. His senior colleagues are very kind to him and always invite him to participate in their group activities, such as going out together for a drink. Sometimes when they go shopping, they will pick some things up for him. This store is just like a big family, bringing warmth to a young worker from an outside locale.

A person who first comes to an unfamiliar place must live there for a while before slowly adapting to the locale. Over the past several months, Xiao Cheng has not only become more familiar with the specific business of automotive decoration but has also made many more new friends, with whom he gets along quite happily. He gets along well with his colleagues at the store and even with the older couple from whom he buys his breakfast. Xiao Chen now has a sunny disposition and more easily engages in conversation with customers. As he satisfactorily performs the work assigned to him, he also quietly makes preparations to open his own store in the future. He has learned from the store manager's management experience how to make the store well-known to the market, how to obtain repeat business from customers, and so on. He also focuses on his communications with customers, to understand customers' various needs. He says he has really gained a lot, and has now further realized that there are still many things to learn.

Xiao Cheng's urban experience vividly reflects the two-way interactive relationship between a person's life plan as an expression of spiritual capital and integration into urban life, specifically embodied in the progressive day-to-day clarification of the life plans of the new generation of rural migrant workers. Dynamic motivation provided by such spiritual capital grows stronger and stronger, to exert a tremendous push to expedite the integration of the new generation of rural migrant workers into city life. And a smooth integration into urban life also gives the new generation of rural migrant workers the confidence and courage to pursue their future development, enabling them to more effectively ground themselves in urban life and duly make plans, thus further accumulating such spiritual capital. Accordingly, the new generation of rural migrant workers' integration into the urban environment is an ongoing progression in this bi-directional positive interaction. They use their own two hands to change their life destinies and to struggle to redefine their identity.

What cannot be overlooked is that since such a positive interaction exists, a vicious cycle is also present. Spiritual capital has a positive effect. However, given varying production and labour objectives, its effect on economic and social development also varies. Embodied in subjects of production and labour – the emotions, beliefs, strength of will, and other such non-intellectual factors of labourers – a duality is apparent: spiritual capital may be internalized as a labourer's "inner driving force", promoting social development and embellishing a person's aspirations. Or it may act as a "spiritual opiate" for the labourer, obstructing his or her development (Wang, 2011).

Xiao Zhu, from Yunyang County, Chongqing province, is a living example of this. Although only 21 years of age, she has been working away from home for six years and currently works at a hotel in Nanjing. Her birthplace is extremely impoverished and isolated, with a restricted supply of electrical power. There is only one television in the whole village, not to mention computers! It seems as if the place is completely cut off from the outside world.

Accordingly, when she first came to the city, Xiao Zhu discovered that she was truly amazed by everything she saw. She began to come into contact with the television and the Internet. She wanted to communicate and explore, so she tried talking on QQ. However, she didn't have any friends to add. She had never heard of WeChat, today's trend. And she still used the most conventional type of mobile phone. Although she had been working away from home for six years, she was still living on the periphery of this world. Not only with respect to the use of media tools, but also with respect to her participation in society, she remained isolated and consistently found it impossible to keep up with the pace at which the city developed. As a result, she felt bitter and lonely. She believed that she was incapable of integrating into society. She currently wants to go back to her native village to marry her boyfriend. She still feels uncertain about her future. Her only conviction is that she must venture out again in the future to give her child the opportunity to experience the world outside, so that they will not repeat what she went through.

From this it can be seen that uncertainty about one's future and lack of clarity about one's life plan will result in the new generation of rural migrant workers lacking the resolve and motivation to fight for their future. During their social inclusion process, they also will encounter various mental obstacles, and feel that no matter what they do, they can't fit in. Moreover, difficulties they encounter in this integration process make them feel greater uncertainty about their future, causing them to despair and to not know what to do, even to the point that they abandon opportunities to change their destinies, and retreat from the city to the village, making them persons who have renounced the group.

In summary of the preceding, after the new generation of rural migrant workers enters the city, they restructure and accumulate spiritual capital which is embodied in their life plans. Clinging to their dreams, they experience the realities of life, begin to modify their life plans, and for the first time are awakened by their desire to obtain social value through social status and respectability. Based on such a value system, the media in the form of mass media, new media, and interpersonal communications plays an important role in the course of their lives, spurring them to achieve turning points in their lives. Moreover, such spiritual capital, through bi-directional interaction during social inclusion, influences and changes the future development of the new generation of rural migrant workers.

4. Media Boost: Towards an Alternative Future

In the flower of their youth, the new generation of rural migrant workers, like their peers of the same age in the city, harbour hopes and desires in pursuit of their ideals. Filled with idealism, they arrive at an unfamiliar and vast space, hoping that they can put down roots in the city to achieve personal value in their lives. Unlike the older generation of rural migrant workers whose objectives in life were to "earn money, build a house, take a wife and have children", the new generation of rural migrant workers are motivated to leave home to work by factors which are manifestly related to their age. They yearn to experience a life of unlimited possibilities in the city and achieve their dreams. Streaming from the villages into the cities, they undergo a gradual growth process in which they mature physically and mentally, and they experience the realities and cruelties of urban life, while their plans for life gradually become clear. During this process, the highly developed urban media exerts a significant impact by guiding and inspiring them, offering them possibilities for moving towards an alternative future.

As members of the new generation of rural migrant workers build their life plans, it can be observed how spiritual capital is reconstructed and accumulated under the influence of the media. Media in this context means mass media, new media, and interpersonal communications, the main media channels. After their spatial migration, members of the new generation of rural migrant workers gradually form their plans for life through a multiplicity of rich media experiences and communication practices. Such plans embody their yearning to express themselves and pursue their ideals, manifesting their efforts to change their futures and their life destinies.

Nonetheless, we must clearly recognize that generalizations cannot be made about the media boost. This media boost cannot possibly provide positive motivation to every member of the group. Such a positive effect is conditionally felt by certain members of the new generation of rural migrant workers. On the one hand, the media provides hope which illuminates the lives of this group living at the bottom of society, helping them to fulfil themselves, achieve value, and actuate their integration into urban life. However, on the other hand, due to the combined effect of a deficiency of subjective factors among members of the new generation of rural migrant workers, the context of the times, and social environment, the media also sets up various obstacles to their advancement to a certain degree. The media generates both positive and negative forces which give rise to dilemmas in the process of pushing and pulling them forward. Accordingly, the new generation of rural migrant workers must rely on improvements in the function of the media and on enhancing their own personal attributes to overcome such difficulties.

It may be said that the media has a dual effect: as it propels the social inclusion of the new generation of migrant workers, it also embodies the worsening conditions of the communication environment. Although a gradual awakening of spiritual needs continues to occur among the new generation of rural migrant workers, and although their pursuit of personal expression is becoming stronger, the contradictions and conflicts between their ideals and life's realities still cause them to feel at a loss. This is also a key issue in their ongoing thoughts and suspicions about where they belong in the future. Accordingly, how to improve the existing media environment to provide them with positive motivation for personal achievement and assist them in smoothly integrating into the city is where the essential significance of our research ultimately resides.

With respect to the current communication environment in urban areas, alleviating the marginalized conditions of media representations suffered by the new generation of rural migrant workers, giving them equal media rights to motivate them to express themselves and achieve their ideals, enhancing their ability to utilize the media, empowering them to more effectively use media tools to serve their personal life plans and dreams, and enabling them to smoothly integrate into the city as they struggle with life's realities, is the real meaning which underlies research on the life plans of the new generation of rural migrant workers.

Further elaborating on this, it can be said that this actually involves the process of reconstructing a person's identity. As a matter of fact, choices made for the future by the new generation of rural migrant workers and their plans for their own lives entail a reconstruction of their identity through conscious self-awareness. Reconstruction of their identity is an internal transformation, expressed externally by migrant farmers' thoughts about their future life. The ultimate objective of personal expression and the ultimate result of integration into urban life is their successful transition from rural dwellers to "new urban citizens".

Notes

1 Translator's note: referring to couples getting hitched even though the groom brings no apartment or car to the relationship, as is Chinese traditional.
2 Translator's note: Lu Tao is a character in the drama series *Struggle*.
3 Translator's note: Another character in the drama series *Struggle*.

References

Bao, L. (2005). An exploration of the time perspective of the life course theory. *Sociological Studies, 20*(4), 120–133.

Chen, F. (2007). From isolation to adaptation: The culture transition of migrant workers in Chinese cities. *Journal of East China University of Science and Technology (Social Science Edition), 3*, 84–87.

Chen, Q. (2010). *Spatial mobility and rational choice – The action logic of migrant workers' migration in the context of financial crisis*, Master Dissertation. Northwest University.

Hamilton, A., Jay, J., & Madison, J. (2009). *The federalist papers* (F. Cheng, H. Zai, & X. Shu, Trans.). The Commercial Press, p. 113.

He, X. (2007). Changes in Chinese farmers' values and their impact on rural governance: A survey of Dagu Village in Liaoning province. *Study & Exploration, 5*, 12–14.

He, X. (2011). A female migrant worker's life of working in the city for 30 years: A perspective based on life course theory research. *China Youth Study, 5*, 37–41.

Li, Q., Deng, J., & Xiao, Z. (1999). Social change and personal development: A paradigm and methodology for life course research. *Sociological Study, 6*, 1–18.

Li, Y. (2006). On mental capital. *Wuhan University Journal (Philosophy & Social Sciences), 59*(6), 741–746.

List, F. (1983). *The national system of political economy* (W. Chen, Trans.). The Commercial Press.

Pan, Z. (2007a). Social exclusion and predicament of future development: An empirical study of migrant workers in China. *Zhejiang Social Science, 2*, 96–103.

Shi, B. (2010). An analysis of the social distance between the new generation of migrant workers and urban residents. *South China Population, 25*(1), 47–56.

Tao, J. (2004). A study on the influence of mass media on migrant workers' perceptions. *Journalism & Communication, 11*(2), 10–15.

Tao, J. (2010). A study of migrant workers' interpersonal communication behaviors and influencing factors. *Journalism & Communication, 19*(5), 97–104+112.

Tao, J., & Xu, H. (2012). Personal modernity and interpersonal communication of the new generation of migrant workers – An empirical study based on survey data in Shanghai. *Journalistic University, 1*, 80–86+108.

Thomas, W. I., & Znaniecki, F. (2000). *The Polish peasant in Europe and America* (Y. Zhang, Trans.). Translin Publishing House.

Tian, Q. (2012). The use of new media and the modernization construction of migrant workers: The case of taxi drivers from Hunan Youxian in Shenzhen. *Modern Communication, 34*(12), 28–32.

Wang, C. (2003). The social recognition and integration of a new generation of rural migrants in China. *Sociological Research, 3*.

Wang, Y. (2011). A sociological interpretation of knowledge of spiritual capital. *Academimc Forum, 34*(2), 169–173.

Xu, B. (2007a). Social networks and interpersonal communication of migrant workers moving to cities. *Journal of East China University of Science and Technology (Social Science Edition), 22*(3), 92–96.

Yang, H. (2010). *The hidden world – Women's belonging and meaning of life in a water village in Southern Hunan*, Doctoral Dissertation. Huazhong University of Science and Technology.

Zhou, B., & Lv, S. (2011). An empirical study on the use and evaluation of new media of the new generation of migrant workers in Shanghai. *Journalistic University, 2*, 145–150.

5 Escaping Isolated Islands

Interpersonal Communication of the New Generation of Migrant Workers

New-generation migrant workers leave their hometowns in rural areas and their familiar social networks to work and live in the city. In this process, they must develop a new social circle that is evidently different from the natural intimate relations they established with family and friends in their rural life. Instead, they must identify new approaches to establishing relationships. Moreover, they must interact with diverse people based on work relationships, life experiences, and everyday consumption.

Interpersonal communication is fundamental to the survival, adaptation, and social inclusion of the new generation of migrant workers in the city. Poor interpersonal communication can affect their work and life, whereas excellent interpersonal communication skills can increase their confidence and generate a sense of belonging in the city. Therefore, the interpersonal communication of the new generation of migrant workers is a suitable observation point for this study to examine the state of their urban adaptation. Different from the older generation, the new generation of migrant workers has relatively weak emotional ties to their rural origins and strongly identifies with the city; thus, they have more active interactions with urban residents. Furthermore, as a generation that has grown up with the Internet, they frequently and abundantly use new media for interpersonal communication. Therefore, they have a stronger willingness and ability to develop interpersonal relationships with others than do older generations. However, they are also more likely to struggle when facing setbacks in interpersonal communication because of their young age and immature mental development. In general, various differences between the new and the older generations of migrant workers at the interpersonal communication level have clearly affected their urban adaptation. Therefore, examining the interpersonal communication of this new generation of migrants is crucial.

1. Residents on Isolated Islands: Triple Isolation in the City

The new generation of migrant workers come from the countryside to work in the cities where they face ubiquitous rural-urban differences. In this unfamiliar place, because of the effect of institutionalized labels, they are regarded by urban residents

DOI: 10.4324/9781003365785-5

as negligible and excludable outsiders; they are also obscured by the media or represented in a stereotypical manner. After being isolated by the urban residents and the media, these new residents absorb, perceive, and internalize this discriminatory information and isolate themselves in work and leisure life. Because of this triple isolation (i.e., isolation by urbanites, the media, and themselves) that these workers experience in the city, they seem to each inhabit their own separate and isolated "islands" in the city. The "isolated island" in the city is not a concept with a clear geographical boundary, and it is neither born nor created overnight. Without spatial barriers, the concept is slowly formed under the combined effect of multiple isolations caused by the dualistic structure system of urban and rural areas. Such isolations have both objective and unavoidable factors as well as the resultant subjective psychological factors in urban and rural residents. The triple isolation experienced by new migrant workers is described in the following sections.

1.1 Isolation by Urban Residents: Neglected and Excluded Migrant Population

The differences between migrant workers and urban residents can most clearly be described from the perspective of the dualistic structure system of urban and rural areas. This difference is reflected in all aspects of social life such as career opportunities, living space, and consumption space; the social living space of migrant workers is isolated from that of the city's residents in a multidimensional and comprehensive manner, which strongly hinders their process of urban adaptation and social inclusion. In the process of interviewing migrant workers in the Yangtze River Delta, apparent differences caused by such social factors were constantly observed, the most prominent of which was the difference in job opportunities. The dual segregation of China's urban and rural labour markets has resulted in new-generation migrant workers seeking employment opportunities in the secondary labour market and having to engage in dirty and arduous work that urban residents are unwilling to do. These jobs offer low wages and are not protected by social security. The human capital of this new generation of migrant workers remains limited despite being higher than that of the older generation, and this renders the new generation of migrant workers helpless.

Xiaoyu, born in 1990, in Xuzhou, has been working in Nanjing for seven years. He used to work at a restaurant next to the Hongshan Forest Zoo. Subsequently, he worked at several small restaurants before his current job at another Chinese restaurant. He works in the kitchen and has pleasant interactions with his colleagues. He goes out to sing karaoke and eat together with his colleagues on weekends, and he occasionally gathers with those who have the same hometown as him. When expressing his feelings about first coming to Nanjing, he highlighted that it was extremely lonely and difficult. Although nonlocals and locals work together in an enterprise, jobs that the locals are engaged in are obviously not available to nonlocals like him.

> An older male friend brought me over to Nanjing. At that time, I was working as an assistant (processing fish and preparing side dishes) at a restaurant

next to the Hongshan Forest Zoo; life back then was tough. Many of my colleagues were from Nanjing. The place where I worked was greasy and dirty, and the local people refused to do such [dirty] work. The locals do management and administration jobs, and they return to their own homes after work. The locals would laugh at my accent. When I felt sad, I would go for a walk. However, work still had to be done. After all, this is not home.

(Xiaoyu, male, from Xuzhou, Jiangsu)

New-generation migrant workers not only experience isolation in their workplaces but also residential segregation in their personal lives. Residential segregation is the most noticeable form of social exclusion in terms of space. Because of their limited financial resources, most new migrant workers live in urban villages. As a result of the clustering effect and word-of-mouth of relatives, those who share the same hometown, colleagues, and other migrants over the years, urban villages have become a spatial symbol for migrant workers. Urban residents are rarely seen in this space except for those involved in certain industries (e.g., manufacturing) that set up factories in the suburbs. To facilitate centralized management, accommodation is provided to the factory workers. These dormitories are also isolated to some extent.

I lived in Shilitin when I first came and started working in Wenzhou. The area was large, and all houses were low, single-story houses. Because of its cheap rent, people who lived there were migrant workers who came from various places for work. Urban residents would not be willing to live here, and we even seldom saw the landlords.

(Xiaoluo, male, from Huanggang, Hubei)

Dormitories are provided in the factory that I work for, so I do not need to rent a room outside. This area is the principal shoe production area in Wenzhou, where large and small factories are located, and dormitories are built for workers. We only have two days off a month, and it takes more than an hour to reach the city without accounting for traffic congestion. Although we work in the city, the place is actually quite some distance from the city.

(Xiaowen, female, from Huanggang, Hubei)

Another apparent social isolation is observed in the consumption space. Although new-generation migrant workers have learned something about urban lifestyles, such as being able to use iPhones just as urban residents would, they are restricted in some consumption areas because of their financial limitations. Although consumption provides an illusion of democratization that seems to reduce the gap between migrant workers and urban residents, migrant workers still suffer from silent isolation in the consumption space.

I seldom go out for entertainment; at most I go grocery shopping at the supermarket. Whenever I have additional time, I go back to my dorm to rest.

Although I live in a major city, I do not have much interest in it. Those grand shopping malls are boring to go to because I can only window shop and cannot afford anything. My clothes are all bought on Taobao; they look pretty and are easy to purchase.

(Xiaoyang, female, from Jiangxi)

In summary, the new generation of migrant workers only manages to break geographical barriers through their work in the cities. They are still isolated from urban residents in terms of employment, residence, and consumption because they form part of the neglected and excluded migrant population. This is the first isolation that they encounter in the city: being isolated by others, that is, urban residents.

1.2 Media Isolation: Marginal Audiences That Are Obscured and Exploited

The so-called media isolation refers to the incomplete media representation of migrant workers. Although they live in cities, they are obscured in the media coverage, as if they do not exist in the city, and are isolated from public view. Even if they receive media coverage, the manner in which they are depicted differs from that of urban residents. They are generally labelled as poor, uncivilized, pitiful, and vulnerable because of the media's entrenched stereotypes of this group. As a marginal audience of the media, migrant workers appear to be unwelcome intruders. This type of media representation indicates a state of isolation between the mainstream urban population and the marginalized migrant workers. Media isolation, a type of isolation encountered by migrant workers in cities, was specifically noted in this study because the media plays a key role in representing and constructing the images of migrant workers.

Xiaojin, a 25-year-old man from Huanggang City, Hubei, has been working in Wenzhou for ten years. He has worked as an apprentice in a barber shop, an assembly line worker in a clothing factory, a waiter in a restaurant, a pedicab driver, and a real estate agent. He is currently working as a catering manager of a canteen in Wenzhou. He reported that he often browses diverse information on the Internet. When he was asked whether he had seen news reports on migrant workers similar to himself, he required a considerable time to recall, but he responded that he had hardly seen any such coverage. This study does not rule out that the media literacy of the new generation of migrant workers results in them having less interest in news reading, leading to their selective neglect of news reports. Nonetheless, media organizations clearly do not pay much attention to this group of people.

I seldom read the news. Every time I use my mobile phone, I only click on [articles with] attractive titles. I have almost no recollection of reading news about migrant workers. I mostly watch television shows and movies, particularly Hollywood blockbusters. Although there are many characters in the movies, I can only remember the protagonists because they are usually handsome and beautiful. These movies and shows do not portray anything regarding migrant workers.

(Xiaojin, male, from Hubei)

Undeniably, apart from the obscuring aspect, the media also plays a role in the representation of migrant workers. Although media representation has increased the social visibility of migrant workers, such coverage is often used for dramatic and sensational effects. The media has continually promoted the differentiated and marginalized treatment of migrant workers in the name of humanistic care by emphasizing their identities and titles, describing their inferiority and humility, and bestowing the kindness of urban residents on migrant workers, which has negatively affected the image of migrant workers. This phenomenon highlights that the media bears some responsibility in the process of stigmatization of migrant workers. Sensational and stereotypical news reports indirectly reflect the vulnerability of migrant workers in the media.

I generally don't read newspapers. National events have nothing to do with civilians like us. I am also not interested in anything related to migrant workers because those stories are all fabricated. The government always claims that it cares about migrant workers, but it has done nothing helpful. The government should allocate houses to us to show that they really care about us; otherwise, why would I want to read those newspapers?

(Liuzi, male, from Jiangxi)

The media report that migrant workers are uncivilized. Indeed, some migrant workers always talk nonsense and behave poorly. We should ignore them, and just take care of ourselves.

(Xiaoli, male, from Sichuan)

Larry Gross proposed that media representation endows various groups with distinct visibility and power. In other words, media representation is a type of power. Urban residents are the primary audience of various media organizations. Under market economic conditions, migrant workers become marginal audiences of the media because of the limitations in their own literacy level and financial strength. If migrant workers are institutionally regarded as second-class nationals and are isolated by urban residents, then they are also classified as second-class audiences at the level of media representation and suffer from media isolation. They are either obscured or exploited, and they may not be aware of this situation.

1.3 Self-isolation: Migrant Workers Who Concede to and Escape From the System

After new-generation migrant workers perceive, absorb, and internalize the isolation by urban residents and media, they developed a self-awareness centred on being migrant workers. Migrant workers are often associated with informal employment, highlighting their characteristic of frequent mobility. Faced with the rigid institutional arrangements and influential urban mainstream culture, new-generation migrant workers feel compelled to or decide to voluntarily limit their interactions to a closed environment. As a result of conceding to and escaping from the system, their leisure life demonstrates monotonous, closed, concessive, and evasive characteristics that constitute self-isolation.

Contacts during work are mostly formal interactions between people in different roles. In an urban society where the labour division is increasingly rigid, new-generation migrant workers do not have much freedom in selecting their field of work, and they must interact with all types of people. As soon as they retreat from the world of work to the world of leisure, they can actively choose their own lifestyle. Many participants responded that they typically remain at home during their leisure time. To avoid conflicts, they opt to marginalize themselves and thus prevent contact with urban residents. Such isolation is mainly reflected in their focus on work, not frequenting the entertainment venues that urban residents favour, and living in groups with other migrant workers.

> I enjoy shopping, but I only shop nearby this area. All the things needed are available here. I am familiar with the people around here, and I sometimes chat with them. Everyone is friendly. However, not all of them are from Hangzhou; many of them are migrant workers. Migrant workers have more common topics to talk about. Hangzhou locals do not like to interact with people like us, but it does not matter.
>
> (Xiaozhang, male, from Anhui)

> When I am not working, I am looking for a job. Apart from smoking and drinking, I have no other hobbies. In terms of entertainment, I occasionally watch television, read newspapers, sing karaoke, and watch movies. It is better to save money than spend it. I want to open a Sichuan restaurant in the future.
>
> (Xiaoli, male, from Sichuan)

The interviews revealed that many migrant workers have a small and limited living area in the city. They prefer to move around in areas they are familiar with, rather than visit crowded places for entertainment. In addition, because of various types of isolation and restrictions in cities, the life of some migrant workers in the city is not substantially different from that in the countryside. By living in an area where migrant workers gather, they feel closer to their hometowns and they are in contact with other migrant workers who also moved from the countryside. They can live comfortably in these areas because they avoid city rules. Moreover, many migrant workers are required to travel to other cities according to the needs of their work, which prevents them from developing a sense of belonging in the city. Therefore, adopting a lifestyle that resembles the conventional rural lifestyle becomes desirable.

I have been staying in Hangzhou for quite some time, but I have not made many Hangzhou friends. The main reason is that I have no chance to make new friends. Except for the boss who hires people to work, no other urban residents would come to work in this area. Even if we get a job, the only person we interact with is the boss. But our lives are extremely different from theirs. Therefore, I prefer to have a casual chat with those who come from my hometown.

(Xiaosun, male, from Xuancheng, Anhui)

The interviews revealed that in addition to the isolation by urban residents and media, new-generation migrant workers in cities also actively self-isolate. Their self-isolation may be a product of the influence of external isolation. After all, pursuing a higher quality of life is the dream of most people. The "urban dream" and moving to urban areas are also the ultimate ambition of migrant workers, but the process of realizing this dream is difficult and long-lasting for various reasons. In this process, the self-isolation of the new generation of migrant workers reveals their helplessness, even though they struggle to overcome the powerful force of self-isolation. The combined effect of isolation by residents, the media, and migrant workers themselves has resulted in a new generation of migrant workers being excluded in the cities.

2. Helplessness in Communication: Interpersonal Communication With "Islanders" and "Non-islanders"

As social creatures, it's impossible for humans to leave society and live alone. Interpersonal communication is an essential means of satisfying one's material, emotional, and self-actualization needs. Because of the isolation by urban residents and the media as well as self-isolation, the living conditions of the new generation of migrant workers can be portrayed as "islands in the city". However, they still inevitably communicate with "islanders" and "non-islanders" in urban life. Because the contacts with the urban residents are one-sided and superficial, and limited to business contacts and interest exchanges, they can only communicate with relatives, those who come from the same hometown, colleagues, and other migrant workers. Although they can rely on each other, this isolation is not conducive to them moving towards an open structure of communication. The emotional support provided by physically separated family members is insufficient for new-generation migrant workers who live in cities for extended periods. These factors reflect a state of communication helplessness.

2.1 Gaining a Foothold: Migrant Workers Whose Destiny Is Mutually Dependent

Migrant workers most frequently and most willingly communicate with other migrant workers in the same city. Moreover, having the same hometown is more conducive to intimate communication. Making friends with a migrant worker who is experienced and willing to help in the city is the beginning of numerous migrant workers' urban lives. Many migrant workers obtain the opportunity to work in the city through the help of others from their hometown who have experience working in the city. Chinese society values *renqing* (moral commitment to norms of reciprocity), and Chinese people have a strong hometown complex; the notion of valuing *renqing* is typically more ingrained in the countryside than in cities. Therefore, for migrant workers who wish to work in cities, seeking a like-minded and more experienced person from their town is the first step to working in cities, because having such support in the city is equivalent to having networks in the city. These allies can use their own experience to guide new migrant workers regarding employment opportunities, living locations, and urban public resources, enabling them to begin their urban lives safely.

> My friends all come from the same hometown as mine. I have no chance to meet new friends in the city. The person I have most contact with is the boss, who would not want to make friends with us [migrant workers]. Most of the time, I am surrounded by migrant workers, and we are not close to each other.
> (Xiaoqian, female, from Wuhan, Hubei)

In the city, migrant workers who come from the same hometown or from the countryside tend to form a homogeneous group wherein most interpersonal communication occurs. Homogeneous groups are composed of individuals with similar characteristics. Homogeneity refers to the commonness of people's internal cultural structure, life style, and ideology. Individuals in a homogeneous group identify with each other because they have similar living backgrounds, occupations, financial status, education levels, personalities and hobbies, social status, values, levels of culture, ethnicity and tradition, and behaviours and habits. These aspects through which people identify with or are attracted to each other become the basis for them to form a community. Therefore, interpersonal communication within homogeneous groups has become the main communication behaviour of migrant workers in the city.

> My friends are my colleagues. We have no chance to meet locals, and locals would not want to make friends with us. It is not their fault; what can we do if we are poor? At least we still have common topics among colleagues. When I have free time, I go to a nearby restaurant to have a good meal and drink with a few colleagues. They are all friends who came from several cities to work here. We have a deeper understanding of each other, which has helped us to form a stronger friendship. We even discussed opening a shop together and being the bosses. However, that was a joke because we are now poor, and we do not know what lies ahead of us.
>
> (Qiang, male, from Xuzhou, Jiangsu)

Because they have similar living environments, cultural backgrounds, and interests, migrant workers in the city tend to focus their interpersonal communication on homogeneous groups comprised of other migrant workers. Such communication is harmonious, but short-lived, and is easily hampered by the barriers of time and space. Moreover, establishing intimate relationships on the basis of such communication has invisible risks because of the high information repetition rate and the limited flow of resources in the group. Although these relationships help migrant workers establish a foothold in the city, such relationships do not assist these workers to move towards an open pattern of communication.

2.2 Hometown Bonding: Mutual Emotional Needs Between Migrant Workers and Their Families

Although the feelings of new-generation migrant workers toward their hometowns have changed, and they no longer have an excessive attachment to the places they come from, they still maintain a psychological attachment to their homes. Experiencing the hardships of working in unfamiliar places helps new-generation migrant workers become aware of a sense of wandering caused by an unstable life. The isolation by urban residents limits them to homogeneous social network communication with those who come from the same hometown and colleagues. Nevertheless, this type of communication is insufficient to address all the difficulties they face in the cities. Therefore, they also seek emotional support from their families. Because of their physical separation from family members, migrant workers often use new media to maintain their emotional connection with their family. As a primary social group in the socialization process, family members have a strong emotional relationship with the migrant workers. Contact with family members can provide a solid motivation for their urban life and help them build the confidence to live in a foreign place. This process also provides the family with a sense of relief.

Nannan, a 22-year-old woman from Lianyungang, Jiangsu, is short in stature, has long hair worn in a ponytail, and has been working far away from her hometown. She first worked in Inner Mongolia because her father was working there. She moved to Nanjing to join her friends after a year. She and her friends have been working at a cosmetics store in Xueze Road (in Nanjing) for more than a year. That is, the interviewee has been working in the city for more than two years, but has been separated from her family for more than a year in order to work in the city. Currently, she receives one day off after two working days. In the interview, she revealed that her job is relatively hectic and that she does not have a standardized contract that offers protection. She has no clear life plan.

> I prefer to chat face-to-face with friends. After all, things on the Internet cannot appropriately and fully show what people are thinking. Typically, I use my mobile phone to make calls or use QQ [an instant messaging software service] to talk with my family members. I prefer calling because I can do other stuff and talk to them simultaneously. For now, I call them every other day. When I first came, I called my father every day, and the phone call ended in four or five minutes. In fact, four or five minutes is quite long. I often tell

him to eat more, drink plenty of water, take care of his body when the weather changes.

(Nannan, female, from Lianyungang, Jiangsu)

Nannan's behaviour of conversing with her family for four or five minutes every other day can be regarded as an emotional ritual. Rituals are repeated behaviours, a transitional phase from the known to the unknown, that people use to manage their emotions and guide their position and direction (Singerhoff, 2009). New-generation migrant workers face an unfamiliar living area after moving from the countryside, and they have to face various challenges alone. During this period, they develop some rituals that help them alleviate various psychological discomforts. These rituals must be feasible. In a new environment, overly cumbersome rituals are unpractical. Therefore, new media are generally favoured for its portable and mobile characteristics. With the aid of new media as a ritual tool, new-generation migrant workers affirm their own existence in the city, maintain their emotional connection with their families, and expel the sense of rootless wandering. Most of them did not live in the era when letters or travel where necessary to keep in touch with families. Instead, they have directly entered the era of communication with new media such as mobile phones and the Internet; communication with their families has thus become more convenient and frequent. For migrant workers who work alone in the city, this hometown bonding provides the impetus for maintaining their urban life.

2.3 *Exploring the City: Interest Exchange Between Migrant Workers and Urban Residents*

To survive in the city, interpersonal communication with urban residents is inevitable. However, the current survey revealed that only a few migrant workers have had a pleasant communication experience with urban residents. Although new-generation migrant workers have a stronger identification with the city, this does not mean that they necessarily have smoother communication with urban residents. A barrier exists between most of the new generation of migrant workers and urban residents. From a cross-cultural communication perspective, migrant workers and urban residents belong to distinct cultures. The migrant workers symbolize tradition and backwardness, whereas urban residents symbolize modernity and civilization. When the two groups interact, the social comparison mechanism is activated. The conscious or unconscious contempt exhibited by the urban residents with superior status exasperates the migrant workers, causing them to generally have a poor or lack of impression of urban residents.

Migrant workers tend to interact with urban residents mostly in formal contexts, where interactions tend to be more stilted. Such interactions may appear to be too impersonal and lacking the human touch. The mobility of migrant workers means their interpersonal communication with many people is short-lived, and they often take large risks when establishing deep interpersonal communications with each other. Because of the lack of private communication, migrant workers and urban residents generally have only one-dimensional communication; the participants in such communication can only grasp minor aspects of their counterparts. Such one-sided and superficial communication is not conducive to the development of deep and fixed interpersonal relationships between migrant workers and urban residents.

> Major cities have excessive rules, which make these cities less free and comfortable than my hometown. I will definitely go back to my hometown in the future. Once I was waiting at the train station early in the morning to return to my hometown. I wanted to take a nap on a bench, but someone came to stop me as soon as I lied down. Those people are too rigid. Why am I not allowed to sleep on a bench when no one is using it? Such incidents always happen. Shanghainese people are indifferent, unlike the hospitable people in my hometown. In addition, you must wait in line when you shop [in major cities], and when you accidentally cut in line, someone will immediately drive you away with an unfriendly attitude. This will not happen in my hometown. We do not need to queue to buy something, and we always let people with an urgent need buy [something] first. Everyone in my hometown gives way to those in need, unlike Shanghainese people.
>
> (Xiaosun, male, from Yancheng, Jiangsu)

Undeniably, interpersonal communication between migrant workers and urban residents is not all utilitarian and accompanied by conflict. The interviews also revealed a few examples of pleasant communication between migrant workers and urban residents. Xiaojiang, a migrant worker from Gansu, shared about the benefactor he met after coming to work in Hangzhou – a local *shifu* (a skilled person, a mentor or teacher) in Hangzhou. He is 23 years old and has been living in Hangzhou for three years. A friend helped him find work in Hangzhou. He also previously worked in Yunnan as a construction worker. Working on construction sites is dangerous, with long working hours, mediocre wages, and little protection. Moreover, wages are only paid after a project is completed. Some unfortunate workers may encounter bosses that do not pay them after they complete a project. His life was completely changed after arriving in Hangzhou. Knowing this particular *shifu* was a crucial turning point in his life. With the support and encouragement of his *shifu*, he gained the determination and confidence to live in the city.

> I made some local friends in Hangzhou, such as my *shifu*. My *shifu* is a nice person. There are very few other Hangzhou colleagues in the workshop, and we do not share common interests. My best friends are those who come from the same hometown as me. I think making friends depends on appropriate opportunities and timing. For now, I just want to work in the factory steadily, and my *shifu* said that he will recommend me for a promotion if he has the opportunity. I think meeting someone like my *shifu* in Hangzhou is my biggest luck.
>
> (Xiaojiang, male, from Gansu)

Overall, negative experiences accounted for the majority of the interpersonal communications between migrant workers and urban residents. Affected by communication channels, communication purposes, and status differences, the communication between migrant workers and urban residents has always been unequal; thus, establishing long-term and stable relationships between these two groups is challenging. Nonetheless, once migrant workers establish a positive and stable close relationship (e.g., marriage and career) with urban residents, the changes resulting from their urban adaptation can be dramatic. Typical communication between migrants and urban residents focuses on mutual benefit exchange, which is simply practical and therefore not long-lasting and in-depth. Urban residents have not had a considerable effect on the lives of the new generation of migrant workers.

3. Escaping the Isolated Islands: Virtual Communication Led by New Media

As long as the dualistic structure between urban and rural areas is not broken, migrant workers have to wear their identity as a cangue. With the channels of equal communication between migrant workers and urban residents blocked and mutual assumptions and misunderstandings strengthened, migrant workers are isolated on their individual islands of self-consolation without progress. As time passes, new-generation migrant workers continue to comprehend and learn the laws of urban survival, their modernity continues to grow, and they begin to attempt an escape from their island. Different from the older generation, the new generation of migrant workers has grown up under the influence of the Internet. New media channels such as mobile phones and computers are ubiquitous, and virtual communication space enables people of different identities and statuses to hide or selectively present their own roles; such platforms provide more possibilities for people in their interpersonal relationship in terms of communication scope, content, and effect. The virtual communication facilitated by new media assists the new generation of migrant workers to escape from the predicament of isolated islands.

3.1 Duplication and Expansion: A Mixed Interpersonal Communication Network

As mentioned previously, the difference between the new and older generations of migrant workers is that new migrant workers have more experience with new media, and they are considerably more proficient in using new media than are older generations; thus, they are more likely to maintain and expand their social circles by using new media. Xiaowang comes from a small village in Yunnan. He has been working in Nanjing for three or four years, and now works in a snack bar on Xueze Road. This snack bar is relatively small, measuring only 50 or 60 square metres. The snack bar has three other waiters, and Xiaowang noted that he has pleasant interactions with them. Judging from his explanation, he seems to be satisfied with his current life.

> I still remember that I received my first mobile phone after completing my National College Entrance Examination. I was so happy, and I exchanged mobile phone numbers with my classmates so as to keep in touch with them. However, everyone went [their] separate ways not long after [that], and many classmates changed their numbers and could no longer be reached. At that time, most [of my] classmates did not have computers at home. Moreover, not everyone was familiar with the Internet, so we had no other contact information. I have not seen several classmates for a long time, and [with] some [I] have lost contact. Now I am often online and keep in touch with numerous friends; our relationships are well maintained. It would have been good if we had Internet back then.
>
> (Xiaowang, male, from Yunnan)

Xiaolin, who has been working in Nanjing for eight years, is a 26-year-old single man. Having been working in the hairdressing industry for years, Xiaolin is now a senior hairdresser. Although his hometown is in Anhui, he can only go home once a year. "I must succeed" was the goal he pursued when he first found work in the city, and now he is working towards the goal of "settling down in Nanjing". He said, "Work is communication, and we must learn new information online to do so". The importance of communicating with customers is one of the major lessons he has learned in his work in the hairdressing industry. Therefore, he pays attention to crucial local news in his spare time, reads news on online forums, learns about the latest trends on Sina Weibo, and watches television, including popular shows. At work, he exchanges contact information with customers and becomes friends with them on platforms such as WeChat and Sina Weibo to establish long-term working relationships.

> I have been working in this barber shop for several years. Because I have to talk to customers when I work, I improve my communication ability by reading student forums as well as watching dramas and shows such as *If You Are the One* and *Sing! China*. I also watch a lot of news-related videos on the Internet, otherwise I would have no common topics to discuss with the customers. Basically, every customer is my WeChat friend, and some are my friends on Sina Weibo. My customers select me as their hairdresser every time they come for a haircut.
>
> (Xiaolin, male, from Huangshan, Anhui)

By the use of new media, migrant workers not only duplicate their primary relationship network but also develop some secondary relationship networks. The Internet makes people who cannot be reached in real life become accessible in a different space. Xiaoqiu, who was born in Anhui in 1993, now works as a waiter in a hotel near Xuzhuang Science and Technology Park, Xianlin Center, Qixia

District, Nanjing. His family are ordinary working-class employees. He dropped out of school in grade 8. He used to work in the kitchen of a hotel in Beijing, and later worked as service staff in the lobby of the Nanjing Premium Club. He first considered opening his own clothing store in the future. However, he later decided to set up his own hotel in the future because his family ran a restaurant. He does not blindly follow the trend of constantly upgrading electronic equipment. He has always used a Nokia mobile phone, believing that it is inexpensive, high quality, and durable. He has many online friends who are not his friends in real life, but he is glad that he can use the Internet to expand his interpersonal communication scope.

> I like to make friends online. I feel that the people I meet in real life are very similar. However, I can meet people of different types, personalities, and classes on the Internet, and I do not need to feel embarrassed about what I say. I contact customers through mobile phone because they usually leave their phone numbers as contact information. Nonetheless, phone calls are sometimes inconvenient. For example, it could be embarrassing when people are busy, miss the call, or are unable to answer the phone. Phone calls are not as convenient as text messages and WeChat, which help people avoid unnecessary problems from direct contact.
>
> (Xiaoqiu, male, from Huangshan, Anhui)

The interpersonal network established by the new generation of migrant workers through new media are not merely a duplicate of the original social network – it is an expansion of the individual's social network. Temporally putting aside their rural origins, migrant workers can build a mixed interpersonal communication network during the process of social inclusion in cities. By using new media platforms, these workers manage to overcome, to a certain extent, the limitation of the homogenous social circle that forms part of their isolated island existence.

3.2 Continuation and Expansion: Content of Interpersonal Communication Between Real and Virtual Situations

In formal face-to-face interpersonal communication, both parties must perform in accordance with their respective role specifications. In private contexts, although people are not restricted by identity, their respective postures, language, expressions, and tone still reveal a considerable amount of information. This makes it impossible for people to fully disclose themselves, and they have to communicate in accordance with a certain "script". According to the well-known sociologist, Erving Goffman, everyone wears a mask – figuratively – during social interaction. Therefore, what people present in their interpersonal communication is a mixture of the real and the false, making it challenging to determine the veracity of what is said. Nevertheless, in the virtual space constructed by new media, the user's real identity is hidden. Thus, the rural-urban divide that hinders interaction between migrant workers and urban residents is greatly reduced on new media platforms. When new-generation migrant workers use these new media platforms to interact with their offline acquaintances, they may retain their real-life interpersonal communication style and topics. In addition, in the face of unfamiliar online friends who these migrant workers have not met in real life, they may become more willing to share about themselves, thus resulting in interpersonal communication that is more authentic. On the Internet, these migrant workers may feel more freedom to express themselves on topics that they may normally avoid, which could relieve their depressed state caused by struggling to survive on their isolated islands.

Born in 1992, Lili is a woman from a rural area of Pingyin County, Jinan City, Shandong province. She has an older sister who is married, a younger brother who is still in school, and her parents work in Pingyin. After graduating from senior high school, she came to Nanjing to work. Currently, she is an employee at the Gulu Gulu bubble tea cafe in Qinhuai District, and she is mainly responsible for the preparation of bubble tea. For her current job, she saw the job posting on the street and went for the interview because she thought the job was interesting and easy to handle. The boss hired her after asking her a few questions and thought that she was a hard-working and attentive worker. She currently has a boyfriend who also came to Nanjing to work. For her, the content of interpersonal communication online is similar to that of face-to-face conversations; the only difference is the form of the interaction. The topics that girls are interested in do not differ between online and offline modes.

> Generally, I browse Sina Weibo with my phone when I have idle time at work. In addition to watching television dramas in the evening [or when I have a day off], I also surf the Internet and chat with my friends on QQ by using my mobile phone. I often chat with my friends online, and we usually talk about topics that girls are interested in. I feel quite happy. Sometimes I play mobile games by myself or with friends. Sometimes when I want to buy clothes on Taobao, I ask my friends to give me some ideas and help me make decisions.
>
> (Lili, female, from Jinan, Shandong)

Xiaoyun grew up in a single-parent family and was once left behind in rural villages while his parent worked in cities. He had many outlandish dreams during junior high school. After failing the senior high school entrance examination, he worked at a construction site during the summer vacation. He later enrolled in a cooking school. After graduating from the cooking school, he was recommended for a job as a chef in a small restaurant in Zhenjiang. The work was quite varied but arduous. Now that he has a girlfriend, he is caught in a dilemma between settling down and saving money and improving his current working conditions. He enjoys chatting on online platforms, and he feels unrestrained when doing so, which is impossible during face-to-face communication in real life.

> I can obtain more information, make friends, chat, and meet a lot of like-minded friends online. I still contact my classmates in junior high school,

mainly through QQ and Renren Network, and the conversation generally [focuses on] [discussing] the current situation and teasing each other. When working in foreign areas, meeting friends from the same hometown is heart-warming. I am close to my buddies from the same hometown. The topics of our chats range from work to sports and to various topics in our hometown. I check Sina Weibo and Renren Network every morning and between work to see if there is anything new to share and comment on. I think this is an effective approach for me to understand the world. Compared with face-to-face conversations, I prefer to chat online because I will [have more confidence to] express my thoughts and the conversation will go smoothly.

(Xiaoyun, male, from Jiangxi)

Xing is employed at a hardware store. His hometown is in Taizhou, Jiangsu. He lived in Nanjing for his elementary schooling, but then he returned to his hometown. He is currently in Nanjing with his parents to help in their store. Business is conducted on the first floor of the shop, and the family lives on the upper floor. Whenever we visited him at his hardware store, we found him attentively sitting in front of the computer. He admits that he chats online whenever he is free.

I am more active in online chat. Sometimes I am shy when talking [with people] face-to-face, but I can have a smooth conversation online. Online text chat and voice chat are different. I prefer to use voice messages when talking to acquaintances because I can talk freely, and emotions in the voice give me more understanding [of the speaker's emotional state]. Moreover, I prefer voice messages because I am [too] lazy to type. For strangers, I prefer typing. When speaking with those who I am not particularly familiar with, I will think before sending the message due to the fear of saying the wrong thing. I dislike detecting the emotions in voice messages from strangers. As for video calls, it is more open and [allows people to] directly see the face of the other person. Sometimes we talk about things that we would not discuss during face-to-face communication.

(Xing, male, from Taizhou, Jiangsu)

In the virtual space constructed by new media platforms, the identity restriction imposed on the new generation of migrant workers is loosened, and they can disclose themselves more authentically. Although the content of virtual interpersonal communication can be either fictitious or real, this communication medium still helps these workers to deviate from having to mask their true feelings in communication during their survival on their isolated islands.

3.3 Assimilation and Alienation: Indistinguishable Positive and Negative Interpersonal Communication Effects

Two critical questions to consider are as follows: (1) What can interpersonal communication through new media contribute to the real life of migrant workers from the new generation? (2) What is the effect of virtual interpersonal communication? Virtual interpersonal communication can provide informational and emotional support to the new generation of migrant workers, but instrumental support is relatively scarce. However, virtual interpersonal communication can also cause trouble in real life. Online interpersonal deception and alienation caused by addiction to online interpersonal relationships are problems these migrant workers must face. Virtual interpersonal communication provides a sense of sameness and assimilation to migrant workers through social support; however, it also has a negative effect on real-life interpersonal communication because such online communication is a solitary activity, which may in turn result in alienation. The positive and negative effects of virtual interpersonal communication are difficult to distinguish because of problems related to assimilation and alienation.

Tingting was born in 1986 in Jiangning, Nanjing. She has worked in Jurong, Zhenjiang; Dongshan, Suzhou; and Jiangning, Nanjing for a total of 12 years. The attitude of her family is one that strongly favours sons. Tingting has an obedient and tolerant personality, and she looked for a job through introductions by relatives and friends or in-person visits. She has been involved in the clothing industry, with roles ranging from basic assembly line work to clothing pattern making, which is her current job. She is an introvert, and when encountering difficulties and problems, she solves them on her own. Furthermore, she has gradually become accustomed to her loneliness without asking for help. Only the use of a QQ group provides her with some emotional comfort.

> Because of boredom, I set up a QQ group for migrant workers with a few friends of mine. Later, many netizens joined in and now there are more than 80 people in the group. There is less pressure when migrant workers chat together, and I feel close to this group. My QQ is online 24 hours a day, but I rarely chat. I do not want to know too many people, nor do I want to know too much. Feeling mentally worn out, I choose to avoid anything I dislike.
>
> (Tingting, female, from Jiangning, Nanjing)

Dawei, born in 1984, is from Huanggang, Hubei, and only has a specialized secondary school degree. He is currently looking for a job. He dropped out of school for work in 2006 and has been to Beijing, Nanjing, and Huizhou in Guangdong, where he worked as a network administrator, salesperson, security guard, and a factory worker. His social circle is small, and he rarely interacts with those who have the same hometown as him and colleagues around him. He feels that they are on the same level as he is and thus do not help in his self-improvement. Most of them focus on family life, and because he is single, he does not have much in common with them. He enjoys watching online news, familiarizing himself with national affairs, and chatting on QQ. Although new media platforms have entertainment and recreational functions, they can also provide some professional information. In particular, through the virtual social network in QQ, he has accumulated a certain amount of online social capital through the expansion of virtual interpersonal relationships; however, transforming that online social capital into offline social capital has been unsuccessful. This suggests that virtual interpersonal communication has some efficacy in providing information and emotional comfort, but its role in substantive instrumental support is yet to be improved.

> I frequently chat on QQ, and I have met various friends who opened online stores and many of them made money. I have learned a lot from them, such as where to purchase stocks. Nonetheless, they will not disclose everything, so I still have to explore on my own. I have also worked for a boss and helped him to pack cosmetics, and then consigned the cosmetics to courier companies for delivery. In the process of observing him establish an online store, I also learned a little bit and wanted to open my own online store; however, I have no money.
>
> (Dawei, male, from Huanggang, Hubei)

Interpersonal relationships that develop on new media platforms can only exist in virtual spaces. Transforming online interpersonal relationships into offline interpersonal relationships may be challenging. As mentioned previously, in the conventional real-life interpersonal communication environment, the interaction between migrant workers and urban residents proceeds according to the premise of mutual understanding of their real information. Virtual space essentially circumvents the exchange of real information. Both migrant workers and urban residents engage in role-plays with their favourite images and identities in the virtual network space. Interpersonal communication on the Internet is essentially risky and fragile communication between two or more parties using virtual images in a virtual space. When a well-established harmonious relationship in the virtual world moves towards reality, the rural-urban dualistic identity differences that migrant workers carefully ignored and avoided online become apparent between the two parties. Moreover, the contrast between the real and virtual context is likely to transform the communication from positive in the virtual space to negative in the real world. Because of deception, the relationship between the two parties is likely to be broken, and the migrant workers who managed to leave their islands behind may face a second isolation.

Xiaoli, who works as a cashier in a concession stand of a college in Nanjing, is only 19 years old, but her QQ has already achieved high popularity with over 100 followers. She participates in various online groups. She said that she was unfamiliar with many things when she was a student, but now she can find all the answers online. She has bought clothes in a Taobao store run by a member of the group. Although the quality was poor, she did not provide a negative review because she felt embarrassed to do so, as she is an acquaintance of the member and they chat online every day. Because she spends much time online, the difference between reality and the virtual world is blurred. She feels that online interpersonal relationships are prone to deceptions and falsehoods.

> I typically use my mobile phone to chat online. I feel that the Internet is different from reality because there is a lot of deceit. I used to know an older

online friend. She opened a Taobao store and asked me to buy something from her. I was embarrassed to reject her, so I bought a piece of clothing for tens of yuan. I was still new to Nanjing at that time and I did not have much money. The clothes I bought from her were of poor quality, transparent, and could not be worn. However, I felt embarrassed to return it and I also gave the clothes good reviews. The clothes looked nice in [the online] pictures, but the actual quality was poor. After that, I stopped buying from her. In addition, I also used to hang out with an online friend. I felt that the way he really was differed from his Internet persona. The things online are unrealistic. These days, I keep an "online" status for a whole day but I seldom initiate a conversation. I just talk when someone starts chatting with me first. I now have real friends here, and it is nice to chat with them after [we finish] work. I used to be on the Internet because I had no friends when I first came here.

(Xiaoli, female, from Sichuan)

Some new-generation migrant workers, however, fail to consciously distinguish between online and offline interpersonal relationships. Because of their lack of interpersonal communication experience, they may struggle to filter true and valid information from the complex network information, thus running the risk of being deceived. Xiaocai from Yingkou, Liaoning, shared an example of his friend.

I like to watch *If You Are the One*,[1] but I will definitely not join the Baihe matchmaking website because the site is full of scammers who cheat [people out of] money. You have to pay if you want to register as a member of that website. I do not mind paying to participate on a show like *If You Are the One*, but I will not pay for Baihe because it is just a website. I had a friend who looked for a girlfriend on Baihe, but he later learned that the woman was a scammer. My friend took her out for a few meals and bought a considerable amount of wine from her. He was embarrassed to reject her, which is the vulnerability that those scammers exploit. Anyway, I have not heard of anyone who actually found a girlfriend on Baihe.

(Xiaocai, male, from Yingkou, Liaoning)

In addition to causing interpersonal deception, virtual interpersonal communication can also lead to alienation in human communication. Xiaobao, from Zibo City, Shandong province, works as a teaching assistant in Jiangsu Education Center. He arrives at his workplace at approximately 7 o'clock in the morning every day for cleaning duties. The teachers arrive in the classroom at 8 o'clock to check student attendance. He is generally busy both before and after school because he must ensure the students' safety, but he has some idle time in between. He has a clear view of the alienation that can result from virtual interpersonal communication, and expressed that he prefers face-to-face offline communication to online communication.

Although mobile phones are said to bring people closer, there will be misunderstandings in reality. In addition, people do not even bother to shorten the geographical distance after getting a mobile phone. Mobile phones can also be responsible for creating distance between people. People express themselves through body language, spoken language, expressions, and tone, but the existence of the phone leaves only language and tone. These two items expand the distance between people. To be exact, technological advancement has only increased the means of communication, but what is really meaningful is face-to-face communication, which is more sincere and more in line with human feelings.

(Xiaobao, male, from Zibo, Shandong)

In summary, virtual interpersonal communication led by new media on the one hand helps new-generation migrant workers assimilate with urban residents and frees them from their isolation; on the other hand, media also results in alienation between new-generation migrant workers and urban residents, which pushes these individuals back to the individual islands they are trying to escape from. The positive and negative effects of isolated island living are closely linked and challenging to untangle.

4. External Expansion and Involution: The Semi-Modernity of Interpersonal Communication

The interpersonal communication of the new generation of migrant workers has also undergone a major transformation. In the countryside, those workers are surrounded by people who are dear to them, and their interpersonal relationships are marked by strong bonding of family ties, emphasizing the emotional nature of these relationships. However, after coming to the city, facing the business relations formed by the division of labour in the society, they must communicate with urban residents in a formal manner. During this process, they gradually learn the rules of communication in the city, and their interpersonal communication begins to become instrumental, rational, and secular. In this sense, their interpersonal communication gradually modernizes. Nevertheless, because of the restriction of their status by institutional arrangements, they are forced to or voluntarily rely on their existing primary social network. Subsequently, their interpersonal communication grows in the opposite direction (i.e., involution), becoming confined to a homogeneous social circle and lacking organic connections with the outside world. However, they also use new media to break the vicious circle of involution, thereby opening up a new network of interpersonal communication. At this time, their interpersonal communication tendency changes from involution to extroversion. In short, on the road to the modernization of their interpersonal communication, new-generation migrant workers have been moving forward and backward, and they have not yet developed a complete urban interpersonal relationship network. In addition, their interpersonal relationships are also markedly different from the conventional interpersonal relationship in their hometowns. Therefore, the status quo of the new generation of migrant workers living in isolated islands reflects the semi-modern characteristics of their interpersonal communication.

4.1 Towards Instrumental Interaction: The Desire for Heterogeneous Social Capital

The popularization of new media has greatly broadened the living space and communication channels of migrant workers in cities, facilitating the expansion of their social capital. Because of their long-term experience with the "mediated society", migrant workers in cities have become increasingly aware of the importance of new media in urban life, and they have begun to clearly recognize that the instrumental characteristics of media can guide their interpersonal communication in cities towards instrumentality.

Heterogeneous capital is the pursuit of urban social capital by migrant workers, including their connections, social resources, urban identity, status, and identification in the city. The popularization of new media has helped migrant workers realize that various social capitals that they might have never considered are actually easy to obtain. From the moment they arrive in the city, diverse types of social capital are at their disposal. The older generation of migrant workers were not aware of and had no opportunity to obtain these capitals. However, under the catalysis of new media, the gap between the new generation of migrant workers and urban residents has narrowed. What the new generation of migrant workers has seen, heard, experienced, and felt in contemporary society differs from the societal experience of the previous generation of migrant workers. Conventional interpersonal relationships and social capital have been unable to meet the growing urban life needs of migrant workers. Their desire for higher levels of social capital is also increasing with the development of media technologies.

The desire for the expansion of social capital is an external feature of migrant workers' interpersonal communication, and their intrinsic motivation and desire have also undergone subtle changes. Among them, changes in the degree of dependence on the strength of social relations have also quietly emerged. In the conventional social relationships of migrant workers, blood relation is the strongest relationship, followed by relationships with those who come from the same hometown; the weakest relationship is with urban residents. On the surface, the social relationship with urban residents is the most dispensable social relationship for migrant workers in the city. However, the opposite is also true: having social relationships with urban residents is a crucial indicator of the degree of urbanization of migrant workers. These relationship dynamics have been changing gradually in contemporary society. Blood relatives are still the strongest moral support for migrant workers, but the homogeneous groups that these workers used to rely on for interpersonal communication are no longer that essential. The popularization of media use has greatly reduced the difficulty of obtaining social capital. Even migrant workers who have recently arrived in the city can easily and rapidly obtain information on all aspects of urban life such as work and housing. The approach of the older generation of migrant workers in similar circumstances would no longer be effective or efficient. Heterogeneous social capital obtained in the city can prompt a qualitative change to the urban adaptation and social inclusion of migrant workers. Urban residents can provide them with far more social resources and beneficial information than can homogeneous groups. Therefore, establishing strong intimate relationships with urban residents can assist in the urbanization transformation of migrant workers.

In a nutshell, in the context of new media empowerment, the demands for social capital by certain migrant workers have begun to display more instrumental characteristics. The ultimate goal they pursue is to safeguard their own interests, rather than emotional dependence. This highlights the importance of heterogeneous social capital.

4.2 Towards Extroverted Communication: The Pursuit of Incremental Social Capital

For new-generation migrant workers who undergo a transformation in their urban lives and enter a highly mobile society of strangers, their interpersonal communication model presents a weak instrumental tendency, and the cost of interpersonal investment in secondary business relationship groups is higher. Nonetheless, the trust of Chinese people is basically limited to their circle of acquaintances. To maintain a sense of psychological stability and order, Chinese people seek social resources from their primary relationship network. The primary relationship network is formed through interpersonal communication in the basic socialization process, and this network is frequently regarded as an emotional community. In the emotional maintenance of this strong relationship, their social capital stock is activated to alleviate their sense of wanderings in real life.

To achieve a better state of urban adaptation and social inclusion, migrant workers must have a certain amount of social capital. The actual stock of social capital often differs from ideal social capital; thus, the new generation of migrant workers must develop incremental social capital to address the ubiquitous demands of urban life on individuals. With the expansion of communication, the new generation of migrant workers is also developing various types of incremental social capital, and the social resources available to them are gradually increasing. They actively maintain their existing weak relationship network (e.g., colleagues at work) through new media, but they also develop social relationship networks through social media to meet strangers with whom they do not have any interaction in real life. They engage in emotional self-presentation and disclosure in the virtual space to obtain emotional and information support from the online society and accumulate social capital. Moreover, when people interact with media, they are interpreting media content and satisfying some of their own needs. Media content is constructed by media outlets, so it is essentially a dialogue with powerful players in the media or the people embodied and shaped by the media (Fang, 2012). In this sense, the contact and use of new media can be regarded as a process of para-social interaction. As a tangible fixed capital, new media's value in use will be depleted over time from the user's perspective. However, the message, information, and entertainment provided on new media are productive and can provide resources to the new generation of migrant workers, enabling them to also accumulate social capital.

The pursuit of incremental social capital generates an extroverted communication trend. As mentioned previously, the cutting-edge social network technology of new media has made the interpersonal communication of migrant workers in the city more active and spontaneous. The successful inclusion of interpersonal relationships with urban residents has further promoted the formation and growth of urban social networks for migrant workers. Migrant workers who successfully enter the urban social circle through new media begin to gradually experience the charms of urban life; these workers become aware of the great significance of the city to themselves or future generations, thereby gradually increasing their willingness to communicate with urban residents. From this perspective, new media have become a large window that displays urban life and the image of urban residents to migrant workers. A mere glimpse is sufficient to attract more migrant workers to overcome difficulties and work towards their desired urban dreams.

The changes in interpersonal communication prompted by new media are even more notable. For migrant workers, new media provides them with equality, diversity, and positivity in interpersonal communication. In the conventional interpersonal communication model, *renqing* is at the core of interpersonal relationships. However, this core position has been shaken in the new media environment. In real life, the so-called *renqing*-based society reflects the characteristics of China's "acquaintance society". In a society of acquaintances, *renqing* is an essential means to maintain a stable relationship. When people get involved in the media use from the real world, their social context disappears. Moreover, they have greatly increased autonomy and mobility so as to confront the temporal and spatial limitations in their media use. In short, people do not intend to establish strong and long-term relationships but to utilize the media environment to establish a short-term relationship that meets their immediate needs. Such a relationship is based on a contract, and the core of communication is to establish a contractual relationship instead of building a *renqing*-based relationship (Guan, 2014). The conventional interpersonal communication model is completely broken in the new media environment. Migrant workers can experience authentic interpersonal interactions, free from discrimination and misunderstandings, with urban residents in the space created by the new media because of the absence of exchange of *renqing* and the concealment of rural-urban differences. In the conventional real-life communication space, migrant workers lack the channels to communicate with urban residents, and these migrants rarely have interpersonal communication with urban residents except for work contacts. By contrast, in the new media space, migrant workers have countless channels to reach netizens worldwide through games, chat, news, or online forums. These netizens include migrant workers, urban residents, and even international friends. Communication on an equal footing with people from different regions and cultural backgrounds is unimaginable for migrant workers in the conventional real space. With convenient communication channels and a communication environment that eliminates rural-urban differences, migrant workers can develop the confidence to communicate with people of different identities and backgrounds.

4.3 Communication Towards Involution: The Limit and Boundary Effect of Social Capital

The media are not developed to help migrant workers communicate with urban residents. Although its existence helps migrant workers break the dual identity opposition and allows them to see the possibility of equal communication with urban residents, we must also be aware of the limitations of this breakthrough. Interpersonal communication in the virtual space appears peaceful and enthusiastic, but it will inevitably be tested by reality if it is to move towards stability. The migrant workers disguise their reality with more favourable images or pursue their urban dreams in the virtual space constructed by the new media; this enables them to have a peaceful, equal, and natural communication with urban residents who once appeared aloof and inaccessible, and even establish a close relationship with them. Nonetheless, once this interaction moves from the relative protection of digital communication to reality, and the rural-urban differences reappear, it remains to be seen how many intimate relationships can survive. Perhaps migrant workers lack the intention to transform digital communication into actual intimate relationships.

As new media have fully penetrated the lives of the general public, its influence on and meaning to people have become increasingly stable. Social networks in new media have experienced a dramatic rise, but their growth is now plateauing. The guidance of the new media has certainly helped migrant workers take major strides in the process of urbanization. However, we must understand the essence of the role of new media, so as not to be dazzled by the progress and become complacent.

Involution, also referred to as over-densification, is an influential and frequently used concept that has become popular in Chinese sociology in recent years because it is closely connected with certain characteristics of Chinese society. With the publication of Huang's book *The Peasant Family and Rural Development in the Yangzi Delta* on the social changes in rural China in the 20th century, this concept has attracted the attention of Chinese scholars. Moreover, after the publication of US scholar Prasenjit Duara's book, *Culture, Power, and the State: Rural North China, 1900–1942*, which focused on social changes in rural north China in the first half of the 20th century, more Chinese scholars have conducted research on Chinese society by using the concept of involution.

According to the American anthropologist Clifford Geertz, "involution" refers to a social or cultural model that has reached a certain form at a certain stage of development and then stagnates or cannot be transformed into another advanced model. Huang applied this concept to the study of China's economic development and social changes in *The Peasant Family and Rural Development in the Yangzi Delta*. He referred to the approach of increasing total output by investing a large amount of labour in limited land (i.e., the method of diminishing marginal utility) as growth without development, which is involution.

With the increasing use of new media, the interpersonal skills of the new generation of migrant workers and their capabilities of social inclusion have improved, but the improvement has stagnated after reaching a certain level, and the trend to oppose urban residents under the new media environment has reappeared. This conclusion is not based on conjecture. By consulting numerous investigations and studies, the current study discovered that although the lower barriers to entry of new media have opened up a path to equitable communication for migrant workers, a gap remains between migrant workers and urban residents in terms of media literacy. Specifically, a gap exists between migrant workers and urban residents in terms of entertainment and information search capabilities in new media. New media platforms may also magnify some of the defects of migrant workers, causing the differences between migrant workers and urban residents in the new media environment to become increasingly apparent. Over time, migrant workers gradually lose their interest in new media, and the new media facilities are reduced to internal communication tools between them and those who come from the same hometown, relatives and friends, and other migrant workers. This study has observed that the major premise proposed at the beginning of this study (i.e., the isolated islands in the city) has begun to appear in another form in the virtual space constructed by new media, and involution has been observed in migrant workers' interpersonal communication.

From a macro perspective, the development of new technologies follows a certain cycle: from the initial stage to the booming period and then to the bottleneck period (involution), as can be observed in the development of the media. The evidence in this study points to a reverse phenomenon: migrant workers are first isolated by the media, followed by full access to the media for promoting urban communication, which is subsequently followed by alienation and isolation of these workers in the virtual space. Evidence suggests that the involution of urban interpersonal communication among migrant workers has already appeared in some groups of migrant workers. However, this observation does not diminish the role of the media in the process of urban adaptation and social inclusion of migrant workers. After all, without new media serving as a catalyst, the interpersonal communication of migrant workers would still be confined to the conventional real space. The enormous effect of new media on the interpersonal communication of migrant workers is undeniable, but its involution is also inevitable. Correspondingly, the interpersonal communication of these migrant workers in the virtual space is also entering a stagnating period, waiting for a possible new change ahead.

Overall, the interpersonal relationships of the new generation of migrant workers have undergone tremendous change in the new media environment. This change has generally been positive and provides reason for optimism, but the effect achieved is not as remarkable as we assumed. Helplessness in communication does not only involve migrant workers but is also a major problem in the process of human development. Nevertheless, such unavoidable problems can still be faced and addressed. From the perspective of communication studies, we should consider the role of the media in these social contradictions, and whether and how the media can positively influence the social inclusion of migrant workers. The ideal situation would be for the media to enable humans to make progress in interpersonal communication, eliminating conventional communication restrictions in terms of time and space. Convenient, real-time, and equitable communication is difficult to achieve in the era of conventional communication without the help of media. Nevertheless, the media seem to have facilitated the urban adaptation and social inclusion of migrant workers. However, in reality, the current urban adaptation situation of migrant workers is not ideal. After the initial support from the media to integrate into the city to a certain extent, migrant workers were unable to go further, causing some of them to isolate themselves again from the city during this semi-inclusion process. Academia tends to assign considerable importance to the media's role in society; however, this may lead to an overestimation of this role. Researchers must still base their findings on facts and realize that the media have no specific responsibility towards urban residents or migrant workers, nor should it be used as a publicity tool for humanistic care; the media thus do not have an obligation to help migrant workers assimilate into the city. Evidence suggests that the media have promoted the interpersonal communication of migrant workers. That is, migrant workers have used new media to promote their interpersonal communication.

Extreme assertions regarding the role of the media are unhelpful. For instance, exaggerating the role of the media and assuming that the media are the biggest contributor to the progress of migrant workers' interpersonal communication practices is just as unwise as ignoring the role of the media and asserting that the media simply constitute one of the many environments in which migrant workers grow up. Essentially, the upbringing of migrant workers has changed their interpersonal behaviour and habits. The clear role of the media in this process is the virtual space parallel to the real space that it offers. In this space, migrant workers can pursue their desire for adaptation in the city as well as construct a make-believe identity that allows them to perceive themselves positively. The urban dream of migrant workers can be temporarily realized in this virtual space. This space has opened up a conflict-buffering paradise for migrant workers in the city, enabling them to temporarily abandon the negative influence generated by differences in status and obtain a transient harmonious relationship in the contradictory urban life. This space is rather flexible and fluid. Migrant workers who enter this space may break through the limitations of real space and complete their urbanization, or they may simply enjoy the urban life experience that matches the atmosphere in the urban life. Regardless, the unique role of new media in the interpersonal communication of migrant workers in cities should not be neglected. High mediatization drives migrant workers to establish interpersonal communication with "non-islanders", whereas low mediatization causes migrant workers to conduct interpersonal communication with "islanders". Although the ultimate goal of this flexible space created by the new media remains unclear, the changes it has caused in the interpersonal communication of migrant workers are significant.

If the ultimate goal is to promote interpersonal communication between migrant workers and urban residents and assist the migrant workers to complete their transformation into urbanites, the new media environment presents a rare opportunity for migrant workers to complete this transformation. The keys to migrant workers' social inclusion in terms of psychology and identity are (1) understanding the role of the media in interpersonal communication; (2) leveraging the favourable platforms created by new media; (3) changing the conventional concept of interpersonal communication; (4) and shortening the distance between urban residents in terms of making friends, job seeking, and communication, in order to create more opportunities and possibilities to assimilate themselves into the city. New media platforms can also help urban residents to adjust their stereotypical views and reduce their prejudice against migrant workers through direct communication, or to simply express concern for migrant workers. Everyone is equal in the virtual space, and mutual understanding and respect have become an integral part of such spaces. Mutual care and understanding are indispensable for promoting interpersonal communication between people of different classes.

Note

1 Translator's note: a Chinese dating television show.

References

Fang, Y. (2012). An analysis of medialized interpersonal relationship. *Journal of International Communication, 34*(7), 52–57.

Guan, L. (2014). Deconstruction and reconstruction of traditional interpersonal interaction patterns in the media environment. *Journalism Research Herald, 5*(13), 55–56.

Singerhoff, L. (2009). *Why we need rituals: The meaning, power and support of the heart* (Y. Liu, Trans.). China Renmin University Press.

6 "Opening the Lock and Scaling the Wall"

Information Literacy Among the New Generation of Migrant Workers

In an era of information explosion, information literacy is especially significant for the new generation of migrant workers. It refers to an ability to realize their information needs, develop information awareness, and avail themselves of information tools for personal purposes. The level of information literacy has a direct impact on their ability to use information tools for urban adaptation and social inclusion. Improving their information literacy is one of the significant ways of assisting them to gain social recognition and integrate into urban society (Yang, 2012). However, considering their relatively low information literacy levels, there is considerable scope for further improvement in developing information awareness, cultivating abilities to disseminate information and to leverage information tools. Metaphorically, there is a wall between the new generation of migrant workers and information-based urban life. To some extent, the wall is a hindrance to their adaptation to urban life.

As an essential means of scaling the wall, urban media are incredibly conducive to the information literacy cultivation among migrant workers. In the urban environment marked by information explosion, thanks to their functionalities, modern media are more than merely entertainment tools and information carriers for migrant workers. Instead, new media are inherently important tools to achieve user gratifications. The new generation of migrant workers can explore the variety of urban life through television, newspapers, magazines, radio, and so forth. In addition to the traditional mass media, other media, including outdoor advertising, electronic billboards, flyers, and Internet-based platforms, are ubiquitous around the city. Entwined with their urban life, those media boost the information literacy of those migrant workers.

1. "Opening the Lock": Leaving a Closed Media Environment

Rural-urban migration doesn't merely mean geographical changes. Moreover, it leads to comprehensive changes ranging from the cultural environment to living conditions, with the most notable and drastic change taking place in the media environment. In the countryside, where living conditions are monotonous, people limit most of their activities to a single village, with a faceless model of life and

DOI: 10.4324/9781003365785-6

a shortage of entertainment resources; in cities, the required working knowledge extends beyond farming to numerous professions. Various recreational activities and living conditions are accessible to the new generation of migrant workers. In the closed rural interpersonal environment, word-by-mouth communication predominates, and the interpersonal relationships form within a limited group of villagers; in cities, the popularity of mobile phones and other communication tools gradually accelerates and extends their interpersonal communication and widens their interpersonal social groups. In most rural areas in China, radio is the only medium for mass communication, which is mainly used by local cadres to give notifications. Even in places with access to televisions, only several local channels are available; by contrast, new-generation migrant workers acquaint themselves with multiple platforms of urban TV and radio stations, as well as the Internet. They begin to voice their opinions and interact with the outside world on such platforms.

Following the changes in the media environment, the new generation of migrant workers is more capable of obtaining information from urban media and is desirous of information. With growing open-mindedness and greater proficiency in multi-media skills, they are more likely to improve information literacy in the urban media environment. Hence, rural-urban migration opens the lock on the information environment for the new generation of migrant workers.

1.1 From Monotony to Variety: Shifts in Lifestyles

In urban life, the new generation of migrant workers embraces new possibilities. In terms of living environments, they mostly live with colleagues or fellow villagers who are primarily about the same age. Compared with the previous household-living model, such a group-living model is more conducive to mutual communication. In terms of working environments, they mainly work in such open spaces as barbershops and restaurants, allowing them to absorb more information from the outside world. In terms of recreational activities, such entertainment places as cybercafes, cinemas, and rinks are popular among the new generation, some of whom occasionally go to high-level consumption places, such as pubs and high-end clubhouses.

Hui, a 20-year-old native of Bengbu City, Anhui province, has been in Nanjing for two years, working as a takeaway delivery driver in his parents' snack bar near Nanjing University. Fashionably dressed, he is an iPhone user and fond of talking Internet slang. Nothing except his broad accent can betray his rural origins. In his colourful urban life, Hui frequents such places as karaoke bars, cybercafes, cafes, and cinemas for recreation. Back in the village, however, life was different.

> Since I came to Nanjing two years ago, my life has undergone many changes. This big provincial capital is in a different league from Bengbu, my hometown. Back there, after dropping out of senior high school in my teens, I became jobless and stayed at home in this small village, which was short of recreational activities. As my parents were working in Nanjing and my

fellows were attending school, I had no company and just idled my time away by watching TV alone at home. Besides, the television set wasn't connected to cable and just offered several channels. Sometimes, I had no choice but to watch my grandmother playing cards, the village's only pastime. It was really boring there. Other diversions were only available in the town, with nothing more than game machines, snacks, and the likes. The cinemas there, poorly equipped, were no substitute for Wanda's[1] in Nanjing. When bored to death, I just stared aimlessly into the sky, slept, or listened to the radio for a whole day. A year later, my parents couldn't stand up with my way of life, and took me to Nanjing. It's awesome.

(Hui, male, Bengbu County, Anhui province)

Hui's story reveals his perception of the migration as a relief, reinforced by the sharp contrast between the frowning face when he narrated the rural life and a smile rested on his lips when he related the urban life.

Having experienced the diversity of urban living conditions, many new-generation migrant workers perceive the monotonous rural life as painful and urban life as their ideal lifestyle. For them, such migration is an escape from dull life. "I struggled my way out of the village, and I don't want to return. I'll stay in cities at any cost", said Liu, the next interviewee.

Liu, an employee of Huazai Hairstyle adjacent to Nanjing University, has a stylish haircut and delicate appearances just as other male hairdressers appear. He describes his hometown, Feng County in Xuzhou City, as "poverty-stricken". Born into a farmer family and graduated from trade school, Liu was once employed in a motorcycle repair shop in the town, where he toiled at work and led a dull life. Having left for Nanjing, he has better experiences in personal entertainment and the overall living conditions.

The urban living standards are way much better! I'm living in a rented house with several roommates on Qingdao Road in Nanjing. The hospital is just a few steps away, and the street is lined with restaurants. However, in my hometown, it's difficult to find a fine restaurant for a drink. In addition, the commuting experience here is better. My workplace is within walking distance of where I live, and my colleague, though residing in Xianlin, the sub-city on the outskirts of Nanjing, can still take the subway for work. Anyway, it's convenient to commute. In comparison, the days when I biked to work in my hometown were real torture. Moreover, supermarkets and farmers' markets are everywhere in Nanjing. However, when my hometown folks buy meat (typically they are self-sufficient in home-grown vegetables), it takes two hours to travel to and from between the market and the home. The better-off families can buy relatively more meat, which they store in fridges. But those without fridges can't afford such a shopping trip every day. So many seniors there just live on vegetables and don't touch meat.

(Liu, male, Feng County, Xuzhou City)

From Feng County to Nanjing City, his living conditions witness significant improvement. Back in the monotonous living conditions in the county, Liu divided his time between the motorbike repair shop and his home only. In contrast, abundant options are open to him in the city. In his words, "When having a meal, I can choose from a number of nearby restaurants. After work, I can either shop in the supermarket and or browse around shops."

Both Liu's and Hui's cases reveal that urban living environments are so diverse that even activities that are commonplace to urbanites are probably a luxury in rural areas, including dining out, shopping, and observing people's comings and goings.

For the new generation of migrant workers, the rural-urban migration is not only followed by the change in the geographical location, but also by more profound changes in the field of their daily lives. Due to the rural living conditions, they worked from dawn to dusk with monotonous regularity. Nevertheless, in the diverse urban living conditions, new-generation migrant workers have various free choices of entertainment activities, including dining out, shopping, and so forth. Even in terms of job search and accommodation, they can also make choices and changes of their free will, adding much flexibility to urban life. Diverse decisions make for the most significant internal motivation behind their desire for urban life. Though many new-generation migrant workers struggle to live a decent life in large cities, and some are even unable to make both ends meet, they refuse to resign themselves to their hometowns' monotonous life. Compared with their older counterparts, the younger generation switch from a monotonous and closed environment to a diverse and open lifestyle (Zhu et al., 2010). This shift is credited to the diversity of urban living environments. Such diversity whets their appetite for more information, with which they can make the most informed choices in the option-rich urban living environments. In addition, in the diverse urban living environments, new-generation migrant workers witness the gradual improvement of information literacy during their ongoing learning and adaptation.

1.2 From Closedness to Openness: The Extension of Social Interaction

In the living spaces of the new generation of migrant workers, social interaction constitutes the bulk of their communication, be it before or after the migration. However, rural interpersonal interaction is different from urban interpersonal interaction. Pastoral interpersonal relationships are narrowly founded on kinship and geographic relationship, where people communicate primarily through word of mouth, resulting in a relatively closed interpersonal environment. By contrast, urban interpersonal relationships cover a broader range of relationships, including business relationship and relationships built on personal interests. New-generation migrant workers communicate by various platforms, including the widely used WeChat and other social networking applications, thereby gaining access to multiple channels to obtain and discriminate information. All leads to much more open interpersonal relationships. Accordingly, the rural-urban migration represents a rapid shift in interpersonal communications.

First, the change in the residential model favours the new generation's social interaction. The urban residential models generally fall into two categories: the compact residential model and the scattered residential model. The former refers to a model where the neighbourhood is inhabited only by migrant workers, of which the urban village[2] is a typical example. In contrast, in the latter, the inhabitants involve their colleagues or other urban residents. Research reveals that such primary groups based on kinship and geographic relationships remain the foundation for the new generation to build social networks. Those relationships provide the migrant workers with emotional support in an unfamiliar urban environment. However, statistics reveal the new generation of migrant workers in the compact residential model is essentially less able to build new social networks except primary group relationships. Some even withdraw into themselves. By contrast, those in the scattered residential model proactively extend social networks. Hence, the business-related secondary group relationships have predominated in their reconstruction of interpersonal networks after migrating into the cities (Wen, 2011).

Born in a village in Luhe District, Nanjing City, Hong now works in a nail salon in the urban area. Before that, Hong's network of contacts was somewhat limited. "My family used to live in the back of beyond, where there are only two households. Both are surrounded by a river, and there is only one way to leave the village." Barely engaging in talks with other villagers, Hong was informed mainly by former junior high school classmates who worked in cities.

> At home, I just watched TV series and seldom watched the news. Mostly, my former classmates told me about significant events when we went out for fun, like the Youth Olympic Games held in Nanjing. One close friend of my neighbour's was nearly as ignorant as me, but she didn't follow me into the city. I guess she is still so ill-informed that she probably doesn't know who the president of China is. Since I worked in Nanjing, I got to know more people and broadened my horizons. It feels good to live with several roommates in a dormitory, from whom I learn much about dressing, the city, and others.
>
> (Hong, female, Luhe District, Nanjing City)

Having changed her place of residence, Hong lives with roommates and enjoys a better interpersonal communication environment, thus becoming better-informed about fashion and blossoming into a stylish girl from a countrified villager. Hong is a classic example of those who leave their parents in rural areas and develop close bonds with colleagues and roommates. Due to the new residential model, they are influenced by roommates in the "habitat". The roommates, whether colleagues or friends, are often more experienced in urban life and offer great assistance to new arrivals. Meanwhile, following the changes of residence, it is probable that the migrant workers live next door to born-and-bred urban residents or rent houses in urban residents-dominated neighbourhoods. Through communication with city dwellers and by osmosis, the migrant workers can learn more about urban lifestyles.

Second, more open working environments are conducive to the social interaction of the new generation of migrant workers. According to research, they not only acquire living wages but also establish valuable interpersonal relationships from work. If their urban accommodation is compared to a relatively closed "habitat", their jobs, especially those from the service industry, are bridging them with the urban lives.

Feifei works as a salesperson for the store on the first floor of the canteen of a Nanjing-based university. Childlike and witty, she looks more like a freshman than a 25-year-old grown-up.

> I never changed my uniform after work, because I didn't bother dressing up, or felt the need to do so. However, I gradually felt envious of the gorgeously dressed college girls and other young female guests, so much that I didn't want to wear the uniform even at work. By observing the beauties on the street, I realized I was equally attractive if I dressed up. My roommate Ms Gao also shares my view. Once she insisted that I should wear one of her clothes, and I followed her advice. As it flattered my waist, I was widely admired. Afterward, through gritted teeth, I bought the same one as hers. I love it very much.
>
> (Feifei, female, Chuzhou City, Anhui province)

In the workplace, Feifei encountered many stylish college girls. The improved interpersonal environment shifted her perception of fashion and propelled her into action, earning her rave comments. Undoubtedly, such improvement of interpersonal communication environment provides fertile ground for shifting her perceptions.

In addition to the living and working environments, advanced information transmission technologies and communication tools also help extend the new generation of migrant workers' networks rapidly.

Located near a Nanjing-based university, the Laodifang restaurant is among the author's frequently visited restaurants. As its youngest waitress, the 21-year-old Jie is more smartphone-dependent than her counterparts in the restaurant. Shortly after its launch, she bought her Samsung smartphone for over 3000 RMB. "It nearly cost me two-month salaries." However, she wasn't discouraged by the prohibitive price. "I had no alternative. My life can't go without a smartphone." The smartphone's networking function plays a significant role in extending her social network in Nanjing.

> I make friends with two male Nanjing locals, one at 28 and the other at 25. I see little of them, and just hang out with them once in a while in my spare time. The 28-year-old works in a bank in Dafangxiang and is helpful. I came to know him when I was grappling with computer problems. Uninformed about them, I asked for help in the WeChat group. He volunteered to lend a hand and shopped for a computer with me. He is very nice. Maybe I was

simply lucky to get to know such a kind person. I usually don't add strangers as my friends on WeChat. The 25-year-old works in a nearby company, and I knew him also through WeChat. When going out with him, I make friends with many others, with whom I dine, watch movies, and sing. Usually we don't chat much, for they are on a different wavelength from me. But I believe it's good to make more friends.

(Jie, female, Hefei City, Anhui province)

Jie makes friends with many urban dwellers via WeChat on the smartphone. Those friends, who can either repair her computer or hang out with her, have played a vital part in her adaption to urban life.

In addition to WeChat, social networking services, including Momo, Tencent QQ, and so forth, facilitate friendship development for the new generation of migrant workers. Some of them even find their life partners through Jiayuan.com and other dating websites. Though none of my interviewees became romantically involved with their chatting partners on those matchmaking websites, some made friends with their dates after personal contact. It's the advanced Internet communication technologies that infinitely extend their virtual interpersonal communications in cities, and transmit the online into offline relationships after a face-to-face meeting, thereby leading to the rapid extension of the urban interpersonal networks and adding variety to the lives of migrant workers.

Accordingly, the living environments in dormitories or rented houses, open working environments, and advanced Internet communication technologies are all conducive to interpersonal network extension for the new generation of migrant workers. Credit for those conveniences goes to more open settings for social interaction. As scholars claimed, "The vast shift from rural to urban life reconstructs their behaviour and content of interpersonal communication. During their ongoing interaction with urban residents, various modern ideas and concepts have deeply influenced each one during the process" (Tao & Xu, 2012). Instead of being shut away in the closed rural areas, the new generation of migrant workers has opened the lock on interpersonal communications after they moved to cities. Such a shift is conducive to enhancing their information literacy.

1.3 From One-way Communication to Interaction: Upgrading in Media Experience

Cities are defined not only by rapid economic development and a convenient life but also by the media-rich environment. Following the rural-urban migration of the new generation of migrant workers, the days are gone when radio and TV were the only entertainment options, and so is the one-way communication model deprived of feedback from recipients of the information.

Mobile phones are the most popular new media for the new generation of migrant workers. According to the survey, there are two overarching trends in their media experience: one is switching from traditional media to new media, and the other is moving away from PC terminals to mobile phones.

Meizi, a native of Hai'an County, Nantong City, has been working in Yaohan, a shopping mall in downtown Nantong since she was 21. It's situated in the Central Business District (CBD), the city's most bustling area, in what is colloquially addressed as "South Street" by local residents. For Meizi, the most challenging part of work is commuting. Living next to Nantong Hi-Tech Industrial Development Zone, she has to spend more than one hour on a bus before reaching her workplace in Yaohan, which is more than 20 kilometres away. However, ever since the smartphone has entered her life, Meizi feels the commuting time flies when she takes the bus.

> My last phone was too pathetic to have an Internet connection. When taking the bus, I was bored and felt the bus move so slowly that it took ages for me to reach the destination. I had no choice but to watch TV on the bus. However, it kept running the same advertisements repeatedly. Earlier this year, I bought a Samsung smartphone with easy access to Internet service. My colleague helped me create a Weibo account and download many other news applications. It's a good way to kill time on my way to work and feel I'll arrive soon. For example, I check the draw results of lottery I buy occasionally, and chat with friends via QQ and WeChat. In this way, I feel the time slips. Not long ago, I lost the phone. Literally, without any hesitation, I bought another smartphone. I can't live without a smartphone, and sometimes I even secretly play with it at work. Of course, my store manager will piss off if catching me doing so.
>
> (Meizi, female, Hai'an County, Nantong City)

The interactivity of mobile phone applications allows Meizi to idle away the long commuting time in her favourite ways, either by freely reading news she feels interested in or conversing with like-minded friends. Mobile phones have become the primary medium for the new generation of migrant workers adapting to urban life. Waiters or hairdressers scroll through Weibo or play games via mobile phones as leisure activities. The interactivity and affordances of mobile phones are the primary reasons behind their user stickiness. "I feel it interesting to join others to write comments, share reposts and roast people." "I can read whatever news I want." "I can download any game I like." Moreover, the portability of mobile phones significantly contributes to their popularity over computers. Most of the interviewees own computers and Internet connections. Nevertheless, they seldom play with computers, mainly because a hard day's work wears them out so much that they want to loll somewhere as soon as they return home. Therefore, they don't reserve much time and energy for computer entertainment. As computers are rendered spare, light-weighted portable mobile phones have been more appealing for the new generation of migrant workers, whether on the bus, taking subways, or on the street.

In addition to mobile phones, upgrading in such traditional media as television, also adds colour to their urban life. The 24-year-old Shi works in a Nanjing-based Huazai hair salon. Before leaving for Nanjing, he lived in a small village in Puyang City, Henan province. He describes his family as "better off" in relation to other local households. Though his family can afford a large-screen LCD colour TV, access to cable TV is denied by the outdated local software, making the television set more like a white elephant in their home. For this reason, he would rather listen to the radio than watch TV. However, after living in Nanjing, his media experience with TV has dramatically improved.

> The living standards in my hometown now have improved as well. We have cable TV, but my parents have seldom watched TV since I left. However, it still paled in comparison with life in Nanjing. Take the digital television in the apartment my colleague Xia and I are renting. It allows us to watch old shows, which my friends back home find hard to believe. Moreover, it offers specialty channels. As a football buff, I subscribed to the European Football channel by Guangdong TV Station (GDTV Station), which runs football programmes around the clock and saves me the trouble of changing channels.

According to many new-generation migrant workers, they feel most relaxed when freely watching TV at home after an exhausting workday. The advent of digital TV transformed one-way communication, marking the beginning of the digital era and the emergence of interactive TV. Instead of passively watching what is being broadcasted on TV, new-generation migrant workers can tune in to programmes of interest to them and broadcasted at other periods. Such interaction means better user experience and the need for better information literacy, which allows the group to select appropriate information. It's the ongoing learning and adaptation that increasingly enhance their information literacy.

Our survey also reveals smartphones and smart TVs are the most popular media terminals among the new generation of migrant workers. Essentially, their Internet connection is at the core of their popularity. In addition, other Internet media platforms are also much appreciated.

Apart from massive information, online communities and communication functions are the most significant Internet attractions for the new generation of migrant workers. Take Shi, mentioned earlier, for example. On Weibo, he offers consultation on beauty and hairdressing, attracting over 10,000 followers and satisfying his ego. He is also fond of browsing through the BBS of a Nanjing-based university for top ten trending topics, to find conversation topics with clients. In addition, some local forums are among the most frequently visited online sites for new-generation migrant workers, where they acquaint themselves with their surroundings, and learn urban lifestyles and life skills.

Accordingly, the new generation of migrant workers has high expectations of media interaction, where such expectations are met with interactive media environments in cities. They find great pleasure in interpersonal communications through such online interactions as chats and games, which offer them a temporary shelter from loneliness. Meanwhile, the urban interactive media environments provide not only comfort but also a great convenience. For instance, DiDi Chuxing, a ride-hailing interactive application, has become an integral part of their daily lives and facilitates their travel. Unlike the one-way communication in rural media, urban media enable more interaction with great variety and openness. Whether through traditional media (e.g., TV and radio) or new media (e.g., the Internet and mobile phone), they can acquire desirous information and give necessary feedback.

The unlocking of urban media environments and continuously improved inter-active experience are followed by the new generation of migrant workers' growing participation in, a new perception of, and new demands for urban life. Therefore, they have a natural desire for higher information literacy. In other words, it's the urban interactive media environment that expects more of the new generation of migrant workers in terms of information literacy.

2. Information Barriers and Real-life Obstacles Encountered During Adaptation to Urban Life

Rural-urban migration lifts the new generation of migrant workers out of a relatively closed information environment and exposes them to various urban media. Such migration brings about high hopes and promises a boundless potential for improve-ment in information literacy. However, the unlocking of the information environment is usually followed by a certain kind of information barrier. The obsolete mindset rooted in rural society can't be changed in the short term; their words carry little weight in communication, because they are slighted for being city outsiders; unfamil-iar with urban life, they encounter unexpected obstacles in leveraging urban media. All constitute the information barriers, an outgrowth of their rural-urban migration.

2.1 Hysteresis: Traditional Mindset Rooted in Rural Society

Some of the migrant workers growing up in the countryside have developed an indelible conventional mindset. Others, who have been raised in cities since child-hood, also embrace such mindsets as rural residents under the influence of their parents, the older generation of migrant workers. Generally, my interviewees stay abreast of the times and are more open-minded, at least more than the older gen-eration. Nevertheless, a significant number of the younger generation are still susceptible to a traditional mindset. As farmers, they will be stuck with the values they inherit for a long time, whose negative parts will be a major hindrance to their enhancement of information literacy.

For example, some of the new generation of migrant workers suffer from severe loss of confidence, as they believe their rural roots lead to a wide gap between them and urban residents. After leaving Chuzhou City, Anhui province, for Nan-jing with her husband, Gao has been a salesperson at the first-floor store in a local university's canteen. Working in the higher education institution, she believes the customers leave her standing, for they all have excellent credentials, whereas she is a junior high school dropout.

> At first, I've been reticent. I come from a village where even college stu-dents are rare. But in the university, intellectuals with high educational levels

abound, and even postgraduates and PhDs are commonplace. They are the backbone of our country. However, I didn't even finish junior high school. I'm too clumsy to talk with them.

(Gao, female, Chuzhou City, Anhui province)

Believing the gap is enormous, she shies away from exchanging ideas with student guests at the cost of many opportunities for information and knowledge acquisition. Moreover, considering herself poorly educated, she isn't an avid reader of books and newspapers for information. "I only buy newspapers casually, and don't take to reading probably for lack of education." When asked whether she searched jobs online, Gao is noticeably unsure of herself: "I think only the well-educated can well navigate the website Zhaopin.com. We the migrant workers don't visit those job search websites, and I know little about them either."

Likewise, Dong, a native of Guizhou province, also feels there is a permanent gap between himself and the locals. To his eyes, the gap lies in entrepreneurial skills.

I notice the exclusivity of Taizhou City, where the locals have a strong bias against us migrant workers. Unlike the city dwellers who mostly have a business head, we aren't cut out for entrepreneurship and could not but work for them. In addition, I see no career prospects in the city, and we can't fit in at all.

(Dong, male, Guizhou province)

In fact, cases abound where many new-generation migrant workers blossom into successful entrepreneurs. As long as they remain positive and work hard instead of disparaging themselves, starting a business is also realistic.

Many of the new generation of migrant workers believe they were born with a gap which can't be bridged. The lack of confidence originates from the conventional belief that country folks should know their place. Once they take this attitude to extremes, they will be exceedingly conservative and cling to the false proposition that fate is predestined instead of improving themselves for a better life. Such a negative mindset discourages new-generation migrant workers from accessing information and knowledge of their own accord, which in the long run will be detrimental to their adaptation to, and assimilation into, urban communities.

In addition to a sense of inferiority and aversion to exchange ideas with the better-educated, there is a mistrust of urban media among the new generation of migrant workers. It is partly because of their unfamiliarity with the tools, and partly due to their prejudices and prevailing presumptions based on hearsay. The mistrust of an online job search is particularly evident.

Qin and Lulu are waitresses in a restaurant around a Nanjing-based university. Skeptical of an online job search, they found current jobs through their contacts. In Qin's case, such mistrust is shaped by her fellow villagers' personal experience where they were defrauded when searching jobs online, so she never has recourse to the Internet.

When changing jobs, I turn to those I'm on familiar terms with or return to my hometown for a new job. I'm doubtful about online job advertisements, as the Internet is overrun with frauds, and many of my fellows were victims.

(Qin, female, Haining City, Zhejiang province)

Though Lulu didn't fall for those scams, hearsay and subjective judgment prejudice her against such an approach. "I don't job-hunt online. Many information about job vacancies is false, and I know those cases. I mainly resort to my relatives and other people I know well when finding jobs."

Many new-generation migrant workers found satisfying jobs through the Internet, which will be amplified in the following. Some hoaxes are attributed to the victims' ignorance of those websites and access to illegitimate websites, rather than job search websites per se. For many of the new generation of migrant workers, their doubts over such a job search approach results in scarce employment information. Though they can achieve employment through networks or job advertisements outdoors, they are bereft of better job opportunities.

In addition to an online job search, Qin also harbours bias against dating or marrying city dwellers. Such discrimination feeds on her own experience.

I still believe my fellow villagers are better partner choices, for it's easier for me to know my fellows like the back of my hand than city dwellers. My ex-husband, a Nanjing native, is annoyingly unreliable. When we were in a relationship, he was somewhat trustworthy. After marriage, however, he showed his true colors and quibbled with me constantly. Real-life marriage is a far cry from the romantic TV series plots, which I think are unrealistic and only have entertainment value. They won't be replicated in the real world. I'm still conservative.

(Qin, female, Haining City, Zhejiang province)

Such rural conservatism puts some migrant workers on the defensive when they are in a new environment. For fear of being hurt, they are resistant to new ideas at the cost of many opportunities. Their sense of inferiority and other objective factors has resulted in a confined network made of their likes, leading to few in-depth chances of exchanging with city dwellers and a vicious circle which adds to such feeling.

Hamstrung by the traditional rural mindset, new-generation migrant workers miss the opportunity where they otherwise could have better-enhanced information literacy and quickly adapted to urban lives. Therefore, it's imperative to help the group keep abreast of the times and strengthen their information awareness.

2.2 Humble and Voiceless: Disadvantaged Positions in Communication

As outsiders to cities, migrant workers also have access to the same resources as city dwellers, thus shrinking the urban natives' share of resources to some extent.

Such shrinkage is minor but deeply felt by city dwellers. As a result, they reject and prejudice against migrant workers. For this reason, migrant workers are both institutionally and mentally underprivileged. With a stronger sense of self-esteem, the new generation of migrant workers is more vying for respect, especially from city dwellers, and better protection for their legitimate rights. However, the group, underprivileged on all counts, are unlikely to be fully spotlighted and find their opinions barely noticed due to their humble origins.

When given a rough deal, the new generation of migrant workers, hindered by subjective and objective factors, may find no outlet to expose them. According to the survey, the group is mainly subject to wage arrears, dilemmas with children's education, employment contract issues, arbitrary charges, miserable working conditions, safety hazards in the workplace, and insufficient social securities. Though those injustices are relevant to their interests, they tend to remain silent, not for the sake of it, but for lack of spheres to air their grievances. Even if they find some ways to express their outrage, they may be given the cold shoulder.

Hu, who has started to work in Shanghai from Hai'an, Nantong, at the age of 24, is employed by an appliance maintenance company. As the local police severely disrupted his sleep by frequenting his accommodation late at night for the temporary residence permit, Hu approached the neighbourhood committee for help, but that was of no avail.

Long, Hu's younger brother, who followed the example of Hu, left for Shanghai for work and was bruised by his first job. At that time, Long was employed on a casual basis as a security guard by a property management company for a high-end residential quarter. According to the company stipulation, security personnel was obliged to carry its residents' luggage or other personal effects to the front of the related block but not to the specific floor. Helpfully, Long sent the TV to the female resident's home, beyond his work responsibilities. However, instead of appreciating his voluntary help, she demanded a large sum of compensation. Moreover, the property management company dismissed Long's explanation outright and insisted he was responsible for the damage. Long was outraged and turned to the media afterwards, but for nothing.

Despite the possible slight from the media, new-generation migrant workers may face a frosty reception when proactively promoting themselves and networking with urban locals. Dong, a native of Guizhou province, longed to strike up friendships with locals in Taizhou City, Zhejiang province, for he was attracted by their business talent. However, he was bitterly devastated by their constant inhospitable response.

> I don't make many contacts with local youth. They don't like making friends with migrant workers and even stay aloof. They are indeed ambitious. But sometimes, I still feel unfair, as their family backgrounds put them in a better position to succeed. Having said that, I have no choice but to work harder to make up for my humble family background. One local colleague of mine went for a drink, and invited me along as I happened to be around. I knew he did so just as a matter of form, not sincerely. But I still went along, for

I thought that might be an opportunity for me to fit in. When I was there, however, I was out of my element. They were talking and laughing, leaving me alone and quiet. Even when I raised a subject after they exhausted their topics, they were lukewarm and just went through the motions before their second chat. After the gathering, they wanted to go to Karaoke. This time I didn't follow them and said I had something to attend to. Though I'm a sociable person, I tried my best and couldn't fit in. It's just they didn't care about me at all.

(Dong, male, Guizhou province)

Unable to integrate into locals' social circles, Dong feels he will be an outsider forever and doomed to rejection. Therefore, he feels exclusivity among Taizhou locals.

Disadvantaged positions in communication remain a barrier to the new generation of migrant workers' integration into cities. Most confine their network to only primary groups based on geographic relationship and kinship. Some never consider interacting with city dwellers, and some, including Dong, fail to find effective means of developing the secondary group relationship with city dwellers.

Whether for self-protection and justice, or for networking and making money, the new generation of migrant workers is assailed by the disadvantaged positions in communication. As significant contributors to urban development, however, they are vulnerable groups in communication, for they have narrow discourse space and little bearing on public opinions. Therefore, this large group may become "aphasic" collectively, as evidenced by an academic paper from the perspectives of their loss of discourse in political rights, information demand, and cultural life (Ye & Wang, 2009). As outsiders to cities, they have disproportionately weak voices due to their rural roots. To change the status quo, not only urbanites should become more welcoming, but also new-generation migrant workers should proactively overcome barriers to enhance their information literacy.

2.3 New Arrivals: Barriers to the Use of Information Tools

As outsiders with rural life experience, new-generation migrant workers are confronted with new living conditions and mechanisms. Accordingly, their integration into cities hinges on their ability to adapt to city life with information tools.

Compared with their older counterparts, new-generation migrant workers are more skilled at information tools, with smartphones, the Internet, and other new media increasingly prevailing in their lives. However, a fair number of them are newcomers who lack urban life experience and have little knowledge of smartphones and other information tools. As a result, they find difficulty in leveraging those tools. In fact, those new arrivals are faced with challenges from learning and can only use auxiliary functions of such media as mobile phones. Moreover, they are supposed to navigate through media information tools peculiar to cities (e.g., bus stops and ATMs). Those urban media, inaccessible in rural areas, will be both immensely helpful and challenging.

The new generation of migrant workers in cities is surrounded by readily available practical information tools and completely capable of mastering those tools. However, it never dawns on them that the tools can be used to their advantage. What's worse, they excuse themselves for not developing such a lifestyle, making it harder for them to take the first step.

Lili, from Fenshui County, Shanxi province, went to a technical secondary school in Taiyuan City at the age of 17 and worked as a masseuse in a local beauty salon after graduation.

> I knew nothing at the beginning of my school life, and I just followed the example of my fellow students. It's normal for those recently moving from the countryside to dress and act differently from the locals. So, I just followed them and learned, like, how to pay the bill in the canteen and wash clothes in the laundry.
> (Lili, female, Fenshui, Shanxi province)

When asked about the fellow students' backgrounds, Lili replied that they included some of the faculty's children, locals, or upperclassmen. "I consulted them since the freshman year, for they were more experienced." Usually, first-year students receive an orientation handbook on every facet of campus life, including E-payment in canteens and guidance for laundry services. However, it was quite an effort for her to recollect the handbook's advice.

> I knew it was a handbook for first-year students, but I didn't know what was inside. I didn't read the manual because it was crammed full of characters. I wasn't academic or a bookworm all along, so reading was really repulsive to me. I didn't even go through the instructions. Instead, I just felt my way.
> (Lili, female, from Fenshui, Shanxi province)

The handbook is all-encompassing regarding campus life, even covering useful information concerning college surroundings and the whole city. Had she finished reading the manual patiently, she would have managed her affairs independently. However, as she wasn't habituated to referring to handbooks, instructions, and other practical reference books, it took her more time to accommodate to a new environment.

Travelling frequently to and fro between their hometowns and working locations, new-generation migrant workers need to tackle transportation problems in cities. Sometimes, they find it inconvenient to master the various but unfamiliar media information tools in the urban transportation system.

The 27-year-old Jun works in a mechanical manufacturing factory in Nantong Hi-Tech Industrial Development Zone. He recalled a failure to board a train several years ago. Although he narrated the story with a smile, as if it was interesting, it sounded like quite the contrary.

> The boarding procedure at Hai'an Station in my hometown was simple. You just bought a ticket and went to the platform straight, and there was no big

screen for notification. But it's not the case in Nantong City. Before boarding my first Hai'an-bound train from Nantong, I sat in the waiting room straight after buying the ticket. However, we weren't allowed to go to the platform even when the boarding time was close. I assumed the train was behind sched-ule as usual, so I kept waiting there until running out of patience and asking a member of staff. It was at that time that I realized I had been in the wrong waiting room. I was told that the notice had been issued by the announcer half an hour ago and the train had already left. Until then, I learned things like, notifications could be broadcast, and there were several platforms and waiting rooms in one station, and you had to wait on designated platforms for different trains. All was shown on that large screen, but I knew nothing about it. Fortunately, the ticket was cheap. It's just that I waited for another four hours before taking the train. It was a great lesson that I learned.

(Jun, male, from Hai'an City, Jiangsu province)

Jun's story epitomizes the challenges for the new generation of migrant work-ers for lack of knowledge of information tools. Likewise, legions of his fellows, after migrating to cities, are subject to otherwise avoidable inconveniences of all magnitude just because of their poor command of information tools.

There are other media information tools for consumers' convenience (e.g., Baidu Maps, DiDi Chuxing, and other mobile applications) or offering discounts (e.g., coupon printer in railway station and group buying website) in fields other than transportation. A poor command of those tools is a high price to pay.

Not knowing group buying, Juan from Anhui province missed an existing discount.

Once, I had a hot pot meal with a colleague in a department store in Xin-jiekou. It was so expensive that we weren't full even we spent 100-plus yuan. A neighbouring table of three gobbled down much more than us. However, when we checked out, we found they spent as much money as ours. Since then, I came to know group-buying costed much less. With hindsight, I was so silly that I lost so many discounts.

(Juan, female, from Anhui province)

Yang from Yunnan province made a fool of himself when going to a hospital, unfamiliar with the queuing system.

During my first visit to Drum Tower Hospital, I knew nothing about the fol-lowing procedure after registration. After asking a nurse, I was told just to sit and wait. However, I was confused about the order, for all just waited but were not in line. After a while, I heard the calling and said to myself, "How can a doctor call me if he doesn't know my name?" For this reason, I ran into the room, and the doctor told me it wasn't my turn. I asked in reply, "How can you tell me it's my turn if you don't know my name?" That's how the embar-rassment unfolded. After this event, I learned about today's hospital queuing system. All information, like the turn, the number of patients queuing before you, are displayed on a big screen outside the room.

(Yang, male, from Yunnan province)

When freshly arriving in cities, most of the new migrant workers have trouble with urban information tools, or fully leveraging some of the tools. For instance, new-generation migrant workers are mainly capable of communicating, listening to music, playing games, and so forth via mobile phones, but know little about other convenient applications. The majority of them can watch videos and play games online, but fail to further explore the Internet's great access to information. Some information tools (e.g., the aforementioned hospital queuing system and utility bills inquiry system), which are common to urbanites, may be even unheard of for some new-generation migrant workers. Those problems are prevalent for those freshly arriving in cities, resulting in their dissatisfaction of the city life.

3. Scaling the Perimeter: Enhancement of Media Use and Information Literacy

After entering cities' open information environment, new-generation migrant workers are confronted with significant information barriers, either objectively or subjectively, like a wall separating them and information-based city life. Only by tearing down the wall can they enhance information literacy and use information tools to freely navigate their way around cities and adapt to city life.

Over time, new-generation migrant workers deepen their exchanges with urbanites. Having perceived the infiltration of urban lifestyle, the group gradually elevates their information awareness to the levels of their urban counterparts. As the government pays increasing attention to the group, so do the general public and media organizations. Moreover, the group's concerns are increasingly gaining publicity. Consequently, the voices of Chinese migrant workers have been heard in cities. Following their gradual inclusion in the city life, the group come to learn media information tools and proactively use them to strengthen their information awareness. Those changes are conducive to overcoming information barriers and rapid enhancement of information literacy.

3.1 Perceived Media Infiltration and Cultivation: Enhancement in Information Awareness

Influenced by the traditional rural mindset, new-generation migrant workers have low-level information awareness when freshly arriving in cities. According to a survey conducted in 2011, 13 percent of the migrant workers surveyed were unaware of the information they needed. Another 42 percent were ignorant of access to the information and failed to take effective approaches. This leads to the conclusion that the group's information awareness remains conservative. They lack the initiative to collect information, the motivation and resolve to solve problems with useful information (Yu et al., 2011).

However, the survey targeted both the new and the older generations of migrant workers. Unlike their older counterparts, the new generation is younger, better educated, more open-minded and receptive to novelties. Consequently, the new generation can be immensely shocked by various ideas circulating in the urban media environment after migration to cities, and impacted by their experience with media tools. They then make their selection and smooth away parts of the traditional rural mindset which are unfit for city life, before switching to the urban one.

First, the living environment will considerably shift following the rural-urban migration of the new generation of migrant workers. Due to years of rural life, they settle for the status quo and are less responsive to new ideas. By contrast, the values advocated by urban media are progressive and enterprising attitudes. With long-term infiltration of urban values, the group finds that their traditional mindset is shocked and challenged, gradually giving way to the new one which is fit for city life. During this process, their information awareness grows stronger.

Bin, a now 22-year-old native of Anhui province, has grown into a chef by starting as a busboy in a Western chain restaurant in Nantong at the age of 19. Without any formal training, he has been teaching himself Western cuisine cooking techniques, mainly by surfing online forums and watching videos in addition to consulting the restaurant's experienced chefs. His motivation to become a chef was inspired by a piece of TV news two years ago.

> It covered a scavenger who passed the self-study examinations for college just by reading in the spare time. If he could move up the social ladder through self-study, why wouldn't I realize my dream of becoming a chef in the same way?
>
> (Bin, male, from Anhui province)

Spurred on by the successful case, Bin began to believe that "knowledge can change one's life or fate" and embarked on a path towards his dream through self-study.

During the earlier days after their rural-urban migration, the new generation of migrant workers still falls prey to the outdated rural mindset. They are trapped in a mental burden, considering themselves incapable of improving themselves through useful information. Over recent years, mass media are increasingly interested in covering the new generation of migrant workers and other vulnerable groups, hence the growing number of reports on those self-made people. Those reported positive role models not only remove the psychological barrier but also expose new-generation migrant workers to the great power of knowledge and information, thus encouraging them to pursue more ambitious dreams with useful information. In addition to greater information awareness, the mass media offer them channels to access useful information. The channels include the Internet media, through which Bin has become knowledgeable about Western cuisine; newspaper columns on related issues; regular broadcast lectures, and TV programmes designed to popularize related knowledge for the new generation of migrant workers. Having perceived the media infiltration, they are motivated to improve their information awareness. Meanwhile, they acquire useful information through media and the information serves its purpose, which amounts to a reward. Such encouragement and reward combine to elevate the information awareness of the new generation of migrant workers.

Second, after the rural-urban migration, new-generation migrant workers not only come to know cities and access information through media, but also extend the possibilities of their life experiences. It is such personal experience that gradually awakens them to the importance of information and elevates their information awareness.

Most new-generation migrant workers are ingenuous and remain defensive rather than offensive. In a complex and dynamic urban society, they need to improve their information awareness and stay more alert. Zhou, a native of Henan province, has been in Shanghai for three years, but didn't become an Internet user until a year ago. As his colleagues told him that there were friend-making websites on the Internet, he began to go to the cybercafe just for striking up friendships and entertainment. Not long afterwards, he was defrauded on Baihe.com.[3]

> Baihe.com is crawling with tricksters, especially here in Shanghai. The sheer number of tricks in Shanghai, really boggles your mind, and I experienced all of them. I have accounts on Baihe.com and several other dating websites. Many girls living in urban districts made the first move and asked me out for meals within one week. In one case, the meal cost me over 4000 yuan, but my date disappeared without a trace the other day. She discarded her original QQ ID and changed her phone number, so I lost contact with her. With my luck, I didn't know she was a decoy. My friend was also tricked in a similar way.
>
> (Zhou, male, Henan province)

Zhou was fooled by a common trick. This type of defrauder, commonly known as a decoy, conspired with a restaurant where they invited their dates out for prohibitively expensive meals. For Zhou, 4000 yuan is a large sum of money, which can last him for more than a month. Having learned a lesson, Zhou took some countermeasures.

> Since then, I have only invited out those whose identity has been verified. After we decide the restaurant we will dine at, I'll search it online, for some other victims getting ripped off by decoys may expose those restaurants online. In doing so, I won't be taken in.
>
> (Zhou, male, Henan province)

Though he was ensnared in online dating, Zhou escaped sadder but wiser, for he learned to search information on the Internet so as not to fall for the same trick. This is a result of his enhanced information awareness. In fact, many of the newly arrived new-generation migrant workers fumble their way to enhance their information awareness. For instance, due to lack of information awareness, many just flip through the employment contracts, thus falling for the traps deliberately set by employers and having the legitimate rights hurt. As one of the vulnerable groups in cities, they learn the lessons the hard way and realize the importance of information. To stay immune to those tricks, they develop "self-protective" primary information awareness, which is significant for them to make a living in cities.

In addition to the ubiquitous infiltration and cultivation of urban media, the intent of the new generation of migrant workers is also a major force behind its information awareness enhancement. After the rural-urban migration, they are faced with various pressures to live, thrive, and communicate. Those stresses inevitably leave them exhausted and numb and prevent them from improving information awareness. However, stresses may also be a motivation. Many new-generation migrant workers proactively elevate their information awareness precisely because of their desire to improve living standards, find better jobs, or make good contacts with people of higher calibre.

Information awareness is progressively enhanced. The traditional mindset of new-generation migrant workers can't be changed overnight. However, in highly information-based cities, with their greater involvement in city life, interpersonal exchanges, and media reports, the traditional mindset is being impacted by new elements. After its transformation and reorganization, a new mindset emerges, enhancing their information awareness. Once the new generation of migrant workers develops sufficient information awareness, they will be prodded into acting on their initiative. In the process, their information literacy is greatly enhanced.

3.2 Making Use of Media Agendas to Acquire the Discourse Power

Compared with their older counterparts, new-generation migrant workers, with a stronger sense of dignity and desire to express themselves, are more eager to make their voices heard and gain recognition in the urban society. Over recent years, China has been increasingly concerned about the new generation of migrant workers. Against this backdrop, urban community and media gradually turn the spotlight on the new generation of migrant workers, and the group's difficulty in integration into cities is added to the agendas of city administrators and the media. These agendas amplified the voices made by new-generation migrant workers, encouraging them to speak up on urban media platforms. For those reasons, they acquire some power of discourse in cities.

First, the new generation of migrant workers begins to speak up on mass media platforms. Following the call of the Central Committee of the Communist Party of China (hereinafter called the CPC Central Committee) to focus on this group, migrant workers' appearances on CCTV Spring Festival Gala and other high-profile events emerge one after another. As some central media have transformed their stances on migrant workers, media of all sizes nationwide are following suit and strengthen their sense of social responsibility for vulnerable groups. They focus on the new generation of migrant workers on an unprecedented scale, and reshape the group's image with adjusted coverage tactics.

Huang is a native of Rugao, which is under the administration of Nantong City. As a taxi driver, he was troubled by natural gas replenishment. The problem wasn't solved until he complained to a journalist from *Jianghai Evening News* who happened to take his taxi.

> One day I drove a very talkative passenger. Among other things, he asked me about the latest chemical plant project. I wondered about his job. He told me he was a journalist from *Jianghai Evening News*. It occurred to me that it was a good opportunity to expose this issue in the newspaper to the government. So, I pointed out the scarcity of gas stations in Nantong and added that I only knew two. In one gas station, the peak time usually coincides with the change of our shift [when most drivers need to refill the car with gas]. The queue was so long that the streets were clogged, and the waiting time was at best half an hour and at worst, two hours! What's worse, out of eight fuel dispensers, only three were available. Did it make any sense? Why were the rest out of service when the drivers were waiting in long lines? Even though we asked for further fuel dispensers in service, they [the service providers at the gas station] said, "We could do nothing to help", for the person in charge wasn't there. What a ridiculous excuse! On top of everything else, taxi drivers were forced to give way to bus drivers. Isn't it crazy? Why were bus drivers superior when we both served passengers? At this rate, I would lose my job and carry passengers on my humble electric tricycle again. To my surprise, the journalist took my complaint very seriously. Having approached a high-ranking official in the local Traffic Management Bureau, he arranged a face-to-face conversation between me and the official and recorded the talk. Afterwards, the journalist told me the scarcity arrested the leadership's attention and would be covered by the press. Indeed, that gas station has truly improved, with all eight fuel dispensers in service. The only disappointment is bus drivers are still given priority. I've been keeping the journalist's phone number till now, and I know he is surnamed Shen. He is such a big help that I will contact him if necessary.
>
> (Huang, male, from Rugao City, Jiangsu province)

The survey also finds newspapers in Nantong set great store by average labourers and migrant workers to respond to CCTV's call to "reach out to the grassroots". For this reason, the new generation of migrant workers has more opportunities to speak out in the media. This is conducive to the development of information distribution awareness to reflect and solve problems through media. By contrast, *Nantong Daily* devoted little space to the new generation of migrant workers and other vulnerable groups. The chief reason is the commercialization craze that sweeps global media leads to growing demands for commercial interests in the industry. Therefore, greater orientation to the market is widely acknowledged in the media industry. The media coverage is mainly crammed with commercials of vehicles, property, cosmetics, delicacies, and so forth, a noticeable tendency to city life and bourgeois tastes. Groups on the fringe of society have little say, and few media are willing to listen to and voice the concerns of migrant workers (Ye & Wang, 2009). Nevertheless, following the CPC Central Committee's emphasis on the new generation of migrant workers, urban media attach increasing significance to this vulnerable group, who also acquires some power of discourse through media agendas.

Second, the new generation of migrant workers boasts greater power of discourse in the workplace. Work is the source of their incomes and the foundation of their survival. Only when guaranteed power of discourse and job security can they have the foothold to put roots in cities and voice their opinions regarding other fields.

In the wake of the CPC Central Committee's growing attention on the new generation of migrant workers, all media outlets nationwide immediately followed suit, with frequent coverage on the group. The media spotlighted many of the problems which migrant workers complained about and put them on the agenda. Their enhanced power of discourse on media platforms exerts pressure on business executives, who can no longer afford to exploit the group or turn a deaf ear to their sufferings and demands. Some enterprises' management have already taken active steps by lending an ear to their troubles and prioritizing their concerns.

In response to the call of the CPC Central Committee, Nantong and other small cities are actively working things out. Unsurprisingly, Guangzhou and other first-tier cities outperform those small cities. Ding is a TV maintenance technician in the Guangzhou-based Jinnuo Appliance Maintenance Company. He also repairs DVDs and VCDs when not occupied with TV maintenance assignments. Normally, Ding is tasked with a heavy workload, because he has to serve several households within a day. In some cases, he even brings broken TV sets back to the company for maintenance and returns them to the owners afterwards. At the age of 22, Ding already turns grey and appears older for his age. Obviously, his work is arduous. However, according to Ding, things have been much better after the Spring Festival holiday in 2013. The boss specifically lessened the burden on the company's migrant workers and offered some perks. Upon returning to work after the holiday, the boss gave each of the migrant workers red envelopes of 50 yuan and a bucket of cooking oil. Those gifts, though not so valuable, were unprecedented. Moreover, after the holiday, the boss organized a meeting with the migrant workers on their life and work and attached a suggestion box to the front gate. Ding once used this suggestion box to reveal a problem:

> Some parts for TV maintenance were often in shortage. It took so much time to apply for the replenishment of our stocks and I had to buy them for the company and claim back their cost, which was really time-consuming. However, after taking my suggestion into account, our company's approval procedure has truly been accelerated.
>
> (Ding, male, now working in Guangdong province)

The company where Ding works is predominated by young people, a majority of whom are migrant workers from Henan, Guangxi, and Hunan provinces.

Fairly speaking, the company is a meeting place for the new generation of migrant workers. To some extent, Ding's story is representative. As the new generation of migrant workers earns wide coverage from the media, many enterprises begin to value the group's concerns and legitimate rights. By seizing this opportunity, the group establishes a foothold in businesses and acquires some power of discourse.

In many ways, urban society is considerate of the new generation of migrant workers. There are migrant workers sections in the newspapers, purpose-built forums, websites, and job fairs for migrant workers. Even in large-scale gala evenings, migrant workers are invited to perform onstage. Given that, the issues confronting migrant workers have already been on the agenda of city administrators. If new-generation migrant workers seize the opportunity and take the initiative to the full by speaking their mind courageously, their voice will reverberate through the cities, and the group will gain increasing attention and recognition, thus obtaining more discourse power.

3.3 Making Use of Media: Extension of City Life Experience

Most new-generation migrant workers have never set foot in cities before their rural-urban migration. Consequently, they are inexperienced in city life and feel confused about media tools. However, following their ongoing involvement in city life and extension of city life possibilities, new-generation migrant workers will gradually learn to use the tools during their social inclusion, which in turn extends their city life possibilities. A virtuous circle thus comes into being.

First, traditional media outlets, including newspapers and televisions, remain the most frequently used media for the new generation of migrant workers. Such outlets are greatly helpful in their city life. Our interviews have revealed that new-generation migrant workers found jobs through recruitment advertisements in the newspapers. In comparison to newspapers, television sets are more influential to migrant workers. Some of the group will be most relaxed and content when watching TV on the bed after an exhausting workday.

Qu, a native of Guizhou province, works in Guangdong province. Unable to speak Cantonese, he was bitterly assailed by his poor work performance. Therefore, he was determined to have a good command of Cantonese. For more than a year, he has been watching Cantonese programmes and actively conversing with local Cantonese. Finally, he has become an excellent Cantonese speaker and can generally negotiate with clients in Cantonese directly.

> I turn on the TV as soon as I return home and have been watching Pearl Rivel Channel for years. As a fan of Manchester United, sometimes I change the channel to GDTV Sports for matches where the team competes and meanwhile listen to commentary in Cantonese. It's really interesting. For example, "Arsenal" and "Chelsea" in Cantonese have different pronunciations from those in Mandarin. Pearl River Channel runs Cantonese-speaking programmes only, including news broadcasting. However, there are subtitles at the bottom. In the beginning, the news was incomprehensible to me, so firstly

I watched with subtitles. Step by step, I could understand the news just by listening. Moreover, those talking with me in Cantonese corrected my wrong pronunciations in daily life. Gradually, I improved my oral ability.

(Mr Qu, male, from Liping County, Guizhou province)

The new generation of migrant workers can acquire more useful information through local TV programmes, just like Qu's case. For information collection, watching TV requires more initiative than reading newspapers but less than searching on the Internet. The Internet, TV, and newspapers are in descending order in terms of the amount of information the medium carries. However, the avalanche of information also renders the new generation of migrant workers tired and disoriented. By contrast, the TV strikes a balance between newspapers and the Internet. Therefore, new-generation migrant workers mainly consider TV the best medium, and most of their city life experience is directly related to TV programmes.

Second, the Internet is a force to be reckoned with. As is mentioned earlier, the new generation of migrant workers is easily disoriented by the jumble of online information. Nevertheless, the highly motivated migrant workers with sound judgment are undoubtedly the chief beneficiary of the Internet.

Born in the prefecture-level city of Zhaoqing in Guangdong province, the 24-year-old Jie has been working in Guangzhou City for more than four years and does administrative duties in a foreign trade company. She found her job through the Internet and has already been browsing recruitment advertisements online, usually on websites about job vacancies. Although she acknowledges how helpful human contacts are in job search, Jie believes in her own initiative most. In addition to the Internet, Jie thinks some news on social affairs is helpful in their day-to-day life. "For instance, it was reported that in Egypt a hydrogen-inflated balloon was exploded. Having read that, I bore in mind that I shall stay clear of dangerous activities in mid-air," said Jie. She also resorts to the Internet proactively. "I renew the Exit-Entry Permit for Travelling to and from Hong Kong and Macao online, and search for high-quality eye creams." To sum up, Jie is a frequent user of the Internet, through which she landed herself a job and has solved many other problems.

Therefore, most new-generation migrant workers have been skilled at searching the Internet for information. A large number of the migrant workers interviewed can keep abreast of the auto market and stock market, and job-hunt skilfully through the Internet. The Internet can be fairly perceived as new media in real terms that new-generation migrant workers are exposed to after the rural-urban migration. Before the migration, most of them had limited knowledge of the Internet, for the rural economy is undeveloped and the Internet media are more demanding in terms of reading, linguistic, and navigation abilities. After the migration, it's easy for new-generation migrant workers to find cybercafes and other places with Internet connections. In addition, steeped in city culture and recognizing the appeal of Internet media, they are eager to learn to use the Internet. Surfing online in spare time is a common occurrence among the new generation of migrant workers. They are receptive to new things and quick learners, and some know searching work-related technical information online. It's widely acknowledged among the group that the Internet can greatly enhance their cultural literacy and information literacy. To sum up, Internet information tools are a powerful weapon for new-generation migrant workers to extend their city life possibilities. Knowledge of the Internet is also a vastly important aspect of the group's information literacy.

Besides traditional mass media (e.g., TV and the Internet), other forms of media are also helpful. Chen from Hai'an County, who often found it difficult to decide everyday meals, makes up the mind more quickly after downloading an application named Meals for Today, which recommends delicious takeaways.

> After I shake the mobile phone, the recommended food will pop out. If the food doesn't suit my taste, I can shake the phone again for other options. The application can also recommend delicious food nearby and offer the telephone number of the restaurants for food delivery. It's very convenient.
>
> (Chen, male, from Hai'an county, Jiangsu province)

Lin from Xuzhou City found his phone bills often deducted for no reason. He consulted in a China Mobile business hall, and it turned out China Mobile subscribed to this service on his behalf without his permission. "I didn't need this traffic data at all. My friend told me that I could check my bills via online business halls, which would save me the trip. From then on, I have been checking the phone bills online."

For Qu, the first Cantonese sentence he understood was from the bus stop announcer system in Guangdong:

> Please get ready if you want to get off and be watchful when the door is open; China has been traditionally extolling the virtues of respecting the elders and caring for the young. Please offer the seat to those in need.
>
> (Qu, male, working in Guangdong province)

Public transportation is among the most frequently used urban medium for the new generation of migrant workers after the rural-urban migration. Taking the bus or subway is their prime choice when they commute, travel, or run errands. When freshly arriving in cities, the new generation of migrant workers, hamstrung by the lingering traditional mindset, may not try some new media of their own accord. However, public transportation is inevitable in city life, through which they may grasp local dialects, or are updated on local events from bus TVs. As public transportation is categorized as a public sphere, it's more noteworthy that the passengers include not only the new generation of migrant workers but also other city dwellers. In such a tiny space, the new generation of migrant workers is more likely to communicate with city dwellers. Whether the communication is a one-way or two-way process, the new generation of migrant workers can acquire useful information and develop skills in the process, even just by listening to the conversations among city dwellers. Although the learning process in such medium space is passive, the impact on their life in the long run can be astonishing.

Zhou, Lin, and Qu are the most typical representatives of the new generation of migrant workers. Most of the group extend their city life possibilities through media information tools: practical phone applications make their lives more convenient; group buying websites slash their recreational expenses; ATMs spare them the trouble of queuing when they withdraw money. Though those media tools are commonplace for city dwellers, the new generation of migrant workers can't feel at home with them without ongoing exploration, discovery, and learning. To their eyes, even signs in the shopping mall are helpful, as the signs allow them to locate the toilets quickly.

To sum up, new-generation migrant workers gradually enhance their information literacy and extend their city life possibilities by seeking and learning information tools in daily life and in the workplace. The extension, therefore, increases their utilization of information tools. Such a virtuous circle brings about a constant stream of the impetus for their adaptation to city life.

4. An Extension of the Physical Body: Information Literacy as Adaptive Capital

By enhancing information literacy after the rural-urban migration, new-generation migrant workers gradually adapt themselves to city life. Along this journey, they have experienced the unlocking of the information environment, but are faced with inevitable information barriers. Over time, supported by subjective and objective factors, some of them manage to scale the information wall and navigate the city's information space smoothly. In fact, the complicated and challenging process is designed solely to improve their adaptation to city life. Meanwhile, for the new generation of migrant workers, adaptation to city life is a massive social project, primarily affected by their personal finances, cultural literacy, mindset, and even political awareness. Notably, information literacy, which our research pivots around, is undoubtedly another indispensable part.

It's highly effective to transform information literacy to adaptive capital to facilitate the urban adaptation and social inclusion of the new generation of migrant workers. First, information literacy enhancement contributes to the accumulation of human resources. Growing information literacy raises their awareness of self-learning and improves their ability to search, discriminate, and analyse professional information, thus accumulating human capital. Second, information literacy enhancement increases social capital. By enhancing their information literacy, new-generation migrant workers consciously broaden their horizons or read the latest news through newspapers, the Internet, and other media platforms. With those topics, they strike up daily conversations with their existing friends and enter the circles of a higher calibre.

The information literacy enhancement of new-generation migrant workers adds to their human capital and social capital, which then improves their sense of identity. Once their human capital and social capital accumulate at a great speed, new-generation migrant workers will see self-improvement across the board, ranging from finances to cultural literacy to professionalism and moral standards. Due to this progress and media reports, the new generation of migrant workers is increasingly more urban than rural.

Media are always helpful alongside the endeavours of new-generation migrant workers to break through the information barrier, scale the information wall, and enhance their information literacy. New-generation migrant workers with higher-level information literacy want more than information or entertainment from the media. Instead, they consider the media indispensable for adaptation to city life. When information literacy development is realized through media, those with higher-level information literacy, by leveraging the affordances of various media, convert their information literacy adaptive capital (e.g., human capital and social capital), thus enhancing their adaptation to city life.

If the new generation of migrant workers uses the media merely for information collection or as a window onto city life, they will end up living in a pseudo-environment represented by the media rather than experiencing real city life. If the media are a stepping stone for new-generation migrant workers to watch from a distance the city life outside the wall, then utilization of the media as instruments allows them to scale the wall and experience city life personally. This is a shift from observation to experience or, more precisely, a shift from fantasy to substance. Such utilization has become a catalyst for the new generation of migrant workers to convert information literacy to adaptive capital. Whoever in the group realizes the connection can make great strides in adaptation to city life, as long as they proactively use media to live and thrive in cities rather than merely for diversion.

Notes

1 Translator's note: a famous real estate property in many Chinese cities with a wide array of recreational offerings.
2 Translator's note: according to Wikipedia, urban villages are villages that appear on both the outskirts and the downtown segments of major Chinese cities. As a unique phenomenon that formed part of China's urbanization efforts, they are surrounded by skyscrapers, transportation infrastructures, and other modern urban constructions.
3 Translator's note: China's first major dating website.

References

Tao, J., & Xu, H. (2012). Personal modernity and interpersonal communication of the new generation of migrant workers – An empirical study based on survey data in Shanghai. *Journalistic University*, *1*, 80–86+108.

Wen, Y. (2011). *Research on the status of information contact and urban integration of the migrant workers in two different residential models*, Doctoral Dissertation. Central South University.

Yang, Y. (2012). Internet media literacy of the new generation of migrant workers. *Journal of China Institute of Industrial Relations*, *2*, 81–85.

Ye, J., & Wang, Y. (2009). The media "discourse" missing in the process of migrant workers entering the city of and its reconstruction. *Chongqing Social Sciences, 10*, 37–40.

Yu, S., et al. (2011). Empirical study on information demand of migrant workers in Guangdong province. *Journal of South China Agricultural University (Social Science Edition), 3*, 67–71.

Zhu, L., Zhao, L., & Wu, J. (2010). Half-initiative pattern vs. constructive pattern: Social adaptation patterns of the new generation of the migrant workers. *Journal of Gansu Administration Institute, 4*, 4–10, 126.

7 The Media as Capital

Continuing Education Among the New Generation of Migrant Workers

Unlike their parents, the new generation of migrant workers is a group "bathing in the spring breeze of a new era". Since the reform and opening up, the improvement of China's modernization has enabled them to receive higher-level education and enjoy a better living and growing environment. It is natural for them to have a higher employment expectation and more robust demand for self-development. Although most of them are still working in manufacturing, services, and construction industries, the proportion of the former two is on the rise, while the latter is on the decline. It can be observed that higher requirements for jobs and labour environment have been added. On the other hand, working away from native homes is no longer a reluctant choice to make a humble living. Instead, they now tend to take self-development and personal dreams into more consideration, hoping to "improve one's ability and learn a useful skill".

Constrained by poor economic conditions, limited social resources, and narrow space for growth, new-generation migrant workers usually find it difficult to obtain diversified and high-quality learning opportunities in urban society. To a large extent, they are confined to the survival and development mode of the older generation, inheriting the traditional skills of their predecessors. Growing up in this environment, they also tend to engage in low-skilled production for the sole purpose of surviving. This is extremely unfavourable to their adaptation and integration into the ever-evolving and unpredictable urban society. At this point, providing convenient and easily accessible channels or learning opportunities for their self-development is the top priority in facilitating their urban adaption and social inclusion.

1. From the Village to the City: The Awakening of Ongoing Intellectual Growth

From the village to the city, the spatial movement means more than the transfer of geographical location. It also includes the resetting of the whole living environment and lifestyle, which further leads to changes in the psychological perceptions and concepts of the new generation of migrant workers. They often embark on the journey with beautiful fantasies about the city, but feel lost in front of real urban life. The repetitive work, the mediocre and uninteresting life,

DOI: 10.4324/9781003365785-7

the difficulties of surviving, and the trust crisis in the urban society make these migrant workers, who have left their hometowns and land, face severe challenges of survival all the time. The double pressure of adaptation and promotion forces them to seek available social support and resources, during which they began to realize the necessity of improving their skills. Being aware of the importance of learning, they start to strive for self-development.

1.1 Mobility Dilemma: The Survival Challenge After Leaving Home and Land

Before the journey from the countryside to the city, the young migrant workers generally have an incredible vision of the modern metropolis and feel the joy of being free from the control and discipline of their families and enjoying true "independence" and "freedom". However, those beautiful fantasies gradually diminish in the modern urban landscape, and the freshness and joy of entering the city are dissipated under the severe survival challenges and heavy living pressure.

Yang, a 28-year-old man who comes from the countryside of Chongqing, is now a chef in Nanjing, the capital city of Jiangsu province. When he graduated from vocational school as a young man, he got a job in Wuxi City in Jiangsu province. He describes his excitement about the first actual departure from Chongqing to the long-awaited metropolis.

> I was pretty silly at that time, Beijing's skyscrapers on the television seemed particularly inviting. Our first night in Kunshan was totally sleepless. Travelling by boat, we spent the whole night thinking about the high salary and good job. That feeling was good.
>
> (Yang, male, from Chongqing)

However, the harsh reality dealt a heavy blow to the hopeful man. With the presupposition of working as a welder after graduation, he was disappointed to find out that he was only assigned to make radiative electronic boards in the factory. After the rigorous military training, this monotonous and uninteresting work made him feel a sense of disillusionment and depression. Novices like him are not allowed to take the actual technical work in the factory; they are not permitted to make use of the key equipment either. Therefore, they could only do some odd jobs. Such a boring life and humdrum landscape in the factory completely shattered his colourful fantasies, and he was gripped by unspeakable disappointment and pessimism all day long. In fact, Yang's psychological transformation reflects the change of most new generation migrant workers' perception of the city. The bright and glamorous urban images created by mass media in rural areas form their unrealistic illusions about urban life, which are ruthlessly disillusioned by reality after they enter the city. In the repetition of monotonous labour and production, they see no self-value and hope for the future.

Nevertheless, the dilemma faced by Yang is more of psychological cognitive dislocation, a gap between psychological expectation and harsh reality. For young workers who have left their hometowns and started empty handed, they are mostly struggling to survive, worrying more about the realistic problems of how to settle down in the city, how to find a job and a place to live, how to earn money. For them, the first priority in the city is to manage to scrape together a living with no relatives and money.

Working in a cafe in Nanjing, Bai has experienced such an arduous and tortuous adventure of survival. For him, leaving his hometown of Linxia, Gansu province, was an unwilling choice. The failure of his father's investment in wooden furniture led to a sharp decline in the family's economic conditions, and the sudden change forced this thoughtful young man to take up the burden of his family overnight, giving up his studies and going out on his own. Therefore, at the age of 16, Bai dropped out of high school and left his familiar hometown with just over 100 yuan in his pocket. His arrival in Nanjing began in total isolation, so he could only find an Internet cafe near the train station. From then on, he ran around for a job and a place to live during the day, and rested his tired body in an Internet cafe at night. It was an excruciating period when his heart was full of fear and anxiety about the unknown future, but he never complained to his family lest they would worry. He could only bear it on his own. He said that insomnia and homesickness were almost part of his everyday life, and of course, he had thought about giving up. Regardless, he gritted his teeth and pulled through. Fortunately, he was rewarded for his efforts, and life did not disappoint him. After such a difficult struggle to survive, Bai has found a good job and successfully settled down in the city.

In traditional rural societies, everything is done on a family basis. New-generation migrant workers who are barely engaged in any agricultural work often move to the city once their studies are interrupted. Therefore, they are, on the one hand, still young and cannot cope with life independently; on the other hand, they grow up under the shelter of their families and have no experience in dealing with life affairs. After entering the city, the young and ignorant migrant workers are completely separated from the care of their families and the protection of the rural acquaintance society. Basically, they are fighting alone in an unfamiliar city. In addition to that, this fast-changing technological society determines information, knowledge, and technology to be the basis for a settled life and development in the city. So, it is only natural that new-generation migrant workers, who have neither education nor skills, can hardly get satisfying jobs in the competitive environment. At the same time, separated from the shelter of their families and the protection of traditional rural customs and institutions, they are just like the rootless "duckweed", feeling a strong sense of anxiety and uncertainty under the pressure of survival. This is precisely the fundamental characteristic of the highly modernized Chinese urban society and the inevitable experience for the new generation of migrant workers to become modern urbanites.

Chinese society is undergoing a transition from a society of acquaintances to a society of strangers, where anonymity and superficiality are the essential features of interpersonal relationships, resulting in indifference and a general lack of social trust. With the increasing frequency of interaction with urbanites and the urban environment as well as their accumulated life experiences in the city, this feature is gradually exposed to the new generation of migrant workers, which can be found in their extreme distrust of urban society. Therefore, they feel that there are traps and crises everywhere after the break of acquaintance society's principle of interaction based on the premise of trust. Accordingly, their sense of alienation and vigilance towards the city is manifested in all aspects of finding jobs and making friends. This is the price the migrant workers must pay to integrate into modern society, and it is also the reality they have to face after the departure of the rural society. As Giddens (1988) once put it, "Modernity is a risk culture". In the fast-changing metropolis, the new generation of migrant workers encounters unprecedented helplessness and profound anxiety. This sense of crisis also stimulates them to make further changes and efforts in order to survive.

1.2 Living in the City: Facing the Double Pressure of Urban Adaptation and Self-improvement

In addition to the pressure of survival, new-generation migrant workers also face serious problems such as how to find a suitable and satisfying job, how to be comfortable at work, and how to take advantage of the fierce competition in the workplace. On the one hand, they need a job to adapt to the city life and settle down through their efforts; on the other hand, finding a job is not the end of the story: excellent professional skills are also needed to excel in their own work, to gradually climb up the ladder from the initial work and seize the opportunity for their career development.

Facing the double pressure of urban adaptation and self-improvement, new-generation migrant workers realize the necessity of reliable support and resources to avoid the fear and insecurity brought by the crisis of modernity. The first step to survive is to get a job. Generally speaking, the traditional interpersonal network based on blood and local ties are the first to provide the needed support and resources. Hua, a 23-year-old young man who comes from Anhui province and is now an apprentice in a famous barbershop chain in Nanjing, has been in the city for six years. He used to be a high school student who did not like to study, and his mind was occupied with the desire of "venturing into the world". So, he turned to his brother in Nanjing, the owner of the barber store, when the latter was hiring new employees.

Yin, from Zaozhuang, Shandong province, is working as an assembler in a high-end restaurant in Nanjing's Zifeng Building. In 2007, he left for Suzhou, but the weary work there was too much for him to bear. So, he went to his relatives in Nanjing and got the current job with the help of a friend, and he commented as follows.

> We mainly rely on our friends to find jobs these days, because they are more trustworthy. And as the [social] circle gets bigger, there are more friends getting around, so they will take us to new jobs when they get promoted.
>
> (Yin, male, from Zaozhuang, Shandong province)

This suggests the critical role of the accumulation of contacts to new-generation migrant workers in their job-seeking. Their reliance on acquaintances can also be explained by the fact that this circle is easier to enter and integrate, without being marginalized by unfamiliar people.

Such a way of finding a job is pervasive among migrant workers. Although they have become less dependent on relationships, especially blood and local ties, compared with their senior counterparts, their perceptions are still influenced by rural culture and traditional interpersonal relationships. Therefore, at the early stage of urban life, a phenomenon of seeking survival by reproducing primary relationship networks appears. As such, they mainly rely on primary group relations to obtain information about work and urban life.

However, acquaintances cannot solve all the problems faced by migrant workers in the risky modern city. On the one hand, the primary circle of new generation migrant workers is characterized by small size, great closeness, strong convergence, and low heterogeneity (Feng, 2011). Such relational resources are necessary for them to obtain basic survival information and low-level adaptation at the early stage. Nevertheless, these resources will gradually fail to meet their demands as their experiences grow and development needs increase. On the other hand, relying entirely on local and blood relations may sometimes result in one-sidedness, which will greatly increase the employment and survival risks of these workers. What's more, in a society full of strangers and lack of trust, the reliability of such relationships will also be significantly reduced.

For example, Fei, a young girl from Chuzhou, Anhui province, went to Shanghai to help in her brother and sister-in-law's printing store as soon as she graduated from junior high school. Although her work was easy and simple, she had been bored over time and realized that complete freedom was impossible when living with family members. Eventually, she went to Nanjing with her fellow villagers and decided to find a job on her own.

In addition to finding job opportunities and adapting to the urban working environment, professional self-improvement is also a crucial important step for the new generation of migrant workers. Only in this way can they get promotion and gain a firm foothold in the city. Bai, the aforementioned young barista, also bears tremendous pressure and hardships in the city before he formally enters the coffee industry. He initially searched for employment information on the Internet, but the high recruitment standards made him realize that there were few opportunities for people like him. Those who possess neither education background nor skills could only serve as a busboy or waiter. Based on such information, he tried some stores but received no offer because of his young age and inadequate experiences. Fortunately, an Internet cafe owner took the initiative to help, so he got his first job: a floral arranger at a flower store in Jiangning District, Nanjing. However, the low salary of 600 yuan a month could hardly satisfy him, so he looked for other job opportunities in between flower deliveries. Later on, he worked hard in a Cantonese restaurant. He also set up his own stall to sell things like slippers, watches, and trinkets before he was appreciated by the owner of this coffee shop, thus entering the coffee industry.

That was how he found his real interest and career development, and resolved to make achievements in this field.

As such, the new generation of migrant workers with a high willingness to develop and a desire to improve themselves, can hardly learn anything or adapt to the urban competition if they only depend on traditional interpersonal relationships to acquire knowledge, skills, and experience. Therefore, they start to look for more supporting resources. That's how the mass media and new media, standing out with open information and easy access, gradually become their primary choice in adapting to urban life and work and improving their knowledge and literacy level.

All in all, new-generation migrant workers, the same as all other citizens in the modern society, face the "individualistic crisis" (Beck, 2004), which is what the German sociologist Beck (2004) called the risk of making their own decisions and taking their responsibility. In this process, they gradually become aware of the adverse effects of over-reliance on relationships and turn to the support of urban media and communication systems. This is a shift beyond interpersonal relations and an evocation of modernity accompanied by the awakening of crisis consciousness.

1.3 "I Need to Study": An Awakening of Self-learning Consciousness

Challenged by the severe pressure of survival and adaptation, new-generation migrant workers gradually feel the need to improve themselves. The city is an ideal destination for these workers who are devoid of independent working and living experiences to "go out and broaden their horizon". Unlike the older generation of migrant workers, earning money is no longer the only pursuit. They now think highly of self-development. They wish to master useful skills to make a better life and develop themselves. However, facing the hurdles of urban society, they are also aware of their deficiencies in various aspects.

Bai, the barista mentioned earlier, felt frustrated when looking for a job. When he first arrived in Nanjing, he searched for a job through the Internet. The wide range of job information made him feel desperate: "There is a lot of information on the Internet, recruiting chefs, waiters, everything. However, those with a low threshold cannot satisfy me, while all the good ones have requirements to enter." All the chefs, for example, are required to have several years of work experience, and be good at cutting or carving. These are all conditions he failed to meet. He also mentioned a particular experience of witnessing a girl who failed several interviews in external recruitment tearing up her resume. At that very moment, he felt very lost. "I once had that feeling too, feeling pity to pick up some low threshold jobs, but unable to get into good companies." While getting disappointed, he realized the necessity to learn. Stuck between expectation and reality, and fuelled by the reference of recruitment information and self-esteem, he understood that learning skills are the prerequisite of urban life. But what to learn and how to learn became real problems for many migrant workers like him.

Similarly, Yang, the chef mentioned earlier, followed his classmates and learnt to be an electrician, only to find later that the work was not suitable for him. So, he left Chongqing and came to Nanjing where his mother worked. At that time, his mother told him that mastering a skill is a must for better development here. So initially, considering the prevailing use of computers in the city, he wanted to become a computer technician with his basic knowledge in this regard. Later, he was enlightened by a comment from a chef friend of his mother, who thought that being a chef is a promising job since there would be one day when people get richer and prefer to dine out rather than eat at home. These words offered hope, so Yang made up his mind to become a chef. When choosing where to learn, he thought of the TV advertisement of the New Oriental Cuisine School, so he learned some more information about the course through newspapers and websites. Feeling good after a thorough understanding, he finally enrolled in a three-year (tuition totalling 20,000 yuan) all-around class with great enthusiasm.

Yang was greatly influenced by the TV commercials when choosing the chef school. At the same time, he said that while it was those urban experiences from his mother and town fellow that solidified his idea of learning to be a chef, he figured out exactly who to learn from and what to learn only by the ads of the training school. Although the impact of the media is not as powerful as a magic bullet, sometimes it (especially TV commercials) can subconsciously influence or even sway people's choices. Therefore, for the new generation of migrant workers, training advertisements of that kind on TV are indeed prompting their shortcomings, stimulating their needs, and triggering their potential learning consciousness.

Some other migrant workers suffer from the lack of craftsmanship when they begin their work at the lower level. Some of them start at the bottom of apprenticeship; some wash hair for several years before becoming a junior barber; some are engaged in the service industry with high turnover rates, earning low income while facing the contempt of the public and difficulties prompted by customers. So, as their age and experience grows, their desire to master a skill or tool becomes clearer and more apparent.

Twenty-eight-year-old Chen is currently working as an electrician in a company in Shanghai, and is responsible for the management and maintenance of the company's plumbing and electrical work. Although he's already a sophisticated worker with more than ten years' experience, he could not help sighing at the mention of the initial struggle. In 2002, this 17-year-old teenager followed others to work as an unskilled labourer on the construction site. In 2003, he went to an electronics factory in Shenzhen, working up to 14 hours a day with a salary of only 700 yuan.

> In 2003, 700 yuan meant a lot to a man without any skills, and my wage only increased by over 100 yuan after another half year. I worked in the electronics factory for a year and a half, then went to another factory, Longhua Foxconn. That was exhausting work which required the worker to stand 12 hours a day with only a one-hour meal break. By 2005, I really couldn't do it anymore, realizing that doing this for life would not work. In 2006, I went back home

and signed up for the Shangqiu Technical School, learning electrical integration. All I thought about at that time was learning some skills, or else I could only be a common labourer, and that was definitely a dead-end.

(Chen, male, from Henan province)

In addition, a few migrant workers have strong foresight and high learning consciousness. The insufficient education in childhood contributes to a strong willingness and tireless practice of further study in the process of going out to work. Zhou, who has a vibrant life experience, is a typical example of this kind. This 34-year-old man, a native of Fushan, Jiangxi province, is a freshman in the adult education class of Nanjing Normal University. Having missed the college entrance exam, also known as Gaokao, he was always yearning for the atmosphere on campus where students can study with no interruption.

My parents couldn't provide me with any guidance; they don't even know the answers themselves. I would love to have someone successful as my role model, but such a person is nowhere to be found. So I accept training at school where I receive formal and systematic education.

For this reason, he has never stopped learning during years out in the world.

Thus, in such a melting pot of rich information and people from all walks of life, the new generation of migrant workers has realized that learning a trade is a necessary ability to survive in the city. The mass media and the Internet, in this regard, play an essential role as catalysts, providing a reference for these workers to survive. In this reference system, they are either stimulated by the information of job recruitment or influenced by the overwhelming advertisements, thus leading to the awakening of their potential learning consciousness and urging them to make great efforts.

2. From Training to Self-Study: Obtaining Multi-Channel Ongoing Learning Resources

The individual is active in learning because he feels the need to learn and sees a personal purpose that could be achieved through learning. And the reason why he tries his best to use all available resources (including teachers and books) is that he considers them as relevant to his needs and purposes (Knowles, 1989). Putting it another way, to achieve a certain purpose, the learner will employ various channels and methods to obtain the appropriate resources. Compared to the rural areas with comparatively blocked information and underdeveloped education, the urban environment is characterized by highly developed media and abundant education and training resources. In reality, the learning of migrant workers in the city mainly includes the following ways and forms: first, the organizational way, including continuing education and work-based learning and training; second, the apprenticeship way, that is, learning in the form of traditional apprenticeship; third, independent learning, including self-study by using various media tools and mutual learning through interpersonal communication. Such study, including both formal training and informal learning, is a dynamic, complex, and constantly evolving process.

2.1 Systematic Learning: Formal Training at the Organizational Level

Systematic learning mainly refers to acquiring work information and improving ability through training in formal or informal organizations. It is an option for a small group of new generation migrant workers to improve themselves, especially for work preparation.

Yang, the chef mentioned previously, participated in several kinds of training before he took a job in the city. Having received both secondary school education in his hometown and training courses in the New Oriental Cuisine School, he had a great say in this regard. He learned to be a chef at the New Oriental in Nanjing, choosing a three-year all-around class with a college degree. According to Yang, the first six months were mainly spent learning knife skills, the next year and a half learning how to cook, ending with an internship assignment. This systematic learning brought him down to the gate.

> Learning still brings some benefits, and those basic skills certainly speed up the cooking process. For example, I can roughly picture a dish only by its name. Those braised dishes, for instance, have a similar colour and look. People who are devoid of such knowledge may be blind to all these and find it completely unimaginable. It is necessary to grasp basic skills such as knife work or turning the pot.
>
> (Yang, male, from Chongqing)

Yang's satisfaction with his technical school experience was delivered through his words. With its institutionalized management and well-developed education system, the training school makes the acquisition of knowledge more convenient and complete. After systematic learning, new-generation migrant workers have acquired more solid skills and a stronger ability to apply knowledge and accept new skills. At the same time, thanks to the training school's model of supplying the education market while providing job-seeking assistance, it would not be a problem for migrant workers to find their first job. Moreover, holding a certification from formal training schools, these migrant workers are quicker to get the hang of their jobs than those who have not received systematic training. For that reason, they are easily preferred by employers when they try to find a job. In addition, as a modern social organization that disseminates information in a purposeful and systematic way, training institutions serve as a window to urban society and a bridge to real life for young migrant workers who have just left school and entered the city.

Yang also said that knowledge could be gained as long as you work hard. While teachers finish their parts, learning or not is students' own choice. He also stressed that students in the school must please the master (teacher), or they will miss some important knowledge. Despite the fact that a training school resembles a miniature society, they can make genuine friends at the training school. Many of his current friends come out of the same training school. This shows that new-generation migrant workers can meet all kinds of people and have a prior experience of complicated urban interpersonal communication in the training institution, thus building up contacts for later urban survival. Additionally, the one-to-many teaching model in the training school also makes them realize that one's efforts and initiatives play a crucial role in modern society.

Zhu, a 16-year-old girl, is currently studying pastry at New Oriental Cuisine School in Jiangsu province.

> I have learned how to make cakes and 60 or so pastry, and the teacher also taught some other skills, such as making the image of the Chinese zodiacal animals. The teaching building is divided into chef and pastry trainings, with the latter in the downstairs and the other at the left. The first floor serves a one-year program, and all the two-year students are taught upstairs. If you sign up for the two-year course, you will pass the preliminary test in the first half of the year, then take the intermediate test after graduation, and the advanced test after another three years. But if you choose the one-year program, you could only graduate with the primary certificate, then wait three years to take the intermediate test, and another three years for the advanced. The one-year program is similar to ours, including both Chinese and Western pastry, yet it includes less courses than the two-year program containing sugar art, flipping sugar, and many other skills.
>
> (Zhu, female, from Changzhou, Jiangsu province)

Zhu has planned to leave for Shanghai to learn Western cooking, get the advanced certificate after finding a job, and get the certification for cake designers. Although Zhu is still young, she already has a specific plan for her future, trying to develop her career through learning and training.

In his seminal work *Becoming Modern*, the American sociologist Alex Inkeles noted the role of modern organizations such as schools in guiding people towards modernization. According to him, apart from the course-based formal education, people become modern through many activities in schools, including reward and punishment, setting examples, modelling, and generalization (Inkeles & Smith, 1992). However, the current training system in China is relatively imperfect, especially for migrant workers. Some people say that many skill-based implicit knowledge cannot be acquired in technical schools and the knowledge learnt at training schools cannot come into full play in the work place. As Yang puts it, considering that teachers have different teaching attitudes and varying levels, it depends a lot on the students themselves, or even on the traditional sense of relationships. It takes a lot of self-discipline to learn the crafts and skills, otherwise it would be a waste of time and money. In addition, we find that some other migrant workers don't have the option to go to training institutions for further study due to their family economic status and their conditions, so they will choose to receive on-the-job training in a specific workplace.

The barista Bai mentioned earlier quit his job as a store manager in order to participate in on-the-job training. He started as a trainee at the Carving Time Cafe, which is famous for its training programs. In his opinion, he is in an industry with a lot of technical flexibility and room for development, so he had to keep abreast of the latest trend. His study at Carving Time turned out to be very useful. He was able to learn everything he wanted to, such as how to manage the staff, how to run a store, and his coffee-making skills were also improved under the guidance of the master.

> In our industry, the Carving Time is the best in terms of its management, and there is this branch in Nanjing located at the Confucius Temple. The militarized management and services ensure quality, and the tuition of 100,000 yuan is really worth it. My master told me that it was good to learn there, and I did so after I graduated. I learnt a lot there, knowing about all kinds of good machines and getting along well with everyone. It was really an eye-opener.
>
> (Bai, male, from Linxia, Gansu province)

Bai, who is doing an excellent job in the industry, has a clear goal of study and self-development. In his opinion, on-the-job training is a kind of learning. Just like him, many other migrant workers choose this way to further develop themselves. Workplaces are considered as a more implicit organizational resource, since what they provide is different from formal technical schools, and is more of practical exercise. The access to information and resources lies in the interaction with the work environment and people. Whether migrant workers can obtain the right learning resources for themselves is contingent on the attributes of the industry in which they are engaged and their willingness to accept new things as well as their ability of self-discipline and adaptation to their surroundings.

2.2 Learning From a Master: Relationship-based Resource Development

For both the older and new generation of migrant workers, relationships remain as their most trustworthy information-gathering channels in the city. When entering an industry or preparing to learn some new skills, most migrant workers seek advice and essential information from their friends and relatives engaged in related industries.

Take Hua from Anhui as an example. Before entering the hairstyling industry, he learned the basics from his brother. Due to the kindred relationship, he could work as an apprentice in his brother's store without going to hairstyling school. Therefore, it can be seen that whether there is a network of relationships available in the city can affect migrant workers' choice of learning methods. Yang, who went to a technical school, expressed his slight regret in the interview. He felt that if his mother's chef friend had found out about the job opportunity at the Jinling Hotel earlier, he might not have gone to study at the New Oriental school.

> If you know someone, you could be taught in the real world, which means you can work with income while learning something without paying the tuition. But if there's no such person out there to teach you, school is your only choice. Moreover, there are things you cannot learn at school. Take carving as example, the master will only teach you the most basic method, and it is only when you get on good terms with him, will he teach more advanced skill of dragon-carving.
>
> (Yang, male, from Chongqing)

Bobo, a 19-year-old young man who has been working in Nanjing for just one year, loves to hang out with like-minded friends. At such a young age, he has some vague but unique ideas about the future, even though detailed plans are yet to be developed. He attaches particular importance to friends in the outside world. Hanging out in his friends' stores a lot, he has developed a certain understanding and interest in the barbering industry, thus intending to learn to cut hair. Thanks to the recommendation of a friend who is the acquaintance of a barbershop owner, he is allowed to learn there in the second half of the year. The store is quite good, and it saves money for school. What's more, he can be looked after by his friends. When asked what is the most important thing to gain a foothold in the city, he said straight away:

> Friends, of course! One cannot get along without help from friends. We should make more friends. The most significant change after I came to Nanjing is the growing number of friends. Friends make my life tasteful; being rich with no friends around is meaningless. A friend once introduced me to the decoration business, but I refused because I was not interested.
>
> (Bobo, male, from Bengbu, Anhui province)

Similar interview data lead us to understand that the new generation of migrant workers prefers to learn crafts from their acquaintances. This is because people they know impart not only explicit knowledge but also a lot of tacit knowledge. Michael Polanyi, a British scholar, once categorized knowledge into explicit and tacit knowledge. The former refers to a kind of specific, systemic, and normative knowledge, which can be understood as knowing what it is. The latter contains some latent knowledge of the industry that is generally unspeakable and needs to be acquired through practical exercise of how to do it (Cheng, 2012). For new-generation migrant workers who have just gained a foothold in the city, they are engaged in industries with high requirements of skills and crafts, so the amount of mastered latent knowledge also determines their abilities to survive and develop in the city. Therefore, they should not only learn skills but also be familiar with the tricks of mastering skills, and, more importantly, they must understand the relevant background and even the inside stories. In this regard, face-to-face interpersonal communications can quickly meet these requirements and provide useful assistance.

In general, there are two main ways for new generation migrant workers to make use of relationship resources for training and learning. One way is to learn from people with higher qualifications and richer experiences in the industry. The other way is to communicate with their co-workers or heterogeneous groups of peers. The most typical example of the first way is to find a master or supervisor to teach them step by step, which is commonly seen in cooking, hairdressing, beauty, and other service industries. For instance, Li, a 22-year-old chef from Anhui province, has been working in Nantong, a city in Jiangsu province, for six years, starting from the miscellaneous work. He comes into contact with a lot of people, mainly colleagues, and is now learning from his most admired "head stove" (nickname), who is the head chef. This seasoned chef often gives him tips on how to cook and make sauces, and Li is grateful for that.

Unlike professional training at the organizational level, people engaged in apprenticeship often acquire vocational skills without having to pay the tuition. They usually start from the basics, and then grasp a comprehension of the work, and further touch the cornerstone through hands-on practices, hence mastering the required vocational skills. Ah Long is a 22-year-old native of Xuzhou, Jiangsu province. He is now working on car decoration in Suzhou, another city in Jiangsu province. When he first started working with his uncle as an employment agent, he had the feeling that such work couldn't last long. He wanted to learn a trade, to master a skill. Therefore, when one of his friends who studies auto decoration introduced him to an auto repair store, he became an apprentice and learned auto decoration step by step. In this process, the store owner, embodying a channel of organizational communication, played a vital role in the instruction of skills.

Judging from the preceding cases, the hierarchical relationship is beneficial to the new generation of migrant workers in terms of improving their professional skills and gaining information. As these "superiors" have been in the city for a long time, their life experiences could be taken as references, by which migrant workers lay the foundation for their adaptation to urban life. Therefore, the mode of learning from masters with the help of a relationship network is also a right path to acquire professional skills and broaden their career development space.

2.3 Self-learning: Channel Expansion in the Urban Communication Environment

When new-generation migrant workers enter the city, they spend most of their time working. Due to the long working hours and few number of acquaintances, they rarely have extra time, money, and energy to attend formal or informal training. However, living in an increasingly competitive city, they long to seek self-development instead of abandoning themselves, so they choose to improve their abilities in all aspects, especially their employability, through self-learning.

In this process, various forms of media have become their main independent learning channels due to low cost and fewer restrictions of time and space. Liang, a 23-year-old girl, graduated from a technical secondary school. She comes from Zhaoqing, Guangdong province. She has been working in human resources in the provincial capital city of Guangzhou for three years. In her spare time, she often reads newspapers, and she learns from local newspapers about the industry conditions in recent years and relevant policies promulgated by the government. She considers it a helpful guide to their human resource planning. Li, the chef mentioned in the previous text, also reads food magazines to learn about the trendy dishes and other relevant content. It is clearly shown that the relevant information obtained through reading newspapers and magazines can provide migrant workers with guidance and deepen their understanding of the industry, thus preparing them for a constantly changing working environment.

If reading newspapers and magazines is to obtain cutting-edge industry information, reading books should be regarded as the best means to tap potential and enrich oneself at multiple levels. As a senior high school graduate, Xiao Tai is 24 years old and unmarried. He has been in Taiyuan, the capital city of Shanxi province, for three and a half years, and currently works as a barman. Working in the bar during the day and learning at night, he prefers reading inspirational books, such as Carnegie's *Human Weakness*, hoping to learn the truth about how to deal with people in the world. "I used to hate learning when I was a student, and only found what I learned was not enough after working. Now I'm eager to learn." He is clear about his future path – to be a manager. Therefore, reading books is an essential way for him to expand his knowledge, accumulate experience, and achieve self-improvement.

From these cases, it is easy to find that many migrant workers do not have access to standardized and organized training of skills. After working in the city, the low income, long working hours and great work pressure hold them back from paying a large sum of money to attend standardized skill training in leisure time. Most of them know that it is difficult to continue their work and life in the city without improving their skills. At this time, the new media that can break through limitations of time and space comes in handy.

Wang, a waitress in a fast-food restaurant in Nanjing, often checks online information to prepare for her dream of being a store owner. And she said:

> I used to surf the Internet for information about opening a store, and had some knowledge of the capital requirement. For example, the decoration fee may vary for different locations. Previously, I thought about opening a jewellery store, which attaches great importance to the source of goods. The Yuqiao Wholesale Market in Nanjing is a choice, but the price there is not low enough because they also source goods from other places. I also checked the online platform Taobao and found lots of cheaper goods.
>
> (Wang, female, from Feidong, Anhui province)

Another example is 31-year-old Yu from Hai'an, Jiangsu province, who is engaging in the decoration industry in Jiashan, Zhejiang province. Yu said he often goes online and looks up things that are useful to him, such as gorgeous decoration pictures, which can serve as a reference, or the latest products like lights and sanitary ware. The barista Bai, on the other hand, follows the industry leaders and some big names in coffee industry on Weibo to acquire the latest industry information. In his spare time, he also downloads apps to learn some foreign language and become familiar with the urban surroundings.

It can be seen that the Internet, with its rich forms of presentation, provides new-generation migrant workers with useful references and guidelines to survive and work in the city. What's more, the rise of new media such as WeChat and Weibo provide diversified channels for people to access various resources faster and more conveniently, so that migrant workers are able to acquire industry information while expanding their knowledge base. In this sense, the new media have not only served as the learning space of these workers but also provided diverse content for them to learn.

In addition to media tools and mediated information, new-generation migrant workers also communicate with others in their daily work and life to fit themselves into the work environment, understand urban life, and better adapt to the profession. This is a form of self-learning based on interpersonal communication. Since few enterprises carry out professional and formal training, these migrant workers mainly become familiar with the business and improve themselves by imitating, learning from and interacting with seasoned employees in their daily work. Gao, only 17 years old, came out to work after finishing her junior high school. Introduced by her sister, she's now working as a waitress in a restaurant in Wenzhou, Zhejiang province. Working for only four months, she is confident about her ability to adapt and acquire vocational skills through observation.

> My sister works in a hotel and she introduced me here. I am adaptable and able to learn through observation and asking questions. Step by step, I got to know all the workflow such as courtesy and etiquette, meal preparation, hygiene requirements, and so on. These things are elaborated by our supervisor and foreman, and could also be found in public notices on the wall, and we need to bear them in mind. Our leader also teaches me many lessons, sharing his helpful work experiences and feelings.
>
> (Gao, female, from Fuyang, Anhui province)

The previously mentioned barista Bai also came close to his dream of opening a cafe through communication. In August 2011, his manager revealed that a cafe was to be opened near a university in Nanjing, so he went there with the mindset of learning things and gaining experience.

> Since it was opening a new store, I've engaged in the whole process, from selecting the venue, decorating, managing the design to the final opening. I watched how they opened the store, recruited workers, and decorated the space, and asked about what I didn't know, thus making preparations for my future. Moreover, this café is right beside the university, which allows me to communicate with the students of Nanjing University in my spare time. From

these students, I began to follow and learn more about interesting things on "RenRen" and Weibo, both of which are Twitter-like social media platforms in China. The cafe was an ideal place for band shows and media interviews, which enabled me to improve my interpersonal skills through interactions with people from all walks of life. Initially, it took me a month or two to get used to such a model of interpersonal communication, since I could hardly start a conversation with others in the past. When I was a chef, I was too shy to look into other's eyes and talk with them, especially girls. A whole month was not enough for me to adapt, let alone maintain a sound relationship with my boss. However, all I need now is a week to adapt to the new environment and get along well with everyone.

(Bai, male, from Linxia, Gansu province)

To sum up, living in the intertwined urban communication environment, new-generation migrant workers begin to seek multiple professional support to improve their ability. In addition to organizational learning and apprenticeship, their practices of learning on media platforms are characterized by multilevel channels and diversified contents. In particular, various supporting media tools and the subtle influence of interpersonal communication further expand their learning channels.

3. From Tools to Platforms: Media-based Diversified Ongoing Learning

New-generation migrant workers differentiate themselves from the older ones with the desire to fight for all the possible opportunities and resources to achieve self-development and transcendence. Unconsciously immersed in the urban culture, they take the initiative to imitate and practice the values and lifestyle of the city, earnestly learn the skills and techniques that secure good jobs, and strive to seize the opportunities to make important breakthroughs. In their views, all these experiences equate to valuable assets, and constant training and learning are the way towards self-improvement. In the closely intertwined and mediated modern cities, diversified learning methods based on various media tools are becoming an important way to acquire necessary skills and enrich themselves. The role of the media is also witnessing a transition from a tool to a platform in the learning and training of migrant workers.

3.1 Acquiring Professional Information: Effective Use of Media Tools

After entering the city, new-generation of workers first need to find jobs to survive. However, they are extremely devoid of capital, outstanding credentials, professional skills, and extensive social support to settle down. Hence, painstaking effort is their only way out. In this process, various forms of media serve as information dissemination tools, enabling their access to information and self-learning and providing them with abundant information to quickly step into the professional field and improve their job skills. As such, media have provided them more autonomy in their choices of employment, training, and learning.

In the past, many migrant workers, similar to Bai, mentioned earlier, did not have a clear picture of their future and could only depend on other resources when they had no relationship to resort to. And mass media, with its wide coverage and easy accessibility, turned out to be their first choice. Recruitment information on TV, websites, and newspapers demonstrates the requirements for wage earners. It provides migrant workers with a preliminary understanding of urban work standards and requirements, and serves as a reference for learning and working, laying the first step for their "adventure" in the city. Others, however, are aware of the importance of learning from the beginning and manage to find relevant information via the Internet.

Zhou is an experienced self-learner since he has attended training schools and taken night school self-study examinations. From the time he embarked on the path of art, he has obtained most of the information online.

> I first studied music education in a bogus college in Sichuan province, because I stumbled across the advertisement when searching "music adult education" online. Being surprised that it had music literacy-related classes available for people like me who had never stepped into college, I went straight to it by plane.
>
> (Zhou, male, from Fushan, Jiangxi province)

He quit the school one year later because of the discrepancy between the advertisement and its actual conditions. Although his first attempt was unsuccessful, it laid the foundation for his improvement of searching skills and learning resources.

> The information about the school is all from the Internet. There are only a handful of schools in China that excel in broadcasting education – Communication University of China in Beijing and Communication University of Zhejiang. After the initial consultation, I went straight to Nanjing. Learning that the Nanjing Normal University was famous for its literature major, and had the broadcasting and hosting classes taught by teachers who give lessons to first-year students, I signed up for the course with reasonable tuition of about 4000 a year. In comparison, Communication University of Zhejiang is far less worthy with more than 20,000 yuan a year (not including food and accommodation) with teachers hired outside. In addition, I was impressed by the hospitality of the consultant at Nanjing Normal University.
>
> (Zhou, male, from Fushan, Jiangxi province)

From fumbling around to a focused and strategic search for learning information, Zhou represents a large part of Chinese migrant workers. Though they are unable to take a shortcut using relationship resources, their urban living and learning experiences can improve their media literacy, laying the foundation for them to better acquire learning information and resources. Moreover, they have developed autonomy in choosing their way of learning.

With the accumulation of urban experiences and the improvement of media literacy, more and more migrant workers are trying to adopt various media tools, especially the convenient and efficient new media to acquire professional knowledge. Like Zhou, many others make use of the Internet and digital technology to solve their problems, to develop further professional expertise, and better adapt to their work in the city.

As we have observed from the chef and hairstyling postings and forums on the Internet, cyberspace has turned into a rather convenient and efficient communication platform where migrant workers share their urban working and living experiences and post information about recruiting and apprenticeships. Such platforms have enabled information sharing and provided a venue of training and learning. Through these various ways, migrant workers can acquire rich professional knowledge, and may even get better employment opportunities.

The 22-year-old Bai, mentioned earlier, not only has a stable job as a barista but also gives training to others occasionally, which is mainly due to his continuous efforts and learning. When talking about how he gets his foot in the door, he mentions that:

> At the very beginning, I was utterly ignorant. So, I searched relevant information on the Internet and learned the basic knowledge of coffee and related culture, including the types and tricks of coffee-making, to grasp a basic understanding of what I am going to handle. When I've gradually mastered the skills and drew the boss's attention, I tried to make coffee on my own with tutorial videos from the Internet.
>
> (Bai, male, from Linxia, Gansu province)

Now Bai is the prospective manager of a well-known coffee shop chain. Having enjoyed the benefits from learning, he continues to tirelessly improve himself by talking with peers, reading books, looking up information on the Internet, attending training seminars and coffee exhibitions, and going to different cafes for internships. Even after the late shift, he squeezes in time to read relevant materials. As he puts it, "most of my knowledge about coffee is self-taught in this way". In addition, he often browses Weibo, a like-Twitter platform in China, to follow coffee masters and the latest industry information. Apart from that, some apps in the cell phone can also serve as an important means of obtaining information. "I have apps such as Carved Time, Starbucks, where I learn marketing campaigns of some great coffee shops."

Different forms of learning have allowed Bai to have a job he loves, concluding the transformation from a handyman to a prospective store manager. His success proves that the post-capital gained through learning is essential for the urban life of the new generation of migrant workers. By finding the information needed for his job through various means, he gradually mastered the knowledge, experience, and skills necessary for a barista, completing the vertical mobility of social status at the personal level. In this process, the use of mass media of all kinds, especially new media, and their roles deserve our attention. As an information channel and a content provider, the media have not only brought fresh job information to migrant workers and reduced their economic risk in urban life but have also guided their self-learning and enabled them to experience different aspects of knowledge through various forms of information. With the immersion of various media, they've gradually gained an understanding of the industry they are working in and improved their working ability, resulting in higher income, more decent jobs, and more promotion chances. All these have provided a solid economic foundation for their self-development and better adaptation to urban life.

3.2 Peer Relationship Building: Information Sharing in Multidimensional Interaction

Existing studies show that the reliance on kinship and geo-relationships runs through the social mobility of migrant workers, with the instrumental primary group relations among fellow townsman and secondary group relations characterized by business relations serving as their major ways of obtaining urban resources (Li, 1996). Apart from beneficial resources for employment and urban survival, meeting new friends also matters in building peer relationships.

Hua, 20, is a junior hairstylist who goes to Nanjing to learn hairstyling as soon as he graduated from junior high school. According to him, the busy daily work stops him from exchanging ideas with people in the store, so he could only resort to professional networks to learn from online peers. Indeed, he feels that they've hit it off online.

> I rarely ask questions on the Internet, but to answer others, especially those junior technicians who just entered the industry with main concerns of how to learn and what to do. Many of them become friends of mine after my initial help and may turn to me when they have other problems later.
>
> (Hua, male, from Suqian, Jiangsu province)

On top of that, platforms like Tencent's Qzone and WeChat are frequently used in the daily lives of the new generation of migrant workers. The QQ chatting group, in particular, has become an important platform for them to relieve their life hardships and seek professional help. In this space, characterized by both openness and closeness, communicative and interactive learning also serve as an important way to acquire skills, expertise, and share experiences. Yang, as mentioned earlier, said:

> I have joined two chatting groups: one for our former classmates in the chef class, and another for those who have worked as chefs, upon invitations from friends in the group. People who have invented new dishes will post the recipe online to teach others.
>
> (Yang, male, from Chongqing)

Although migrant workers in the group do not know each other well, the common interest and learning needs determine their willingness to share in such a platform that combines synchronous and asynchronous information as well as anonymous and non-anonymous group members (Wan, 2012). Everyone who enters the platform can enjoy accessible and much-needed information about industry insiders, job seeking, and cooking skills. The interactive learning with others also facilitates the exchanges among migrant workers, exerting a positive effect on their urban adaptation and social inclusion.

It can be said that the virtual social network constructed by the new media has a positive effect on enriching the professional knowledge and improving the vocational skills of the new generation of migrant workers. Zhiwei, who likes to chat and make friends on QQ, is a 29-year-old man who comes from Huanggang, Hubei province. He has accumulated a certain amount of online social capital by such means.

> I chatted a lot on QQ and met many friends who gain profits through running online stores. I learned a lot by helping these store owners, such as where to purchase goods and how to pack cosmetics and then consign them to the courier company for mailing. The knowledge accumulated through observing the process of running online stores inspires me to start my own, but money is a big issue.
>
> (Zhiwei, male, from Huanggang, Hubei province)

Although it is difficult to convert this online social capital to real life, he is getting more familiar with the sense of proactive utilization during this process.

Constrained by personality and competition, many migrant workers are reluctant to exchange technical and industry knowledge with their peers or co-workers offline. Rather, they prefer to communicate and get problems solved in the anonymous virtual space. People become friends through such professional interaction guided by common interests, and the prerequisite of all is such a platform provided by the media. Professional forums and QQ groups bring together these like-minded workers, enabling them to enlarge their networks and make friends in a virtual space. According to the data from online observation, closer relationships could stimulate more information sharing among these people, covering the industry, employment, and daily life. In this way, the media fulfil the function of resource reproduction.

Moreover, the new-generation migrant workers are not only concerned about work-related knowledge and information while learning, but they also read social and local news. Various media, especially the mass media, expose them to things beyond their work space and expand the radius of their social interaction. Although they are not fully integrated into the city, the sense of alienation from the city and its dwellers is diminishing. In addition, this conscious supplement of information about urban life and society also provides topics for their communication with colleagues and customers.

The older generation of migrant workers has little exposure to the media and rarely pays attention to current events and information about urban life. As a result, their conversation was confined to their own work and the small circle of the primary group. The new-generation migrant workers, however, form a life-style of reading or watching the news and searching for life and social infor-mation to strike conversations and make social connections. The information on the media provides them with "agendas" for chatting. In this way, these migrant workers exchange ideas with their colleagues and customers, thus building closer relationships that further enable the construction of a new social network. As the primary access for migrant workers to gain material resources in the city, such a reconstructed social network is essential when the rural network filled with coun-try fellows and acquaintances cannot provide them with the expected resources to achieve social inclusion in the city (Zeng, 2003). Hence, the new-generation migrant workers leverage the information resources provided by the media to interact with their colleagues and urbanites, whiling maintaining and extending their established social networks to build bridges for social adaptation.

3.3 Multiple Emotional Solace: Positive Energy Transmission in Mediatized Self-learning

As the new-generation migrant workers leave the familiar rural environment and enter the unfamiliar city, they inevitably suffer from significant psychological and emotional fluctuations due to the complex urban setting and the challenges of life and work. However, this uncertainty and insecurity are partly alleviated through mediatized self-learning.

First, the vast amount of information and easily accessible knowledge from the media help them mitigate their fear and anxiety about the unknown urban envi-ronment, be it work or life related. Studies show that many migrant workers are utterly ignorant of what they are going to do and how to do it at the beginning of their urban lives. Bewildered and helpless, they will first resort to people around for consultation, and when this doesn't work, the Internet and various newspa-pers and books become their second choice. After they have learned about the industry and accumulated a certain amount of expertise, their anxiety diminishes and their confidence strengthens. Moreover, the positive information in the media could ignite their inspiration and motivation, fuelling their desire to create a bet-ter future.

Bobo, as mentioned earlier, likes to watch some entrepreneurial TV programs.

> I often watch some entrepreneurial TV programs to learn the practical steps of starting a business, see the potential difficulties and how to detect, improve, and finally solve them. The Financial Channel is one of my favourites. It feels good to occasionally watch this kind of program, because the stories of those people from grassroots backgrounds make entrepreneurship an attain-able goal to me. The key to success is to seize the moment to invest, so the start-up capital is an essential requirement. People starting their own business are those who have gained more than a decade's experience.
>
> (Bobo, male, from Bengbu, Anhui province)

Second, informal learning spaces such as industry websites and forums based on the Internet and other forms of media could provide them with both information resources and psychological support. By means of self-expression and venting their frustration in the virtual space, as well as interpersonal communications and interactions in real life, they can alleviate the negative emotions brought by the difficulties in their work and life. The anonymous virtual world is like a huge reservoir that reduces the pains that cannot be dissipated in real life. What's more, it provides opportunities for strangers who share the same hardships to meet each other, so that they can encourage one another and regain their confidence in life.

A chef apprentice nicknamed X is an active user in the chef post-bar of Baidu. After initially asking about how to cook well, he began to keep daily records of his work experience. Here are a few excerpts from his diary:

> I was scolded by the head chef at the end of today's work, criticizing me for not being watchful enough. I was wronged, but I was already used to it. You have to finish what you have chosen to do, regardless of all the troubles and hardships.
>
> (X, male, a netizen in the chef post-bar of Baidu)

It is clearly shown that he has encountered numerous difficulties in his life and work at the beginning of his career. When he was desperate or felt badly, it was the post-bar that provided such a platform for him to vent bad emotions and resonate with peers who share the same experience by responding and encouraging each other.

A user named J commented after reading his diary,

> I could feel your positive attitude from your diary. It's for sure that you will make it someday. Your words reminded me of my early years when I did a lot of laborious work. But never mind of that; this is the kind of job that requires accumulation. So keep it up!!! I believe in you! Keep fighting!
>
> (J, an internet user)

It is observed that the aforementioned phenomenon is more common in professional websites and forums. One of the reasons is that most migrant workers who have left their hometowns feel it is hard to talk about their hardships with families or colleagues, lest the former couldn't help but worrying about them, and the latter may not have the empathic ability to understand such feelings. The anonymous online network, however, makes it possible. These online spaces are similar to those spontaneous "supporting groups for learning", which are not only a place for them to gain work experience and acquire skills and knowledge but also a tiny world to interact and exchange with others in the industry. Here, these workers seek help on the platform and justify their personal demands for self-improvement. In this online public sphere, they no longer feel isolated and atomized. Rather, they have gained the courage to overcome the difficulties of work and life. Accordingly, the identification of their profession is achieved with the support of their peers. And the feeling of being needed and relied on helps them achieve a state of psychological or spiritual peace.

The process of acquiring knowledge, information, and skills through one's own efforts to settle down in the city and improve one's social status is itself a manifestation of increasing autonomy. It is delightful to see that the new-generation migrant workers begin to recognize their own efforts and professional identities. At the same time, the media literacy of these workers is continuously improved during learning, and converges with that of urbanites. The media has become an essential part of their lifestyle. It is believed that a closer relationship between the workers and the media, especially the new media, and the improved capacity of media use will also be conducive to their urban adaptation and social inclusion. In this sense, the media plays an essential role during migrant workers' search for spiritual belonging and self-identity.

4. Media Empowerment and Self-generated Capital: Achieving Self-Efficacy

The tortuous urban experiences make the new generation of migrant workers gradually realize the significance of knowledge and skills, thus arousing a sense of self-improvement and development. As a convenient and efficient information channel, the media have been utilized to conduct diversified and multilevel mediatized self-learning. With their awakening consciousness of learning and proactive media practice, they have enjoyed media empowerment and self-generated capital, or a new type of resource restructuring in the complex urban communication context, which has profound implications for their urban adaptation and social inclusion.

4.1 Media Empowerment: Resource Restructuring in the Communication Context

One of the most significant differences between urban and rural environment lies in the accessibility of a developed media network. In the background of mediated society, televisions, cell phones, and the Internet spread across cities and villages, reaching every corner of the world. Even before living an urban life, new-generation migrant workers have already had initial contact with the media, especially the new media represented by cell phones. And after entering the city, the migrant workers are reduced to a disadvantaged group in all aspects of urban society. In this case, convenient media and advanced information systems play an essential role in obtaining their much-needed resources and facilitating the reproduction of resources.

Empowerment is a multilayered conceptual system with broad implications. The term can generally be understood at both individual and collective levels. From the perspective of individual motivation in psychology, empowerment refers to "self-efficacy" that stems from the individual's intrinsic need for autonomy. In this sense, empowerment is a process that allows individuals to feel in control of a situation by promoting a strong sense of personal efficacy and enhancing their motivation to achieve their goals (Conger & Kanungo, 1900). Some scholars also view "empowerment" at a collective level as a dynamic, cross-level, and relational conceptual system. It is therefore regarded as a process of social interaction, a theory and practice, a goal or psychological state, a developmental process, and a form of intervention (Chen, 2003).

Scholars point out that empowerment has three orientations. First, the empowerment target is mainly the marginalized groups in society who have little or no power. Second, empowerment, as an interactive social process that cannot be separated from information communication and interpersonal exchanges, has a natural connection with the most basic human communication behaviours. Third, empowerment theory is practice-oriented: it goes beyond theoretical discussions and has been widely applied to social practices (Ding, 2009).

Some scholars believe the meaning of empowerment lies in challenging the existing power structures while elevating the status of individuals or groups. Empowerment allows people to voice their concerns, and communication serves as a mechanism that makes empowerment a reality (Pamela, 2003). As such, communication provides a practical tool for empowerment to achieve social changes in a tensional relationship-based society (Xie, 2008). In recent years, Chinese scholars began to adopt the concept of empowerment and the related theory to explore the self-awareness and power aroused by the new media technology. For example, studies have shown that cell phones can meet the living needs of self-employed and itinerant employees in low- and middle-income groups, facilitating their social mobility and upgrading their social status (Fan, 2010). Similarly, scholars argue that the cell phone can not only facilitate female hourly workers in Shanghai to adapt to the new urban life but also enable them to perform their maternal duties by remote monitoring. The widespread use of communication technologies and the marketization of productive labour have reshaped the social status and gender position of women in rural areas (Cao, 2009).

It may be more enlightening to adopt the media empowerment theory to understand the mediatized learning process of migrant workers. First, under the combined effect of media and the urban environment, the new generation of migrant workers' learning consciousness has been ignited, accompanied by a stronger desire to obtain resources and improve social status in the city. On the one hand, they rediscover themselves during the process of mediatized job-seeking, realizing that they have no advantages in obtaining the job information. It further motivates them to improve themselves and obtain more resources. On the other hand, the ubiquitous advertisements and training information come into their view through the media, suggesting their deficiencies in life and professional capability, and providing them with information on where and how to learn.

Second, the new generation of migrant workers actively participates in media platforms, using all the needed information and content to prepare for self-development and obtain social resources. It is found that migrant workers with higher developmental and training demands strive to get industry information and expertise via all forms of media, especially new media. They also have their preferences in fulfilling their different needs and demands. For example, they may take advantage of social media and mass media to gain job-related information, while resorting to professional forums and websites for specific expertise and skills. Such preference enriches their learning experiences and brings along better job opportunities and career mobility.

Moreover, these migrant workers also interact with urbanites through mediatized self-learning. Such interactions range from solving problems, gaining experiences and skills, to seeking peer or group recognition. Accordingly, their employment resources increase, and social networks become even broader, helping them realize psychological belonging and construct self-identity. The people they interact with are not only country fellows and urbanites, but also colleagues and peers in different cities. This heterogeneous network of relationships and resource channels has greatly enriched their learning process. The support and encouragement of their peers also contributes to the self-realization and urban adaptation of these migrant workers.

In terms of accumulating social capital, the new-generation migrant workers' mediatized learning is a way to acquire capital through their own efforts. These migrant workers are disengaged in the social security in the rural society. Yet, they have no access to the institutional capital that is only available to urban residents. Hence, the primary goal of their city life is to get a job and acquire the organizational capital. Therefore, relational capital is the main form of resources they can obtain at the early stage of urban migration. Over time, they have realized that a single form of relational resource is not enough to achieve what they desire. They've begun to seek low-cost and convenient means of capital accumulation. As one of the most commonly used information tools in the urban society, the media not only provide professional learning resources but also reconstruct the social capital network of migrant workers. Here, the media have taken a dual role of capital accumulation and resource regeneration. Whether these workers adopt the media tools and how they use them result in differences in their resource acquisition ability, and the forms and degrees of capital accumulation, exerting a profound influence on all aspects of their urban lives. In this sense, the media are more than a form of resource, but carry attributes of resource reproduction and accumulation. This kind of capital is a form of "latent" capital behind the relational, organizational, and institutional capital, which could only be obtained through migrant workers' own efforts and life practices.

4.2 Self-generated Capital: Two-way Interaction Between Media and People

Notably, empowerment is not about the delegation of power or authority to migrant workers, but about tapping or stimulating their potential. In other words, media empowerment does not mean the media itself gives power to migrant workers. Rather, it means the media ignite their potential by providing information resources and reorganizing social resources, so that they can manage social resources and their destiny through their efforts. This is a two-way process comprised of the interaction and communication between the media and people. American scholar Thomas Ford Brown divided social capital into three levels, namely, micro-, meso-, and macro-levels. More specifically, micro-level social capital presents in the form of relationships and provides access to resources such as information, job opportunities, knowledge, influence, social support, and long-term social cooperation through kinship, schooling, and geographic connections; meso-level social capital exists in the form of informal institutions, organizational practices, and customary rules; and macro-level social capital emphasizes the possession of social resources by member groups in social organizations at the national level (Cui & Chen, 2007). In short, they are relational, informal institutional, and contractual social capitals. Since contractual social capital is underdeveloped in China, and remains unavailable to the migrating population, the first two are preferred by migrant workers, especially relational capital. However, blood and locality ties are not enough to form the urban identity of migrant workers and achieve the psychological assimilation, despite its positive impact on migrant workers' employment (status), job security, urban life and development, as well as the construction of their social relationship network (Zhang, 2007). As some scholars suggest, migrant workers need to cultivate and develop more localized capital after entering the city (Ren, 2012), which can be realized through interactions with urbanites and making use of the easily accessible capital in the city.

For the new generation of migrant workers with less social power, they have an even stronger desire for an open access to the localized capital. Compared with their parent's generation, they are better educated, and less tolerant to dirty or laborious work. As such, they have higher job expectations and stronger demands for good employment opportunities. Meanwhile, thanks to the improved family economic conditions, exchanges among friends and relatives coming back home, and the mass media exposure, their goals go beyond earning money to developing themselves and even establishing a foothold in the city. Nevertheless, few channels for organizational and relational support are available for these workers, while the relational network, which is based on primary relationships such as kinship and geo-relationship in the traditional rural society, may even inhibit their information acquisition and continuing learning. Taken together, these elements hinder the migrant workers' personal development. In addition, migrant workers pale in comparison with the urban residents in their job stability, income levels, educational background, and vocational skills. Such a gap has become even larger, as the urban-rural dichotomy of the household registration system has kept them away from reaping the benefits of China's urbanization process. Therefore, they are in a relatively disadvantaged position in the acquisition and possession of economic, cultural, and social capital. In this regard, they are in urgent need of more publicly accessible capital, and the media's role should be in full play.

Media capital can only be acquired when the new generation of migrant workers fully recognize its role in obtaining resources within a rich and convenient media environment. Clearly, the information environment in which migrant workers live has experienced drastic changes, as can be seen from the improvement of rural infrastructures, especially the penetration of information networks in rural areas. The new-generation migrant workers have not only got access to traditional media such as TV and newspapers, but also utilized the computers at school and Internet cafes ever since they were at the elementary schools. Hence, they are endowed with wider media exposures and higher media literacy. Furthermore, the all-encompassing city provides access to more organizational, interpersonal, and media resources, enhancing their continuing learning and even changing their lifestyles. Some scholars point out that the lower and middle classes, the majority of Chinese society, have become the manufacturers and owners of new communication tools. In this sense, new-generation migrant workers' urban survival and self-development can be contributed to lower thresholds and relative accessibility of mid- to low-end communication technologies, the spread of cell phones and the Internet, as well as more accessible and affordable information in the urban environment.

The new capital theory emphasizes individual actions or choices, and considers capital as independent atomized elements randomly distributed in society or mainstream values that have been instilled into individuals, accepted, and later become investments or production of individual actors. Lin Nan, the master-mind of social capital theory, states that one of the tasks that social capital should accomplish is to show how individual actors make a difference in their access to the embedded resources of these structures, that is, opportunity structures, through interactions and social networks (Lin, 2004). Our study shows that the media also have this tendency to differentiate the access to opportunity structures. Specifically, migrant workers with more media resources are likely to be given higher social status, thus enjoying more opportunities to act freely within structural constraints. And those who are more capable of making use of media tools to gain information and continue self-learning, have more choices in their job seeking and a higher probability of social mobility. What's more, they may have more advantages than those who do not use media or have a poorer learning capability in terms of interpersonal interaction and establishing a sense of belonging. In this regard, the media is also a type of latent capital embedded in the urban society.

In contrast with structural and institutional capital, media capital can be acquired later through one's efforts. Hence, the lower middle class has become the largest beneficiary of information acquisition through the new media. The accumulation of media capital hinges on one's media literacy, educational levels, family environment, as well as economic status. In particular, differences in migrant workers' media literacy – that is, knowing how to find needed resources, remaining skeptical when exposed to different media platforms, and adopting media tools creatively for one's survival and development – will result in disparities in their accumulation of media capital. Therefore, media literacy and personal education may even become a bottleneck for migrant workers who lack money, time, and technical capability for media use, thus widening the gap between the members of lower and middle classes.

Therefore, the core of gaining media capital lies in the communication practice of new-generation migrant workers with their subjective initiative. That is, they can take advantage of the media's instrumental properties as information resources and communication platforms to obtain the needed learning information and resources, to realize economic, social, and cultural gains. This is a process of self-generated capital with the new generation of migrant workers as the mainstay. In the complex and ever-changing urban society, these workers lacking institutional capital can utilize the information and resources provided by the media to lay the foundation for their settlement and self-development in the city.

First of all, the new generation of migrant workers, stimulated by the information network formed under an intertwined urban media environment, begins to use multiple media to obtain learning information, thus expanding their learning channels and dispersing potential risks. At the same time, they adopt different media to acquire new knowledge, reduce transaction costs, and improve professional skills, so as to enjoy better employment opportunities and a higher social mobility. As a result, they gradually form the economic capital for their urban survival. Second, they interact positively with the others and with the urban society by participating in the information production on various media platforms. From problem-solving to mutual comfort, from exchanging the industry rules to talking about the urban life experience, the migrant workers, either actively or unconsciously, share urban experiences and feelings with different groups. This not only extends their original social networks but also strengthens their connections with the urban society, which is beneficial to their social capital accumulation. Finally, such an act itself points to the realization of self-efficacy. The emotional support gained during their continued learning process is often accompanied by the improvement of their literacy skills. In so doing, Chinese migrant workers have established a sense of belonging regarding their occupation and self-achievement, and felt less alienated and isolated in the urban society.

In conclusion, the media, as a form of latent capital embedded in the urban structure, have made up for the migrant workers' lack of institutional resources, and provides them with much-needed social support during their ongoing learning process. However, we must be aware that media empowerment is only possible with the advance of media technologies and information networks (as objective substances) and the self-initiatives of the new generation of migrant workers (as subjective efforts). Only when the two are intertwined and interact with each other can the effect of media empowerment be achieved.

References

Beck, U. (2004). *Risk society* (B. He, Trans.). Yilin Press.

Cao, J. (2009). Communication technology and gender: A case study on the use of cellphone by migrant domestic women in Shanghai. *Journalism & Communication, 16*(1), 71–77+109.

Chen, S. (2003). Empowerment: A new perspective of the theoretical and practical approach for social work. *Sociological Studies, 5*, 70–83.

Cheng, C. (2012). College students' social network, knowledge and status attainment: An empirical analysis based on investigation of college students in western China. *Youth Studies, 4*, 22–34+94–95.

Conger, J., & Kanungo, R. (1900). The empowerment process: Integrating theory and practice. *The Academy of Management Review, 13*, 3 (Cited in Ding, W. (2009). New media and empowerment: A practical social research. *Chinese Journal of Journalism & Communication, 10*, 76–81).

Cui, C., & Chen, H. (2007). A survey of social capital theory. *Journal of Tongling University, 4*, 25–30.

Ding, W. (2009). New media and empowerment: A practical social research. *Chinese Journal of Journalism & Communication, 10*, 76–81.

Fan, P. (2010). From communication technology to productive tool: A sociological research on the use of mobile phone by Chinese mid-and-low income classes. *Journalism & Communication, 1*, 82–88+112.

Feng, J. (2011). From strong ties to weak ties: A sociological analysis on the transformation of migrant workers' social network. *Journal of Southwest Agricultural University, 9*(12), 79–93.

Giddens, A. (1988). *Modernity and self-identity* (X. Zhao & W. Fang, Trans.). Shanghai Sanlian Bookstore.

Inkeles, A., & Smith, D. (1992). *Becoming modern: Individual change in six developing countries.* China Renmin University Press.

Kalbfleischet, P. J. (2003). *Communication yearbook* (Vol. 27). Editor's Introduction LEA. Inc.

Knowles, M. (1989). *Andragogy in action* (Y. Lin, Trans.). People's Publishing House.

Li, P. (1996). The social network and social status of migrant workers in China. *Sociological Research, 4*, 42–52.

Lin, N. (2004). *A theory of social structure and action.* Shanghai People's Publishing House.

Ren, Y. (2012). Localized social capital and social integration of migrants in urban China. *Comparative Economic & Social Systems, 36*(5), 47–57.

Wan, L. (2012). Research on social interaction of online learning community based on QQ group. *E-Education Research, 33*(9), 54–58+68.

Xie, J. (2008). Empowerment in communication studies. *Chinese Journal of Journalism & Communication, 4*, 33–37.

Zeng, Z. (2003). The re-established social network of migrant workers and its internal flow of resources. *Sociological Research, 3*, 99–110.

Zhang, Z. (2007). Social capital and employment of migrant workers. *Comparative Economic & Social Systems, 6*, 123–126.

8   Media Support
Professional Adaptation Among the New Generation of Migrant Workers

Compared with the old generation, new-generation migrant workers, who just started their careers, have incredibly different motives for working in cities. They have distinct career positioning, career planning, and professional role identification. In the old days, off-farm workers entered cities only for material benefits, and they would always end up returning to the farmland. For the new generation, however, with limited farming experience, they show strong resistance to the rural identity and farming work. For them, working in cities is not only for livelihoods but also for integrating into a new environment. Beyond salary and working environment, the new generation of migrant workers starts to care about career development, organizational culture, and professional values. Many of them have shown professional awareness, started to plan their careers, and yearned for different job opportunities.

In fact, migrant workers' adaptation to city life is a continuous flow of actions formed by their experiences in life, rather than a process with an explicit boundary (Fu & Jiang, 2007). The professional adaption of the new generation of migrant workers is also a continuous flow, where job seeking, skill learning, group adaptation, workplace communication, psychological adjustment, occupational mobility, as well as career planning all take place. During the process, these young people learn to observe, recognize, comprehend, imitate, reflect, identify, and internalize, wherein the media play an essential role in facilitating, influencing, and even changing their work and life experiences in cities. As such, we start with their work and professional adaptation, to investigate the role of the media in the process of their urban adaptation and social inclusion. Next, we try to figure out how the media can promote these young migrant workers to complete their career acquisition and achieve the transition from the countryside to the city, and how the media is used to help them achieve self-empowerment and establish professional awareness.

1. "My Life's in Turnaround": Challenges in Obtaining Employment After Switching Communication Environments

Except for a few who moved to cities with their migrant-worker parents, most new-generation migrant workers spent the earliest part of their lives in the countryside.

DOI: 10.4324/9781003365785-8

As a geographical environment separated from the city, rural villages constitute an occupational territory where rural families are mainly supported by the farm work. In cities, people's work is based on uniform time order. Within a fixed time frame, people rely on a specific organizational communication environment and cooperate on the basis of the division of labour. The hierarchical relationship in the workplace is deeply embedded in all aspects of people's professional life. Moving from rural to urban settings lead to spatial changes in their lives. In urban areas, they would encounter different communication environments and face new professional adaptation challenges.

1.1 Farming: Monotonous Communication Environment in the Rural Memory

Although nearly half of new-generation migrant workers have never got their hands muddy, they know something about farming. Since they grew up in villages where the work of agriculture can be seen everywhere, they have developed a perception of the communication environment in agricultural activities, though such kind of perception could be directly acquired or indirectly observed. Our interview data indicate that the farming life in their memory was generally dirty, tiring, monotonous, and trivial. Such an occupational perception comes into being partly due to the boring and monotonous communication environment in the countryside.

One phenomenon has been mentioned repeatedly: the scope of interpersonal communication in farming life is relatively fixed, and "familiarity" can bring stability and monotony. In rural areas, working time and leisure time are intertwined and connected. Professional interactions among people overlap with general social interactions, and are mostly confined to interpersonal communication networks based on kinship and geographic proximity. In the society of acquaintances, the exchange of information is limited in terms of scope and frequency. Distant relatives and close neighbours have little to do with each other in terms of business. They are connected with kinship and geopolitical relationships.

Born in 1991, Wenxiu entered the city at an early age, from Huanggang, Hubei province, worked for a long time, and what she said is much more mature than her peers. She thinks farming is monotonous. In her eyes, her parents always started working at sunrise and rested at sunset. Occasionally they would invite some relatives to give a hand. In most cases, however, her parents barely interacted with others when doing the farm work.

> My parents only grow sesame, cotton, and other crops alike. They do the same thing every day – nothing changes in the field. What they need to do is quite repetitive, requiring no skills. Most of the time they can do it by themselves and don't need others' help. Only occasionally when it is about to rain, they would ask some relatives to help and offer a home-made meal. But now such things rarely happen, since our relatives live sparsely and many neighbours have moved to the town or the city.
>
> (Wenxiu, female, from Huanggang, Hubei)

Compared to the limited interpersonal communication in the farming process, the characteristics of decentralization and low organization of rural households make agricultural production mostly unorganized. In rural areas where a general division of labour has not formed yet, the family is the basic unit of action in agricultural activities. A qualified farmer needs to master the entire process from sowing to crop harvesting. In most cases, mutual cooperation is unnecessary for the farm work since the older generation of Chinese farmers has gone through the period of collectivized agricultural production,[1] and believed that individual incentives might be undermined by the intervention of organizations and collective groups. Therefore, they do not mind the absence of organizations in agriculture. Twenty-six-year-old Jin San is also from Huanggang, Hubei. Now he works as a catering manager in a canteen in Wenzhou. When he was a child, he saw his parents doing laborious work on the farmland and, at that time, he thought it was way more difficult for farmers to make a living. In his impression, farmers only mind their own business and do not feel it necessary to form into groups or agricultural organizations. In their views, farming itself is a private business after all.

> Farming requires no skills. You can do it as long as you are strong and hard-working. In rural areas, people grow their crops and plough their fields on their own. [There is] no need of organizational guidance or formal organization. Village cadres come to the door only to collect grain and taxes. Since these cadres have rarely done farm work before, they may not be able to offer you any guidance. In recent years, the younger generation of farmers has been reluctant to take any farm work, leaving their old guys busy in the field. Farming for years, the older generation know exactly how to sow seeds, water the crop and hoe up weeds. For sure, farmers do not need an organization to help with their farm work.
>
> (Jin San, male, from Huanggang, Hubei)

In addition, the penetration of mass media and new media in rural areas is rather limited. Except for radio and television that have maintained a high penetration rate, most farmers have not been used to reading newspapers, magazines, and surfing the Internet. Field studies in the rural areas of economically developed Jiangsu province show that the mass media has not achieved a "soft landing" in disseminating information of agricultural science and technology, without generating real benefits to farmers in terms of media content, distribution channels, access opportunities, and production costs (Zheng, 2011a). If this holds true for rural areas in developed regions, the situation in underdeveloped rural areas wouldn't be any better. According to the present study, the mass media plays an entertaining role in the countryside, helping farmers relax in their leisure time. In a nutshell, Chinese farmers have exhibited a "non-agricultural" pattern of media use.

The farming experience of migrant workers is closely related to the level of regional development, their family's economic conditions, their parents' time away from home as well as their personal characters. Those born in 1980s and

1990s have less farming experience than the older generation. Due to their limited farming experience, they show great resistance to their rural identity and the farm work.

For example, Wen Tao, born in 1981 in Luan, Anhui province, did all kinds of farm work when he was still a child. By now, he has been engaged in Internet maintenance work for many years, and sits in the office every day. According to him, "working in the city is way much better than before". As for Jin San, mentioned previously, he has been in the city for a decade and said that he will not do farm work anymore because "it is laborious and fruitless [making little money]".

In a nutshell, they believe farming is monotonous and repetitive. Under the unique geographical conditions in the countryside, human communications mostly take place within the network of kinship and geographic relationship. Information exchange is rather limited in an enclosed space with clear social boundaries. Organizations are rarely seen in the rural environment, not to mention the division of labour and cooperation within the organizations. Therefore, mass media and new media are used less often, due to two main characteristics of China's rural society: (1) farmers mainly relied on farming to live and the weather for harvest, and (2) acquaintances lay the foundation of interpersonal relationships in the rural society. As a result, new-generation migrant workers generally lack interest in farming and resist the role of farmer in their occupational identifications.

1.2 Working in Cities: A Three-dimensional Communication Network in Personal Experience

Entangled in a closed rural communication environment, many migrant workers have little access to external information and lack sufficient stimulation. On the contrary, the urban society is a highly organized social system. The social division of labour enables it to develop a set of mechanisms where organizations play different roles and meet various needs. Among all the organizations, business enterprises are the most common form of organizations in urban areas and serve as the essential cells of modern society. As such, new-generation migrant workers also rely on a certain organization to start their careers in cities. After gaining access to the organization, they need to work within the system and follow the organizational norms and culture. The organization, therefore, functions as an objective environment influencing all aspects of their life.

An extensive division of labour in the urban society helps them build up working relationship networks, including their leaders, colleagues within the organization, as well as customers and partners outside the organization. Yang Zi was born in Huanggang, Hubei, in 1988. He left the countryside after finishing the first semester of high school in 2005 and started to make moulds. Now he works as the head of the product development department of a shoe company in Wenzhou, mainly designing shoe soles. After ten years of experience, he has been able to talk eloquently about his work, though he used to be very timid when he was a rookie. He has to deal with strangers from all walks of life in the city, which is entirely different from the acquaintance society back home.

> The biggest difference between a large city and our village is communication. In our village, people are familiar with each other. In the factory, however, people were from different places including my county fellows, and those from other places of Hubei province, some of whom are even from other provinces. They were also at different ages: some were in their forties or fifties, much older than me; some were 20 or 30 years old, while I was under 18. Watching people hurrying back and forth in the city, I was too timid to say a word.
>
> (Yangzi, male, from Huanggang, Hubei)

Although rural areas have been widely involved in local commodity markets and global trade markets since the beginning of modernization, farmers still make a living in the self-produced and self-sold household-based rural economy, which is a case especially true in the middle and western rural areas. In fact, the tradition of farming that has lasted for thousands of years in rural areas remains unchanged. Farming is always a matter of autonomy and flexibility based on farmers' self-regulation – farmers decide whether to do it or not, and to do more or less. However, working in cities requires comprehensive plans and a hierarchical organization which can coordinate allocation of resources. In order to achieve development goals, especially profit targets, most organizations in corporations will establish a set of management mechanisms.

Haiting, from Nanjing, Jiangsu province, is 28 years old. She has worked in Jurong of Zhenjiang, Dongshan of Suzhou, Jiangning of Nanjing, and other places for 12 years. Growing up in a family with a patriarchal tradition, she is always obedient and tolerant. She has worked in the clothing industry, and the job opportunities were introduced by her relatives and friends or found by herself. When she first started working for a company, she encountered an embarrassing incident from which she realized the absolute presence of corporate organizations in urban workplaces.

> After leaving school, I went to work on the assembly line of a clothing factory. At the start, I assumed working was just like being in school and I could take a break every 40 minutes. But truth is, I had to work nonstop and could barely take a break. To be honest, I was not used to that at the beginning. With time passing by, however, I got used to that. After all, everyone worked nonstop in the factory.
>
> (Haiting, female, from Nanjing, Jiangsu)

In addition, working in cities can offer greater access to a wide range of mass media and new media. Unlike the conservative agricultural society, industrial society is driven by innovation and requires continuous technological improvement, process reorganization, and service renewal, which puts forward higher requirements for workers. Various work-related mass media products are often placed in corporate organizations, such as fashion magazines in barbershops and newspapers in real estate agencies. Walking into the era of new media communication, many corporate organizations have even set up their own websites or official Weibo or WeChat platforms. Apart from the media access opportunities provided by enterprises, some industries, especially the service industry or sales industry, require interpersonal communication skills due to the nature of the industry. The new generation of migrant workers also needs to constantly acquire media information and use it to develop topics or recharge themselves, where media devices such as laptops, smartphones, and tablets play their parts.

Advanced organization has become one of the basic features of modern society (Xin, 2005). After entering the city, migrant workers need to work within an organization with clear goals and follow the rules, the commands, and the coordinative orders within the organization. They also need to deal with different working groups beyond the primary relationship network, and be constantly exposed to various mass media and new media. Under a more complex and diverse urban communication environment, these migrant workers have encountered ups and downs through their working experience. For example, Hongtao, born in 1994 in Fuyang, Anhui province, works as a waiter at a snack bar in Nanjing. When asked about the early experience of working in the city, he said, "When I first came to work, I felt very comfortable, and everything was fresh to me". Jiajia, a girl born in 1995 from Lianyungang, Jiangsu province, described her bitter work experience. After graduating from a junior high school, she came to Nanjing with her mother and worked in a restaurant near a university. She said, "We can only leave until the guests leave. We don't have fixed vacations. [We have] no time for entertainment. The work is exhausting since we don't have enough time to sleep." Noticeably, such working experience is enhanced by the stimulation of the urban communication environment.

1.3 From the Rural to Urban: The Transition of Professional Adaptation Environment

Unlike the household-based rural economy where the family remains the core production unit, the commodity economy characterized by commodity production, exchange, and sales, is based on the division of labour and mutual cooperation. The scope of interpersonal communication at work has been greatly expanded, thus highlighting the importance of handling interpersonal relationships within and outside the organization. At work, there are not only face-to-face communication activities but also one-to-many and even many-to-many mediated communications. With the ubiquitous use of media devices, migrant workers' urban professional adaptation has become a complex process.

First of all, such kind of complexity is prominently manifested in the interpersonal communication among migrant workers. The problem facing the new generation of migrant workers is how to get along with other senior workers. Pang, born in 1980, is from Yangzhou, Jiangsu. After graduating from high school in 1997, she was introduced by an acquaintance to work in a clothing factory, working on an assembly line for three years. Later, she followed her boyfriend, who is now her husband, to Nanjing to start a business. Since then, they have settled in Nanjing and run a barber shop for 14 years. Pang recalled that when she started working at a very young age, "interpersonal communication often presents too much of a challenge", especially with people who were much older than her. Fortunately, as she integrated into her peer groups later, the psychological distress caused by interpersonal communication at the early stage of work gradually faded. Similarly, many interviewees admit they have encountered the same problem with Pang. It is quite common because the new generation of migrant workers is generally younger than their colleagues when holding their first job. Therefore, they have to interact with adults who are much older. The generation gap and its negative effect trigger many problems in interpersonal communication. Those with good interpersonal communication skills tend to be more capable of adapting to the organizational environment.

Pang was facing the communication problems in the interpersonal relationship within an organization. Thanks to the nature of their work, some other migrant workers have to deal with customers or partners outside the organization, which is especially common in the service industry or sales industry. Xiaoya is from Suqian, Jiangsu. After graduating from a junior high school, she first worked in the factory in her hometown, doing repetitive and monotonous work nonstop and staying in the factory all day. She described this job as "dull and boring". She then left the boring job arranged by her parents, and took another job in a nail salon in Nanjing. As a manicurist, she communicates with customers frequently at work. Although she is easy-going and always builds a good rapport with customers, she can still feel helpless when encountering demanding customers.

> We are all tired up at work: we open at 10 am and close at 9 pm, and only have one day off on Monday. Sometimes customers come one by one and we don't even have time to eat. Occasionally I will miss home and my parents, especially when I am sick. Lying in bed, I feel quite sad and heartbroken. Quite often encounter very picky customers. It is them who picked the colour and pattern, but when everything is finished, they will blame me saying they are not satisfied with my work. I have no choice but to swallow my anger silently and carry on.
>
> (Xiao Ya, female, from Suqian, Jiangsu)

Second, the complexity of urban professional life also determines that adaptation in organizations cannot be accomplished overnight. New-generation migrant workers, generally young and yearning for freedom, are not quite used to being restrained and managed by corporate organizations. Some of them express their resistance directly through actions, such as frequent job-hopping. Some have psychological aversion even though they do not leave their work, which has become a problem in their professional adaptation.

Xiaogao, as mentioned earlier, was born in 1997 in Fuyang, Anhui province, and stayed at home for half a year after finishing her third year of junior high school. Then she moved to Wenzhou and has worked there a waitress in hotel for four months. Although it was the first time for her to work far away from home, and she has worked for only a few months, she spoke appropriately and decently, leaving us an impression of her being sensible, independent, and self-reliant. She feels that the biggest difference between the urban and rural is that urban workers are "restrained and managed by a company", and she is not quite comfortable with such a feeling of restraint.

> I think working in the city is different from farming in the countryside. In the countryside, of course there are many things that need to be done, but I can arrange my own work. Yet working in the city, I have to do the work even if I don't want to do – I am not allowed to make my own choice. After all, I am under the control of the company. Only by doing the work the company arranged can I get paid. As my mother said, "paid by others, controlled by others". Sometimes I really don't want to go to work, but these is no choice for me since I need to survive in the city.
>
> (Xiaogao, female, from Fuyang, Anhui)

In addition, the nature of urban occupations also determines that they cannot just use mass media and new media for entertainment. Working in the city requires them to learn skills, recharge themselves, and constantly learn how to adapt to an evolving society, which has led to a renewed understanding of the function of mass media and new media. The aforementioned Jin San, who dropped out of school in 2004 after just finishing half of the first semester of his second year in middle-high school, went to Wenzhou to make a living. In the past decade, he changed many jobs, including hairstyling, selling houses, and pedalling tricycles. Currently, he has a family with two children, so he started to pursue job stability and work as a catering manager in a staff canteen. He only used new media for entertainment at a young age, but gradually started to use it to learn software skills and recharge himself, such as posting recruitment information and learning marketing skills, to lay a good foundation for his long-term career development.

From rural to urban areas, the communication environment faced by new-generation migrant workers in their career lives has also undergone significant changes with the deepening of social division of labour. Their communication network has expanded from primary relationship networks to a three-dimensional communication network comprised of secondary relationship networks, organizational channels, mass media, and new media. Working in a complicated urban environment, they have to overcome professional adaptation challenges, dealing with interpersonal communication within and outside the organizational channels, and setting up an appropriate positioning of mass media and new media in the work. These are all problems that need to be solved in their professional life, and the media play an extensive role during this process.

2. Convergence of Collective Power: Occupational Attainment and Urban Adaptation Under the Influence of the Media

In the advanced urban communication system, the new generation of migrant workers often remains a vulnerable group when seeking job opportunities. Regardless, out of humanity and morality concerns or the protection of interests, the media have provided all kinds of help to promote the occupational attainment and urban adaptation of the new generation of migrant workers. This includes (1) the primary relationship network based on family ties; (2) the secondary relationship network established by business connections; (3) the organizational channels consisting of the labour department, the talent market, and the business enterprises; as well as (4) the mass media (i.e., newspapers, televisions) and new media (i.e., the Internet).

2.1 Career Opportunity Search and Employment Choice: Information Distribution From Multiple Sources

As the reforms of traditional institutions in the social and political fields lag behind the rapid advancement of the economic reform, China's labour market is segregated, and the formal and subordinate labour markets co-exist (Li, 2002). To be more specific, the subordinate labour market provides a large number of low-end job opportunities. For job seekers to effectively grasp these opportunities, the dissemination of employment information is essential. Despite the fact that the information dissemination in the labour market is asymmetric, a highly developed urban communication system has helped to bridge that gap.

On the one hand, intergenerational inheritance is a common phenomenon in the first-time occupational attainment. In other words, most new-generation migrant workers find their first jobs through occupational information provided based on kinship and geographic relationships. Although job-seeking is usually fairly haphazard for each of them to engage in different jobs, the choice of their first job is often influenced by the people around them (Tong, 2011). The primary network of parents, relatives, country fellows, and classmates provides them with various employment information clues, driven by the ethical obligations and the sense of responsibility derived from blood, kinship, and geographical ties.

On the other hand, market-based job search methods are gradually deployed among the new generation of migrant workers (Xu, 2010), thanks mainly to the gradual improvement of China's labour market and the upgrade of the new generation of migrant workers' literacy levels. Employment information is disseminated in various ways based on the operational needs and profit considerations, as can be seen in the job vacancy announcements posted everywhere in the city, the recruitment columns in newspapers and on the Internet, and the job referrals from employment agencies. Additional to these market-based channels, neighbourhood communities, government labour departments and the job fairs are also building platforms that facilitate the communication between rural migrant workers and their potential employers.

Zhiwei was born in Huanggang, Hubei province, in 1984. He has only got a degree from a technical secondary school, and is currently busy finding a job. He came out to work in 2006 and has been to Beijing, Nanjing, and Huizhou (a city in Guangdong province). He has been in cities for eight years, trying his luck working as a web administrator, a sales person, a security guard, and a factory worker. He has a small circle of friends, and he rarely socializes with colleagues or peers because he believes people of similar age and background are not very helpful. Moreover, most of his colleagues are married while he is still single, leaving them few common topics. Zhiwei likes to watch news on the Internet and cares more about national affairs. When hunting for a job, Zhiwei used the information provided by primary social networks to find his first job, but soon he turned to the Internet, hiring agencies, the job market, and other channels.

> I majored in computer science, but I did not learn it well enough to find a job in this field. After I graduated from a technical secondary school, an acquaintance introduced me to work as a web administrator. Later, I tried jobs like sales, security guard, and factory workers. I felt so tired and always failed to hold on to one job. Every time I was just a temporary worker working for a short period. I am surrounded by people who are exactly the same. It is impossible to count on them to find a reliable job. Now I resort to employment agencies, the talent market, and sometimes I will see whether there are good jobs available online, although most of them are not suitable for me. Many opportunities posted online are deceptive. As for agencies, if you give the agency money, it will take you to the company you like for an interview. This time, I heard from an acquaintance that there is a migrant labour market in Andemen, Nanjing, so I came to have a look.
>
> (Zhiwei, male, from Huanggang, Hubei)

After the initial job acquisition, new-generation migrant workers have significantly diversified their job search channels, highlighting the importance of work-based secondary networks in their career transitions. In Granovetter's view, this is due to the fact that the overlapping part of the social network of strong ties provides a lot of redundant information, and the heterogeneous information circulating in the weak ties is more effective for job hunting. Some scholars have revised Granovetter's "strong-weak relationship hypothesis" to a "strong-weak trust hypothesis" in the Chinese context (Zhai, 2003), arguing that the key to the effectiveness of interpersonal communication is not the strength of the relationship but the authenticity of the information. However, scholars also acknowledge the explanatory power of Granovetter's theory for the job search behaviour of those individuals with a high level of human capital. For new-generation migrant workers who have improved their expertise to a higher level, interpersonal relationships built in the circle of business-related acquaintances could be a key source of information that hardly appears in formal recruitment channels.

Xiaojin was born in Huanggang, Hubei province, in 1988. After finishing junior high school, he came out to work. He married the year before and had a daughter.

He has opened a computer after-sales service store in Wenzhou City. He often needs to provide after-sales service door to door. When talking about job search, he emphasized the importance of friend circle or network.

> No one is looking for a job through a newspaper. The talent market is flooded with companies that are unable to recruit people. Generally speaking, job hunting relies on people in the circle referring each other. People in the same circle know each other well. You can always get a line on some information if you keep inquiring after these people.
>
> (Xiaojin, male, from Huanggang, Hubei)

Career search is not only about getting information but also about selecting and processing the information from these channels. When the information available is limited, things are relatively simple. However, when faced with abundant job information, it is often necessary to make comparisons and filter the information. In this process, new-generation migrant workers often make decisions alone, or they may refer to, learn from, or even listen to outside opinions. Different from the older generation of migrant workers, the new generation has more diversified channels to obtain career opportunities. Although the channels are currently mainly based on interpersonal relations, the market-oriented channels that appear in the form of organizations have gradually gained recognition. In addition, the talent market established by the government also provides them with more choices. Taken together, the new-generation migrant workers are able to start brand-new professional life experiences.

2.2 *Professional Skill Acquisition and Norm Mastery: Organization-led Resources Transfer*

Compared with their parents, new-generation migrant workers have improved their educational levels. Overall, they are still doing dirty, tough, and tiring work. In labour-intensive enterprises, labour is the most important resource to organize and arrange production and service activities. As such, modern enterprises adopt a series of skill training, system management, production instructions, and reward and punishment measures to shape the young migrant workers into qualified labourers.

Haiting, a native of Nanjing, Jiangsu, has been working for 12 years. Having engaged in the garment industry for over a decade, she has become quite familiar with every detail of the whole production process, from the most basic assembly line work to her current position of garment plate making. As she recalled her work experience in the early years, she felt that assembly line work did not require high skills, and everyone could adapt quickly. Therefore, the organization's skill training remains invisible in assembly line production, and only the low-level leaders will occasionally show up and give some work guidance.

Compared with the assembly line where practice makes perfect, the service industry is more demanding of training. Hence, the scope of organizational participation and guidance is wider. As such, formal training systems include lectures, internships, outbound training, qualification examinations, etc. There is not only verbal experience conveyed by the leadership, but also written declaration of rules. The corporation/organization carries out the norms of labour production, which serves as the principle that guides the work of employees. Less formal trainings are often carried on the guidance of low-level leaders and seasoned colleagues.

Maoer from Xuzhou, Jiangsu, did not enter university after graduating from high school. After staying at home for more than half a year, she came to a Nanjing beauty and body leisure club. She used to be a masseuse in Xuzhou, and later she was recommended to the head store in Nanjing. Maoer's company has a formal skill training program ranging from the theoretical knowledge of meridian acupoint to practical massage techniques. Employees also need to pass institutionalized assessments and obtain nationally recognized qualification certificates before they can officially start their work. The six-month training also shows that the enterprise has attached great importance on staff training.

> I participated in the training of our store after graduating from high school, and started to work after six months of training. At that time, I had to learn the meridians of the human body and the techniques of massaging acupoints. The techniques were complicated, and I had to take exams to prove I truly mastered them. After passing the exam, I was required to understand the effects of various essential oils and learn how to mix them. The essential oils used in our massage are adjusted according to the customer's skin types. I learned quickly and passed the certification exam in only six months. Then I got a nationally recognized beautician qualification certificate. Some of those who prepared with me have taken the exam for two years and still failed to pass it.
>
> (Maoer, female, from Xuzhou, Jiangsu)

Regardless, few companies provide formal trainings like Maoer's company does, because migrant workers mostly have to take arduous manufacturing work. Although the service industry pays more attention to vocational skill training than assembly line work, it's also dependent on the real situation of each organization. Some service providers only carry out fragmented skill trainings for their employees.

It should be admitted that many migrant workers have entered vocational training schools to receive certified trainings of skills. They pay for the training, the school teaches them skills, and then the school recommends jobs to these migrant workers, or they find a job by themselves. This is market-oriented process of resource allocation. Twenty-three-year-old Xiao Sheng is from Chuzhou, Anhui. He failed in the high school entrance examination. Eager to make money, he went to a chef school for training, where he met many people who are talented and passionate about cooking. He also worked hard to participate in some cooking competitions, although he didn't win any medals or awards. After graduating from the chef school, he was introduced by his uncle to work in a small restaurant in Zhenjiang City. His vocational skills were first obtained in the chef school, and then supplemented and perfected by working as an assistant chef. It is difficult to judge which experience matters most, but there is no doubt that organizations dominate the process of acquiring professional skills.

Vocational skills, as an explicit and instrumental resource, lay the foundation for migrant workers to gain a foothold and develop within the organization. We can see that various organizations have decided to provide basic or advanced vocational training to their employees. The scope and depth of the training varies by industry, scale of operations, management style, and the vision for development. During these processes of organization-led resource allocation, the new-generation migrant workers gradually acquire various skills, master the professional norms of the work process, and prepare themselves for professional adaptation in a urban environment.

2.3 Embracing a New Professional Community: Interpersonal Reciprocal Emotional Communication

With the different length of time employed in a corporation/organization, employees are divided into newcomers and seniors. Seniors may gang up on the newcomers, or they may offer their hands to help the newcomers adapt quickly, depending on how these newcomers behave. To be accepted by professional groups, the newcomers need to acknowledge the importance of seniors and make them feel respected. In the Chinese culture emphasizing seniority and ranking, senior employees, as the old-timers in an organization, normally enjoy psychological authority and obtain emotional satisfaction of being recognized, respected, and admired by helping and supporting the newcomers. The newcomers, on the other hand, obtain guidance from the senior colleagues using certain emotional communication skills. Gradually, they will be accepted by existing professional groups. By this kind of emotional interactions, newcomers achieve emotional adaptation within the workplace.

Xiangyu, who is about to turn 19 years old, is from Zigong, Sichuan province. His father works for meagre wages, and his mother has been sick for many years. Instead of finishing high school, he chose to learn cooking. Now he works as a chef in a big hotel. Working from 8 am to 11 pm every day, he barely has days off. Weekends are the busiest time of a week, and he now earns 3800 yuan on a monthly basis. It has been almost a year since he came to Nanjing. His mentor and a group of old colleagues have taken good care of him. With a cheerful and optimistic personality, he quickly adapted to the working environment of the hotel he currently works in, and the people around have created a harmonious atmosphere. The emotion established on the division of labour and daily communications is different from the feeling of strong trust and mutual attachment built within a primary network. It is more like a kind of emotional investment of interpersonal reciprocity. New employees gradually integrate into the established circle of professional groups and become one of them amid such emotional interactions.

However, compared with those seniors, newcomers tend to get familiarized with the workplace environment through their peers. Most new-generation migrant workers start with colleagues of similar ages, because they share similar status in the organization, and the growth trajectory of young people makes it easy for peers to find topics of common interest. Although peers may encounter certain frictions or even conflicts at work, they have similar life experiences outside of their working organization, so they can form a sense of dependence and shared destiny. Xiaoluo, from Huanggang, Hubei province, is 18 years old. His parents work outside all year-round. Left behind by his parents in the countryside, he feels confused. Fortunately, he is optimistic and open-minded, believing that people will know each other over time. Daily interactions make all colleagues naturally familiar with each other. It is also in the process of being accepted by the professional group of colleagues that they gradually build up a sense of familiarity with their organization.

> The atmosphere among colleagues is quite harmonious. I am an easy-going person. At the very beginning, everyone was not familiar with each other, which is the same in every company. Now I know them well, and not to mention we are all young people. And we never beat around the bush. Faced with difficulties at work, I always ask my colleagues for help, and then solve these problems by myself.
>
> (Xiaoluo, male, from Huanggang, Hubei)

Not everyone can be as lucky as Xiaoluo. Due to the various conflicts of interest, it is difficult to achieve mutual recognition among colleagues. In many cases, many people, being rejected by the original professional groups, can only be reduced to a narrow loop of social circle. Xiaodu is 20 years old and works as a receptionist at a beauty shop in Xinjiekou, Nanjing. She comes from a rural village in Tianshui, Gansu, and she has five younger siblings in the family. Xiaodu dropped out of school at the age of 17 and then left her hometown to work with one of her classmates. Before coming to Nanjing, Xiaodu had worked in a garment factory in Hangzhou. The female workers in the factory crazed to vie with each other and always asked newcomers to do all the work, which made Xiaodu quite uncomfortable. Later on, she developed a smaller social network. Her story illustrates the complexity of emotional communication in the process of interpersonal adaptation. If people are not emotionally accepted by the established group, they can only exist as a subgroup of the organization.

> When I first came here, I didn't know anyone, and I saw a lot of things I hadn't seen before. I was scared and dared not to talk to people, so I had no friends. There were many female workers who entered the factory earlier than me. I talked to them but they always felt superior. I had no other friends at that time. I had to hang out with them as companions. But sometimes, they can be really annoying and I want to keep a distance from them. Later, a few colleagues and I formed a sub-group and we always gathered as good friends.
>
> (Xiaodu, female, from Tianshui, Gansu)

Colleague relationship brings emotional satisfaction, such as a good working atmosphere and a mutual assistance mechanism, but it also leads to emotional disconnection, that is, miscommunication, misunderstanding, jealousy, and underhanded attempts to compete. Yige, from Suzhou, Jiangsu, is 20 years old. He is quite outgoing and knows about the relationship between colleagues. He used to work in Wuxi and Suzhou. Currently, he is engaged in the machinery industry in Hefei as a CNC lathes operator. In his eyes, a good relationship among colleagues helps the new generation of migrant workers quickly adapt to the professional environment and be accepted by professional groups. However, adverse relationships among colleagues generate an "anti-adaptation" effect. The conservativeness and bullying of colleagues may make it difficult for new employees to integrate into the working atmosphere.

> When working together, colleagues can establish dynamic relationships through both cooperation and competition, involving personal interests in relation to promotion and pay raise. Some [migrant workers] make good friends with their colleagues and share privacy with each other. Sometimes, they express their dissatisfaction with the boss in private, only to find someone snitch on them to their supervisors. Some are promoted based on their capabilities, but their "good" friends think that he or she has played tricks to get the promotion. Felt cheated, they would retaliate by leaking his or her privacy. That being said, the relationship among colleagues really matters. Work can only be accomplished through collaborations among colleagues; many difficult problems can be solved by regularly consulting with colleagues. Colleagues can put forward opinions and suggestions on your work performance. Fair competition with colleagues can generate motivation and learning opportunities, which will keep you in a good mood at work.
>
> (Yige, male, from Suzhou, Jiangsu)

Most of the new generation of migrant workers said that "you will have friends after a long time" and "people will get familiar over time". "Familiarity" is essentially a sense of adaptation after being accepted by the group. Individuals feel that they are gradually accepted by the group. Through mutual help and mutual assistance, they get to understand both formal and informal rules in a professional environment. Whether this process can go smoothly depends on the industry that a company is engaged in, its business scale, organizational structure, and management system. As such, workers in the service industry are more likely to get familiarized with one another and communicate in a trough period of a business cycle. In comparison, it takes relatively longer time for workers to get familiar with each other in the manufacturing industry. Due to the large scale of manufacturing work, employees are atomized by various processes and the work on the assembly line allows no slackness. In addition, the piece-rate wage system makes them quite busy at work, so they barely have time to communicate and interact with each other. In any case, only when they are emotionally accepted by the group of colleagues can they find a sense of familiarity.

3. "I Can Only Rely on Myself": Utilization of Media and Professional Consciousness in Self-Empowerment

The Western empowerment theory believes that empowerment, as an interactive social process, cannot be separated from the communication of information and interpersonal exchange, suggesting a natural connection with the most fundamental communication behaviour of human beings (Ding, 2011). Although the professional adaptation of the new generation of migrant workers has been pushed by various media from the outside, it goes beyond the level of job acquisition and role fulfilment aided by the media. In their daily professional life, migrant workers are not just simple performers of tasks. They have their own emotions, thoughts, and strategies, and they can also use the media to accumulate professional experience, expand their network, and update their professional cognition. Through the use of new media and interpersonal communication practices in urban and rural areas, they actively plan their careers, play their professional roles, confirm their professional values as time progresses, and develop a professional self-identity in their work. These basic communication behaviours tap their own potential, bring them a certain sense of self-efficacy and a control over their professional life, hence empowering themselves.

3.1 Upgrading Technology Literacy: Migrant Workers' New Media Use and Career Planning

We are living in a highly mediated society. The media of the current era has exerted a far greater influence than any other time in history (Zhang, 2006). As the whole society is undergoing a huge revolution in accessing information and forming relationship networks, it is not surprising to witness the penetration of the new media in the daily lives of migrant workers. They can obtain useful career information by using the new media, including ongoing learning materials, recruitment opportunities, pay range, and opportunities to start a business, all of which have a catalytic effect on their career planning. The social attribute of the new media can also provide them with a network of relationships they need for career planning.

Despite of the short entrepreneurial experience of Wenxiu we mentioned earlier, her new media literacy is instrumental in making her dream come true. After she developed an awareness of career planning, she was able to find relevant professional training information. For example, the keywords she used (e.g., "Wuhan", "Snack", "Training School") when searching online included both regional and vocational elements. Therefore, the information retrieved from the web page was quite effective. She also chatted with customer service staff via QQ, to compare and filter the information gained from multiple sources. After her new career kicked off, she took the initiative to use the new media to gain customers' attention and facilitate the arrangement of her store operations. In so doing, she has purposefully used the new media to have a better career development.

The new media can also help migrant workers find virtual social networks which can benefit their career planning. Zhiwei, mentioned earlier, is an avid reader of online news and also likes to chat through QQ. Although his use of new media are partly for entertainment and recreation, they can also provide some career information, especially the virtual social network built on QQ. By expanding virtual interpersonal relationships, he has accumulated a certain amount of online social capital. However, the transition from the online social capital into offline social capital remains a long way to go, because what he had learned from his net friends is superficial. He also worked for an online store to learn some knowledge about online store operations. Although these self-empowering attempts eventually failed due to the lack of social support, Zhiwei had already understood the importance of using the new media proactively.

In addition, the new media per se can become a platform for their career development. In spite of the entry barriers, ordinary people can still manage to learn the Internet technology. Many new-generation migrant workers have felt the influence of the Internet since they were young. Driven by their natural interests in computer technology and strong self-learning abilities, they can start up quickly. Many migrant workers achieved their career transitions through the new media. They have been engaged in more decent and well-paid jobs like web art design, graphic design, website construction, and Internet promotion.

Compared with Zhiwei's failure in his career planning, Xiaowu mentioned earlier is a typical example of a successful career transition using the new media. After finishing high school, Xiaowu first worked in Foxconn as an assembly line worker and later as a real estate salesman for a short period. He is smart and has learned some network technologies. When he was at Foxconn, he wanted to build a dating website to meet the needs of young people. When working in the real estate industry, he also used the network platform to attract potential customers. To some extent, he has consciously adopted the new media to enrich his career possibilities. After many twists and turns, he is now fully dedicated to website development, maintenance, and Internet promotion and becomes a practitioner in the IT industry.

I have worked in the Foxconn workshop for several years. At that time, Foxconn's Shenzhen factory had almost 200,000 people. There were a lot of young people who were at the age of dating and starting a relationship, and all of them would go online. Under the influence of *51.com*,[2] I wanted to set up a dating website called *Dashuikeng Dating.com*, since the Foxconn factory was located in Dashuikeng Village. The website had successfully been built but didn't last long due to poor promotion. Thereafter, tired of the two-shift working schedule, I left Foxconn and went to a real estate company. The manager would provide us with a contact list of potential customers, whom I eagerly made calls. Other people in the company knew nothing about the Internet, but I knew how to use it. I posted ads on *51.com*, and a lot of phone calls naturally came, which was aspired by my colleagues. Later, I realized that there were a lot of tricks in selling real estate properties, and I couldn't make it because of my conscience. With the help of one of my friends who worked in the IT industry and some online tutorials, I learned website design by myself. This how I changed my job.

(Wu, male, from Anshun, Guizhou)

E-commerce has developed rapidly in recent years, which is close to the lives of ordinary netizens. Driven by the trend of consumerism, many people have dreamed of opening their own online shops, as a goal in their career planning. A'miao is a 20-year-old girl from Huaiyin, Jiangsu. After finishing high school and failing to pass the college entrance examination, she went to a vocational medical school in her hometown. But after less than a year, she was still not interested in her caring major, so she dropped out of school and came to Nanjing with the help of relatives. In Nanjing, she has been working in a clothing store owned by her relatives. In her spare time, she often takes some part-time job. She loves shopping on Taobao[3] and dreams of opening an online store in the future. For her, opening an online store is relatively easy as compared to opening a brick-and-mortar store. So, she plans to make more money and carry out her career plan when the time is right.

> Girls love to shop on *Taobao* now, and so do I. The more I go shopping, the more I want to open a store online. And my shopping experience would to be an attempt to accumulate online experience. I rarely make purchases though, unless I really like something or there is a good deal. I really want to open a *Taobao* shop, because [by doing this] I can make money and save energy. I heard that many [Taobao] shop owners earn tens of thousands of yuan a month! You don't need to rent a store or hire people to open an online store. Just take photos and upload them and send the goods to customers by express. How great! I prefer to sell clothes because I think I have a taste for fashion. I don't want to be a worker all my life. I can't always rely on my family to make a living. But I don't have a specific plan yet. I guess no one will support me. My family is relatively conservative. After all, I don't have enough money to start my own business.
>
> (Amiao, female, from Huaiyin, Jiangsu)

The access to and use of new media go beyond simply obtaining professional information. New generation migrant workers make different career plans based on their personal characteristics, professional capabilities, and social support networks. New media is more than a tool for career planning; it can also help people obtain information and get recharged for their work. Even the new media per se can serve as a professional platform for migrant workers. They have been proactive in making the most of the new media in digging for information, while their media literacy began to upgrade, achieving a certain degree of information empowerment.

3.2 Improvement of Career Quotient: Identity Management and Professional Role Playing of "Organizers"

Studying in school requires IQ (Intelligence Quotient), falling in love requires EQ (Emotional Quotient), and winning in the workplace requires CQ (Career Quotient). In short, CQ is a combination of IQ and EQ at work. It is a kind of comprehensive wisdom that includes judgment ability, spiritual temperament, and positive attitude. It is about the compatibility of self and work, as well as status quo and development. At first, new-generation migrant workers have little experience in the real world after leaving school, and do not understand what the workplace is like. Weathered through the years, they have gained some insights about the way of survival in the workplace. They also figure out which kind of mentality, habits, and styles are conducive to career development, and which behaviours are taboo. Additionally, they know how to strike a balance between organizational goals and personal interests.

Twenty-nine-year-old Long is from Chongqing. His family is quite poor, and he once fell for a pyramid scheme. Later, Long went to Nanjing to live with his cousin and studied in a massage school. After graduation, Long was recommended to work in a massage and pedicure salon in Changzhou. Coming from humble beginnings, he was later promoted to be a store manager running three stores in Changzhou. He had a good professional mentality from the very beginning. With a firm belief that everything starts small, he has won the respect of his boss through hard work. He has paid attention to building good interpersonal relationships with colleagues and learning from leaders and customers during work. This way, he has climbed to the pinnacle of his career through successful professional role-playing.

> At that time, I was a technician. When there were no customers in the store, I offered to help other staff – basically I would do everything. I knew nothing at first, and I learned things by doing. To get a promotion and peer recognition, you need to do your job well. In fact, every dog has its day. We should learn from each other because it is helpful to your own development. I also like to consult successful people, such as my boss, and others around me. Chatting with them is pretty enlightening.
>
> (Long, male, from Chongqing)

As for how to maintain a balanced interpersonal relationship in the workplace, Yangzi, mentioned earlier, has made a good attempt. Working for over ten years, Yangzi felt tired and was stuck in a dilemma: he was unwilling to accept low-paid jobs earning three to four thousand yuan while not capable of doing work worth hundreds of thousands of yuan. Besides, it was still impossible to settle in Wenzhou for someone like him, who only earned 10,000 yuan a month. After careful consideration for over half a year, he finally decided to resign and start a small business. In retrospect, he fully recognizes the importance of interpersonal relationships. Meanwhile, he believes the most essential thing is the value one creates for the company. Interpersonal relationship is not a castle in the air. It can only promote career development if it is based on one's own value. Thanks to his understanding of professional roles and interpersonal relationships, he has managed to climb up the corporate ladder, all the way from a lower-level employee to the director of R&D Department.

Although the relationship among colleagues makes a significant part of interpersonal communication in the workplace, it is still a horizontal and internal relationship. In contrast, the relationship with leaders and customers is more complicated and requires a specific communication strategy. This is especially true for the new-generation migrant workers who have reached a certain level in a company. Wentao, mentioned earlier, is from Luan, Anhui. Now he is doing network maintenance in a hotel in Nanjing. He has been working for several years, and his outstanding performance is valued by his boss, who intended to give him a promotion and make him duty manager. His achievement can be attributed to his rational communication strategy. When the boss does not provide the solution to a problem, he will put himself in others' shoes and adjust his professional mentality, so as not to fall into a destructive organizational communication relationship. The proper management of personal emotions also reflects his good professional quality. Now he also takes charge of a small shop in the front of the hotel. The boss sets an annual sales target of 500,000 yuan and the net profit must reach 100,000 yuan, which puts a certain pressure on him. Fortunately, he knows how to relieve professional pressures through multiple ways.

> If I encounter difficulties at work, I will report to my boss and seek his help. I think teamwork is very important. Though I may feel uncomfortable if my boss leaves me down here on my own, I won't be emotional. I will try my best to cooperate with my boss. After all, he has his own reasons for doing things, and I should try to think in his way. Bosses in the hotel industry are very realistic as poor business performance can deny all the efforts. When I am upset, I sing the blues to my families. When I am free, I go to the market and send out my business cards to some bosses, trying to develop them into potential customers. Work is more or less stressful. Sometimes I travel with my families and relatives, and we have almost visited every scenic spot in Nanjing. Now I start to travel to nearby cities, watch TV and play basketball to relax.
>
> (Wentao, male, from Lu An, Anhui)

Regardless, their professional role-playing requires a particular stage provided by the organization. When the organization cannot meet their demand for professional development, the new-generation migrant workers tend to seek better performance space by job-hopping. Occupational mobility is an important feature of the market economy. As a factor of production, human labour can move freely because the market mechanism recognizes individual ability and efforts. So occupational mobility is an important way to seek instrumental resources such as job compensations and development space. When occupational mobility occurs, the new professional adaptation process starts again, and a new round of occupational role-playing takes place.

As such, new-generation migrant workers play their professional roles in the organization through differentiated communication strategies to achieve professional growth and obtain various resources within the organization. Both the increase in job compensations and the promotion of professional positions can be regarded as an instrumental level of empowerment with a practical nature.

3.3 Enhancement of Self-efficacy: Urban and Rural Interpersonal Communication and Recognition of Professional Value

People always attach certain emotions to work. Working does not only mean earning money to support the family, but also means fulfilment and satisfaction brought by work. It is in the pursuit of fulfilment and satisfaction that the new-generation migrant workers confirm their professional values. The value of occupation can be embodied both in the production process and in the distribution field. The value ranges from the superficial level of compensations to a more profound change of professional achievement (Gu, 2001). When interacting with colleagues, customers, and relatives, the new generation of migrant workers, like the older generation, attaches great importance to the surface layer of material benefits. However, unlike the older generation of migrant workers who pay more attention to personal income, they care more about promotion opportunities and professional prospects.

Wentao, mentioned earlier, is earnest and diligent. He has been working in a hotel for several years. His boss thinks highly of him and promises that he can be promoted to duty manager if he excels at his work. He is satisfied with the job and has received much recognition in the company due to his great performance and good relationship with company executives. Most of the colleagues are female and of different ages. At work, they are busy with their own business, while living in different places after work. It makes sense that there is not much interaction between colleagues. He said that as long as he is honest and reasonable, others will not talk behind his back. His families are also quite satisfied with his work and place great expectations on his career development. The recognition from the company, the harmonious relationship between colleagues, and the support of his family all make him full of confidence in his future career development.

> Generally, I feel good about my current job. Now I am allowed to participate in company meetings, mainly to coordinate the work of each department, set up the guest room, do some cleaning, check the equipment, and so on. I have been working here for a long time, and my performance is satisfying. The boss plans to promote me to be duty manager. I shared the joy with my families, and they thought it would be nice to be a duty manager in the future, since I could learn more things at this position. I get along well with colleagues. And I think there is a bright future for a qualified duty manager, because you can bring economic benefits to the company.
>
> (Wentao, male, from Anhui Luan)

In addition, they pay more attention to the deep values in professional production. Their choice to take a job or change a job is based on whether the work itself is interesting and can reflect one's creativity. Many workers move from the manufacturing industry to the service industry or the sales industry because they think manufacturing is procedural and modelized and lacks professional autonomy. When working in the manufacturing industry, they cannot feel the professional value, whereas the service industry and sales industry can provide more flexibility, which is often reflected in the interactive business relationships. To be more specific, recognition and affirmation from the outside world can provoke their sense of professional accomplishment, thus enabling them to recognize their own professional value.

Afang, born in 1990 from Jingzhou, Hubei, is now a clerk in a cosmetics shop in Jiaxing. He has been working as a packaging worker in a garment manufacturing factory since the age of 17. Talking about the repetitive packaging work in the factory, he felt there was no room for career development and no professional value at all. Two years later, he resigned and began to work as a salesperson at a cosmetics store in Jiaxing. Comparing the two jobs, he believes that his current job of sales is "more challenging" and generates a stronger sense of achievement.

> The most significant difference between selling cosmetics and packaging clothes lies in its resilience. Different customers come to our store with distinct requirements of skincare, and we need to recommend suitable cosmetics from person to person. Still, customers have different understandings of their own needs: some may know how to protect their skin so they can choose products by themselves, while other customers may have no idea about their skin types and the kind of cosmetics suitable to them. In this case, we need to pay more attention and provide appropriate suggestions. That's why my current job is more challenging.
>
> (A Fang, male, from Jingzhou, Hubei)

Maoer, mentioned earlier, is quite satisfied with her work. She is a masseuse in a beauty salon. It is in the narrow massage room that she has more interpersonal interactions with urban customers. Since she has great massaging skills, and she is so honey-lipped that she knows how to tailor her words to please the ears of different people, she has won the recognition and trust of customers, albeit on an instrumental and shallow level of interaction. On the one hand, frequent customers would refer new clients to her to improve her work performance. On the other hand, these customers would invite her to have a meal and go shopping. In some service industries, the recognition of customers constitutes an important source of professional value. Customer experience is the utmost decisive factor in the beauty and body health industry that Maoer is engaged in. With the respect, trust, and praise from the customers, they discover their own professional value while the mental and physical exhaustion caused by work has been dissipated.

> I am satisfied with this job. However, the working space is too small. I can only see a few people each day, and they are all ladies. The job does not offer me opportunities to expand my horizon. In this industry, if you want to get promotion, you must rely on your working experiences and your popularity. After working for a long time, many customers come back and they will also recommend you to others. I have been with my customers for a long time, and

gradually we are like friends. I hang out and go shopping with a few customers I met when I entered the industry, and they always take care of me.

(Maoer, female, from Xuzhou, Jiangsu)

The deliberation and preliminary confirmation of professional values forms a
series of information about the effectiveness of professional life. The information comes from a wide range of interpersonal communication between urban
and rural areas. It may be a message of trust and recognition sent through the
process of serving city customers. It may be the affirmation and approval of their
work in the process of getting along with colleagues and leaders. It may also be
the positive comments about their work when they are chatting with relatives
and friends. These positive interpersonal communication practices bring a certain
degree of professional self-efficacy to the new generation of migrant workers. It is
manifested not only in the sense of control over the work process, but also in the
satisfaction of completing the work, as well as the sense of confidence in career
development, so as to realize the emotional empowerment of migrant workers.

4. Successful Transformation: Media Support During Professional Adaptation

Unlike their urban peers, new-generation migrant workers' professional adaptation process tends to be more complex as they move from the countryside to the
city. Their professional adaptation is not a linear process of transiting from the traditional society to the large-scale mass production in modern society. Rather, it is
a multidimensional process influenced by personal characters, work experiences,
organizational norms, social networks, and policy systems, in which media plays
a pivotal role. In the early days of entering the city, the new generation of migrant
workers was in a critical period of youth socialization. With new career possibilities ahead of them, they are embracing an unknown professional life and is particularly vulnerable to the impact of the urban communication environment. By
using various forms of media, they obtain job opportunities and fulfil their professional roles. While gaining more work experience, they are no longer simply
reacting to the stimulus of the urban communication environment but have begun
to deploy the means of communication to advance their professions, carry out a
series of social communication practices, eventually realizing self-empowerment
and construct professional self-identity. The extensive involvement of the media
has facilitated their professional adaptation process and helped them achieve professional development.

4.1 From Media Promotion to Self-empowerment: A Two-way Process of Career Adaptation

The starting point of career adaptation is job search (acquisition of job opportunities), and information becomes the most helpful resource in this process. Apart
from the family and its associated social network, the mass media, government

organizations in labour importing and exporting regions, talent markets, occupational agencies, employers, and other organizations are widely involved, bridging the gap between employers and job applicants. Media from different sources and in various forms serve as a channel for the flow of information, providing information support for the new generation of migrant workers to make the right decision. Compared with the older generation, the new generation of migrant workers is endowed with a broader and more diversified channel of job search, reflecting the fact that a wider range of media has been involved in the employment information market alongside the progress of social modernization.

Once the process of acquiring career opportunity is completed, there is an immediate career adaptation period, of which the adaptation of vocational skills matters most. After enterprises hire the migrant workers from the labour market, they need to transform free and undisciplined individuals into self-disciplined and efficient "organizational people" to realize their organizational goals. This requires a systematic training of their vocational skills in order to quickly fit workers into the modern mass production and maximize the value of human resources. The range and depth of these trainings vary according to the actual situations of each company, that is, the industry background, its business scale, management style, and development vision. It is in these formal or informal trainings that the new-generation migrant workers gradually acquire the vocational skills necessary to adapt to their jobs. Apart from corporations, some market-oriented organizations are also involved in this process. In addition, the skill transfer in private social networks is also common in the daily operations of organizations. Overall, this is an organization-led and goal-oriented process of resource exchange.

While the adaptation of professional skills can be achieved by doing their jobs well, the new-generation migrant workers also need to smoothly integrate into the professional groups within the enterprise. As such, they can adapt to the "hard" organizational environment quickly by following the formal rules and regulations and through personal observation. In comparison, the "soft" environment of interpersonal relationships takes them a long time to fit in. The traditional Chinese culture values interpersonal harmony. Initially, newly employed migrant workers might be treated as outsiders and bullied by some senior employees. Yet the boundaries between insiders and outsiders are blurred. Senior employees might develop reciprocal relationships and have emotional interactions with new employees, albeit on a limited scale and different from the natural attachment in primary relationship networks. Such altruistic behaviours could help new employees familiarize themselves with the professional environment, thus effectively facilitating their adaptation to the organizational culture.

In addition, the individuality of professional adaptation is mainly embodied as "the work depends on oneself". In this regard, the new generation of migrant workers makes use of various communication practices in their efforts to empower themselves. They have formed a certain degree of professional consciousness in media use, which can be analysed from the following three aspects.

At the personal level, the rapid development of new communication technologies and the extensive adoption of laptops, smartphones, and tablets have enabled the new generation of migrant workers to extend the primary interpersonal communication channel to obtain more professional information. Those who tend to have more successful career development are also better at searching, filtering, and integrating information. Through the access and use of new media, they can obtain career information and make specific career plans. Because of the easy access to grassroots, the new media per se can serve as a platform for the new-generation migrant workers to develop their careers. In their attempts to maximize the value of information, they are closer to realizing the goal of information empowerment.

At the interpersonal level, new-generation migrant workers acquire occupation-related information through interpersonal communications with customers, leaders, colleagues, relatives, and friends. During this process, they examine and try to confirm their professional value, which reflects the recognition of their professional identity. On the one hand, it comes from an individual's interests, enthusiasm, and self-evaluation of the profession. On the other hand, it is closely related to the external evaluation of the profession. The positive feedbacks from the outside world greatly promote their recognition of professional value, and even dilute the negative emotions brought about by the "dirty, tough, tiring" nature of the work per se. It can be said that the generation of professional value reflects a certain degree of emotional empowerment.

At the organizational level, as a channel of organizational communication for the new generation of migrant workers, the enterprise holds abundant practical resources that migrant workers want to obtain, such as incomes, bonuses, and professional power. In their professional life, migrant workers consciously play the role of "organized workers" by meeting the expectations and following the norms of such a role, and handling the relationships with colleagues, superiors, and subordinates. Accordingly, they deal with the workplace pressure, set up their career development goals, and make corresponding career plans, so as to be well prepared for their career adjustments like promotion and salary increase. In this way, they've drawn on various resources that are beneficial to their career development. This is essentially a kind of practical self-empowerment.

4.2 The Logic of Professional Adaptation and the Construction of Media Support Systems

In an urban society, various media have been widely involved in all aspects of people's professional life. This includes opportunity seeking, skill acquisition, and familiarization with the environment at the surface, as well as career planning, role playing, and value seeking at a deeper level. Taking into account ethics, humanity, interests protection, or moral considerations, various media have promoted the occupational adaptation of the new generation of migrant workers in every aspect of information dissemination, resource transmission, and emotional communication. At the same time, the new generation of migrant workers takes the initiative to use the media to realize self-empowerment. Whether it is driven the continuous impetus of various media or migrant workers' proactive utilization of media, what cannot be ignored is the important role that the media have played in their professional life. In this sense, the media supports the professional adaptation of the new generation of migrant workers. During this process, the interpersonal communication network based on the blood, geographical and professional ties, together with the organizational communication channels such as the government and business enterprises, as well as the mass media and new media, constitute a mediated support system for their professional adaptation.

First, the media serves as a channel to create an information environment. According to McEvers, the urban expansion inevitably triggers social mobility, which in turn leads to increasing demand for communication (Qiu, 2013). New-generation migrant workers need to find jobs, learn about salary levels, acquire vocational skills, and seek job-hopping opportunities, all of which are inseparable from adequate information. There has always been a tension between the demand and satisfaction of information in the labour market. To a certain extent, the developed urban communication system has relieved the tension in information dissemination. But the empowering effect of information would be limited if it is confined to a certain node in the network. In other words, information can only play its part when it flows through the Internet. This is an innate feature of the media in facilitating the information flow. Hence, the new generation of migrant workers has been surrounded by various media in an information environment connecting the communicators and recipients at both ends of the network. In so doing, the media protect the information rights of new-generation migrant workers and prevents them from becoming "the information poor".

Second, the media act as an intermediary to provide social resources. Individuals' career adaptation always takes place within a certain organizational communication environment. While the organizational channels (referring mainly to companies) provide explicit knowledge resources such as skill trainings, secondary relationship networks (mainly composed of kinship) are deeply embedded in migrant workers' work and life. In the secondary networks, various resources (especially implicit knowledge resources) bring useful help to those who are willing to act. Through the investment in the network of relationships, individuals gain social capital and access to social resources from the network when needed. At the same time, the primary relationship network is at the core of the life circle of the new generation of migrant workers, which bears an obligatory nature in the Chinese context, as their acquaintances tend to reflect their sense of responsibility in the "selfless" giving of resources (Shen, 2003). In addition, the access to and use of the mass media and new media also play a vital role in facilitating resource acquisition within the business organizations. As an intermediary that provides resources, the media run through the whole process of communication practices. Likewise, the process of media access, maintenance, and expansion is essentially a process of generating and accumulating social capital.

Finally, the media serve as a carrier of emotional attachment. It is impossible for a person to engage in work without any emotional involvement. To achieve a deeper level of emotional adaptation, it is necessary to use the media to "narrate" emotions in various forms. This is because emotions are expressive, that is, people always have a need to express. Whether it is emotional exchange or communication, human emotions always need to be carried on (Guo, 2008). In the interaction of social relationships, on the one hand, the media maintain the most basic channel of emotional communication in the workplace, thereby achieving harmonious interpersonal relationships within the organization. In so doing, individuals have established the sense of familiarity and security in their professional life. On the other hand, the media help individuals to pursue positive emotional energy and to affirm their professional values in order to gain a sense of belonging and identification with their professional organization. Whether it is social networks in interpersonal interactions or the mass media and new media in symbolic interactions, the media have been a practical carrier of emotional attachment, facilitating the emotional adaptation of the new generation of migrant workers.

It can be seen that the career adaptation process of the new generation of migrant workers is actually a process supported by the media. As a channel to create an information environment, the media provide information support. As an intermediary that provides social resources, the media provide instrumental support. As a carrier of emotional attachment, the media provide emotional support.

A sound mediated support system is comprised of two essential parties: one party needs help, and the other party is willing and able to provide help. If the two parties and the relationship between them are regarded as a stable structure, a mediated support system should not be one-dimensional, ignoring the interaction between the supporter and the one being supported. Specifically, a mediated support system provides the new generation of migrant workers with all levels of information dissemination, resource transfer, and emotional communication. This system regulates their organizational behaviours and promotes their organization adaptation and social inclusion. At the same time, migrant workers also need to take the initiative to use the mediated support system to develop their professional awareness, exercise professional mentality, and cultivate professional identity. Only in this way can they achieve information empowerment at the personal level, emotional empowerment at the interpersonal level, and material empowerment at the organizational level.

Notes

1 Translator's note: Chinese government collectivized its agricultural production in the 1950s and decollectivized it approximately three decades later.
2 Translator's note: one of China's largest social networking websites and community portals.
3 Translator's note: one of China's largest e-commerce websites.

References

Ding, W. (2011). New media empowerment: Theoretical construction and case analysis – A case study of online self-organization of rare blood groups in China. *Open Times*, *1*, 124–145.

Fu, P., & Jiang, L. (2007). Limitations and breakthroughs in studies of migrant workers' integration into city life. *The World of Survey and Research, 6,* 14–17.

Gu, X. (2001). Initial exploration on the structure of vocational value. *Exploration of Psychology, 21*(1), 58–63.

Guo, J. (2008). *Emotion sociology: Theory, history and reality.* Shanghai Sanlian Bookstore, p. 156.

Li, J. (2002). Multiple separation of labor market in China and its impact on labor supply and demand. *Chinese Journal of Population Science, 2,* 1–7.

Qiu, L. (2013). *The world factory in the information age: New working-class network society.* Guangxi Normal University Press, p. 126.

Shen, Y. (2003). Obligatory relationship: Beyond the emotional or instrumental relationship. *Chinese Journal of Sociology, 9,* 21–25.

Tong, Z. (2011). Career development and work adaption: Urban practice of the new generation of migrant workers. *China Youth Study, 1,* 10–14+41.

Xin, B. (2005). A new interpretation of modern people's way of life. *Theoretical Investigation, 5,* 46–48.

Xu, C. (2010). Ways of migrating into the city and occupational mobility of migrant workers: Comparative analysis of two generations of migrant workers. *Youth Studies, 3,* 1–12+94.

Zhai, X. (2003). Research on Social mobility and relationship trust: Relationship intensity and job-seeking strategies of migrant workers. *Sociological Studies, 1,* 1–11.

Zhang, T. (2006). Public opinions in the context of a mediated society. *Modern Communication (Journal of Communication University of China), 5,* 12–15.

Zheng, X. (2011a). *Rural communication: An empirical analysis and strategy discussion based on the audience.* Zhejiang University Press, p. 169.

9 Media Experience

The Leisure Life of the New Generation of Migrant Workers

Leisure is an essential human need and a basic human right. For the new-generation migrant workers whose education levels are considerably higher than those of their predecessors, "making money" is no longer their only internal motivation for leaving their homes to work. These workers are also pursuing a higher quality of life and the same services and culture as people living in cities enjoy. Additionally, the new-generation migrant workers hope to achieve personal development, realize their value of life, and experience modern leisure and entertainment. The relatively underdeveloped environments of the countryside are unable to provide the new generation of migrant workers with culturally rich and highly developed urban environments offering frequent opportunities for social interactions. Various media have revolutionized the leisure life of these migrant workers by changing their living conditions, psychological attitudes, and how they "blend in" in their cities.

The leisure lives new-generation migrant workers in cities reveal changes in their ideas, self-awareness, and social psychology, as their "identities" change in the presence of complex social factors. Changes in their leisure lives both before and after they arrive in cities and the effects of new urban media experiences on their leisure lives are both topics that merit further investigations. Therefore, we examined the leisure life of this new generation of migrant workers to gain insight into the effects of media, a crucial social development variable, on their daily, leisure, and city lives as well as on their individual development.

1. Different City Lives: Bittersweet Youths

Workers of different ages, family backgrounds, city experiences, and life experiences have different life situations and personality traits. However, these workers do share some similar traits. For example, their childhoods were generally dull and boring because their villages had little infrastructure and the available recreational activities were monotonous. New-generation migrant workers left their villages to work in cities because of unfavourable family financial situations and poor school performance, and their leisure life changed through their city experiences. Their city experiences may be challenging, enjoyable, arduous, or demanding in the beginning and pleasurable in the end. These experiences are

DOI: 10.4324/9781003365785-9

a memorable part of their youth. Overall, some workers must focus on making ends meet and thus have little time for leisure; their leisure activities are also relatively monotonous. By contrast, the younger group of migrant workers born in the 1990s who are not required to support their families financially get weary of the "colourful" leisure activities offered by cities over time and subsequently grow up and comply with norms. Older new-generation migrant workers participate in various leisure activities, since they have lived in cities for a long time and have accumulated wealth over years of hard work without the burden of taking care of their families. Thus, the leisure lives of individuals in the new generation varies chronologically according to their stages of life and personal situations.

1.1 No Time for Leisure Activities: Heavy Financial Burden

Xiaobo was born in 1988 in Huaibei, Anhui, and now works at a university canteen in Nanjing. She left her home to work at the age of 17 for eight or nine years, and is now a mother of a three-year-old child. Similar to most new-generation migrant workers of similar ages, she had a difficult life. Her father passed away when she was young, and she had to support her elderly mother and young brother. She came to the city of Nanjing alone, and was finally able to make a stable income after many years of hardship. To her, life is challenging rather than enjoyable, and leisure is a luxury, not a necessity.

> When I was little, all I did was school; I didn't get to play much. My family was poor. Anhui isn't an affluent province, and the small city of Huaibei is less so. When I was a 15-year-old student, I had only been to the inner county two or three times. Just going shopping was a huge deal back then. We didn't have any money and it wasn't like I could ask my mom for it. However, boarding schools cost money; meals and accommodations cost money. It was really hard, and saving money was really difficult. The thought of buying clothes and going to a county capital to have fun never even occurred to me.
> (Xiaobo, female, from Huaibei, Anhui)

Xiaobo thought that she had a monotonous, boring childhood, and lamented how poor the standard of living once was.

> On Saturdays and Sundays, I fed sheep. Life is so much easier today compared with what it was like in the past. Look at my little girl; I think she really has it good. I get anxious when she's picky about what she eats. When I was little, I didn't get to eat even when I wanted to. The same goes for playing. Back then, school was all there was . . . well, that and coming home to cut grass to feed sheep.
> (Xiaobo, female, from Huaibei, Anhui)

For most new-generation migrant workers in the same age group as Xiaobo, rural life was primitive, boring, and low-quality. Although not everyone had as much financial pressure as she did, factors such as incomplete rural infrastructure, low quality-of-life, and undeveloped communication environments contributed to the difficulty of this lifestyle. As young students, this generation had few leisure activities to choose from.

Xiaobo did not pass her senior high school exam; thus, due to her family situations, she decided to work temporary jobs to help out with family expenses. She fantasized about working in cities.

> I really wanted to visit the city because I never had a chance to. My uncle, who worked various temporary jobs in cities, used to tell me how wonderful city life was. He would bring me candies, sweaters, and scarves, and I would tell myself that I would visit the city when I grew up. I didn't care which city; any city would be better than home.

She later realized that city life was not as pleasant as she thought it would be. Her first city job was at a university cafeteria affiliated with the military in Nanjing. Because her work was incredibly demanding, she quit and went home after six months.

After taking a break at home for a time, Xiaobo visited Hangzhou with other people who had experience working in temporary jobs and found a job at a clothing factory. However, she was wronged and was subjected to unfair treatment, driving her to resign and go to Suzhou alone. As a stubborn individual, she sent a text message to her mother saying that she would not come back home until she had made a lot of money. Looking back, she feels that she was too naïve at that time.

After working in cities such as Hangzhou, Suzhou, Yiwu, and Nantong, Xiaobo returned to Nanjing in 2009 and has remained there since. She initially worked as a hotel attendant but subsequently resigned, saying

> I took the hotel exam for the qualification to be promoted to head waitress. However, I later found out what it took to become a head waitress. They had to drink and socialize with customers. Additionally, competition between my peers was fierce. Although I had an opportunity to work as the head waitress, I didn't drink and disliked the job requirements.
>
> (Xiaobo, female, from Huaibei, Anhui)

She subsequently quit, found a job at a university cafeteria affiliated to the military in Nanjing, and found a place she could call home.

As she drifted from place to place, Xiaobo learned that the most important thing in life is to survive, not to have high quality of life. As long as one can survive in the city, one will continue to have faith in life. Although she was heavily burdened by her family responsibilities, she did not and was not willing to back down from the "cruelty" of the cities. She travelled from city to city to find a home. Xiaobo's memories of cities were mostly of pain and hardship. She did not have time to enjoy what life had to offer; her only goal was to make money to support her mom and younger brother. Although not all new-generation migrant workers have such a heavy burden, the pressure of daily life is a major factor preventing new-generation migrant workers from enjoying leisure in the city.

Despite being in her mid-twenties, Xiaobo is already married and has given birth to a child. She found a home with her husband in his home region of Luhe District. Although her job at the university cafeteria is stable, it is also demanding and requires that she works most days. However, she is happy with the life she has now and believes that the hard times have passed.

> The job that I'm working now requires that I wake up slightly past four in the morning and work until one in the afternoon. Then, I get a one-hour break and work until 7:30 in the evening. It's a tough job, but I'm okay with it because this is what I decided to do. Although life is still hard, it's much, much better than what it used to be. We're definitely making progress.
>
> (Xiaobo, female, from Huaibei, Anhui)

The nature of her work leaves her little leisure time for herself. Her lunch break is not long enough for her to do anything but eat, and she has little time to do anything but sleep after getting home at night because she must wake up early for work the next day. She only has two days off a month; she uses this time to return to Luhe District and see her child. Her child is what she worries most about. "Every time I leave for work, my child won't let me go; it's really sad. But there's nothing we can do about it." Changing jobs is not an option.

> Jobs with many vacations have lower wages. If you find a job where you work less often, your pay is lower and you can't support your family. Now, I have two families to support – my own family and my mother's. I can still do it because I'm still young. If you don't work hard when you're young, life loses its purpose.

Not only does she have to support her family financially, she has to support her mother and brother. For Xiaobo, the pressure of life remains.

Because she has little time for herself, her leisure activities are relatively monotonous. Nonetheless, media become an essential part of her leisure activities, including surfing the net, watching TV, and playing on her cell phone. These activities all involve the use of media. Before she got married, she often went to Internet cafés. She also wanted to learn about computers. For TV, Xiaobo said "I normally watch the Jiangsu channel. I watch whatever is on to kill time." However, she remains sceptical about the authenticity of the programs. For example, she felt that *If You Are the One* is a TV show with little value.

Xiaobo's cell phone is one of the most important tools for her leisure life. "Every month, I use over 30 megabytes of network traffic on my cell phone alone. I mostly read Tencent news and stuff that I am interested in."

Xiaobo now has a stable income and happy family after years of hard work. In particular, she was able to make the down payment on a house in Luhe District, Nanjing for her brother, fulfilling her dream of taking care of her mother and brother. The day that we interviewed Xiaobo was the day after she got the mortgage, and her face was brimming with pride and joy. Xiaobo shouldered a heavy burden and embarked on an extremely difficult journey as she moved from a village to the cities; this burden prevented her from enjoying leisure in city life. She worked tirelessly to make ends meet. She is an epitome of the new generation of migrant workers who permanently shoulders the pressures of life. To these people, leisure is a luxury that they do not have. Nonetheless, the ways that they kill time has changed considerably as they moved from villages to the cities; before they had nothing and now they use media. This is one influence of city life.

1.2 Reduced Interest in Entertainment: From Immaturity to Complying With Norms

Xiaocao and Xiaoding are two young women who are relatively lucky compared with Xiaobo. They were not exposed to unfavourable family conditions forcing them to financially support their families from a young age. Born in the 1990s, they are single today and live relatively free lives; they only need to support themselves. Thus, they still seem somewhat naïve and innocent. City life has not been difficult for them; in fact, it is a life without consequences. Therefore, their leisure lives are comparatively more abundant.

Born in 1991 and 1994, Xiaocao and Xiaoding are from Baoji in Shaanxi and from Feidong County in Anhui, respectively. They are in their early twenties and do not have the same sense of fatigue from years of hard work that Xiaobo does. Similar to may new-generation migrant workers in this age group, they came to cities to work because their poor academic grades forced them to find jobs.

Xiaocao, a girl from northwestern China, is slightly older than Xiaoding; she is calmer and more reserved. She is the youngest of four siblings. Because she is much younger than her two brothers and sister, she was treated well by her parents and was not exposed to hardship. As a person who is eager to perform well in everything, failing the senior high school exam was the first major disappointment in her life.

> Back then, there were only two senior high schools where we lived. One was good, and the other was average. My exam score was only good enough to be admitted into the average one. I felt disheartened because enrolment rates at that school were low. I ultimately decided not to go. Working away from home was never my plan; my plan had always been to finish junior high school, senior high school, and university. When I received the admission letter from the average school, I was devastated. I ripped all my certificates of merit to pieces. I didn't think my life would be like it is now. What a pity. Going to any school would have been better than what I am doing now.
>
> (Xiaocao, female, from Baoji, Shaanxi)

Xiaocao made the decision to make a change and work in the city.

> My parents wanted me to give it a try. If not, I could always come back
> and finish my education. However, as someone with high self-esteem, going
> back home after coming here was too embarrassing, so I stayed here. Most
> people come out here for six months or a year before going back; I just
> stayed here.

When she first arrived in Nanjing, she was too young and had a difficult time
adjusting. She then went back to Xi'an and worked at a textile factory for a couple
of months before returning to Nanjing to work at a school cafeteria near Mochou
Lake. Later, her older brother opened a restaurant, and she worked there for over a
year. Then, she worked in the Nanjing University cafeteria. She has been working
there for three years.

By contrast, Xiaoding recently turned 20 and has worked as a waitress at a
restaurant for four years. Because she hated school, she left her home at a young
age and came to Nanjing.

> During my junior high school days, I played computer games in school and
> read novels. My grades dropped and I had to go to my teacher's office for
> a consultation. However, I really hated school. I did okay in Chinese but
> was horrible in math and even worse in physics and chemistry. I did try to
> study hard one time; I went to cram schools and all that, but it was too dif-
> ficult, and I eventually gave up. My parents suggested technical schools,
> but I simply didn't want to go to school anymore. The frequent tests were
> a headache, and if I did poorly on them and my relatives asked about it, I
> felt even worse.
>
> (Xiaoding, female, from Feidong County, Anhui)

After moving to Nanjing, Xiaoding first worked as a waitress at two restaurants. Then, she switched jobs and worked at a university cafeteria in Nanjing.
She works there because the owner of the cafeteria knows one of Xiaoding's relatives. Xiaoding continued to work there because her family members feel that she
is safe at the cafeteria. Xiaoding thought that going to the city and working at such
a young age was normal, stating "My younger brother did it as early as 1997. Kids
today are more mature than we were."

Similar to many new-generation migrant workers, Xiaoding went to different
cities not only because of her academic setbacks but also because of her desire to
experience city life. Xiaoding said,

> I did not come to Nanjing to work at first; it was because my aunt was here
> and I came to visit. I had a lot of fun and ended up working here. I wanted to
> know what fun places were in Nanjing.
>
> (Xiaoding, female, from Feidong County, Anhui)

She did not have any financial responsibilities and did not have a plan for the future; she went to cities merely to expand her horizons and begin life experience to the unknown.

The urban and rural environments experienced by new-generation migrant workers born in the 1990s were much more developed compared with those experienced by migrant workers born in the 1980s. In fact, urbanization in China facilitated rural development and increased the prevalence of mass media, enabling middle-income families in villages to have access to media such as television. Thus, individuals such as Xiaocao and Xiaoding had a more diverse leisure life than Xiaobo did prior to moving to the city. This leisure life included shopping and eating with their classmates, watching TV and reading novels at home, and visiting willow forests or lotus ponds in villages. However, because they were still students, they had little time outside of class and no financial freedom. Coupled with the fact that leisure activities in villages were fewer than those in cities, the young and inexperienced girls frequently went to parties when they left their parents' households and enjoyed their financial freedom and everything the cities had to offer.

This phenomenon was clearly observed in Xiaoding, the younger of the two girls. As a waitress, she works during the busy periods (i.e., from 9 am to 2 pm and from 5 pm to 9 pm) and has more time for herself. She mentioned that, when she first came to Nanjing, life was wonderful because she did not have to worry about school, had her own income, and had access to Nanjing's fascinating leisure activities.

> When I first arrived in Nanjing, I was young and wanted to have fun. Because I was only a student and that there wasn't much to do back home, when my new friends introduced me to leisure in Nanjing like bars and KTVs, I went there at night and had a blast. So, I went there all the time.
>
> (Xiaoding, female, from Feidong County, Anhui)

However, these feelings of freedom and novelty typically do not last long. Experiencing the city life that migrants had imagined may be gratifying at first, but this feeling fades over time as migrants understand the realities of city living. For these young and inexperienced migrant workers with no financial burdens, the freedom to make their own decisions results in bars, KTVs, and dance halls becoming their top choices for entertainment. They desire at this moment merely to expand their horizons, find places to relax, and learn about cities' leisure life.

As they become more familiar with this lifestyle, new-generation migrant workers are no longer fascinated by the new activities that are available in cities. They are weary of this entertainment, and their lifestyles return to normal. They go to work, collect their salary, and do not always go to parties in their free time. Instead, they comply with city norms. They move past the novelty phase and learn to live responsibly as they mature.

Xiaocao, now 23, is currently in this phase. She is fairly satisfied with her job. Every day, she works from 7:30 am to 7 pm, with a lunch break from 1:30

pm to 4:30 pm. Her work schedule is not very demanding, and she has a day off every week. She thinks that wages and quality of life should be balanced; she would rather be paid less than be overworked and depressed. Her leisure activities mostly involve various types of media.

> I watch TV and read books in my spare time. My favourite TV shows are idol and romance dramas. At school, we watch CDs in our dorm rooms because we don't have TV or Internet. I like the show *Happy Camp* because it's funny. *Only You* is another show about job hunting that's really informative. I realize, though, that the stuff in *Only You* might be exaggerated and not completely real.
>
> (Xiaocao, female, from Baoji, Shaanxi)

Contrary to most young migrant workers, Xiaocao enjoys reading the newspaper.

> I love reading *the Jinling Evening News*. I like the feel of holding the newspaper in my hands, so I read it from time to time. Our store gets the newspaper delivered. I used to read it a lot more than we do now, and would purchase it when I was on break,

said Xiaocao. She reads Tencent news and entertainment news online; she also plays simple games on her cell phone. The biggest difference between her hometown and Nanjing is the level of access to information and the media, particularly the Internet, which are comparatively "inaccessible" in her hometown.

Xiaoding, now 20, is not as calm or mature as Xiaocao is but is nonetheless calmer and more mature than she was a couple years back. She stopped seeing the fun in going to bars and KTVs and began to realize how bad they are for her body; she now goes only occasionally. Today, her leisure activities mostly involve surfing the Internet on her cell phone, reading novels, browsing on Weibo (a dominant social media platform in China), shopping on Taobao (a Chinese online shopping platform), and chatting on QQ and WeChat (instant messaging and social media platforms). Cell phones have thus become an indispensable part of these young women's lives and a key part of their leisure lives.

> I used to read the newspaper and magazines, but I don't anymore. I read almost everything exclusively on my phone because in addition to reading the newspaper and magazines, you can also watch dramas and do other things. Cell phones have replaced everything else, basically.
>
> (Xiaoding, female, from Feidong County, Anhui)

The preceding examples reveal how new-generation migrant workers born in the 1990s initially love to have fun and are fascinated by various recreational activities that cities have to offer. However, this feeling fades over time and they settle down. They do their jobs, just like everyone else. Although their wages and standards of living do not compare to those born in the city, they find a place in the city. Unlike people like Xiaobo, who has no leisure life, or older new-generation migrant workers who have accumulated wealth after working in cities for years, these new-generation migrant workers live lives that conform with the norms of society.

1.3 Maturation: Quasi-City Youths

To have an enjoyable leisure life, one must have time and money. Thus, new-generation migrant workers from rural areas must first earn money before they can engage in leisure. For someone like Xiaobo, who is relatively busy and must support her family, having sufficient money and time to participate in leisure is difficult. By contrast, the extent of the leisure life of young people like Xiaocao and Xiaoding is primarily influenced by their earning potential. Another migrant, Xiaoguo, had a different experience:

Born in 1985, Xiaoguo is over 30 years of age and old compared with most new-generation migrant workers. He left his hometown of Luhe District to come to Nanjing in 2001, and made a career as a hairstylist after 15 years of work. He dropped out of junior high school due to poor academic grades and came to Nanjing alone at 16. He worked as an apprentice hairstylist under a distant relative, and said that it was a difficult period in his life.

> Working as an apprentice was probably the hardest time of my life. As apprentices, we had to do chores like washing towels and preparing meals. Normal hairstylists could go home after working hours, but I had to stay to sweep and mop the floor, clean the hair salon, and even dust the hairstylists' shoes. It was midnight when I left the hair salon, and I went straight to bed after I got home. In a hair salon, the apprentices have to learn on their own; their teachers don't teach them one step at a time. The teachers only teach the basics, and the apprentices have to learn everything else on their own by watching. It was normal for apprentices to mess up a customer's hair.
>
> (Xiaoguo, male, from Luhe District, Nanjing)

The hairstyling industry has high turnover rates. Xiaoguo left that hair salon after three years. A studious individual, he felt that he could still improve as a hairstylist; he then went to Guangzhou to learn advanced hairdressing. After mastering these skills, he returned to Nanjing and worked at different large chain hair salons (e.g., Jutao and Huazai) that he was referred to by acquaintances. He had a negative experience working in these salons.

> I had no personal freedom at all. There were meetings every day and we always stayed late after work. The meetings were about the business, hairdressing techniques, company culture, and how to treat customers. There were many rules to follow, and we had to meet revenue targets that were set every month. The hair salons used indicators to assess these targets. Bonuses were given if the targets were met, but we had heavy penalties if we missed

them. Those salons divided hairstylists by rank into clear categories – low-level hairstylists, high-level hairstylists, directors, store managers, and supervisors. I reached the level of high-level hairstylist at Jutao and director at Huazai (two other hair salons), but there was more pressure as you moved up. The salary was better at a higher ranking, but the pressure, demands, and performance indicator results were also greater. I had opportunities to go further, but it was too much for me and I decided to give up.

(Xiaoguo, male, from Luhe District, Nanjing)

The hairstyling industry values hierarchy. In the past, apprentices would learn through mentorship. The teachers had total control over their apprentices; they told the apprentices what to do and decided how much to pay them. After apprentices could work on their own, they became low-level hairstylists and continued to work their way up in the company. However, as their rankings increased, the pressure increased as well. Xiaoguo identified one instance as the "straw that broke his back" and caused him to leave large chain hair salons.

Although they paid you a lot, they also took a lot away from you. You were penalized at different ratios according to how much you missed the revenue targets by. The pressure of that number hanging over your head every month was unbearable. Although I became a director, it was just a title – that was all it was.

He ultimately decided to leave that system and work at an ordinary hair salon. Now, he has worked there for six or seven years.

Ten years have passed since Xiaoguo first worked his way up as an apprentice. Working hard in the hairstyling industry for over a decade is exhausting. However, his life is much more enjoyable now. He has more time for himself and more opportunities to enjoy life. His lifestyle has only improved over the past few years.

He began to feel that life was slowing down after he started working at his current hair salon. "I've had more time to rest since coming here. There wasn't a revenue target hanging over my head, I had more freedom, and there weren't as many customers coming in and out of the hair salon." He was no longer overwhelmed by simply trying to survive and could spend time traveling to relax and recharge.

Over the past few years, I went on a trip every summer to relax and recharge if I felt tired from work. Because summer is the off-seasons, I would take a few days off and go on a trip. I visited Qingdao and Hengdian recently. I've visited basically everywhere you can visit around here, like Yangzhou, Suzhou, and Hangzhou. Life is rich and fulfilling nowadays.

(Xiaoguo, male, from Luhe District, Nanjing)

Xiaoguo usually hangs out with his friends in his spare time.

I have more time for myself so I often meet up with my friends and go out to eat, sing, watch movies, skate, or whatever. Sometimes, we went to bars like 1912 to drink and chat. My friends used to take me to a place called Sleepless Town; it's a bar and dance hall. I enjoyed it a lot, and it was kind of addictive. Disco dancing is crazy and a lot of fun, but I'm getting too old for it and don't go as often.

(Xiaoguo, male, from Luhe District, Nanjing)

Now, Xiaoguo uses media, especially on his smartphone, to kill time.

I have more time to watch TV now. When there aren't any customers, I watch TV series on my iPad. I watched so much that it killed my iPad, so I started watching them on my phone instead. My favourite TV shows are historical costume dramas. I used to also read the newspaper sometimes too, but I can do that on my cell phone now. To be honest, I feel that I spend more time on my phone than doing anything else every day.

(Xiaoguo, male, from Luhe District, Nanjing)

Although Xiaoguo's leisure life cannot be compared to that of non-migrants, the appearance, demeanour, and lifestyle that he developed over the last 15 years are no different from those of young non-migrants. He has purchased a car and made a down payment for a house in Jiangbei with both money he saved and with help from his family. To enjoy a rich leisure life such as Xiaoguo's, certain conditions must be met: first, one must not be required to support their family (such as Xiaobo); second, one must not be married because marriage comes with responsibilities; third, they must have lived in the city for some time to become familiar with the environments, develop social connections, and accumulate wealth; fourth, they must have jobs that allow sufficient free time. These conditions enable Xiaoguo to live the leisurely and comfortable life he enjoys today.

These four cases reveal how personality traits and leisure life change over time and how they differ between new-generation migrant workers of different ages, backgrounds, and occupations. However, their leisure lives share some traits determined by factors such as their financial conditions and the number of hours they work each week. The new-generation migrant workers who must do a lot at work and support families do not have the time, energy, and money to engage in leisure activities. Those workers born in the 1990s have been in cities for a shorter period of time; thus, they are less familiar with the cities and lack the wealth to enjoy these activities as frequently as they might wish. Only migrants such as Xiaoguo who are not subject to financial constraints can enjoy as many leisure activities as they desire.

A review of the leisure activities of new-generation migrant workers as they relocate from villages to cities reveals that these activities that were previously monotonous have diversified. These migrant workers are inevitably affected by urban entertainment, and their lifestyles gradually shift to resemble the lifestyles of non-migrants. The media plays a crucial role in this modernization process.

2. Diversified Life Experiences: Leisure Life in Urban Media Environments

When studying new-generation migrant workers, one cannot overlook the information societies they are in as well as their communication environment. As media rapidly advanced in the 21st century, China's informatization has evolved to an environment where only the elites possessed information in the 1990s to one where both the low- and middle-class also possessed information (Qiu, 2013). In fact, the colossal number of low- and middle-class people has made them both producers and consumers of the media content that is enabled by China's new media technology. As for the leisure life of new-generation migrant workers, they have been able to enjoy diversified mediated urban experiences because of the cities' complex media environments. Media are the most important cultural entertainment tool in both normal citizens and new-generation migrant workers' leisure lives. However, media are more than just an entertainment tool; they also provide alternative experiences, satisfying new-generation migrant workers' lack of material and cultural resources. Additionally, media construct experiences for workers, influencing new-generation migrant workers' perception and raising their cultural awareness through diversified information, prompting them to search for self-development opportunities in their leisure life. New-generation migrant workers also use media to build interpersonal relationship networks in cities, combining media use and leisure activities together to create their city lives.

2.1 Media Use Promotes Adhesive Social Relationship in City Life

Samuel asserted that leisure activities can change lifestyles and structural factors such as social relationships and norms. Leisure activities have value; thus, individuals and communities allocate time to select leisure activities and engage in those activities (Hu, 2001). In modern society, media plays a crucial role in leisure life; this is one of the most basic functions of media.

The media experience of new-generation migrant workers is essentially the media usage experience. The media environment of a migrant workers leaving the village to work in a city changes drastically. This phenomenon is especially true for new-generation migrant workers born in the 1980s. These migrant workers grew up in undeveloped villages with immature communications infrastructure. Thus, their childhood activities mostly entailed spending time outside and playing with their friends. As such, media were irrelevant or even dispensable. Interviews with new-generation migrant workers born in the 1980s support this assertion; most of their leisure life involved nature and had characteristics typical of primitive agricultural societies.

"In the past, when we had free time at home, we went out with friends our age to fish and catch lobsters; we rarely stayed home", said Xiaosun. Xiaosun is a man born in 1987 and from Feixi County, Anhui. He has worked in Nanjing for nine years and currently works at a university cafeteria in Nanjing.

Migrant workers departing rural societies with limited access to information and a slow pace of life are blown away when they enter cities, which feature rich, bustling urban media environments. The media has become a deeply embedded part of cities, and the subtle effects of city life have gradually changed the migrant workers' leisure activities; the media have become a major, indispensable part of their leisure lives. For example, Xiaosun no longer fishes or catches lobsters but instead chooses to consume media in his spare time.

> I read e-novels and online novels, take naps, and watch TV in my spare time sometimes; there's a TV where I live. Online, I chat on QQ and surf Qzone (the cloud space of QQ). For news, I read Tencent news on my cell phone and occasionally listen to the radio.
>
> (Xiaosun, male, from Feixi County, Anhui)

The new-generation migrant workers born in the 1990s are more accustomed to changes in the mass media than those born in the 1980s, mainly because of the media transformation in villages during their childhood. By then, mass communication and media could then be found in villages, and many families began to have access to mass media such as TV, radio, and even entertainment venues such as Internet cafés and KTVs. Thus, this generation of migrant workers grew up with media.

Nevertheless, the complexity and diversity of the urban media environment is unmatched by that of villages. As media technology improved, people gained greater access to media, and media consumption became a crucial part of their leisure life.

> I download TV series on my cell phone using Wi-Fi and watch them at home. I enjoy watching [the TV series] *My Love from the Star*; it's so popular and all of my friends watch it. I'm also watching *The Four Literary Masters*. When I'm not watching TV, I do my laundry, play games, or chat with my friends. I used to watch *Happy Camp* a lot and was a huge fan of the variety show *X-Change*; it was incredibly touching. I access the Internet through my cell phone and see what my friends are up to on Qzone, I chat, and I play games. If I see that a friend wrote something good, I click like and share it. I also read entertainment news online and search for celebrity pictures on Baidu. My favourite celebrities are Lee Min-ho and Do Min-joon (renowned South Korean actors).
>
> (Xiaohuang, female, from Sihong County, Jiangsu)

The interview data show that compared with new-generation migrant workers born in the 1980s, those born in the 1990s can master different media technologies more quickly, better enjoy media entertainment, and keep up with pop culture. Accordingly, they are influenced by the city culture promoted by the mass media.

Moving from a village to a city is equivalent to moving from an agricultural society to an industrial society; people who do so experience drastic changes in their leisure activities. For example, in the relatively conservative rural societies, leisure activities are typically outdoors; people may go to the river or play outdoor games. By contrast, leisure activities in cities are primarily indoor games or activities at people's homes or at leisure businesses. Leisure activities in villages tend to focus on the community, conversing with others, social engagement, or the community. Conversely, leisure activities in cities are observational, such as watching professional entertainers and using mass media and are centred around personal interests (Geoffrey, 2000). These differences can be clearly observed in new-generation migrant workers; their leisure life gradually shift from community, society, and nature to individual, observational, and media-oriented as they relocate from villages to cities.

Therefore, for the new generation of migrant workers, the mass media is the most important tool for leisure and entertainment, accessing mass media content, cultural consumption, and enjoyment. Media comforts them when they experience negative emotions, emptiness, homesickness, pressure, exhaustion, or ostracization. Entertainment is representation of reality and a source of self-comfort and self-satisfaction when facing reality. Although the entertainment provided by media is short-lived, it enriches their dull lives, enabling them to persevere in their attempts to integrate in city lives.

2.2 Alternative Experiences Provided by Media: Another Form of Satisfaction

As mass media and communications become more and more ingrained in information societies, the entertainment that it provides can better meet people's leisure needs. For the new generation of migrant workers, entertainment media provides them with alternative leisure opportunities, compensating for their lack of material and cultural resources and providing a sense of satisfaction.

Field surveys have revealed that most new-generation migrant workers, regardless of ages, prefer to watch TV in their leisure time. Empirical research cited earlier also supports this finding. Kelly conducted a study on involvement in leisure activities, and observed that watching TV is a casual leisure activity in two senses; enjoying television requires no attention or technique and requires no interpersonal skills. These characteristics result in TV being a popular option for leisure and entertainment among the public as well as among migrant workers. However, for socially or financially vulnerable people, watching TV is their only choice for leisure. Albert Bandura, a psychologist from Stanford University, introduced the concept of self-efficacy. Self-efficacy is an individual's belief about their capability to achieve specific outcomes. Jeffrey Goby adopted this concept in his health-oriented leisure research and stated that people with lower self-efficacy are less active in pursuing leisure. These people are more inclined to choose passive leisure activities instead of active ones.

The roles and characteristics of new-generation migrant workers have been described in detail in the background section of this study. From a social identity perspective, new-generation migrant workers are socially and financially vulnerable people compared with normal citizens and possess less material and cultural resources. To normal citizens, these people are an "outside group" and are low- to middle-class citizens. Such identity tends to lower new-generation migrant workers' self-recognition and self-efficacy. Because watching TV is immediate and low in cost, demands little material and cultural resources, and offers both audio and visual experiences that evoke a sense of reality, it provides a realistic alternative experience. By using the idea advocated by Goby, one can see that watching TV is more than just a preference; it is also deeply connected to social institutions.

TV series are the most common choice of TV entertainment for new-generation migrant workers. The content of these series offers them novel experiences. For example, watching TV series enables them to temporarily forget about their lives and share the emotional experiences of the actors and actresses in the series. These experiences have no negative effects on migrant workers' roles in life. Alternatively, they can engage in surreal social interactions with the characters in the TV series, which are unlikely to occur in real life. TV series offer diverse, fictional social environments that give migrant workers an opportunity for escapism when they have grown tired of the real world (Liu, 2008).

In addition to alternative psychological experiences offered by TV, information technology and the mobile Internet have developed explosively and provide new-generation migrant workers with functional alternative experiences for enriching their leisure lives. This phenomenon can be observed by studying cell phones – the most integrated type of media. For example, the creation of text messages enabled cell phones to offer "first media" (i.e., newspaper) functions; that of multimedia messages enabled cell phones to offer "second media" (i.e., radio) functions; that of mobile TVs empower cell phones to offer "third (and most powerful) media" (i.e., TV) functions; and wireless application protocol (WAP) and broadband Internet services enabled cell phones to offer "fourth media" (i.e., the Internet) functions. Cell phones have become the dominant communications medium; they are the fastest, most popular, and most convenient.

Mobile phones offer new-generation migrant workers alternative leisure options because of their diverse functions. As the mobile Internet has developed, 3G and LTE high-speed broadband speeds have increased and intelligent terminals have become widespread; these substantially elevate the user experience of cell phone apps. Thus, cell phone usage has grown exponentially in recent years. Today, tens of thousands of apps have been created for clothing, food, accommodation, and transportation. These apps subtly change people's lives and work.

For the new generation of migrant workers, the development of media technology is deeply connected to their lives and influences their lifestyles. This group possesses relatively less material and cultural resources as well as financial capital, inhibiting them from frequenting entertainment venues in cities. However, as young adults, they typically desire to try novel experiences by participating in the various entertainment and leisure activities offered by cities. Compared with older-generation migrant workers, new-generation migrant workers are younger, able to learn faster, and have higher media literacy, enabling them to master the use of smartphones more quickly. The various functions of apps satisfy new-generation migrant workers' leisure life demands conveniently and at low cost, which thereby offer an alternative source of entertainment.

> I enjoy singing. I used to sing on a mobile app called Let's Sing; I downloaded the software at the recommendation of a friend and found it pretty entertaining. So many people on there are horrible. Just the other day, I heard a little girl singing off key; it was hilarious. Although the software can't recreate the atmosphere of a KTV, singing and listening on the app does scratch the itch to go singing.
>
> (Xiaosong, female, born in 1994 and from Chuzhou, Anhui. She has worked in Suzhou for three years and currently works in a fruit shop near Guanqian Street, Suzhou.)

Smartphones offer numerous functions and various apps to enrich new-generation migrant workers' lives; these apps provide these socially and financially vulnerable people some level of satisfaction to compensate for the time and money that they do not have. On a certain level, the media is more than just leisure tools for new-generation migrant workers – although this is what they are designed to do. They are also a form of psychological comfort, resource compensation, and a way for urban development to benefit all. The media is like the sun in the winter; these tools warm the hearts of migrant workers.

2.3 City Experiences Constructed by Media: More Than Just Entertainment

Sections 1 and 2 about media usage experiences and alternative experiences focus on the methods and content of media that entertain new-generation migrant workers. However, media are more than entertainment; regardless of form, media are designed to disseminate information that influences cognition, inspires thoughts, and informs people about the world. Mass media have failed to teach us how to think but have succeeded in teaching us what to think (Littlejohn, 1999). The urban media environment influences the individual perceptions of new-generation migrant workers and their thoughts about both the world and their own lives; it raises the cultural awareness of young new-generation migrant workers and guides them to use media for entertainment as well as for self-development.

The leisure activities of new-generation migrant workers have become diversified because of urbanization. However, they still pale in comparison to the leisure activities of other city dwellers. Nash divided leisure activities that people enjoy in their spare time as illegal or unethical activities, sensual activities (e.g., gambling and online games), passive viewing activities (e.g., watching TV and absent-mindedly reading), viewing activities with emotional involvement (e.g., watching performances), mentally or physically engaging activities (e.g., playing sports or learning), and creative activities (e.g., inventing or creating things) (Ma, 2012). Leisure activities that new-generation migrant workers engage in are mostly recreational sensual enjoyment activities and passive viewing activities, and migrant workers seldom become involved in leisure activities such as mentally or physical engaging activities or creative activities.

However, there are exceptions. Field research results showed that among new-generation migrant workers, those with high cultural awareness sometimes use their leisure time to self-improve and self-develop; they use the diversified information provided by media, which is more convenient and inexpensive compared with other learning resources.

Xiaosun and his girlfriend were childhood sweethearts; they work at a university cafeteria in Nanjing selling breakfast at the window. They plan to marry in May. He left his hometown at 16 and had his first job at a clothing factory in Kunshan. He later found another job in Beijing, and he worked there for a while before quitting and starting his own business. He purchased clothing-processing equipment for his business. He then relocated to Nanjing for his girlfriend, and currently works at the university cafeteria. His leisure activities are similar to those of others. Nevertheless, his entrepreneurial experience in the past has fuelled his desire to make money. Thus, in his spare time, he would spend some time learning related knowledge.

> I used to watch Li Qiang (a trainer and lecturer on entrepreneurship)'s entrepreneurial seminar videos online. I think he is a fabulous speaker and very insightful; I'm convinced by everything he says. The suggestions he made have been practical and incredibly helpful. I noticed the things that I was doing wrong when I watched his videos. I learned a lot from him and know what to do next time I start my own business.
>
> (Xiaosun, male, from Feixi County, Anhui)

From Baoji, Shaanxi, and born in the 1990s, Xiaocao has a stable life but feels both satisfied and dissatisfied with her job.

> I'm satisfied with my job because it's simple and stable; there aren't any rivalries between me and my colleagues. However, I'm dissatisfied with my job because it pays very little; coming all the out here for such a meagre salary is really frustrating. The only thing good about this job is that my co-workers are nice, but there's no opportunity to get promoted or for professional development.
>
> (Xiaosun, male, from Feixi County, Anhui)

Thus, she looks for potential career opportunities in her spare time.

> I always wanted to take the college entrance examination for adults because I truly care about my educational achievement. I've thought about it for a while but I never knew how to do it. I searched online a lot and found some good information. I saw that Nanjing University has lots of colleges that provide a college entrance exam for adults. I think that might work; I could do

my work here while studying in my free time. I feel like enriching my knowledge is necessary.

(Xiaocao, female, from Baoji, Shaanxi)

Xiaosun and Xiaocao have an awareness of and desire for self-improvement and take initiative to use media to search for specific, useful information. For example, they use the Internet to search for potential career opportunities. Other new-generation migrant workers live life without clear goals, and come up with ideas based on what they see in the media. Their perception of the world is informed by the media, and the information transmitted by the media influences how they think. For example, Xiaohuang, a young female migrant worker who just recently moved to Nanjing and now works as a restaurant waitress, does not know what she wants to do in life. When asked about what she would like to learn in her spare time, she answered as follows:

I want to pick up some skills in my spare time like how to do makeup or how to make desserts and cakes. I think those skills would be useful; just look at how many makeup commercials there are on TV. That means that knowing how to do makeup is valuable. And, I want to learn how to make desserts and cakes because I learned from TV series that dessert stores are incredibly pleasing and cheap to open. I like their atmosphere.

(Xiaohuang, female, from Sihong County, Jiangsu)

This quote reveals the unrealistic thoughts of a young, naïve girl, but these thoughts are inspired by media and showcase the influence that media has on people's perceptions and beliefs. This influence has driven Xiaohuang and other young girls to search for and learn from online makeup videos in the hope of achieving their dreams.

Contrary to older-generation migrant workers, who have a love for and desire to defend their local culture, new-generation migrant workers possess higher city awareness and agency, the former of which elevates their media consciousness. Media strongly influence their leisure life entertainment choices, shape their knowledge of cities and their lives, and fuel them to fulfil their dreams. Because they have media literacy superior to that of older-generation migrant workers, they can utilize media to search for relevant knowledge and information for their own self-development outside of work.

In addition to shaping people's perceptions and awareness, media can construct social relationships. New-generation migrant workers form small-scale, self-centred relationship networks as they share and transmit information with/ to others in their daily lives; such relationships are closely tied to media. In other words, they may form relationships online and strengthen such relationships live. This was how Xiaoding made new friends in Nanjing.

All of the friends I have made here are new, either friends from work or those I meet via online software such as WeChat and QQ. If I find friends I get along with, we hang out and eat together privately. Knowing more people exposes you to more information, like about their jobs and interesting things that happen. Sometimes it's insightful.

(Xiaoding, female, from Feidong County, Anhui)

Some relationships are first formed in real life and are strengthened online. for example, Xiaoguo often spends time with his friends in his free time.

I met pretty much all of my new friends in Nanjing like this. My friends introduce me to new friends when we go out to sing or eat together. We form new circles. Although the people we meet come from all over, most of them come from Nanjing suburbs, and many of them work in the hairstyling industry. We meet quite frequently – maybe once every other week. But we don't always meet with the same group of people; we go out with new friends. My friends from the hair salons normally do the inviting. The people we invited bring other people so we meet new friends. We add each other on WeChat and hang out together later.

(Xiaoguo, male, from Luhe District, Nanjing)

The preceding reveals how media influence new-generation migrant workers' experiences. First, media provides diversified information, shaping the new-generation migrant workers' perceptions of their lives and themselves and raising their cultural awareness. They subsequently use media for both entertainment and self-development purposes. Second, they use media to construct their social relationship networks in cities, enabling these "lonely individuals" to form their own social networks. They solidify and maintain such social relationships through online and offline interactions. The relationship networks that they voluntarily establish in their leisure time enable them to access more information and obtain emotional support, satisfying their needs for security and belongingness.

3. Field, Habitus, and Capital: City Life Practice Shaped by Media

After investigating new-generation migrant workers' leisure lives and the effects of media on this leisure life, we explored the "logic" behind these phenomena. For new-generation migrant workers, moving to the city is a life-changing decision. They require time to adjust their habitus and adapt to city life because the village environment differs considerably from the city environment. Their living habits and leisure life subsequently shift towards those of non-migrant citizens. During this process, media plays crucial roles in influencing new-generation migrant workers' leisure lives through information provision and dissemination.

3.1 Leisure Life Changes: Collisions Between Fields and Adjustments in Habitus

New-generation migrant workers left their villages to work in cities. They gradually adapt to the cities and become self-sufficient; this process is magnificent yet demanding. They must cope with changes not only in geography but also living environments, interpersonal relationships, values, and psychological and behavioural patterns. According to Pierre Bourdieu's Theory of Social Practices, this process is a transformation from the rural fields to the city fields; the collision between these two fields causes people to change their habitus for leisure life.

Bourdieu defined "field", a major concept in his Theory of Social Practices, as a network or configurations connecting different locations together, with such locations being objectively defined (Wacquant, 1989). In other words, he believed that each field is a unique space, circle, or "game" with different rules. To Bourdieu, fields are not fixed structures or empty locations; they are game spaces. Individuals who believe in fields and contribute to those fields participate in these "games".

Bourdieu posited that fields are social spaces rather than geographical spaces. That is, fields are formed as a result of the high differentiation of modern social worlds. Bourdieu indicated that fields are spaces with different effects. These effects influence all agents related to these fields. Because of these influences, the agents can no longer be solely defined by their intrinsic traits (Bourdieu & Wacquant, 1998). Therefore, new-generation migrant workers relocating from the countryside to cities cannot be viewed as immediately becoming a part of the city field. As such, spatial segregation arises in the sense that villages and cities are geographically different, and rural fields and city fields are socially different. The differences between rural and city fields include different field environments, relational structures, psychological patterns of "agency" in the relational structure, and daily life practices. New-generation migrant workers who grew up in agricultural societies have indelible rural characteristics. Thus, despite moving from the village to the city, their daily habits are still based on those of rural societies. Simply put, in the beginning, new-generation migrant workers relocate physically but not psychologically. However, because they stay in cities for an extended period, the influence of the rural fields decreases, and that of the city field increases. Due to the effects of both the rural and city fields, new-generation migrant workers' life practices subsequently change.

These changes are not without friction. As spaces with both latent and active power, fields maintain and protect the balance of power between agents. These agents fight for the right to control valuable resources or capital in their fields, and both ruling and ruled individuals exist for various types and quantities of capital. This rule is not peaceful; the rulers and the ruled continue to compete. To Bourdieu, even the process of defining the fields and their boundaries entails a power struggle (Bourdieu & Wacquant, 1992). Thus, new-generation migrant workers' rural and city fields are involved in constant struggle over capital and positioning. New-generation migrant workers leaving rural life fields and entering city life fields experience drastic changes in their social statuses; typically, their lack of capital causes them to become the ruled, and non-migrant citizens are the rulers. These differences in social status also contribute to power struggles. Fields are fluid, open spaces without fixed boundaries and thus are constantly changing. When new-generation migrant workers enter the city field and fight for power, various forms of capital are redistributed and converted, and the field's power dynamics change accordingly.

As these life fields are converted and reshaped, the habitus of new-generation migrant workers also changes. Habitus is a dynamic and open system with internalized beliefs and dispositions that individuals acquire; habitus structures their perceptions, judgments, and actions. Such a structure is constantly adjusted and improved based on experiences (Bi, 2004). Bourdieu asserted that habitus is the subjective adjustment made by agency (based on its objective social status and subsequent social positioning) in fields and is the result of the internalization of external situations (Gong, 2007).

On the basis of this assertion, a new-generation migrant worker's leisure life may be viewed as a manifestation of their habitus. Social status changes when an individual moves from the rural field to the city field. New-generation migrant workers exercise agency and make proactive adjustments according to their objective social positions, enabling them to change their habitus in the new field. As they accumulate experiences in cities over time, they gain city experiences and learn about the patterns of city life. This knowledge is then internalized, affecting their cognitions and driving their actions, social behaviour, survival strategies, lifestyles, and behavioural strategies. Their leisure life also changes under these conditions, and their city experiences result in their leisure lives becoming similar to those of their non-migrant counterparts. The migrant workers' external behaviour ultimately influences their internal cognition, causing them to form new habitus.

Habitus can change and be replaced due to the accumulation of experience and conversion of different forms of capital within a field. All fields contain habitus, and habitus exists only in relation with fields. Each habitus is shaped by the power relations with its generating field; thus, the relationships of one field cannot be duplicated in another field; they are incompatible. The relationships between fields and habitus transcends determinism: they are actual practice-based dynamic relationships that involve "generation" or "construction" (Bi, 2004). Similarly, city fields and rural fields have different survival rules and lifestyles. Thus, the rural life of migrant works is incompatible with city life; they must undergo experiences in the actual city environment and make adjustments accordingly. Likewise, leisure lifestyles are products of the city field. New-generation migrant workers living in cities with highly developed media environments are exposed to a complex communication environment with affluent affordances. Media influence city residents, causing new-generation migrant workers to be "brainwashed" by the cities' habitus; they thus behave in a manner similar to that of non-migrant citizens and follow city rules.

The concepts of fields and habitus can be used to explore the leisure life of new-generation migrant workers. Their habitus does not change instantly as they move from villages to cities because they are still sentimental and cherish their childhood memories of rural lives. They may fight to resist urban lifestyles. Nevertheless, as they gain experiences in cities, those two fields conflict and collide; the dominant influence of the city field changes the migrant workers' habitus, thus forming a new, stable habitus. This new habitus then affects the migrant workers' leisure lives. During this process, the rich and diverse transmission capabilities of media play crucial roles.

3.2 Media Empowerment: Building New "Life Worlds" in Cities

Leisure life refreshes people spiritually, enriches their lives, and offers them an opportunity to achieve self-actualization. Individuals' abilities are reflected in their interest in leisure activities as well as their pursuit of knowledge and information. Numerous leisure philosophy-related studies have demonstrated that leisure activities are spiritual activities that are closely tied to both social practices and life experiences. People have little control over their jobs. They must follow rules and do what they are instructed to do as "a part of the system". By contrast, they have full control over their leisure life; they can freely and fully do what they want to do. Leisure life makes them feel alive, reinvigorates them spiritually, and is key to elevating their life quality (Ma, 2005).

Human beings differ from other animals in that they gain and accumulate social culture collectively while individually pursuing spiritual self-actualization (Ma, 1998). Leisure life is closely related to people realizing their values and "permanent spiritual stipulation", constituting a crucial, long-lasting part of people's lives and enabling people fulfilling their personal and social goals (Ma, 2003). Previous studies on the leisure life of new-generation migrant workers have mostly defined leisure life as the entertainment activities of these workers without considering how some of them use their leisure life to modify their lifestyles and achieve self-actualization. The relatively richer and more complex media environments offered by cities are a primary influence on the leisure lives chosen by migrant workers. They select a leisure life which is acceptable and that they wish to experience; this leisure life also enables them to pursue their values. The field surveys of this study revealed that, compared with non-migrant citizens, most new-generation migrant workers had more limited leisure lives because of their lack of time and commercial resources. We also found that most new-generation migrant workers only used media channels for their leisure activities. This study did identify some new-generation migrant workers with richer leisure lives and identified workers who used media both for entertainment and to acquire knowledge and skills. These workers converted media capital to cultural and social capital. These phenomena and trends reveal that leisure life is more than just entertainment for new-generation migrant workers; it is a way for them to pursue their dreams and to self-actualize. The different leisure lives chosen by different new-generation migrant workers exemplifies their differing choices; some choose leisure activities hedonically whereas others engage in these activities to expand their knowledge and skills.

What role does media play for migrant workers choosing their lifestyles and attempting to achieve self-actualization? Media empower new-generation migrant workers to have a leisure life. The term "empowerment" first appeared in Western social science in the 1960s and 1970s. It is a multilevel, broad concept of providing people with power and enabling them to attain self-efficacy from an individual perspective. Empowerment originates from individual demands for autonomy and elevates awareness of individual efficacy to motivate them to achieve their goals. Throughout this process, they feel that they have control over their situations (Ding, 2014). Typically, media empowering individuals are information and communications technology devices such as cell phones, computers, and the Internet (including the mobile Internet) that employ communications technology to spread information in societies. Accordingly, this study investigated how media empowers new-generation migrant workers to enjoy leisure life, choose their lifestyles, and achieve self-actualization.

In 1883, Marxist socialist Paul Lafarge considered different social classes and advocated giving the working class the right to leisure. Despite social advances, new-generation migrant workers are still frequently deprived of their leisure rights (compared with non-migrants) because of their lower social statuses. Fortunately, the development of digital technology has enhanced the migrant workers' self-efficacy and compensated them for the lack of various resources and basic rights. The spread of media use enriches new-generation migrant workers' leisure life choices, compensating them for having fewer material resources than non-migrant citizens. In a way, giving them the freedom to choose their leisure activities is comparable to giving them the freedom to make lifestyle choices. Media empower people by providing them with information, social networking, and emotional support. Migrant workers in cities use cell phones and the mobile Internet to search for social resources to achieve their goals. Outside of work, they consume urban social news and information to imitate the lifestyles of non-migrant citizens and to adapt to the city. They search for useful information on topics that interest them to expand their horizons and acquire knowledge, enabling self-actualization. Cell phones are more than a technological device; they are a manifestation of a social resource. Media theorist Paul Levinson suggested that cell phones are similar to biological cells in that they enable new societies, possibilities, and relationships (Levinson, 2004). In this study, cell phones were crucial to the establishment of interpersonal networks among participants from low- and middle-income families, enabling them to develop their personal relationships, accumulate social capital and information, acquire financial resources, and connect networks and information together, which in turn can generate financial profit (Fan, 2010). For new-generation migrant workers, cell phones are a tool for entertainment and communication and provide them with the emotional and psychological support necessary to cope with their lonely, monotonous lives in cities. In other words, the penetration of media technology carries profound social meaning; for migrant workers, low- and mid-level information-dissemination technological devices are convenient, enable financial gain, provide them with social and cultural resources, and enable them to keep in touch with and support one another. Thus, media technology affects their lives and facilitates their pursuit of happiness (Qiu, 2013). This "empowerment" increases new-generation migrant workers' self-efficacy and allows them to accumulate the capital necessary for achieving self-actualization.

For new-generation migrant workers, leisure life is more than just entertainment; it also represents their life choices and self-actualization. These are made possible due to media empowerment. Their leisure life creates a new "lifeworld" during this process. "Lifeworld", a philosophical concept proposed by Edmund Husserl in his later years, indicates not the world observed by the objective logic of science, but rather the world of a person's subjective experience. Alfred Schütz expanded on this concept and asserted that the lifeworld consists of three dimensions: the reach of an individual's experience, the reach of an individual and his/her partners' experience, and the contemporary world. Martin Heidegger and Jürgen Habermas explained the lifeworld as follows: people, who perform actions, experience constantly changing psychological states. People, regardless of where they are from (i.e., from cities or from villages), must adapt to the lifeworld; that is, they must find ontological security in their lifeworld (Li, 2003). Because people's daily lives are closely related to their leisure lives, one can interpret migrant workers' leisure lives in cities as their adaptation to the urban lifeworld. Migrant workers gradually change their leisure lives to those identical with non-migrant citizens to achieve ontological security in their new lifeworld. Chinese scholar Xiang Biao noted that migration for work is unlike movement from the kitchen to the bedroom or relocating from one social system to another. Rather, it includes the change of the social systems during the migration process and connecting the "kitchens and bedrooms" together to create new systems and spaces. Both traditional networks and flow networks are adopted to develop more complex networks and structures (Ding, 2014). Therefore, new-generation migrant workers create lifeworlds through their leisure life. These lifeworlds are unique and belong exclusively to the migrant workers; they are unlike city lifeworlds and contain village lifeworld characteristics. These lifeworlds are constantly changing, and migrant workers regularly "rebuild" and "integrate" them in accordance with their experiences to achieve self-development and seek ontological security. This process of life field transformation is one in which migrant workers endlessly adapt to city lifeworlds. During this long and complicated process, media play crucial roles.

4. Beyond Entertainment: Exploring the Value of Leisure Life Through Media Use

Media play critical roles in new-generation migrant workers' lives and their myriad functions offer migrant workers diverse leisure experiences. Media are more than just cultural entertainment tools for new-generation migrant workers; they enable migrant workers to live modern lifestyles (i.e., the lifestyles of non-migrant citizens), develop themselves, and achieve self-actualization.

Currently, media are used as a form of entertainment. The use of digital media to create value is also a future trend. Whether new-generation migrant workers effectively use both media and their leisure time determines the quality of their leisure life, the extent of their self-improvement and self-development, their lifestyles in cities, and the extent of their integration with their cities. However, only a small portion of culturally conscious new-generation migrant workers are aware of this fact. As such, media have been used more for entertainment than as a means of value creation; changing this situation may require a long time.

Leisure life enables people to feel alive, reinvigorates them spiritually, and is key for elevating their quality of life (Ma, 2005). Leisure life is closely related to the realization of individual values and to "permanent spiritual stipulation" (Ma, 2003). Leisure life is a part of new-generation migrant workers' lifestyles; and lifestyles are how people live and include the allocation and use of various material and cultural resources of societies to meet individual needs while complying with social norms (Wang, 1995). After new-generation migrant workers are able to satisfy their basic needs, they begin to seek a higher quality of life. This phenomenon is reflected by their leisure life choices. Advances in media functions offer new-generation migrant workers more leisure life choices, giving them more freedom to do what they wish and to live lifestyles similar to those of non-migrant citizens, diminishing the social and cultural gaps between them.

New-generation migrant workers use their subjective agency to have a leisure life and gradually adapt to their cities; this is a living process. As migrant workers depart from villages to work in cities, their lifestyles change completely and they form new, unique lifeworlds. These migrant workers imitate non-migrant citizens' lifestyles to find ontological security in their city lifeworld. These efforts are necessary for them to successfully settle in the cities and are also the prelude to a complete change in their identities.

New-generation migrant workers do not readily assimilate to urban life after moving to the city. Migrant workers differ from normal citizens because of their complex migration experiences, life journeys, and emotional and psychological changes. They develop lifeworld according to their life experiences and find new identities, becoming a new type of citizen. These lifeworlds are constantly changing, and the migrant workers regularly "rebuild" and "integrate" them according to their experiences, making the lifeworlds new "spaces" and "paths".

Because the new-generation migrant workers differ from one another, they accumulate different experiences and adapt differently to cities. This study revealed that not all new-generation migrant workers are satisfied with simply surviving by meeting their fundamental needs. They also have dreams, a desire for self-development and self-actualization, wish to be respected and accepted for their hard work, blend in with their cities, enjoy urban life, and change their identities for the better. For new-generation migrant workers, leisure life is a way of achieving self-actualization, self-construction, and self-representation. These efforts may be small, but they may eventually enable the migrant workers to achieve their goals.

References

Bi, Y. (2004). On the Bourdieu's theory of "field-habitus". *Academic Exploration*, *1*, 32–35.

Bourdieu, P., & Wacquant, L. D. (1992). *An invitation to reflexive sociology*. The University of Chicago Press.

Bourdieu, P., & Wacquant, L. D. (1998). *An invitation of reflexive sociology.* Central Compilation and Translation Bureau, p. 138.

Ding, W. (2014). *Mobile homelands – Community communication and identity practices of the "you county cab driver village".* Social Sciences Academic Press (China), p. 24, 272.

Fan, P. (2010). From communication technology to productive tool: A sociological research on the use of mobile phone by Chinese mid-and-low income classes. *Journalism & Communication, 1,* 82–88+112.

Geoffrey, G. (2000). *Leisure in your life.* Yunnan People's Publishing House, p. 49.

Gong, L. (2007). The different fields of view between Bourdieu and Marx on practice ideology. *Journal of Henan University (Social Science), 3,* 76–80.

Hu, J. (2001). Mass media and leisure cultural life of urban youth – A questionnaire of 592 urban young people. *Research of Youth, 1,* 6–10.

Levinson, P. (2004). *Cellphone, the story of the world's most mobile medium and how it has transformed everything.* China Renmin University Press.

Li, J. (2003). Urban and rural psychology and life world – From Simmel to Schutz. *The Journal of Humanities, 4,* 149–156.

Littlejohn, S. (1999). *Theories of human communication.* China Social Sciences Press, p. 600.

Liu, N. (2008). *Study on leisure lift style of rural labors in urban architecture industry – Based on investigation of rural labors in Wuhan architecture industry,* MA Thesis. Huazhong Agricultural University.

Ma, H. (1998). On leisure theory in the field of cultural spirit. *Qilu Journal, 3,* 98–106.

Ma, H. (2003). The evolution of leisure, historical cultural and philosophical perspectives. *Studies in Dialectics of Nature, 1,* 55–65.

Ma, H. (2005). Culture, cultural capital and leisure: More reflections on recreational issues. *Studies in Dialectics of Nature, 10,* 68–73.

Ma, S. (2012). Investigation and reflection on the leisure life of the new generation of migrant workers – An empirical study based on 186 new generation of migrant workers in Beijing. *The Border Economy and Culture, 12,* 164–166.

Qiu, L. (2013). *The world factory in the information age: New working-class network society.* Guangxi Normal University Press, p. 124.

Wacquant, L. (1989). Towards a reflexive sociology: A workshop with Pierre Bourdieu. *Sociological Theory, 7.*

Wang, Y. (1995). Review of lifestyle research. *Sociological Studies, 4,* 41–48.

10 Blending in With City Lives Through Consumption

Today, new-generation migrant workers are exposed to systemic changes and social transformations. Their needs have evolved from survival-based to development-oriented as they obtain increasingly greater material wealth. Advances in mass media and communication technologies have also enabled them to access information about modern civilization quickly, broadening their minds and values and transforming them into aficionados and promoters of urban civilization and city life. These migrant workers, who left their villages to pursue dreams in cities, are no longer "the silent majorities". Instead, they engage in similar consumption behaviour and lifestyles to non-migrant citizens; they make their own choices to enrich their lives. These migrant workers have differing city-living experiences and form their own communities in cities. The daily consumption behaviour of these communities is key to how they blend in with the mainstream culture of the cities. New-generation migrant workers are exhibiting increasingly identity-oriented, urbanized consumption behaviour and culture, a trend that attracts extensive attention from society.

Migrant workers' adaptation to cities entails more than relocation from villages to cities; it also involves their culture, values, and psychological and behavioural patterns changing from traditional to modern (Zhu, 2002). Traditional migrant workers resemble "migratory birds" relocating between temporary jobs and live half-agricultural, half-urban lives. They view themselves as passers-by in cities. By contrast, new-generation migrant workers feel that they are a part of their cities. They consider themselves to come from cities rather than from villages, and their lifestyles are influenced by their jobs and by their resource-rich cities. In addition to serving as material and wealth producers at construction sites and production flow lines, migrant workers blend in with city life by engaging in modern consumption behaviours; they begin to use the Internet, go shopping, and visit KTVs after work, achieving a colourful and diversified leisure life. The consumption behaviours and culture of new-generation migrant workers reveal how they actively blend in with their cities, adapt to city culture, develop themselves, and increase their awareness of their self-identities in their daily lives.

DOI: 10.4324/9781003365785-10

1. New Cities and New Citizens: Imagined Community of Consumer Culture

In modern societies, mass communication and media create an urban image and consumer culture that influence the lives of new-generation migrant workers, imperceptibly changing their consumption behaviour and habits as well as their views of urban life, non-migrant citizens, and themselves. These migrant workers make purchases not only to satisfy their basic needs, but also to meet their social and cultural expectations of themselves as "new citizens".

Mass media and consumer culture create a rich, abstract city image that affects the lives of city residents, altering their daily decisions. In modern societies, newspapers, periodicals, fashion magazines, TV screens, websites, and even cell phones are flooded with ads and promotional or brand information. Bars, KTVs, 3D theatres, and major brands such as Starbucks, McDonald's, Nike, and Apple are seen everywhere, tying everyone to city life and experiences. As the primary form of mass media, television introduces a new and attractive urban consumer culture to new-generation migrant workers' lives, shaping their leisure lives outside of work.

Today's new-generation migrant workers are exposed to products and technologies that traditional migrant workers, who lived frugal lifestyles, had never seen. These items include modern clothing, food, daily necessities, MP3 players, digital cameras, and personal digital products such as smartphones and computers. They are also exposed to the transformation from material consumption to cultural consumption, the change from cash transactions to electronic transactions and e-commerce, diversification of urban commodities, an increase in information accessibility, diversified consumption patterns, and convenient shopping methods. These changes create cultural shocks and fuel the consumption desire of today's new-generation migrant workers. Consumption is not only a matter of consuming capacity; it is a trendy cultural pattern. Many migrant workers are involved in modernized and citizen-oriented lifestyles that have subtly and profoundly affected their consumption behaviour and culture.

1.1 Pursuing "Trendy" Products and Services: New-Generation Migrant Workers' Avant-garde Consumption Demands

Studies have shown that migrant workers' consumption patterns have been changing subtly. More specifically, their consumption behaviour has changed from simple to complex, their consumption tools have changed from traditional to modern, their consumption behaviour has changed from conservative to open, and their consumption psychology has changed from primitive to forward looking (Yan, 2007). These changes are clearly evident among new-generation migrant workers.

In our field research, we interviewed many migrant workers born in the 1980s and 1990s who had their ears pierced, had trendy hairstyles, listened to music on MP3 players, played QQ games on their cell phones or wore modern clothing such as sunglasses, T-shirts, jeans, or plimsolls. They looked no different from non-migrant citizens of the same age. The numerous buildings, fashionable and bustling shopping districts, entertainment activities, businessmen, and modern girls wearing makeup in cities all symbolize the liveliness of cities, which enriches the leisure lives and experiences of new-generation migrant workers outside of work. These migrant workers follow fashion trends in their own unique ways; Xiaojin is a perfect example.

Xiaojin, now 18 years of age, is a graduate of a vocational high school from Zhenjiang. She has lived in Suzhou for nearly a year and currently works as a cashier at a local restaurant in Shaanxi near the North Campus of Soochow University. She lives from paycheck to paycheck.

> You know how it is with young people; they want to look fashionable, go shopping, and buy clothes. Aren't all girls like that? In Suzhou, looking fashionable may not be a requirement, but people look down on you if you don't dress up.
>
> (Xiaojin, female, from Zhenjiang in Jiangsu)

Living in a city with a high consumer price index such as Suzhou is financially stressful for Xiaojin. She reported finding countless gourmet food options after moving to Suzhou, and wanted to try them. She also often goes to entertainment venues such as KTVs.

> My mom nagged me when I used to live at home. Now, I live alone and pay for food and clothes using the money I make; I can do whatever I want. So, I live from paycheck to paycheck and am more careful with my money sparingly when I only have ¥200 or ¥300 left,

said Xiaojin.

The effects of urban consumer culture on female migrant workers are reflected by their purchases of clothes and skincare products. Xiaoxia, 24, and from Anhui, now works at a fruit shop in Suzhou. She stated the following:

> I rarely bought clothes back home. In Suzhou, everyone seems to be dressed up, so I feel an urge to always buy clothes and dress up. Dressing up and looking fabulous make me feel good.
>
> (Xiaoxia, female, from Anhui)

For male migrant workers, the effects of urban consumer culture are reflected in how they spend money at entertainment venues such as bars and KTVs. One example is Xiaohu, who is 26 years old and works as a hotel chef in Xuanwu District, Nanjing.

> I like to make friends. In my spare time, I hang out with my friends and go to Internet cafés to play games, go KTVs to sing, and go to bars to drink, or flirt with girls. That's what being young is all about. After all, I am spending

my own hard-earned money. I won't be able to enjoy that freedom when I get married and have children in a few years.

(Xiaohu, male, from Anhui)

Products purchased by the new-generation migrant workers have deviated considerably from those purchased by traditional migrant workers. In addition to purchasing clothes, food and beverages, and daily necessities, new-generation migrant workers also purchase personal electronic products such as MP3 players, cell phones, and computers. Purchases of personal electronic products account for their increasingly higher personal spending.

This MP3 player was from back home. We didn't have TV back in the day, and I listened to this in my spare time. My cell phone is a knock-off and it only cost a couple hundred yuan. I didn't spend a lot of money on it because I can just replace it with something else when it's no longer popular or when it dies.

(Xiaofeng, male, 34, is from Huai'an in Jiangsu and works as a foreman at a construction site in Suzhou.)

My first job paid a little more than ¥500 per month, and I used it to buy a Nokia cell phone for ¥1580. It took me a while to get used to a full touch-screen cell phone, but it grows on you once you get used to it. It's really convenient because I can use it to save songs and movies. I also use it to call my colleagues and my friends back home. My monthly bill is about ¥150.

(Xiaoshi, male, and 22 years of age, is from Xuzhou, Jiangsu, and now works as a company intern in Suzhou.)

In urban spaces, advertisements and promotional information on outdoor billboards (e.g., those for major brands such as KFC, McDonald's, Starbucks, Nike, and Apple), city news, fashion magazines, TVs, websites, and even cell phone text messages subconsciously influence the shopping desires and consumption behaviour of workers, engendering ideas such as "I will be out of date if I do not look at advertisements", "advertisements will make me want to try new things", and "cheap products tend to break; I should buy name brand products with better quality". Their attitude towards advertisements is open and rational, and they have relatively high brand awareness.

Many advertisements are fun and creative, such as those for Sony Ericsson, and Yunnan Baiyao (a medical product).

(Xiaoluo, female, 19, is from Zhengzhou in Henan and works at a factory in the Suzhou Industrial Park.)

Most of the interviewed new-generation migrant workers purchased products in physical stores and paid with cash. They have not grown accustomed to paying using credit cards, stating that "using credit cards feels unsafe". They also disliked the idea of TV shopping. However, as computers and the Internet become more prevalent, some of them have begun to make online purchases and are starting to get used to it.

> I often shop on Taobao (an online shopping platform in China). Typically, I look for products that are less likely to become damaged during shipping, such as children's school bags, sneakers, and frameless paintings. Before buying something online, it's best to go to the mall in person to check the models, sizes, colours, and prices of the products you want and try them out to see if they fit. Then, you can go on Taobao and search for the same products and compare the prices and customer comments. Additionally, you could choose online stores based in Jiangsu, Zhejiang, or Shanghai. Shopping online can save you a lot of time and energy, and you can also find products that aren't available in physical stores. I like it a lot.
>
> > (Xiaotang, male, 32, is from Anhui and works as
> > technical staff at a construction company in Suzhou.)

Because new-generation migrant workers born in the 1990s have more financial freedom (i.e., they do not have to make money to support their families), some and live from paycheck to paycheck like Xiaojin because they are unable to resist the "temptations" offered by big cities. However, most of them do purchase rationally and do not try to follow trends blindly due to their income levels, family responsibilities, and traditional consumption philosophies. In other words, they make purchases within their means to improve their lives in the city.

> You spend within your means. You don't spend two months' wages to buy a piece of name brand clothing or a luxury watch just because someone else is wearing it, and you don't think about buying name brand products whenever you see a discount. A piece of regular summer clothing should cost only ¥100. I'm not denying the quality of name brands, but not all name brand products are right for everyone; you should only buy ones that are right for you.
>
> > (Xiaojin, female, from Zhenjiang, Jiangsu)

Consumer culture created by city spaces and mass media "creep" into the city experiences and daily lives of new-generation migrant workers, subtly changing their consumption philosophies, behaviours, and patterns. Compared with old-generation migrant workers, new-generation migrant workers are more willing to leave village traditions behind; they no longer and work and shop as farmers do. Instead, they imitate the consumption behaviours of non-migrant citizens from the same age groups in search of a city-based social identity. New-generation migrant workers' tendency of pursuing mainstream, avant-garde consumption demands and orientations reveal their longing to be recognized as new citizens.

1.2 The Desire to Become "New Citizens": Constructing Urban Identity Through Consumption

Unlike traditional migrant workers, the new generation remembers little about their villages. They did not have day-to-day farming experiences and thus did not develop tight bonds with the land. Traditional farmers prefer villages because of the low housing prices and cost of living, the chance to return home after years of residing elsewhere, and the ability to live free and pastoral lifestyles. New-generation migrant workers desire to accumulate capital to open a business, gain a foothold, and build a future in the city.

> There are still many things for me to learn. Once I have learned what I need to know and have made enough money, I want to open up a business in Hangzhou. It could be any business like a restaurant or a snack bar. In the future, I want to make enough money to open my own business and be my own boss.
>
> (Xiaohe, male, 21, and from Anhui;
> he works as a security guard at a bank lobby in Hangzhou.)

> I want to enjoy life like a normal citizen. I'm optimistic about the future and hope that I can have my own house in Suzhou after a few years of hard work. I like Suzhou a lot and want to stay here. I want to buy a house here and slowly pay off the mortgage.
>
> (Xiaojin, female, from Zhenjiang, Jiangsu)

By contrast with traditional migrant workers, who were like "migratory birds" as they relocated between temporary jobs, living half-agricultural, half-urban lives and viewing themselves as "just passers-by" in the city, new-generation migrant workers are influenced by urban work, lifestyle, and social norms. These migrant workers are fascinated by convenient, modern, and vibrant city life, making them feel that they are a part of and establish a sense of belonging to their cities.

> Life in Shanghai is much more convenient than that in my hometown, where the houses are broken, roads are muddy, and there's nothing for you to buy. The people in my hometown are also really bad at what they do. I don't want to go back home at all. Although the cost of living is really high here, my time off is a lot more fun than when I lived in my hometown. My plan is to develop and stabilize my business here for a few years and then to get married here.
>
> (Xiaoxiong, male, 25, and from Zhoukou in Henan,
> worked as a salesperson in Shanghai for six months.
> He now owns a small company.)

> I love my life here in Suzhou. I get to go home and chat on QQ or watch South Korean dramas and entertainment news every night. This laptop was actually an impulse buy, but later I realized that it was worth it because there are just so many interesting people and things on the Internet; it's actually

a great way for me to kill time. I will continue to get social experience in Suzhou and will definitely stay here in the future.

(Xiaodi, female, 27, is from Hubei and has lived in Suzhou for nine years. She currently works at a clothing store in an underground mall.)

Cities provide new-generation migrant workers with the dream of modern life. They wish to be recognized, respected, and accepted by their cities for their efforts and hard work. They also long for city life, hope that their identities as new citizens are recognized, and hope to blend in with city society.

Living in cities is really convenient; there are so many shopping spots, supermarkets, and restaurants that you can go to. Just the other day, I bought an electric vehicle for ¥2300 at the Auchan Supermarket (a retail group chain); another townsman recommended it to me. I also bought this Gionee (a Chinese phone brand) cell phone because everyone else had one and they seemed pretty good. My dream is to save enough money to open up my own restaurant and be financially stable in the city. Despite being a restaurant manager, I don't have a work contract or even medical insurance. I'm scared of getting sick. In fact, I can't even ask for leave if I am sick. I have no sense of security, so my dream is to open up my own restaurant. My husband and I have been saving money for many years, and we have saved up over ¥100,000. We are getting closer and closer to fulfilling our dreams.

(Wanjie, female, 32, is from Shaanxi and has worked in Suzhou for over a decade. She is currently the manager of a wonton restaurant in Guanqian Street, Suzhou.)

My wife and I normally go to Xinjiekou (a commercial area in Nanjing) to buy clothes. The thing with clothes is that you get what you pay for. Because we live in Nanjing, we can't afford to dress poorly. We buy name brand clothes to try to feel like other people in Nanjing. For me personally, I prefer small things like cell phones and MP3 players, and I listen to music or text my family in my free time. We plan to save money and rent a place here first after a few years. After all, we've lived here for a few years and have stable incomes. If we can, we want our children to go to school here. Education in Nanjing is so much better than it was in my hometown. We don't want them to grow up and still have to work odds jobs like we do. If things pan out, we'll buy a house and settle down here in Nanjing.

(Xiaoma, male, 27, is from Linxia County, Gansu, and has lived in Nanjing for nearly four years. He is a chef at a Lanzhou beef noodle soup restaurant in Zhujiang Road, Nanjing.)

Migrant workers occupy a space between traditional farmers and non-migrant citizens and do not form a predefined social class; they form new cultural "communities". Stuart Hall defined cultural identity as culture (a "true self") shared by its members. This identity embodies shared historical experiences and cultural symbols and brings its members together more tightly, providing them with stable, uninterrupted meaning frame.

Because new-generation migrant workers relocate from schools to factories quickly (i.e., their role changes from student to worker), they have few memories of their villages and thus do not have a strong awareness of farming. Their identities as farmers and shared historical experiences with other farmers are weakened and are replaced by the culture of the city and the media. During our field research, we learned that new-generation migrant workers feel that becoming "normal citizens" entails changing their identities, setting up their homes, establishing their businesses, and blending in with their cities both culturally and in life. They hope to participate in urbanized and modernized consumption and lifestyles. Sisi and Luojie are two examples of how these "new citizens" culturally identify and how changes can be observed through city life.

Sisi is from Jiangxi province and is 21 years of age. She has been working odd jobs (e.g., as a hotel attendant in Nanjing for over a year) since she graduated from a technical secondary school four years ago. She now works at a fruit shop in Wangtianjing Alley. Since moving to Suzhou, she has spent considerably more on clothes than she did in the past.

> I buy clothes from department stores now, so the clothes I buy are pretty expensive. I also pay attention to how I dress now. That's unavoidable. In Suzhou and Nanjing, you can't dress the same way you did in Jiangxi. The stuff we buy is also more expensive in Suzhou or Nanjing than it was in Jiangxi. But I guess the cost of living is determined by the price levels where you live.
>
> (Sisi, female, from Jiangxi)

Sisi has her own views on the city,

> This is where I will work and I might even live here in the future. I don't plan on going back to my hometown. Since I'm out, I'll stay out. So, finding an environment that I like is important. I like Suzhou a lot, but houses here cost a fortune, so whether I can eventually settle here really depends on how hard I work.
>
> (Sisi, female, from Jiangxi)

Sisi said that her current job is just a temporary one. "My boss provides me with food and accommodation; that lowers my monthly costs by a ton." Sisi is currently learning computers and foreign languages. "I want to change to a higher-paying job like one where you use computers and foreign languages. Those jobs also come with higher social status." To Sisi, migrant workers who come from villages like hers have low social status.

> Working blue-collar jobs must be different from working white-collar ones in office buildings. I want to become a white-collar worker. I see them on TV or on

the street sometimes. I think that they're living good lives with a decent income and high social status and everything. It's better than being blue-collar at least.

(Sisi, female, from Jiangxi)

When talking about the future, Sisi's eyes glow, as is typical of young people.

Since I've come to the city, I definitely want to blend in here and live a good life. I see a lot of people like me who complain about making too little but don't do anything about it. I'm different. I think we have to take initiative to improve ourselves and we have to change to have a better life.

(Sisi, female, from Jiangxi)

In an alley near Changle Road, Shanghai, 34-year-old Luojie and her son are watching a movie on DVD and having a good time. When Luojie left her home-town of Anhui to work, she had no plans and no dreams; she just wanted to earn a living. Now, after working in Shanghai for over a decade, she has purchased a small house and opened up a small shop in the alley. "We make five or six thou-sand yuan a month on a good month; sometimes we make over ten thousand. I'm happy with my life now."

Luojie watches TV and surfs the Internet in her free time. When she's exhausted from work, she takes a few days off to visit her friends and drink and dine or to go out and have fun. In the past, she would go back to her hometown once or twice a year. Now, she rarely goes back; instead, she invites her parents and relatives to celebrate Chinese New Year in Shanghai. She remembers her trip to Yunnan four years ago vividly.

I went with my friend – just the two of us. We were there for 15 days and spent over ¥20,000. We left by plane and came back by train and visited places like Dali City, Shangri-La City, Lijiang, Kunming, and the Jade Dragon Snow Mountain. We had a blast.

(Luojie, female, from Anhui)

Luojie has lived in Shanghai for more than a decade. However, she still retains her family registration at her hometown. "There's no need to change the family register to Shanghai now. If my children are admitted to a university in Shanghai, we'll change it then. It'll be easier for them to find work that way too," said Luo-jie. Living in Shanghai is great for Luojie.

First, it's much easier to make money here. Second, the pace of life is fast here and the cost of living isn't too high, so Shanghai is a better city to live in than other nearby cities. Look at me, I'm no different from people from Shanghai; I speak Shanghai dialect well enough, and I'm used to life here.

Fisk (2001) contends that lifestyles separate people into different groups within a social domain. The lifestyles of members of different groups also differ and are affected by the social order. Lifestyles are unlike economic class in that the latter cannot be changed immediately whereas the former can; thus, people have greater control over their lifestyles (Fiske, 2001). "Culture" has been integrated into commodities; thus, people's consumption behaviours differentiate them from each another and divide them into different categories. People make purchases to symbolize their social statuses, highlighting the social and cultural significance of consumption. To new-generation migrant workers, making purchases in cities reveals the existing social order and rural-urban divide. Thus, they consume in certain ways to eliminate these external differences.

> I feel that I'm no different from other people from Hangzhou. For example, people don't ask where I'm from when I walk down the street, and our business is starting to pick up. We can buy the same things that normal people from Hangzhou do, so I do not see any clear differences between us.
>
> (Lanlan, female, 32, is from a village in Jiaoxian, Hangzhou, and now owns a fruit market stall on Dacheng Road, Jianggan District, Hangzhou.)

Because they imitate the purchasing habits and lifestyles of modern citizens, new-generation migrant workers such as Sisi and Luojie perceive themselves as normal citizens by shaping their collective cultural identity flexibly. Their increasingly high purchasing power is a method of identifying themselves as normal citizens.

> A lot has changed since I moved to Hangzhou. I lived a frugal life when I first arrived here. For instance, I bought food from markets at night because it's cheaper even though I knew it wasn't the freshest food. The same goes for clothes. I did my budget everyday so that I knew how much I spent and what I spent it on. Because I made and saved more money later on, I was able to live a better lifestyle where I purchased snacks and attractive, name brand clothes. I am able to be more 'generous' to myself now. In our spare time, we enjoy strolling in the park and often end up by the West Lake (a beautiful lake in Hangzhou city, in eastern Zhejiang province, also known as "Xihu") because it's not too far away from here. At times like this, we feel that we are truly blessed.
>
> (Xiaozhou, female, 24, is from Nantong, Jiangsu, and now works as a shopkeeper at a boutique shop in Xihu District, Hangzhou.)

I have lived in Hangzhou for 15 years, so I'm basically a native of this city. My wife is also a Hangzhou native. Having lived here for so long, I truly believe Hangzhou to be a better place because of its welfare system. We pay a little every year and we get social insurance and welfare in return. My first impression of people in Hangzhou was that they were quite lazy, enjoyed living a comfortable and leisurely lifestyle, and were reluctant to spend a lot of money. However, in reality, Hangzhou people love to enjoy life and aren't afraid to spend. I pretty much spend all the money that I earn on food and entertainment. I tend to buy name brand products. For example, I almost exclusively buy clothes from *Air Jordan* and *Li-Ning* (a domestic sports brand). I think that name brand products are just better, both in quality and image. They're expensive for a reason. I see myself living here for the rest of my life. Although I'm not a Hangzhou native, I actually am better off than many of those who are.

(Afu, male, 33, is from Qingliu County, Fujian,
and currently owns a fruit market stall in Hangzhou.)

One of the crucial features of consumer culture is that goods, products, and experiences can be consumed, maintained, planned, and dreamed. Purchases are made not only to satisfy people's basic needs, but also to build an image. This is a consumer culture created by commercials, the mass media, and product displays. These new, created images stimulates people's consumption desires (Featherstone, 2000). Urban consumer culture affects new-generation migrant workers by using a rich variety of goods to arouse their purchasing desires, inspiring city-based dreams, and offering them channels to realize these dreams. For example, the value of buying name brand clothes, owning smartphones or laptops, going to KTVs and bars with friends, going on short vacations, making purchases on Taobao, and watching movies at home is more than simply functional or practical for new-generation migrant workers. These actions indicate that they live the same lives as non-migrant citizens; these lives include pursuing fashion, paying attention to quality, and knowing how to enjoy city life.

New-generation migrant workers blend in with their cities through two processes: long-term and short-term. In the long-term process, the migrant workers work tirelessly at their temporary jobs, set up their homes, establish their businesses, obtain their identities, and elevate their financial statuses. In the short-term process, the migrant workers make immediate, "learned", and "urbanized" purchases to satisfy their desire to live city-based lifestyles and eliminate the gap between themselves and non-migrant citizens. They seek to win the respect and acceptance of non-migrant citizens, and to rebuild their cultural identities and social statuses. Migrant workers work assiduously to accumulate the wealth required to make these purchases, and they make purchases to stimulate themselves to continue to work assiduously. Despite being relatively unnoticed by society, they are full of energy and work hard to achieve their dreams in the city.

2. Decoration, Change, and Possession: Presenting Selves and Struggling for Urban Identity

The mass media depicts migrant workers as "marginalized people who are unable to blend in with the city and are unable to return to their villages". These migrant workers "from the outside" live in prosperous, modern cities with young, fashionable non-migrant citizens in the same age groups. However, similar to traditional migrant workers, new-generation migrant workers are exposed to problems such as job insecurity, lack of social networks, prejudice and discrimination, imperfect systems, and urban-rural dichotomy barriers.

New-generation migrant workers' consumption culture is shaped by various internal factors such as their personal characteristics, memories of their villages, and city experiences as well as external factors such as real-world situations, public opinions, and media environments. What the migrant workers purchase shapes their image as new citizens, and they use their "capital" (i.e., money) to make purchases to fight off the stigma that media have created for them and change their culturally vulnerable position, showcasing their identity awareness and cultural strength as new citizens.

2.1 Physical Struggles: Dress Well to Leave Behind Traditional Rural Characteristics

China's rural societies are built on the agricultural economy. People who live and reproduce in these societies rely on the land and are only able to live a farming lifestyle. They have worked on the land for generations and are tightly bonded to the land. Famers have lived in their villages for generation after generation, and land is their means of survival. Traditional farmers' connection to their land and their village awareness is closely tied to the presence of the land; it is the means by which they make a living, and farming is the most fundamental of all economic activities (Zhou, 1998). The Chinese proverb, "At sunrise I get up and work; at sunset I rest; I dig wells to find water; and I farm the land to produce food" illustrates the typical lifestyle of a villager.

The rural characteristics of traditional agricultural societies are not only observed in farmers' ideologies and values, but also in their physical appearance. In traditional societies, farmers and citizens can be easily distinguished from one another. Typically, farmers have darker and rougher skin and dress rustically. By contrast, citizens have fairer complexion and dress well, neatly, and in Western fashion. These characteristics were evident among first-generation migrant workers even as they left their hometowns.

Although new-generation migrant workers resemble traditional migrant workers in that they leave their hometowns to work in cities, they differ in that the new generation leaves behind the village culture and accepts city culture and modern civilization. These migrant workers reflect on their traditional rural lifestyles and modern city lifestyles; they ultimately choose the latter. They replan their lives by changing their physical appearances (Ma, 2006). The effects of cities on their psychology are internal and hidden, whereas those on their physical appearance are conspicuous. Temporary jobs in cities typically require new-generation migrant workers to engage in scheduled manual labour (Ma, 2006). These migrant workers no longer follow the traditional work schedule of "At sunrise I get up and work; at sunset I rest". Instead, they are strictly trained to work during office hours to elevate their productivity and marketability.

These "restraints" cause the migrant workers to make purchases to release their psychological stresses. They purchase commercially available urban commodities to feel a sense of control over how they look and what social status they wish to convey.

> You know how it is with women; we all care about outlooks and spend more on skincare. We also spend more on clothes because you can't look too shabby if you live in a large city. I buy name brand clothes. For shoes, I like Kappa and Nike.
>
> (Sisi, female, from Jiangxi)

> Back home, everybody buys cheap products from market stalls, so it's not a big deal there. However, people look down on you if you don't dress up in Suzhou, so I normally buy clothes from specialty stores here.
>
> (Xiaoxia, female, from Anhui)

They begin to pay attention to their self-image and, like their normal citizen counterparts, get manicures and ear piercings, dye their hair, and wear fashionable, modern clothing. By learning about and imitating urbanized fashion styles, new-generation migrant workers leave behind their traditional rural characteristics, covering their rural-originated bodies with modern, urban clothes.

Purchasing urban clothes is more common for female new-generation migrant workers. Because these women are labelled as cheap, humble, and secondary, they make purchases as a way to find freedom, equality, values, and respect (Yu & Pan, 2008). They use clothing and cosmetics to cover up the rural characteristics of their bodies and achieve an urbanized, feminine appearance.

> I love beautiful clothes and accessories and don't like how cheapskates live. You should be spending the money you earn and should be living a happy life. I read magazines like *Ray Li* (a Chinese fashion magazine) all the time to learn how to dress up and put on makeup. To adjust to the life here, these changes are necessary. In fact, I like these changes.
>
> (Xiaodi, female, 27, is from Hubei and has lived in Suzhou for nine years. She currently works at a clothing store located underground.)

> Back home, there are not that many clothes for us to choose from, so everyone pretty much wears the same thing and doesn't dress up. After arriving in Suzhou, I saw that girls on the street were all dressed up, so I wanted to purchase more clothes. I think buying clothes that I like and dressing up to feel good is a good thing.
>
> (Xiaoxia, female, from Anhui)

Female new-generation migrant workers learn not only from non-migrant female citizens of the same age group, but also learn from the celebrities and white-collar workers depicted in fashion magazines and TV commercials. By making purchases and dressing up, these female migrant workers hope to resemble those celebrities and white-collar workers with fashionable, refined, perfect, and modern bodies.

However, by contrast with non-migrant citizens, new-generation migrant workers are spending in a manner inconsistent with their financial status; this spending typically exceeds their means. For these workers, spending is experiential and conspicuous as opposed to natural and common.

> The outfit I'm wearing today is too uncomfortable. This isn't how I normally dress. I only wear suits and ties when I have meetings because I need to look formal. Normally, I wear clean, simple clothes. I prefer sportswear and have shoes from Puma, Nike, and Adidas. However, I don't get to wear them often now, so I don't buy them as much.
>
> (Xiaohuang, male, 25, is from a village in Shaanxi and now works as a salesperson in Shanghai.)

Nevertheless, some new-generation migrant workers make purchases that are within their means; they purchase rationally and selectively.

> I buy name brand products from time to time when shopping malls are having end-of-season sales. There is no need to purchase them at the original prices; that would be a waste of money. Although I normally dress fashionably, these clothes are actually purchased from Laidi (an online shopping platform) and Taobao so they are inexpensive. As hairstylists, we must have cool hairstyles and wear fashionable clothing. We usually dye our hair at salons because we only need to pay for the hair dye, so we don't have to pay as much as our customers do to get our hair done.
>
> (Xiaojiang, male, 24, is from a village in Hubei and is now a hairstylist in Nanjing.)

Learning to dress in an urban style and reducing their traditional rural characteristics is not a one-time process. Instead, they gradually shift towards urban and away from rural characteristics. When observing new-generation migrant workers, an interweaving of urban and rural characteristics as well as a mix of traditional and modern characteristics is evident.

Human bodies are manifestations of culture. Although they consist of natural elements, their appearance, states, and activities are all affected by culture. Who people are and how they are treated are both closely related to their appearances and their activities. Consumer culture "commercializes" human bodies; people accept this fact and display their bodies to portray the hierarchy of social class (Baldwin, 2004). Consumption not only marks urban-rural and hierarchical differences, but it also enables room for autonomous negotiation and resistance to the hierarchy.

New-generation migrant workers dress differently to eliminate rural characteristics and cultivate urban characteristics (e.g., looking fashionable, dignified, and urbanized). However, this appearance is superficial and materialistic. The mass media have stigmatized new-generation migrant workers, reporting that they look "rustic" and consume low-grade products. Thus, their consumption behaviours are a manifestation of their constant struggle against media stigma and stereotypes.

2.2 Struggling Against "Stigma": Making Purchases to Change Stereotype Created by Mass Media

Psychologists have observed that people often use their social categorization knowledge to make judgments and perform social reasoning. In this regard, stereotype is one of the most common and influential types of social knowledge. Stereotype is the fixed concepts, ideas, and social cognition of the characteristics of certain groups of people and has profound effects on the social cognition and behaviour of those who hold such conceptions (Fiske, 2001). In *Public Opinion*, Walter Lippmann (2002) proposed that prejudice and mental images have marked effects on people's cognition of things. He described stereotype as a simplified and typological cognition in which people ignore differences between individuals in groups and consider group characteristics to be shared by all group members. In both media and on public opinion platforms, migrant workers are portrayed as socially and financially vulnerable, causing people to have strong stereotypes towards them. These stereotypes can be observed by their effects on new-generation migrant workers' daily lives and how these workers are collectively identified as a community.

Sun indicated stigmatization[1] of migrant workers is common in Chinese cities. These workers are labelled as "dirty, impolite, and thieves", and they "like to spit" among other pejoratives. If violations or crimes occur, the culprits are first assumed to be migrant workers (Sun, 2003b). In modern societies, mass media such as TVs, newspapers, magazines, and the Internet shape stereotypes towards migrant workers.

Since 2003, news reports about migrant workers committing suicide by jumping off buildings can be found in all major metropolitan newspapers. In media coverage, migrant workers are often portrayed negatively. For example, in articles released by the *Yangtse Evening Newspaper* in the second half of 2001 and of 2003, migrant workers were portrayed negatively 66.7 percent and 45.5 percent of the time, respectively (Cao & Liu, 2004). Between 2003 and 2004, *Workers' Daily*, *Beijing Evening News*, and *Chengdu Economic Daily*, migrant workers were portrayed as socially and financially vulnerable people and were most frequently depicted as people who were insulted and harmed (48.8 percent) (Li & Qiao, 2005). An analysis of the articles released by six newspapers from Beijing, Shanghai, and Guangzhou (e.g., the *Beijing Youth Daily*, *Xinmin Evening News*, and *Nanfang Daily*) between 2007 and 2009 revealed that migrant workers were portrayed negatively 66 percent of the time. The reports included their suffering (e.g., work-related accidents, delays in wage payment, being deceived, and living in poverty), requiring social assistance (e.g., needing protection to ensure employment rights, financial aid, injury diagnoses and treatment, and psychological adjustment), and performing antisocial actions (e.g., violating laws, committing crimes, engaging in misconduct, and having low cultural quality). Migrant workers were portrayed as individuals performing dirty, dangerous, and physically strenuous manual labour, as requiring assistance from the government and society because of their lack of work and living rights, and as posing potential harm to normal citizens' lives (Xu, 2009). Movies released between 2001 and 2010, such as *Blind Shaft*, *A World Without Thieves*, and *Wave of Migrant Workers*, mainly focused on issues such as migrant workers returning home during the Spring Festival travel season, unpaid wages, rights violations, unequal treatment in their work experiences, and criminal violations by workers. Migrant workers are portrayed as both socially and financially vulnerable people working diligently and as creators of social problems (Wang, 2011).

Analysis of news covering migrant workers released by Sina.com from 1998 to 2011 reveal that their portrayal of migrant workers has increasingly focused on the human element of the story and on diverse mentalities. However, netizen comments are often irrational. The Spring Festival travel season, delayed wage payments, psychological problems, social assistance, and endangerment of public order remain the predominant themes of news about migrant workers. Migrant workers are still portrayed as the benefactors of relevant government policies, people that need social assistance, and as "outsiders" trying to survive in cities (Guan, 2011). Media are legitimate platforms disseminating information and often release stereotype-based reports for communities that fail to comply with social norms and values (Fiske, 2004). Although the portrayal of migrant workers varies between different media types, and each medium focuses on various aspects, all media paint the following image of migrant workers: workers in modern cities are marginalized, work assiduously, live low-quality lives, are socially and financially vulnerable, and have no future.

Compared with traditional migrant workers, new-generation migrant workers have considerably higher education levels, professional skills, increasing awareness of protecting their own rights, stronger ability to mobilize, and higher consciousness of modern civilization. Traditional migrant workers lack these characteristics; if their rights are violated, they may not know how to respond and simply accept the violation or passively wait for social assistance. By contrast, new-generation migrant workers have greater awareness of equality and of their rights and expect equal rights in employment, social security, education and self-development, and freedom of expression. They actively protect their rights in order to survive and to live in cities. Traditional migrant workers are hostile towards cities and distance themselves from the city. By contrast, new-generation migrant workers have affection for cities. The environments in which they grow cause them to be closer to cities, and due to their young age, they are fascinated and mesmerized by city life. They prefer modernized, urbanized lifestyles and are better at learning and adaptation. New-generation migrant workers make efforts, in various areas, to fight stereotypes and change their images as marginalized or socially and financially vulnerable both in real life and in public opinions. Instead of simply trying to survive as traditional migrant workers did, they take action to establish their own presence in the city.

Since the 1980s, many talented novelists, poets, singers, theatre directors, folk artists, and art groups have emerged from migrant workers. Examples include An Zi, Wang Shiyue, Zheng Xiaoqiong, Xu Qing, Sun Heng, the Xuri Yanggang Group, the Beijing New Worker Art Group, and the Suzhou Kunshan New Art Troup. These artists and groups have showcased their abilities for rich and diverse cultural production and self-expression in the mass media, gradually generating more positive public views towards migrant workers. Similarly, migrant worker Zhou Shuheng's web fiction *Chinese Migrant Workers* has a click-through rate of over 500,000, exemplifying the efforts of new-generation migrant workers to represent themselves and vie for greater negotiating space in mainstream media.

During our field research, we discovered that many new-generation migrant workers attempt to overcome stigma by making and displaying purchases, engaging in self-actualization, and subsequently achieving self-development and representation. They use active, healthy, urbanized material lives and cultural consumption patterns to counter and change stereotypes towards them created by the mass media. Instead, they attempt to create an image of themselves as optimistic, motivated, and energetic.

Xiaocui is 22 years of age and was born in a suburb of Wuhan in Hubei. She looks mature for her age, with cool short red hair and light, natural makeup. She graduated from junior high school at the age of 16 and later worked as an intern at a relative's chain hair salon in Wuhan for a few months. She then left the city on her own and found temporary jobs in Shanghai. Xiaocui loves Shanghai.

> After all, Shanghai is a large city with many shopping malls, which is great because I love shopping. The environment, income level, and purchasing power here in Shanghai are better than in Wuhan, so I'm motivated to work harder.
>
> (Xiaocui, female, is from a suburb of Wuhan in Hubei)

In her spare time, Xiaocui likes to go shopping, watch TV and entertainment shows online, chat with her friends on QQ, and play games. Xiaocui loves foreign languages.

> There are many foreigners in Shanghai. I run into them when I go shopping. I try to chat with them. In addition to English, I speak a little Korean and Japanese. I studied in language classes when I was in Wuhan, and I bought language books and studied them with my friends here.
>
> (Xiaocui, female, is from a Wuhan suburb in Hubei)

Xiaocui is a fan of foreign songs and movies. She easily name many popular American dramas. Xiaocui is unsure about her future plans at this point.

> I'm not a language expert yet, so I continue to study hard. There's so much that I still have to learn. At the same time, I have to be knowledgeable. That's what I've been trying to do here – to learn and to expand my horizons. I hope

that I can become a hairstylist one day, and if I could do it overseas, that'd be even better!

(Xiaocui, female, is from a Wuhan suburb in Hubei)

Despite living in Shanghai for many years, Xiaocui does not miss home. Many of her friends back home have gotten married, and some have even given birth to babies who have already grown into children. Xiaocui, who is still single today, says firmly, "I am different".

In our field research, we encountered many new-generation migrant workers born in the 1980s and 1990s such as Xiaocui. These migrant workers are clean-cut, young, and fashionable; some even look "fly". They also work relatively higher-paying jobs, expect a lot of themselves, are positive and optimistic about their future. They live materialistic lives and enjoy modern culture (e.g., they go shopping, listen to MP3 players, and watch American dramas online to study English). They improve themselves to keep up with modernity, and long to live the same lives as non-migrant citizens their age. These migrant workers live increasingly urbanized and modern lifestyles. For example, one migrant worker said, "I work out using hula hoops every night so that I can stay in shape; sitting in the office all day makes you fat"; and another said, "I carry my cell phone with me so that I can search for information on Baidu whenever I want". On the surface, these migrant workers look like tourists or college students returning to school and are nothing like the hardworking, underdeveloped, socially and financially vulnerable, and hopeless migrant workers portrayed by the mass media.

In a nutshell, new-generation migrant workers make similar purchasing decisions as those of city dwellers to emulate non-migrant citizens' consumption behaviour and lifestyles, thereby blurring the boundaries between them and city folks, and overcoming media stereotypes against migrants.

2.3 Cultural Battles: Making Purchases as a Response to Unequal Social Resource Allocation

In cities, the formation and dissemination of consumption culture for new-generation migrant workers is contingent on various factors, such as politics, economics, systems, fashion, and social norms. Their consumption strategies are also affected by multiple dimensions and variables comprised of individual and social factors, their status in cities, as well as their capital endowment.

The employment and living situations of the new generation are considerably better compared with the previous generation, despite the new generation still being relatively excluded from official systems and social organizations in cities. Compared with non-migrant citizens, these migrant workers have lower job stability, wages, education levels, and professional skills. Their social relationship networks consist of members from their own clans and/or geographical regions. Additionally, they lack urban social resources to make their voices heard in mainstream mass media. Because of the different social order of villages and cities, new-generation migrant workers are less able to obtain economic, cultural, and social resources in cities compared with non-migrant citizens.

According to research conducted by the Ministry of Culture, new-generation migrant workers have new cultural demands. Their entertainment activities have evolved from passive observation-based recreational activities to active participation in engaging activities. They are no longer satisfied with their current monotonous situations of cultural life and have higher expectations and potential for cultural consumption (Ministry of Culture of People's Republic of China, 2011). During our field research, we noticed that many new-generation migrant workers paid close attention to social news and current affairs as reported by the urban mass media, and attached great importance to cultural knowledge, vocational skills, and education for their children. "Most boys like watching sports, but I prefer to watch domestic and international news so that I know what's going on around the world." "I normally read everything on *Modern Express* (a daily newspaper). I also watch current events and social, domestic, and legal news on *Xinwen Lianbo* and *Nanjing Prime Watch* (daily news programmes)." "Our children must know what we don't know early so that they don't fall behind."

Economic capital is typically accumulated by providing labour and is a long-term process. By contrast, social capital has a relatively closed network and a high barrier to entry. In the media environment of modern societies, knowledge and cultural products are generally presented in the form of media information; they are updated in real time and transmitted ubiquitously throughout society. The acquisition of cultural capital is an open, instant, and autonomous process, offering users a wealth of opportunities for self-study and education. Currently, the purchase and possession of cultural capital have become a method for new-generation migrant workers to develop and consolidate their identities.

Pierre Bourdieu divided cultural capital into three forms: embodied, objectified, and institutionalized. New-generation migrant workers acquire all three forms of cultural capital through media information and city culture.

First, field actors accumulate cultural capital through "embodied" actions such as cultural education and cultivation. They invest time and energy in improving themselves (Bao, 1997). Our field surveys revealed that many new-generation migrant workers spent a considerable amount of time and energy learning new, modern information and skills away from work, endeavouring to engage in actual learning behaviours to improve and elevate themselves.

> When I come home from work, I watch TV, play computer games, and surf the Internet. Additionally, I study Microsoft software such as Word, Excel, and PowerPoint to improve myself. There's no specific reason that I study these programs; I just feel like it'll help me in the long run when I find a better job. I work on the 'front line' right now, and want to work in an office in the future.
>
> (Xiaozhu, female, 19, is from Sichuan and works at a
> power company in Zhejiang.)

Second, cultural capital is found in objectified cultural products and commodities such as pictures, books, monuments, and tools (Bao, 1997). Because cities possess rich and diverse media environments, new-generation migrant workers' media information and cultural purchases are accounting for increasingly higher proportions of their daily consumption. They read books and news, listen to the radio, watch TV, surf the Internet, and access various media to obtain cultural knowledge and search for useful information.

> For magazines, I read *Duzhe* (a biweekly Chinese general interest magazine), which has really well-written articles. Because I love reading the newspaper, I purchased mobile news for ¥2 a month; that lets me read all types of news including the latest domestic and international news. Online, I read the news, chat with friends, watch movies, and listen to music. I don't play games because I don't think they're interesting.
>
> (Xiaozhu, female, 19, is from Sichuan and works at a
> power company in Zhejiang.)

> Because I'm worn out from work every day, I rarely watch TV when I get home; I do read the news, though, and I do it even more often than I did in the past. When I'm at work at the shop, I read everything that's in the newspaper, like domestic news, cultural and entertainment news, financial news, ads, and employment news, to kill time and find useful information. When I'm online, I chat with my friends, read the news, and search for information; it keeps me busy.
>
> (Xiaogao, female, 26, from Langzhong in Sichuan.
> She is a shopkeeper at a small supermarket in
> Minhang District, Shanghai.)

Finally, cultural capital is institutionalized and formalized through education. The institutionalization of cultural capital is the use of academic qualifications and cultural competence certificates to demonstrate that the cultural capital possessed by an individual is established, recognized, and legally guaranteed (Bao, 1997). As new-generation migrant workers move from traditional rural societies to modern urban societies, they are exposed to fiercely competitive market environments which influence and change their values, increasing their understanding of the importance of cultural education in these environments. Changes in their cultural demands and educational beliefs are directly reflected by their daily consumption behaviour. They participate in vocational skills training and adult education courses; moreover, they invest in the education of their children.

> I finished compulsory education and began working at the age of 16 – after I completed junior high school. I worked in some good companies – ones that reimburse me for the training and let me pick up useful skills. I'm jealous of city people because they have the money to buy computers and cars. To make my life easier, I bought a second-hand computer and an electric vehicle. However, unlike others, I don't use the computer to play games; instead, I

search for information about work like technical training information, which is really useful. I don't use my computer for anything else. I used to think that school was unimportant; I was dead wrong. Your educational background is crucial when you're applying for jobs in big cities. If I could afford it, I would definitely have my children study in a big city because big cities can give them with the education they need to get in to good universities and land great jobs. Those jobs will give them a foothold to live in big cities.

(Xiaojiang, male, 23, from Gansu and an apprentice
working at a rubber factory in Hangzhou.)

Xiaojiang, who just turned 24, came from a less-advanced village in Gansu. He now works as apprentice at a rubber factory in Xiacheng District, Hangzhou.

I began working at the age of 16. It was common for people to do that where I lived. Most people started working as migrant workers as soon as they finished junior high school. It was either that or staying at home to work on the farm. Working on the farm wasn't the answer, though, because you would make no progress. Right now, I'm taking some advanced courses offered by Hangzhou municipal government to assist migrant workers. Our company reimburses us for the training provided so that we can acquire the skills we need to meet the factory's demands and make up for our lack of education.

(Xiaojiang, male, 23, from Gansu and an apprentice
working at a rubber factory in Hangzhou.)

In factories, dorm rooms are only provided to undergraduate and graduate students who hold managerial roles. Thus, Xiaojiang and his wife are forced to rent an apartment outside. The apartment is 10 square metres and the monthly rent is slightly over ¥300. Inside their apartment, they have an assembled desktop computer that cost them more than ¥3000. Nevertheless, Xiaojiang felt that it was worth it.

I use the computer to search for information. Some of the training classes that I'm in right now also teach us how to use computers. I don't really play computer games; being able to work at a nice job and support my family is much more important. I learned much more from the computer training classes offered by the Hangzhou General Labour Union. Occasionally, I do use the Internet for entertainment, like playing *Happy Farm*. I think it's pretty fun.

(Xiaojiang, male, 23, from Gansu and an apprentice
working at a rubber factory in Hangzhou)

Xiaojiang indicated that his hometown is relatively backward in its thinking; little attention is paid to education. All families have multiple children but do not provide them with the education they need.

That was the reason we didn't really go to school. I'll definitely send my children to good universities when they grow up. Having been to Hangzhou,

I don't want to go back to my hometown anymore. If I ever save enough money, I would start my own business and live a good life. I want to live and prosper here.

(Xiaojiang, male, 23, from Gansu and an apprentice working at a rubber factory in Hangzhou.)

Mr Tang, 32, came from Anhui and graduated from a vocational high school. He has been working for over a decade and is now technical staff at a construction company in Suzhou. When he first arrived in Suzhou, he did not have a specific plan in place; all he wanted was to learn a technical skill that he could use to support himself financially.

Living in cities now comes with pressure. In the past, that pressure was whether one could put food on the table and have clothes to wear. Today, after the rapid changes in material and cultural lifestyles, the pressure is whether one can learn continuously to keep up with the times, find better jobs, and live a better life.

(Mr Tang, male, from Anhui)

Mr Tang has a highly regular daily routine. Every day, he watches the morning news for half an hour, takes a 30-minute noon nap, surfs the Internet (including chatting online) for an hour, works out for an hour at night, and studies for two to three hours. He prefers the Internet to TV because the Internet allows him to work, find entertainment, watch the news, and shop. He cherishes his current job and is dedicated to fulfilling his job responsibilities. However, he still hopes to develop his professional skills in his spare time and pass the National Personnel Examination (a national public servant examination in China) to obtain professional qualifications. Mr Tang said, with a smile, that he has never stopped learning.

When I'm at work, I sometimes publish professional papers. I do it to summarize my work experience and to elevate my specialized professional titles. We're living in a competitive world today; we have to have professional qualifications and titles and we have to constantly accept and learn new things so we don't get wiped out by the changing times. Regardless of whether we continue to be employed or we own a business in the future, we must have the basic working skills to ensure that we can make money.

(Mr Tang, male, from Anhui)

Cultural capital is similar to weapons used in battles or investments in stakeholder relationships. The battles do not end in the fields of cultural products (e.g., art and science) or social class. During these battles, people use their cultural capital to obtain profits and gains.

New-generation migrant workers make purchases to present a better version of themselves and to overcome media stereotypes. They accumulate cultural capital as a response to the unequal allocation of social resources and to fight for higher social status, indicating their awareness of cultural identity and the efforts they make to be viewed as "new citizens". By possessing and accumulating of cultural capital, new-generation migrant workers are taking concrete and decisive actions to pursue their dreams of succeeding in cities.

3. Imagination-based Purchases: Symbolic Capital of Daily Revolts

All consumption behaviour creates culture because consumption gives birth to meanings (Fiske, 2001). New-generation migrant workers' consumption culture is affected by various internal factors within the field, such as their personal characteristics, memories of their villages, and city experiences as well as external factors such as real-world situations, public opinions, and media ecologies. The purchases of the migrant workers shape their image as new citizens, and they use their "capital" to reduce mediatized stigma and unequal social statuses. Subsequently, these people are able to blend in with their cities and adapt to their culture.

3.1 Imagination-based Consumption: The Identity Awareness of Collective Communities

In *Imagined Communities*, Benedict Anderson elaborated on the importance of reaching consensuses for members from the same geographical location. He used national identity to reveal that the imaginary characteristics of communities is a group-based cultural process (or one between subjects). In this process, the members and their "foreign" characteristics create a community; the characteristics of these communities are created by writing fictional stories and history, creating landscapes and paintings, and planning parades and celebrations. Characteristics obtained from community character as well as from key historical events and locations are then "assigned" by their respective communities. Renato Rosaldo criticized constructivist theories of ethnicity, contending that imagining the characteristics of communities does not solve problems, but rather creates them. For example, if the characteristics of communities are imagined, who were the people doing the imagining, and what cultural systems did they use to do the imagining? Moreover, what effects does this imagining have, and what are its influences and implications? (Rosaldo, 1994).

In human societies, consumer goods are symbols defining people's natural "habits". Jean Baudrillard contended that commodities do more than satisfying people's basic needs; they also connect people to social order. Consumption is not merely the purchasing of commodities; it is also a system and a language in which purchased commodities reflect what people think. In modern societies, purchases are symbolic, and people are recognized according to the commodities that they purchase. Consumption patterns and identities are closely tied together; people utilize the commodities they purchase to represent cultural identities and achieve symbol recognition. As a form of social behaviour and cultural patterns, commodities have a greater significance other than their practical use; they also symbolize social status.

In Yangtze River Delta metropolitan areas, urban space and mass media have created an urban image and consumer culture that pervade new-generation migrant workers' daily lives in cities, imperceptibly changing their consumption behaviour as well as how they view their cities, non-migrant citizens, and themselves. Consumption surpasses simple economics and is part of culture. Many migrant workers have modern lifestyles. They have changed their consumption behaviour from conservative to open, their consumption structure from simple to complex, their consumption philosophies from primitive to forward-looking, and their consumption patterns from traditional to modern. The effects of urban consumer culture on female new-generation migrant workers are reflected in their purchases of clothes and skincare products. For male migrant workers, the effects of urban consumer culture are reflected in their spending at entertainment venues such as bars and KTVs. In addition to purchasing clothes, food and beverages, and daily necessities, new-generation migrant workers also purchase personal electronic products such as MP3 players, cell phones, and computers. Purchases of personal electronic products are also accounting for increasingly higher ratios of their personal spending. Their attitudes towards advertising are open and rational, and they have relatively high brand awareness. As computers and the Internet become more and more prevalent, some of the migrant workers have begun to become acclimated to online purchasing as well.

Urban consumer culture affects new-generation migrant workers by using a rich variety of goods to arouse their purchasing desire and by offering them a dream of the city and methods of blending in and realizing those dreams. By imitating modern citizens' purchasing habits and lifestyles, new-generation migrant workers perceive themselves as normal citizens. They live city-based lifestyles to eliminate the gap between themselves and non-migrants and to win the respect and acceptance of local citizens. Their increasingly high purchasing power enables them to construct and maintain their collective identity as new citizens.

American scholar Edward W. Soja proposed the notion of a "thirdspace", where the first space is a real, geographic space, the second space is a conceptual space emphasizing ideas, and the third space is a living space in which reality and imaginations are reassembled. An example of thirdspace is a postmodern city pervaded by mass media and consumer goods (Soja, 2008). In the first space of the city, new-generation migrant workers from the same regions are connected in a geographical community. By contrast, in the second and third space of the city, they are united as a cultural community. Imagination plays a crucial role in this third space because it enables mass media and cities to form relationships; mass media "narrate", construct, and produce urban space through imagination, enabling new-generation migrant workers to form material and emotional bonds with their cities. New-generation migrant workers make modernized purchases to reconstruct and reproduce the cultural identities of their communities. The migrant workers themselves also exert substantial effort to incorporate city culture into their daily lives.

The communities described by Anderson are groups from the same geographical regions who share the same memories. Unlike traditional migrant workers, the new-generation migrant workers remember vaguely about their villages. Some of them obey their parents' (i.e., old-generation migrant workers') wishes and continued to work in villages, whereas others accompanied their parents to work temporary jobs in various cities. This latter group does not have day-to-day farming experiences and thus does not develop tight bonds with the land. Cities provide new-generation migrant workers with the dreams of modern life. The migrant workers are more fascinated by vibrant city life; they feel that they belong to their cities. Their tendency to pursue mainstream, avant-garde consumption demands is unlike that of traditional migrant workers. Instead, it resembles the flow narratives of new citizens with identity awareness.

City-based consumptions enable new-generation migrant workers to form a "circle of comfort", warming their hearts in the "desert" and filling their hope to their lives, which are lonely, hard, boring, and revolve around their unstable jobs. They work tirelessly to make purchases to eventually be recognized as new citizens with more freedom of self-representation and equal social status.

3.2 Consumption as a Form of Capital: Tensions in the Fight for Self-identity

As the "third community" moving between cities and villages, migrant workers are marginalized in formal urban societies despite living in the same modern cities as non-migrant citizens do. Migrant workers face problems such as poor working environments, discrimination, and institutional barriers in cities. Their struggle for self-identities has become a popular topic of academic research.

James Scott divided farmer "revolts" into daily and public revolts. In the present study, we mainly focus on their daily revolts. Daily revolts are unorganized, unsystematic, individualistic, opportunistic, self-indulgent, and without revolutionary consequences. These revolts are centred on integration with the ruling systems as well as conflicts about symbols and ideologies. Daily revolts are social movements without formal organizations or objectives; they also require no proof. Nevertheless, this type of revolt is the most meaningful and effective over the long term (Scott, 2007). By contrast with passive daily revolt activities as described by Scott, which include "being lazy, playing dumb, sneaking off, pretending to obey orders, stealing, slandering, engaging in arson, and sabotage", active revolt entail activities such as people actively blending in with mainstream societies, reshaping the identities of their communities, and fighting for their social status.

Consumer culture, which is centred on institutionalized commoditization and the deployment of consumption as cultural symbols, has two meanings: First, from a cultural perspective, material products serve more than just their physical functions; they also symbolize social statuses. Second, from an economic perspective, the supply, demand, capital accumulation, competition, and monopoly of cultural products and commodities operate together to become a part of people's lifestyles. Today, nobody purchases and uses commodities purely for their physical functions; they purchase them also to show their identities, statuses, and social classes. People categorize others mostly by what they buy as opposed to what they do (Poster, 2000). The rule of "people purchase according to their social classes" has been rewritten, and people make purchases to give off the impression that they are from social classes higher than their actual ones, engaging in daily battles to fight for recognition for themselves and their communities.

In modern societies, mass media such as TVs, newspaper, magazines, and the Internet depict migrant workers as a community of workers who are marginalized, work assiduously, live low-quality lives, are socially and financially vulnerable, and have no future. New-generation migrant workers emulate local citizens' consumption behaviours and lifestyles through a shared consumption space and shared content in daily life to continuously diminish the gap between themselves and other city dwellers.

New-generation migrant workers' purchases of cultural capital (which comprises embodied, objectified, and institutionalized cultural capital) are based on media information and their spiritual and cultural demand. They make these purchases to fight against unequal resource distributions and to obtain higher social status. They spend a considerable amount of time and energy to learn modern information and skills away from work; they make use of all forms of media to obtain cultural knowledge and search for useful information. They also participate in adult education and invest in knowledge accumulation and pursuit of higher education for their children.

New-generation migrant workers make purchases to connect with urban societies; they use the social status symbolized by these purchases to achieve autonomy over their social status and how they are perceived by others. Thus, materialistic, recreational, media information-based, and culture-based purchases have more than a physical function and symbolize citizen identities. By making these purchases, new-generation migrant workers achieve recognition as new citizens as opposed to as migrants. The rules and symbols of consumer culture as well as people's identities remain controlled by mainstream society and the core class, yet new-generation migrant workers' consumption serves as a method of revolt against this control by the daily process of making purchases.

Trivial actions in large numbers can overcome all obstacles. The daily purchases of migrant workers are quiet yet powerful ways for them to fight for identity recognition. Although these battles do not have immediate results and cannot completely change the structural differences between cities and villages, they can potentially change the images of migrant workers with small but persistent efforts, enabling them to blend in with the urban community.

4. Purchase-based Integration: Adapting to City Life

For migrant workers to blend in with their cities and adapt to their environments, they must make adjustments to their work styles, lifestyles, social interactions, and social psychology (Zheng, 2011b). These adaptations include replacing their traditional rural societies with modern urban societies; these migrant workers are thus not only spatial but "cultural migrants". Additionally, they must adopt modern values, psychology, and behaviour (Zhu, 2002). The process of migrant workers blending in with and adapting to their cities is not passive but is rather dynamic and full of agency accumulated gradually.

According to Michael Schudson, the power of culture in societies is comparable to that of politics and economics. This power is inescapable and extends across various areas and along the temporal axis. The people from these regions consider themselves members of their imagined communities; culture brings everyone together and becomes a part of their awareness (Crane, 2006). New-generation migrant workers blend in with their cities economically, politically, culturally, and psychologically according to their imagined urban life and by constructing and internalizing their cultural identities.

As a part of modern city culture and mass culture, consumer culture diminishes the barriers between non-migrant citizens and new-generation migrant workers through the use of mass media in cities. For new-generation migrant workers, becoming urban natives is more than just a change in identity by moving hukou or getting a citizen ID number. It also includes the opportunity to set up their homes, establish their businesses, become a part of their cities culturally, and live a modernized lifestyle. These migrant workers are no longer excluded and marginalized by their cities. They create their own life experiences outside of their jobs, gaining a sense of achievement and a feeling of self-actualization. Purchases have become a major part of how they blend in with mainstream urban culture and live their daily lives.

The growth experiences and environments of the new generation enable them to feel closer to urban natives than those of traditional migrant workers. The new generation of migrant workers can also better identify with cities and adapt to urban life. The "richness" of city life creates a modern life dream, inducing new-generation migrant workers to long for the approval of as well as win the respect and acceptance of urban natives. New-generation migrant workers wish to enjoy city life just like other citizens and be identified as new citizens. To achieve these goals, they make relevant purchases in their daily lives, and they emulate non-migrant citizens' consumption behaviours and lifestyles through shared consumption spaces and content. Compared with traditional migrant workers, the new-generation migrant workers are more willing to set aside their identity labels and consumption methods, imitating the consumption behaviour of non-migrant citizens instead.

New-generation migrant workers blend in with their cities in both long-term and short-term processes. In the long-term process, migrant workers work tirelessly, set up homes, establish businesses, obtain identities, and elevate their financial status. In the short-term process, the migrant workers make immediate, "learned", and "urbanized" purchases to satisfy their desires. By living city-based lifestyles, they eliminate the gap between themselves and non-migrant citizens and effectively blend in to the city. Through this process, they rebuild their cultural identity and social status. Migrant workers work assiduously to accumulate the wealth necessary to make purchases. As new-generation migrant workers depart from traditional rural societies to blend in with modern urban societies, they are subjected to urban influences, causing them to make urbanized purchases in their daily lives. The two processes infiltrate and interweave with each other to enable the migrant workers' daily consumption practice in the city to present traits of citizen-oriented and modernized lifestyles.

Meanwhile, in modern societies with numerous media choices, knowledge and cultural products are typically presented as mediated information; they are updated in real time and transmitted ubiquitously to offer users opportunities for education. New-generation migrant workers are exposed to a fiercely competitive market environment that influences their values and emphasizes the importance of cultural education. Changes in their cultural demands and educational beliefs are directly reflected by their daily consumption behaviour. They pay attention to the social news and current affairs reported in urban mass media, and attach great importance to learning cultural knowledge, improving their vocational skills, and providing education for their children. They accumulate cultural capital constantly by consuming media information and cultural products.

As such, consumption surpasses the economic scope to become a social behaviour and a cultural pattern. Modernized and citizen-oriented lifestyles have subtly and profoundly affected the consumption behaviour and culture of migrant workers from simple to complex and from traditional to modern. Their mainstream, avant-garde consumption demands reveal that they do not wish to simply be an improved version of past migrant workers; instead, they want to be new citizens filled with identity awareness.

The consumption behaviours of migrant workers shape their image as new citizens, and they use their "capital" to make purchases that reduce media-created stigma against them and to seek social equity. Subsequently, these people attempt to blend in with their cities and adapt to city culture.

The autonomous consumption behaviour of new-generation migrant workers illustrates their needs for material life and for spiritual culture, their increasingly urbanized and modernized consumer culture, their active attempts to blend in with their cities and adapt to city culture, and their self-representation and identity awareness in daily life. These are aspects that future studies on migrant workers must address. To better understand new-generation migrant workers' urban practices, identities, and how they blend in with their cities, future research should shed light on the agency and human elements of migrants with the goal of providing guidance in how to integrate themselves into cities, enrich their city lives, help them successfully relocate from villages to cities, and evolve from traditional to modern city life.

Note

1 Author's note: "stigmatization" includes a one-way power relationship of "signifying", which means to stereotype the negative characteristics of the group, so as to cover up the characteristics and become "the signified" essentially corresponding to the group characteristics.

References

Baldwin, E. (2004). *Introducing cultural studies*. Higher Education Press, pp. 275–276.
Bao, Y. (Ed.). (1997). *Cultural capital and social alchemy – An interview with Bourdieu*. Shanghai People's Publishing House, pp. 194, 198, 200–211.

Cao, Y., & Liu, H. (2004). Urban migrant workers' cognition of self-image in mass media – A case study of Nanjing. In *China communication forum conference proceedings* (pp. 83–91).

Crane, D. (Ed.). (2006). *The sociology of culture: Emerging theoretical perspectives*. Nanjing University Press, p. 19.

Featherstone, M. (2000). *Consuming culture and postmodernism*. Yilin Press, p. 166.

Fiske, J. (2001). *Understanding popular culture*. Nanjing University Press, p. 41.

Fiske, S. T. (2004). *Social beings: A core motives approach to social psychology*. John Wiley and Sons, pp. 398–400.

Guan, J. (2011). *Portray, the media image of the mutation, and perspective – Analysis of media image of migrant workers on sina.com during the prosperity of network media*, MA thesis. Southwest University.

Li, H., & Qiao, T. (2005). Stigmatization and labelling: The media image of migrant workers. *21st Century, 7*.

Lippmann, W. (2002). *Public opinions*. Shanghai People's Publishing House.

Ma, J. (2006). *Bar factory: A study of urban culture in southern China*. Jiangsu People's Publishing House, p. 17, 42.

Ministry of Culture of People's Republic of China. (2011). *Opinions on further strengthening the cultural work of migrant workers*. www.mcprc.gov.cn/xxfbnew2011/xwzx/lmsj/201112/t20111203_213449.html

Poster, M. (2000). *The second media age*. Nanjing University Press, p. 145.

Rosaldo, R. (1994). Others of invention: Ethnicity and its discontents. *Voice Literary Supplement, 82*, 27.

Scott, J. (2007). *Weapons of the weak: Everyday forms of peasant resistance*. Yilin Press, p. 35.

Soja, E. (2008). Postmetropolis. In M. Wang et al. (Eds.), *The city culture studies, a reader*. Peking University Press, p. 39.

Sun, L. (2003b). The new dual structure between urban and rural areas and the flow of migrant workers. In P. Li (Ed.), *An economical & sociological study of Chinese migrant workers*. Social Sciences Academic Press, p. 155.

Wang, C. (2011). Analysis on the media image representation of migrant workers in films – A case study of the films with the theme of migrant workers in China from 2001 to 2010. *Southeast Communication, 8*, 49–51.

Xu, X. (2009). Media projection of a special group – A study on the image of migrant workers in media representation. *Journal of International Communication, 10*, 42–45.

Yan, C. (2007). The transformation of the consumption mode of migrant workers in cities of the Yangtze River Delta – An investigation on the consumption of migrant workers in eight cities of Jiangsu province in the Yangtze River Delta. *Jiangsu Social Sciences, 3*, 224–230.

Yu, X., & Pan, Y. (2008). Consumer society and remarking the subjectivities of "new generation of female migrant workers". *Sociological Studies, 3*, 143–171+245.

Zheng, X. (2011b). On the new generation of peasant workers' adaptation to city life: From the perspective of communication. *Nanjing Journal of Social Sciences, 3*, 71–77.

Zhou, X. (1998). The impact of migration and rural experience on the modality of off-farm workers in Chinese cities: A comparative study on two local communities in Beijing and Wenzhou City, Zhejiang Province. *Sociological Research, 5*, 14.

Zhu, L. (2002). On the adaptability of rural-to-urban migrant workers. *Jianghai Academic Journal, 6*, 82–88+206.

11 Ruptures and Bridges
Cultural Identity Among Rural Migrant Workers

In research on the adaptation of the new generation of rural migrant workers to urban life, "urbanization" and "modernity" are frequently linked to "adapting to an urban environment". Researchers believe that "adapting to the city" involves a process of ongoing urbanization and modernity. Becoming completely assimilated by urban culture and being fully integrated into urban society truly define adaptation to city life. Therefore, contradictions between rural identity and urban culture are inevitable. Accordingly, some people have proposed that the migration of rural migrant workers from villages to cities to earn their living is itself a process which involves pursuing a "modern identity" and at the same time breaking away from a "rural identity" (Wang & Sun, 2015). In a broader context, rural identity is not merely defined in the usual sense of being "rustic" but is also a type of culture, a type of social memory. Relevant research also indicates that memories of home impact the self-identity of the new generation of rural migrant workers. Memories of home result in a crisis of urban identity among the new generation of rural migrant workers. In other words, rural social memory hinders and obfuscates rural migrant workers' integration into urban society (Hu, 2008).

Accordingly, negotiating the relationship between rural identity and modern identity is an issue which should be given special attention in research on urban adaptation and social inclusion among the new generation of rural migrant workers. Naturally, viewed from the antagonistic positions of urban and rural culture, this implies that the ultimate result of rural migrant workers' adaptation to urban life is the complete abandonment of rural culture and full identification with urban culture; otherwise, such adaptation will produce unsatisfactory results. Research on cultural adaptation can indeed provide a new reference point for research on urban adaptation among the new generation of rural migrant workers (Li & Li, 2014). In fact, the development of individual modern identities among the new generation of rural migrant workers is not antagonistic to their rural identities; on the contrary, both identities can co-exist with each other. The conflict between urban and rural culture is merely one expression of the urban adaptation process and is not a result. Unrestrained convergence with urban dwellers is merely an idealized state of being among the new generation of rural migrant workers adapting to the urban environment. However, the reality is that rural culture as a type of culture which embraces rural customs, practices, and living habits, cannot

DOI: 10.4324/9781003365785-11

possibly be completely eradicated from the hearts and minds of the new generation of rural migrant workers. Accordingly, the search for a new balance between urban culture and memories of rural culture should forge a new path to urban adaptation based on ideals and reality.

1. Rural Identity: Social Memory as "An Alien Culture" in the City

Rural identity is not what is usually defined as "rustic". It is types of village customs and habits, habitual ways of life. Accordingly, it is essentially a form of rural culture. In fact, it may also be said that memories of rural culture are a type of collective memory; collective memory is primarily formed in the minds of members of a society who are in a specific space. When collective habits and customs are deeply imbedded in people's minds, individuals will form connections with each other based on such similar habits and feelings. The dialogue between the new generation of rural migrant workers and the rural village is also like this. Identification with specific memories of home and cognition of deep emotions related to rural identity are propagated to establish a community based on shared feelings. This is a form of emotional resonance which can thus generate collective memory. When embedded in an urban environment, these types of memories of rural homes, as an alien culture, inevitably give rise to conflict with urban culture. To avoid such conflict, the new generation of rural migrant workers has a sense of urgency to gravitate towards the city. As a result, memories of home gradually fade out of the live of the new generation of rural migrant workers. Nonetheless, this approach fails to fundamentally resolve the issue of conflicting cultures.

1.1 Spatial Shift and Inner Retention: Contradictions Between Physical Setting and Mental State When First Entering the City

Mental contradictions among the new generation of rural migrant workers frequently arise because they are still psychologically tied to their rural homes despite the fact that they have left them behind. In addition, during their city life, they begin to experience a variety of urban situations. It is not difficult to see that when they initially enter the city, the lives of the new generation of rural migrant workers on the surface merely involve a shift in living space. They are usually influenced by their friends from the village and by their relatives to leave their native place to go to the city to work for a living. In the city, there are not many people whom they know well. Every day they repeat the same work and labour routine, living by themselves, with a relatively narrow social circle.

Xiao Zhang, a young man from Jiangsu born in 1992, came to the city four years ago. He currently works as a digital lathe operator at a factory in Suzhou. Although he grew up in a village, his family did not support itself through agriculture. His mother and father both worked at nearby factories, and only farmed the land during their spare time. The difference between Xiao Zhang's family and other workers was that Xiao Zhang's family's economic situation was satisfactory. The real reason why Xiao Zhang left home to work was not "poor economic conditions", rather it was because he did not like to attend school, and proposed to voluntarily quit school to lead the life of a worker. Having come to the city not long ago, he expressed that he felt "extremely homesick".

> After I graduated from junior middle school, I left home to go to work. A relative of mine introduced me to a job in a district of Suzhou. At that time, I was just 17 years old. This was the first time I left home. I took a worn suitcase with me and there was no one to send me off. I went alone to the station to make the trip to Suzhou. I cried for a whole day, because I had never left home before. Later, I felt a little better, but still felt very homesick and would call home once every week.
>
> (Xiao Zhang, male, from a village near Suzhou in Jiangsu)

Xiao Wu, who comes from a rural village in Hubei province, also expressed the same sentiments. He currently works as a hairstylist at a hair salon in the city of Nanjing. Living away from home for the past six years, he has become accustomed to life in Nanjing. Working as a hairstylist, he has the advantage of coming into close contact with all kinds of people from the city. Six years earlier when he got on a train to take him to an unknown place, he felt reluctant to leave, and felt afraid in this strange environment. This fear intensified the contradictions raging in his mind.

Both Xiao Zhang and Xiao Wu are typical among workers in the generation born after 1990. Although they are registered as members of rural households, they have no experience doing farm work and also left home to become workers after they graduated from junior middle school. Whether working as a digital lathe operator or a hairstylist, they both have new survival skills which are different from those depending on working the earth (farming) to live. From the perspective of their memories of when they first came to the city, leaving their homes to come to the city was merely a spatial transfer. In their hearts they still felt an intense love for their "native places". Of course, this "native place" is not defined merely in terms of the "land" but represents "home" and "people".

This state of living represents a true picture of the lives of most of the new generation of rural migrant workers. They have no acquaintances or friends in the unfamiliar cities where they live, and can only utilize a limited amount of time, leading monotonous lives travelling back and forth from home to work. They have not yet formed any social circles in the city, with each of them living as an independent individual in the city. In addition, urban society is no longer the society of the rural village filled with friends and acquaintances. On the contrary, it is a society filled with strangers in which relationships among people are not so close. Accordingly, developing and maintaining social relationships has become a new challenge facing the new generation of rural migrant workers.

The life of "migrants" is not so comfortable. "Staying at home in the village, they didn't have much of a future, and wanted to leave to make their place in the world, to live independently." "My friend worked away from home in another place, and took me with them to leave home", is the reason they give for initially coming to the city. Although, in today's society, with highly developed transportation, leaving home is not a difficult matter. Frequent moving and job-hopping also robs them of the stability they previously enjoyed in their lives. However, they are still willing to untiringly explore the direction of their professional development, continuously changing their living space. Among our interviewees was a single mother named Xiao Fang, who worked as a cashier at a bubble tea shop in Nanjing. Born in 1989, she showed signs of aging. She had left her home only several months before, filled with expectations of finding work as a cashier in a bubble tea shop such as this one in Nanjing. Nonetheless, her heart was filled with contradictory feelings.

> I changed jobs many times. In the past, I had learned to operate a crane, and worked at this job at home for almost two years. I was still working at this job last year. Although I made a lot of money doing this work, it was too tiring, and I did not want to continue doing it. My younger brother was attending school in Nanjing at that time, so I accompanied him to Nanjing, where I found a job. The boss has provided us with a place to live, but the living conditions there are very poor. After working here only several months, I don't want to continue anymore. Nonetheless, I must keep at it for at least a year.
>
> (Xiao Fang, female, from Huai'an, Jiangsu)

Xiao Fang's contradictions and uneasiness are caused by the uncertainty of urban life. Urban work and the beautiful environment attracted her. However, various unstable factors caused her to continuously suffer from anxiety. In fact, quite a few members of the new generation of rural migrant workers have lived the same life as Xiao Fang, changing their living space and environment to experience different jobs, continuously exploring the road to their future. The new generation of rural migrant workers initially suffer from an acute lack of planning, are often influenced by their relatives and friends, and thus embark on a drifting, transient life of "just picking up and leaving", even to the point of developing an attitude of going with the flow, "living each day as it comes".

From this we can see that the new generation of rural migrant workers' initial experiences of the city are unforgettable and bitter. Even if they have never done farm work, their spatial shift has not brought about an essential separation from their rural homes. They leave the land to come to the city to lead the lives of migrants. Desiring to go out and make a place for themselves in the world, they feel fearful. They want live independent lives but must endure loneliness. This is the reality which they must pass through in their attempt to experience city life. On the surface, it appears that they have left their rural homes to come to a new social space in the city, that they have embarked on new life and work experiences. However, the relatively recent duration of their entry into urban life and work in the city causes the new generation of rural migrant workers to rely on family ties and ties to their native villages as their fundamental relationship networks (Ding & Tian, 2009).

Before coming to the city, members of the new generation of rural migrant workers are filled with imagination and longing. They are determined to live independently as masters of their own lives, and to return in success to their home villages. However, rural society is the environment on which they once relied for their survival. They have deep-rooted feelings for their native homes. Their dependence on and emotional need for their native homes makes them fully realize that their homes remain in their hearts which prevents them from being able to psychologically identify with the city. This state of mind is a normal emotional condition for the new generation of rural migrant workers, because people cannot possibly merely exist in the geographical realm where they are living, while separating themselves from the social and cultural realm (Wang, 2010). Accordingly, they attempt to find the best solution to this problem by connecting with their family members via telephone and other means when living in an unfamiliar city. On the one hand, this enables them to maintain their family ties, while on the other hand they are able to resolve their feelings of loneliness.

Although when compared to the city, their homes in the countryside are relatively isolated and impoverished, members of the new generation of rural migrant workers will really miss home when they feel sad. They feel that their homes are places which they can reach at any time. This phenomenon is most common among the new generation of rural migrant workers, especially among those of them who are rather young and who lack sufficient experience in urban living. Having left their native villages not long ago, in the city they are clearly characterized by an emotional state of "holding on to the past in their hearts and minds".

In summary, when members of the new generation of rural migrant workers first come to the city, their initial memories of their home villages are still very deep. Some rural migrant workers are only 15 or 16 years old when they first arrive in the city, and afraid of their new environment. Even if certain members of the new generation of rural migrant workers leave home to experience the city for the first time at the urging of their friends or relatives, this does not completely enable them to develop a strong sense of belonging to this unfamiliar environment. "Being homesick" and "wanting to cry" are feelings often described by interviewees during interviews. Some interviewees even expressed that "At the outset I didn't want to do it. I just wanted to return home and forget about it." However, ultimately, after struggling in their minds, most people persisted at their work in the city with the attitude that "If I don't prosper, I won't return home" or "I can't just [give up and] return home like this". For the new generation of rural migrant workers, after they encounter setbacks, their rural homes become a psychological preoccupation and refuge. Living in the city, they inevitably suffer considerable mental trials and tribulations.

1.2 Seeking Cultural Common Ground: A Fervent Desire to Assimilate Into Urban Life

In our research on the new generation of rural migrant workers, we customarily view urban adaptation and social inclusion as a one-way process: it seems that the new generation of rural migrant workers must completely fade out their rural identity and fully adapt to all kinds of urban values to become completely assimilated into the city. Facing tangible and intangible pressures when they come to the city, the new generation of urban migrant workers naturally seeks to receive approval and recognition. They have a fervent desire to assimilate into urban life. Faced with being completely immersed in urban culture, they are also highly conscious of seeking cultural common ground. They hope to maintain a similarity with urban residents in their outer appearance, ways of behaving, manner of speech, and thought. After coming to the city, they begin to live their lives with reference to how urbanites behave.

Xiao Wang, a service staff working at the front counter of a restaurant in Shanghai, is from southern Hunan province and is 24 years old. When remembering how she felt when she had just come to the city, Xiao Wang believes that her village identity and rustic accent caused her to "really lose face".

> My native village is far away, and I must transfer vehicles many times to arrive there. During a period of more than a year, I have returned to my native village twice. Now when I get off work, I go home and watch TV. I like to watch Hunan and Shanghai (TV channels). . . . When I first came here, I didn't understand the local dialect. They all spoke Shanghainese. I felt there was a great distance between me and them. Moreover, Hunan dialect is too rustic. I did not dare to open my mouth to talk. Now I have learned a little Shanghainese.
>
> (Xiao Wang, female, from Hunan)

Understanding Shanghainese dialect can help Xiao Wang to quickly assimilate into city life, while also serving as an important means by which she can assimilate into the urban environment. Xiao Wang described how she felt when she first arrived in the city and did not dare to speak. Because she really wanted to speak with the people around her, she made every effort to speak *Putonghua*[1] well, and to appropriately imitate a few words of Shanghainese, to make herself appear to be "half Shanghainese". "Not being the same as the people around us" and "standing out as different from local people" have been a source of pressure for the new generation of rural migrant workers living in the city. They especially hope to be able to close the gap with urbanites in many ways.

After coming to the city, the new generation of rural migrant workers begins to form certain ideals. Faced with increasing demands, they begin to adopt the lifestyle of an urbanite as the plan for the lives they have designated for themselves. This change is rooted in their fervent desire to assimilate into city life. Xiao Guo, a hairstylist from Liuhe District, Nanjing, who was mentioned earlier in the text, has experienced this type of feeling. At the time he initially came the city, he merely felt that Nanjing was not far from his hometown and was also a good city, so he had decided to come here. While experiencing urban living for a period of time, he came into contact with many types of clients, who exerted a considerable influence on him. He began to feel that a person should have their own goals in life. When asked what his goals in life were, he answered without hesitation. From this we can see that Xiao Guo early on had formed a rather complete picture of the plan for his future.

> I really hoped that I could open my own hair salon in Nanjing and that I would be able to purchase a home in Nanjing. This is something I had never considered before I came to the city. In addition, my experience in changing jobs exerted a great influence on me. Within a certain time, I had become a senior hairstylist at the hair salon, which caused me to think about starting my own business.
>
> (Xiao Guo, male, from Liuhe, Nanjing)

In addition to Xiao Guo, quite a few young rural migrant workers fervently harbour the beautiful desire to assimilate into city life. They make every effort to free themselves of their past marginalized predicament, to learn to adopt values similar to those of urbanites. In their real lives, the beautiful aspirations they hold fill a void in their minds, to compensate for their desire to assimilate into city life.

On the surface, the new generation of rural migrant workers under the influence of living long term in the city, seem to have separated themselves from their rural identity. During the process of continuously changing jobs, their work begins to become stable. Xiao Ying from Guizhou is 29 years old. She has now been living in the city for ten years. She has a younger brother back home who is attending school. Accordingly, she has shouldered heavy responsibilities for her family. She has been employed as a factory worker and has also worked as a sales person at a shopping mall. She has moved from city to city many times, and now works in Nantong Municipality as a cashier at a hair salon. She dresses fashionably and has shoulder-length hair dyed yellow on top and red at the bottom. She says she now earns over 3000 yuan per month, which is extremely satisfying. When she recalls events that occurred when she first came to the city, it seems like they happened only yesterday.

> At the time, my two elder sisters had already left to work away from home, and my younger brother was still attending school. My parents had no income. At the very beginning, I went with my elder sister to work in Shanghai at a silk factory. I spoke with a very heavy accent, dressed like a country bumpkin, and did not speak *Putonghua* very well. If I spoke my native dialect, I was afraid that the people around me would laugh at me, so I didn't talk much. I was very ashamed of myself and did not have many friends then. I felt very lonely. In a big city like Shanghai, there are so many things to learn. It seemed like I did not know how to do anything. At the time, I felt a little afraid.
>
> (Xiao Ying, female, from Guizhou)

Xiao Ying recalls how she felt when she first came to the city: her feeling of helplessness at having to live the life of a person working outside away from home; her dislike of school and her decision to quit and leave home to make a living ... rural migrant workers when first coming to the city experience difficulties beyond their imagination. They feel inferior and fearful, even to the point of avoiding people to hide their rural identity.

When asked about what she did to cope with the fear she felt about her new life in the city, she responded: "I made every effort to do my job well. What else could I have done?" From her tone of voice, one could sense the resignation she felt towards urban living. She also admitted that "In a large city such as Shanghai, there are so many things to learn". From this we can see that she realized that if she wanted to live a better life in the city, she must master a key concept: "to learn from people in the city". Learning became a vital means of assimilating into city life.

Even if the rural village is the place where they have lived since childhood, in their minds they believe that the village symbolizes a "rustic" way of life, with predominantly traditional factors, while the city represents a "stylishly modern life", with predominantly modern factors. Accordingly, they invariably have a certain fervent desire to seek common ground in a cultural sense. In their daily lives, they often feel an intangible pressure which causes them to feel afraid of urban life, while this pressure also becomes the motive force which drives them to fervently adapt to urban culture.

1.3 Native Places in Transition: Disintegration of Rural Identity and Indelible Emotional Ties to Home Villages

After the publication of Fei Xiaotong's[2] classic work *From the Soil: The Foundations of Chinese Society*, "rural identity" became an important term for describing the characteristics of Chinese society. Following the ongoing urbanization of China's society and modern development among Chinese people, "rural identity" also gradually became an adjective to describe China's rural society.

"Rural identity" as the term implies from its wording, represents the rustic nature of rural dwellers. Although some proposed that the term "rural migrant worker", along with "rural dweller" and "rustic" seemed to connote certain feelings of contempt or disdain, if "rural identity" is taken as a neutral term in exploring its meaning, in reality it represents a type of culture. The rural village is a society of acquaintances. Through the power of identity people can bond with one another in a group, to give rural villagers a sense of belonging.

The rural identity of the rural village also includes relationships among acquaintances in the society. Acquaintances in their relationships share "unspoken rules" which can only be realized but not verbalized. Since they share a mutual familiarity, accordingly "giving face" forms the foundation of their behaviour towards one another. If the principle of common sense is violated, a member of the village will suffer a loss of face. Sometimes people must cooperate with each other to save face, and to reach a tacit understanding and trust. This type of tacit understanding, which is understood by everyone, remains unspoken.

In addition, habits and customs embodied in the local dialect are also representative of rural identity. The new generation of rural migrant workers in its respective localities has already formed types of language systems which may be termed "dialects". In layman's terms, dialects are also called "vernacular language".

Judging from their feelings when they first come to the city, we observe that the new generation of rural migrant workers feels that they are at a great disadvantage with respect to language. This is especially true for those who come from the Yangzi River Delta, a region which has a complexity of dialects. Such people suffer from even greater insecurity with respect to their language skills. They believe that their dialects are vernacular. The rustic quality of vernacular language is also a vital component of rural identity.

In addition, the rustic quality of rural identity originates from the roots of the rural village which belong to the land. Even if China's rural villages are now undergoing continuous modernization, fundamental conditions in most villages are still tied to directly obtaining benefits from the land. The land is the parent providing the villagers with clothing and food, an important means of production for the villagers' survival, and a source of potential wealth.

In summary, rural identity is a type of social order in the rural village. The maintenance of this social order always requires a series of rules and the power to guarantee that these rules will remain valid.

All societies always require certain means to control the actions of individuals and cause them to comply with standards which are acceptable to everyone. In the rural village, the local order is quite different from the city. Rural society is a society of acquaintances governed by courtesy, while urban society is a typical society of strangers. In an environment such as the rural village, villagers can organically unite. This type of organic unity is built on virtuous relations among acquaintances and based on social norms. Because people living in a rural village must frequently contact each other, they will form familiar relationships. And it is precisely this mutual familiarity or feeling of intimacy that enables them to have a tacit understanding in their normative behaviour and refrain from doing as they please.

Accordingly, in the village people share relatively strong relationships based on trust. All people are familiar with each other and clearly understand the other person's personality and qualities. It is precisely due to such familiarity that relationships based on trust between people have a comparatively reliable foundation. And it is precisely due to the pressure in this society of acquaintances that the living environment in the village is characterized by rather strong ethical responsibilities and pressure from public opinion.

Everyone harbours special feelings for their native place. With respect to members of the new generation of rural migrant workers, the special emotions they feel in their hearts are inseparable from the people in their local society and the longstanding habits of local life, while also being intimately tied to the land and to their patriarchal families. Emotional ties to one's locality cannot be extinguished. However, with the passage of time, they undergo change. Farmers depend on their native place for their survival. Their native place is the foundation of their existence, a key channel for achieving future possibilities.

The new generation of rural migrant workers relies on its memories of home for the following reasons: from their brief urban experience, we can see that their unhappy experience in the city is indeed one reason why they miss their rural homes; certain experiences have detracted from their sense of security and sense of belonging. In a space filled with setbacks and unfamiliarity, they begin to have a greater sense of the pure, simple life of their rural homes, and the relatively uncomplicated nature of social relations in rural society. Over the long term, this environment filled with friends and acquaintances narrows their social networks. Accordingly, when faced with a multitude of strict rules in the city, they miss rural society even more.

The factory's work shift system, the coldness of interpersonal relationships, and being swindled by friends are situations frequently encountered by interviewees in our survey. Their initial setbacks cause them to gradually become mature, and after understanding the complexity of interpersonal relationships, they gradually become re-socialized as a group. Throughout all this they are always supported by everything in their rural memories, which after all are an expression of their emotional ties to their rural homes.

However, after coming to the city, certain aspects of rural identity are forced to disappear, while certain other aspects remain. Faced with the new environment of the city, the new generation of rural migrant workers also consciously and voluntarily rids itself of rural identity, while certain parts of their rural identity under the subtle influence of urban life gradually fade away.

That set of rules in the village, which are tacitly understood by everyone, seem to be not so practical in an urban context, with the village's fundamental system of courtesy being transformed into another system of etiquette. Changes and substitutions also constantly occur in the language system, while customary practices in communication between friends and acquaintances also seem to gradually undergo a transformation. Step by step, the new generation of rural migrant workers is freeing itself from bondage based on a "rustic" identity. They have broken the status quo of satisfaction with village life and reluctance to migrate, to begin to meet the challenges of an urban life filled with uncertainties.

Their coming to the city has caused the living space for their family to disintegrate. The opportunity to be with family members has been lost by the new generation of rural migrant workers. Their living space has undergone a complete transformation and they have begun to live the lives of migrants. However, spatial changes are unable to instantaneously remove their heartfelt feelings. Physically, they find themselves in a strange place, but emotional ties to home sum up the intense feelings shared by most of the new generation of rural migrant workers after they arrive in the city.

When they first come to the city, they are still not fully immersed in this new world. They have tasted bitterness and suffered setbacks. Nonetheless, their feelings for home do not change. Their feelings for home always provide them with spiritual support in their drifting sojourn in the city. It may be said that these inextinguishable emotional ties to home form the spiritual support of the new generation of rural migrant workers. Such spiritual support helps them overcome obstacles they encounter in urban life while comforting their inner insecurities.

Among the existing research, scholars proposed the concept that rural workers in the city will form their own kinship circles, which are channels for them to obtain emotional support while living in the city. Subsequent to the continuous enrichment of their urban experiences, the new generation of rural migrant workers no longer excessively relies on their ties to home. In addition, their memories of home begin to gradually be replaced by the rich lives they live in the city. Accordingly, their memories of home begin to become blurred.

2. Identity Crisis: The Survival Dilemma of Being "Unable to Enter and Unable to Exit"

In essence, the greatest difficulty faced by the new generation of rural migrant workers in their adaptation to urban life is finding their self-identity. Self-identity is constructed during interaction with other people. A person's sense of self is a reflection of how other persons see him/her, a conception of oneself which is formed by imagining how other people evaluate oneself.

The new generation of rural migrant workers is making every effort in its desire to integrate into the city and in its attempt to become new urban dwellers. During this process, references to other groups, interpersonal communication, and widespread media use enable them to obtain social capital for integrating into the city. Their rural identity is also worn down during this process.

The contradiction is that in the eyes of villagers, they are persons who have lived in the city, who have become disconnected from the rural village. They are no longer plainly dressed, and are no longer traditional, while in the eyes of urbanites, they are labourers who have come to the city to work, with no social status. Thus, the new generation of rural migrant workers are people who dually marginalized.

Many symbols of the city have been engraved in the new generation of rural migrant workers. However, whether they have really adapted to urban life must be confirmed in terms of their cultural identity. It can be said that most rural migrant workers have experienced an identity dilemma. Although, the new generation of rural migrant workers has made great efforts to integrate into urban life, they have not fundamentally achieved this goal. Even if they were separated from their land a long time ago, they have never truly left behind the social aspects of their home life.

2.1 "A Home to Which There Is No Return": The Rupture of Memories of Home

The survival of memories of home relies on the collective environment of home, since memory is a product of their communities, and people can only possibly produce memory through participation in specific social interactions and communication. Such memories of home are also a type of cultural memory.

When members of the new generation of rural migrant workers leave behind their village identities and go alone to the city, they lose their community, the original group which may possibly enable them to continue their memories, and enter into a collective group closely related to the city. Accordingly, in this context, the rupture of memories of home seems to have become an inevitable phase.

Xiaoqin comes from a remote mountain district of Guizhou and came to the city 11 years ago. In her late twenties, she already has a ten-year-old son, and currently works in Nantong, Jiangsu province, as a salesperson selling clothes. Her home district in Guizhou is terribly impoverished. Coming from a traditional village household which places importance on boys and disregards girls, she was forced to leave home to make a living. Initially, she went with her elder sister to Nantong, to work as a service personnel in a place which is something like a dance club. Afterwards, she met Wenhua, her current husband, who is from Nantong. Although she married a local person, her life has not been as good as her other sisters imagined it would be.

She has encountered many twists and turns during her stay in the city. She has worked as a cosmetics salesperson in a large shopping mall and has also worked as a labourer at a garment factory. Finally, she decided to take a job as a clothing salesperson at a boutique. Xiaoqin looks very pretty, with thick eyebrows and big eyes. She dresses fashionably. She is unconcerned about her interpersonal communications with people in the city. Nonetheless, she quickly recalls the time when she first came to the city:

> Wenhua also came from an impoverished family. He didn't have much formal education and performed hard physical labour. He was eight years older than me. The fact that he was a local person meant nothing. Like me, he lived in a rundown dwelling, of only several dozen square meters. Nonetheless, transportation to and from home was much better than at home in my village. When I came here at age 18, I knew nothing, and was even unable to communicate well with others. Because I married someone from this place, my husband's family treated me like one of their own family members. They are all from this locality. Naturally, I know them well. All of them cared a lot about me, and didn't want me to continue working at a KTV. So, they introduced me to various jobs.
>
> (Xiaoqin, female, from Guizhou)

Xiaoqin believes that the long trip she would have to make to return home caused her to lose her enthusiasm for going back. Her home village's concern for males and disregard of females also fuelled her desire to find a husband from Nantong to enable her to "lead the life of a local person".

Initially, she felt overwhelmed by many language barriers because she didn't speak standard *Putonghua,* and couldn't understand Nantong dialect. Soon afterward, she married a local person, and has not returned to her home village since. Other than her parents, there is nothing there worth missing. Although her husband is a local resident, he belongs to the working class. He speaks Nantong dialect with Xiaoqin while Xiaoqin also speaks Nantong dialect to him with an accent, and they can communicate well.

Xiaoqin's interpersonal relationships in the city stem from her marrying a local person. Although her husband comes from the working class, her marriage to him was a big turning point in her life. He introduced her to a job, which enabled her to better adapt to life in this city. Her job as a clothing salesperson requires that she speak often. Accordingly, she often deals with many local persons, which enables her to establish relationships with them in her work. Marrying into the city has made integration into city life easier for her than for other members of the new generation of rural migrant workers, and for her personally, has enabled her to obtain more relationship capital.

Living in the city, this status of hers will prove very helpful in enabling her to build future relationships. The modern nature involved in human relationships during the process of urban adaptation and social inclusion has enabled her to completely adapt to her role in the city while any feelings for her native place seem to have completely disappeared. Her home village has become a place to which she will never return, "unfamiliar terrain with which she is most familiar".

> When I first came to Nantong to work, I came here with people from my home village. I felt that cities, especially cities in eastern China, would be very fashionable. Selling clothes at the mall, I gradually became very fashion conscious, and rather particular about how I made up and dressed.
>
> (Xiaoqin, female, from Guizhou)

When asked "whether at that time she had thought about returning to her village", she forced a bitter smile and said:

> Since I had already come here, I didn't want to return home. My home was in very remote area, and there was no way I could go back there. I also did not want to go back. After coming here, I gave no further thought to my life in the past. Other than my parents, there was nothing I missed.
>
> (Xiaoqin, female, from Guizhou)

We learned from Xiaoqin's husband, Wenhua, that during the past seven or eight years they had returned to Guizhou only once. He described Xiaoqin's circumstances:

> Her home was indeed located in the mountains. Her home was quite empty and the floor was mud. Next to the place where cooking was done was a bed. When we slept on the bed at night, we dared not turn over. The bed shook badly and seemed as if it would fall apart.
>
> (Wenhua, Xiaoqin's husband)

Xiaoqin is very cognizant of circumstances in her home village. She expressed that after leaving home she never wanted to go back again, for the only reason that it was too impoverished and too poor, virtually lacking everything. There was no way she could accept going back to her former life. From Xiaoqin's case we can see that the main reason she could not return to her native home was that she had developed strong relationships in the place to which she had now moved. When the language, customs and events of the village no longer appeared in her daily life, under the joint influence of the intense pull of city life and weak memories of home, Xiaoqin had almost lost all memory of her native village.

In addition to Xiaoqin, Xiaohe who works in a beauty shop in Wuxi, also believes that after staying in the city for a long time, she will never return home.

Xiaohe, female, 22 years old, from Jingzhou, Hubei, came to the city five years ago. As a member of the "generation born after 1990", Xiaohe has worked in the beauty industry for five years. She said that most clients in the beauty industry are people who are relatively well-off. The persons she encounters every day are generally certain "affluent housewives", who at the very least are people with money.

Because she left home at a young age to come work in Wuxi, Xiaohe is almost completely accustomed to living in Wuxi. She is able to completely understand Wuxi dialect, and sometimes can even speak a few words of Wuxi dialect herself. Since each client spends a rather long period of time on each beauty session, holding a conversation is a necessary part of her daily work. Her bright personality has won praise from many of her housewife clients. During her five years of work, Xiaohe has accumulated many regular clients.

Although she is young, she frequently comes into contact with such wealthy housewives and certain women who have successful careers. Xiaohe believes that it is quite easy to better one's life and has accordingly adapted her values. She would find it very difficult to return to the past, because if she went back to the village, she would feel out of place in every way, not to mention that her skills would basically have no value in a rural village. She also feels that "They [local villagers] don't watch movies and don't pay attention to new things, so there is nothing I can talk about with them".

From these two cases which share similarities we can see that reluctance to return to the village is due to barriers caused by spatial distances. In other words, spatial barriers are insufficient to form "a field" of memory. Memory is a type of collective behaviour. When the domain and medium which carry memory no longer appear in the lives of the new generation of rural migrant workers, not returning to one's native village becomes an inevitable trend.

Our interviews showed that many members of the new generation of rural migrant workers had abandoned many of the customs of the rural village, while expressing that such customs belonged to the older generation and were not intimately related to their own lives.

2.2 *"Failure to Assimilate Into the City": Ostracized Rural Identity*

The two difficulties encountered by the new generation of rural migrant workers are psychological difficulties which often confront them during their lives in the city. Strangers see Xiaoqin as a "successful person" who has married into the city, while, realistically, she cannot return to her native home and has been excluded from the city during a certain phase of her life there. Integrating into the city requires time, while also requiring a memory "field". When city dwellers describe their own collective memories, the new generation of rural migrant workers is often unable to enter the domain shared by city dwellers in their survival.

On the surface, the weakening of ties to their rural homes has not effectively enhanced the new generation of rural migrant workers' integration into the city. For Xiaoqin, although she has lived in Nantong for a long time, during the time when she first came to the city, she continued to exist in her identity as an outsider who had come to the city to work. Physical adaptation to the city and psychological adaptation to city life are two completely different situations.

Even if self-identity refers to a type of self-evaluation by the new generation of rural migrant workers, a perception of one's own identity, nonetheless, creating self-identity and social identity actually involves a process of mutual construction. Self-identity, in fact, includes outward acceptance and inner acceptance. In this regard, many members of the new generation of rural migrant workers feel they are incompatible in every respect (with city life). On the other hand, Xiaoqin, who had married a local person, and worked in the service industry, had also experienced the same feeling (as other rural migrant workers of her generation):

> I was only 18 years old when I got married. Many of Wen Hua's relatives said that he had married a girl from another locality. At that time, I was still young and also very nervous. I dared not speak, and didn't know what I should say to them.
>
> (Xiaoqin, female, from Guizhou)

From an outsider's perspective, Xiaoqin did indeed possess the qualifications to integrate into city life. Nonetheless, she objectively expressed the dilemma she felt in being segregated physically and psychologically. To a certain extent, a rural identity is ostracized by outsiders. From the perspective of other female rural migrant workers, Xiaoqin has already become an urbanite. However, from her own perspective, after becoming intimately familiar with the families of local people, the feeling of being ostracized become more intense. In addition, living in places away from home, the new generation of rural migrant workers feels relatively deprived. This feeling of relative deprivation results from comparing oneself with other people in society, when people take those around them as a reference group with whom they compare themselves. For rural migrant workers, their feeling of relative deprivation indeed arises when they compare themselves to urban residents. This feeling is a type of subjective emotional response. Accordingly, regardless of which phase they are in, all of them will compare themselves to others. The feeling of deprivation which arises from making such comparisons is produced when differences between oneself and local people are discovered as comparisons are made during their adaptation and inclusion into city life.

Xiaohe who works at a beauty shop in Wuxi, mentioned earlier in the preceding text, shares similar feelings. She has always worked at a beauty shop, with all her clients being persons from the upper middle class. Even if she has always felt that her appearance is no different than that of urbanites, in her mind she lacks an affinity with them.

When I came to Wuxi, I was still quite young. However, after I arrived here, I learned quickly. Although there were certain things I couldn't afford to buy, I was able to learn a lot from them since I provided services to many different people. The more contacts I made, the more I realized that there was a huge gap between me and those wealthy people. In fact, I felt I had no status, that I was only a service worker. Especially certain affluent persons who drove their own car to the beauty shop to receive services, who would talk about their problems at home. What they told me I thought only happened in TV dramas. I had no understanding of what they were talking about.

(Xiaohe, female, from Jinghou, Hubei)

Xiaohe believed that she "did not share a common language" with them, that the cultural differences between them, in fact, resulted from the mutually exclusionary relationship between rural culture and urban culture. Loss of reliance on their rural homes coupled with their failure to blend into city life, have caused the new generation of rural migrant workers to be caught in a double dilemma.

Naturally, not everyone feels the same as Xiaohe. Yuting, who is 27 years old, from Lianyungang City, Jiangsu province, sells cosmetics in Nanjing and came to the city five years ago. She once studied cosmetology in Shanghai, and after finishing her studies, decided to stay in a big city to work. Yuting has a vibrant personality, enjoys learning and is dedicated to her work. She has always worked in cosmetic retail sales, and has achieved a measure of success in her work. She feels that she has found a place where she belongs in the city. She believes that everything she is doing now revolves around her work, that her work is her life. She doesn't acknowledge that there are any differences between herself and other city dwellers. She believes that she is now a Nanjing local. She is not only economically independent but also has a family and children.

Nonetheless, like many members of the new generation of rural migrant workers, she has also gone through a hard time. However, Yuting always has a positive outlook, and is filled with passion for living. She is rather unwilling to speak about her past experiences. She is even unwilling to admit that she once held the status of a "labourer".

We can see from the circumstances challenging Xiaohe and Yuting that struggling with a double dilemma is a situation encountered by most of the new generation of rural migrant workers. They have pre-existing conditions, certain fashionable lines of work such as beautician, hairstylist, and cosmetologist, which enable them to have zero distance contact with urbanites. Externally, they have become quite intimate with city dwellers, and entertain certain ideas which are almost identical to those of urbanites. However, their lines of work in service industries also cause them to believe that they are service staff, not persons who are receiving services. They believe that as service staff, they have a low status. Accordingly, with respect to self-identity, the new generation of rural migrant workers does not view itself as the equal of urban residents.

To a great extent, whether the new generation of rural migrant workers can integrate into urban life will be determined by whether they are able to identify with urban culture and develop their own identity. And their self-identity frequently will be determined by the environment in which they live and the course of their daily lives in the city. When living in the city causes them to feel an intangible pressure, the balance between urban and rural is broken. In particular, the mutual exclusion of urban and rural domains of memory affects the ability of the new generation of rural migrant workers to identify with the city. And striving to find a shared memory "domain" is a vital means for the new generation of rural migrant workers to integrate into city life. Accordingly, under the double impact of a ruptured memory of home and exclusion from urban culture, the new generation of rural migrant workers has fallen into a double dilemma which is difficult to resolve.

2.3 Cultural Amnesia: Deficiencies of Marginalized Self-awareness

In our research on the new generation of rural migrant workers, we tend to believe that when the new generation of rural migrant workers loses its rural identity, it will be able to complete its urban adaptation and social inclusion. In our research we have discovered that integration into the city is not as simple as disinterested parties may have imagined. Such integration not only requires external integration into city life but also demands a recognition of one's own identity. The so-called self-identity involves an evaluation of self-identity by the new generation of rural migrant workers, which includes self-awareness and external evaluation. Based on the preceding exploration of "who I am", one can find an answer to this problem.

The new generation of rural migrant workers is filled with hopes and desires when it enters the city. However, their working and living environment in the city cause them to feel that they are discriminated against and isolated. The distance between them and urbanites causes them to feel that they are completely incompatible with city life. When they return to their native homes, in the eyes of their kinsmen and neighbours, they appear to be well-off financially and to view things from a higher perspective, which makes them infinitely proud. However, at the same time, they are individuals whose ways of thinking have undergone external and internal transformation, people who appear to be incompatible with certain traditional practices of rural society. Most of them work in the service industry in the city. Even if they are members of urban society, they feel inferior to others. It is precisely their closeness to urbanites which makes them realize their distance from urban dwellers. Members of the new generation of rural migrant workers see themselves as dually marginalized, on the one hand different from urban residents and on the other hand, different from the farmers in their home villages. Although they appear to be urbanites, they are unable to rid themselves of their rural status. Even if they free themselves of their reliance on the land, they cannot separate themselves from their deep-rooted rural lifestyle and concepts which have been with them since birth. When they return to the rural village, they feel different from others and encounter an intangible exclusion from rural life. When they come to the city, they feel that their rural style is incompatible with an urban environment.

It is not difficult to see that this marginalized deficiency of self-awareness is caused by the absence of a sense of belonging to the city while also lacking a sense of belonging to the rural environment. Even if the new generation of rural migrant workers has been exposed to an urban setting over a long period of time, with opportunities to contact urban dwellers and understand urban culture through a more modernized media, nonetheless, they lack confidence and certainty when it comes to their self-identity construction. This lack of self-confidence on the one hand comes from the pressure of being ostracized as they live their lives in the city, and on the other hand comes from media reports which stigmatize rural migrant workers, causing them to realize how they are seen in the eyes of certain urbanites. Such intangible pressures are encountered by the new generation of rural migrant workers living in the city. As our interview data shows, a lot of discrimination they encounter in the city remains hidden. However, such discrimination causes psychological estrangement between rural migrant workers and the local population.

The reason why members of the new generation of rural migrant workers feels marginalized is because they "have homes to which they cannot return". An external force originating from their rural villages makes it impossible for them to return to their rural homes. On the one hand, as mentioned earlier, the ongoing process of modernization experienced by the new generation of rural migrant workers determines that they will fall out of step with the village. On the other hand, mobility among village residents is growing. Villagers often believe that if young villagers fail to go to the city to find their way in the world, and choose to remain in the village, they will fail to make anything of their lives. Under the intangible pressure of the village, the new generation of rural migrant workers has become a group which cannot return to the village, and which is also unable to integrate into urban life.

Social memory theory proposes that the past is a useful resource for expressing how people feel at the present, and when the past is overlooked in what we feel at the present time, memory goes missing. This type of cultural amnesia is caused by a vacant cultural field. Cultural memory, first of all, is not simply a recalling of past events. It is socially constructed behaviour at a certain stage in time, with certain factors determining the process of constructing social memory, what things can be deleted and what can be retained and revised. Simultaneously, people in society who experience a loss of memory will also construct memory in the context of their new living space (Yan, 2009).

Memory is frequently selective. Cultural memory is a type of collective memory, while preservation and intensification of collective memory often relies on media and images (Liu, 2009). During the transformation from rural village to city, the new generation of rural migrant workers, through contact and association with urban dwellers, completes its modernization and obtains urban characteristics under the influence of mass media. However, regardless of the means by which they improve themselves, they all feel intangible pressure from society.

This intangible pressure and feeling of rejection cause them to have contradictory feelings about whether they should identify themselves as urban or rural, which results in a lack of self-identity, because they are not members of the rural village, and also do not belong to the city.

In their outward appearance, members of the new generation of rural migrant workers look very much like urban dwellers, and are inclined to integrate into the city, nonetheless, as urban service personnel and labourers, they are also unable to truly be accorded the same treatment as urbanites. As a result, they encounter multiple difficulties. In fact, cultural conflict is a major factor leading to identity dilemma. Fusing urban and rural culture is perhaps the best outcome for the new generation of rural migrant workers in their adaptation to city life. However, realistically, it is very difficult for urban adaptation to produce a definite outcome. The new generation of rural migrant workers is perpetually searching for balance in its dilemma, while this attempt to balance gives rise to contradictions. Rural culture may very possibly become obfuscated or even extinct. Whether or not they can integrate into the urban environment depends, to a large extent, on self-identity and cultural identity among the new generation of rural migrant workers. As the new generation of rural migrant workers strives to integrate into the city, rural culture becomes obfuscated. To a certain extent, this helps to avoid the ongoing cultural conflict, while creating an identity dilemma. And reconstruction of rural memory is possibly a fundamental and effective way of constructing their cultural identity.

3. Restoring Self-identity Via Media Use and Communications: The Reconstruction of Rural Memory as a Cultural Sphere

In the process of cultural conflict and reconciliation, urban and rural culture continuously clash, while rural culture gradually exits the urban stage: this is the outcome of cultural conflict, which causes the new generation of rural migrant workers to sink into an identity dilemma. Naturally, the passage of the new generation of rural migrant workers from marginalization to integration is not accomplished overnight. Moreover, this integration does not involve systems but involves an integration of culture, social intercourse, and identity. Actually, a person's modern identity and rural identity are not mutually opposed and are not incapable of co-existing. As such, the reconstruction of rural memory proposed in this chapter may be able to eliminate cultural conflict, and achieve a balance in the transmission of urban and rural culture and form a multiple cultural identity. In other words, the rebirth of rural memory does not represent a retrogression in the modernization of the new generation of rural migrant workers, but is an adjustment made by the new generation of rural migrant workers in their adaptation to the city.

The media experience which is present everywhere in the city takes the new generation of rural migrant workers into a new world. Members of the new generation of rural migrant workers strive to enter into professional circles of relationships in their work, strive to gain acceptance among circles of friends in their living space, and strive to enter into a new social space which integrates blood relations, geographical ties, and work relationships in their use of new media. Mass media, on the one hand, serves as a tool for their communication, and on the other hand also plays the role of messenger, to transmit multidimensional information. Under the impact of numerous urban information elements, from their initial entry into the city to their adaptation to city life, changes occur in the daily habits and values of the new generation of rural migrant workers. Such changes enable them to "localize", to become more like urbanites. Over the long course of their living in the city, the new generation of rural migrant workers has long term contact with various types of media, from television and other traditional media to the Internet and other new media, in addition to other We Media represented by WeChat and Weibo. After the rupturing of their rural memory, the memory of the new generation of rural migrant workers is awakened under the influence of the media, enabling them to restore the culture and customs of their rural homes.

3.1 Media as a Tool: Maintaining Rural Ties in the Use of Media

When initially coming to the city, members of the new generation of rural migrant workers all seem to "fawn on things stylish (foreign)". They often feel that customs, culture, and ideas from back home are backward, even to the point of imagining that urbanites view rural migrants as "superstitious" people. On the contrary, urban culture is what they long to pursue. Urban culture is stylish (foreign), scientific, and progressive. Accordingly, in the city they pursue individualism, worship of wealth, hedonism, and consumerism. During their several years after coming to the city, they madly pursue an identity based on material acquisition and engagement in the spirit of materialism. However, the diversity of their social networks determines that they not only have relationship networks of their own in the city, but also maintain contact with family members. From the perspective of dynamic change, as the new generation of rural migrant workers are being "pulled" in by urban culture, rural culture is also continuously undergoing change. Over a long period of time, utilizing the media to maintain contacts, the new generation of rural migrant workers gradually begins to identify with the culture of their native homes once again. Such identification is primarily dependent on maintaining connections with one's native home.

Empirical investigation demonstrates that connections maintained with one's native home originate from the existence of human ties with society back home in the village. Human feelings become a medium in behaviour which awakens rural memory. Traditional society places great emphasis on collective ideas and maintenance of family ties. Most family members and close friends of the new generation of rural migrant workers are in the same village or in the same city, thus giving rise to various types of connections. From banquets at weddings and funerals to customs at traditional festivals, such large and small affairs are sufficient to cause them to generate ties with their native homes. In this regard, the media often serves as a transmitter of information, a messenger for communicating emotions.

Yating, born in 1982, comes from a rural village in Anhui and currently works as service staff at a hotel in Nantong. The hotel is quite large and has a strict work system, which has resulted in her having very little free time for herself. Tempered over a long period of time during her work at the hotel, Yating has metamorphosed from an ignorant little girl into a highly effective assistant lobby manager. Yating left home to work at the age of 18: she has worked as a quality inspector at a garment factory and as a shop assistant at a boutique. After going through ups and downs in her professional life, she finally came to work at the hotel. Moving from service staff to her current position as assistant manager, her perseverance and effort have finally paid off. In the future, she plans to continue working at the hotel. Although she is quite busy every day, she uses her free time to go out with colleagues to sing and have fun. During her life, memories of her home village have been forgotten and then remembered again. Long term adaptation to the city has enabled her to find her place in the city. As such, media has brought her modern lifestyles while also bringing her emotional ties to home. She has ten years' work experience, during which she has travelled a complicated psychological journey.

> Before when I went alone to work at the factory in Wenzhou, I did not even have a mobile phone, and felt a bit afraid. Later, when I went with my friend to a store in Suzhou to sell clothes, I changed a lot. At the time, I hadn't gone home to Anhui for quite some time and hadn't even called home once.
>
> (Yating, female, from a rural village in Anhui)

When we asked her about customs back home in her village, she recalled some memories of the time she was married:

> My husband was from my locality. Later when we got married, we held the wedding in my home village in Anhui and my family prepared for it long in advance. As I was working away from home, how could I possibly find the time to make such preparations? All preparations were discussed over the phone.
>
> When I married, my family hosted a banquet for several days at our home. As I now recall, the event was extremely exhausting. . . . I didn't have many friends in Nantong and all my relatives were back home in my village. So, I had to hold the wedding banquet back home.
>
> (Yating, female, from a rural village in Anhui)

Remaining in the city while following certain social customs from back home are traits which typically characterize Yating's life. Even if she comes from a rural village and only has a senior middle school education, she finds herself more and more removed from village life and farming activities after living in the city for many years. The land, harvest time, and rural life for her are distant memories. For a member of the new generation of rural migrant workers such as Yating, who has lived in the city for over a decade, a mobile phone is the most convenient tool for connecting with people on an emotional level. When she first came to the city, Yating experienced confusion, low self-esteem, and bewilderment, having no direction and having no objective. However, her determination to develop professionally enabled her to move closer and closer to her goal of integrating into city life. She learned from her experiences living in the city, while accepting urban values. Throughout all of this, her mobile phone proved effective in maintaining contact with folks back home. The process of acquiring a mobile phone and then establishing contact with her family aroused memories of home which had lain silent in her heart. When making wedding arrangements, her mobile phone proved to be even more convenient as a bridge connecting her with her family. Such a wedding ceremony deepened her memories of home to a certain extent.

Dawei from Sichuan province, age 26, has worked at a hair salon in Wuxi for six years. He described himself as once being a "delinquent youth". When asked about his initial arrival in the city, he expressed without hesitation, "I felt the city was highly developed, and especially wanted to go to Internet cafes and bars, which we didn't have in our mountain village". During the first year when he followed his uncle to work in Wuxi City, he was young and didn't know anything. He spent the whole day at Internet cafes playing video games and spending a lot of money. Furthermore, he was not allowed to show up late for his job at the hair salon. He found it quite difficult to adapt to this type of restrictive life. When he first began working at the hair salon, he arrived late every day and was penalized for his tardiness by deductions made from his wages.

His former girlfriend made him change his work attitude. He said, "I met my girlfriend at a bar. We had only been together for a month when she grew tired of my being poor and broke up with me." He has no reservations when speaking about his past, and adds, "However, now I am the most senior hairstylist at the salon. Now that I enjoy a different status, my thinking has also changed. I want to stay in Wuxi. It's better than living in the mountains."

> These two years, every time I return home, my family urges me to get married. I don't have much education. At my age, 26, most kids in our village are married with two children. I still have no potential marriage partner right now, so they criticize me. Every time I call them, after saying a few words they begin to nag me about when I will get married. They want to introduce me to a girl from the village, but I want to stay away from home. There are many people here who are 26 and unmarried. Moreover, my work must be stable, and I must do better if I want to succeed.
>
> (Dawei, male, from Sichuan)

From this we can see that Dawei's setback in his love life made him realize the importance of "earning money". Although he has achieved a certain status at the hair salon through his hard work, he is nonetheless holding the traditional concept of love and marriage, influenced by people back home. Under this dual pressure, he consistently maintains his own way of thinking. However, when the question of work is raised, he has become accustomed to the city's fast pace and high income and has developed an individualistic and hedonistic spirit nurtured by modern society, while at the same time he has been profoundly influenced by his family's ideas. He has no choice but to neutralize such contradictions time and again in his telephone conversations with his parents, while trying to find the best solution. At such a time, media is mostly used as a tool for connecting with people at an emotional level. Such exchanges using media tools mostly involve communication with parents who are back home in rural society.

Moreover, a significant difference exists between these children and their parents with respect to their ability to accept new things, thus restricting media use between both parties primarily to merely "making telephone calls". For members of the new generation of rural migrant workers who have lived in the city for many years, after they reluctantly leave their homes to work in an urban environment, they begin to become infatuated with certain new things which they discover in city life. Certain urban scenarios may be imagined when living in the village. However, in the city you can experience them at a personal level. However, after their initial indulgence, they come to develop a deep understanding of urban life. At this point in time, most members of the new generation of rural migrant workers have reached an age where they begin to feel the need to get married and start their careers. While adapting to certain urban practices, their memories of home, which had faded in the depths of their minds, are gradually reawakened. Driven by various social rituals and observances, memories of home appear once again. And such memories of home gain new life through the use of media, to become a component which cannot be bypassed in their adaptation to the city.

3.2 Information-rich Media: The Arousal of Memory in Content Distributed by the Media

Media content is highly varied: from news reports to film and television drama, all include large and small things pertaining to city life and also include emotional ties and matters pertaining to rural society. From traditional media such as television, to various platforms on the Internet, different ways of life and cultural attributes are shown to the new generation of rural migrant workers. In urban life, media content guides them in developing a perception of urban culture and rural culture. The new generation of rural migrant workers is affected by subtle influences of media agenda-setting. With the strengthening of their subjective cognition, the new generation of rural migrant workers no longer blindly pursues the materialism and culture of the city. At the same time a certain urban identity is produced, the media's description of rural culture arouses in them feelings for their villages back home. The language, customs, and emotional ties of home will often bring back memories to members of the new generation of rural migrant workers who have lived in the city for a long time.

These also constitute memories of home for the new generation of rural migrant workers.

They often use the media as a platform to establish a connection between content shown on television and historical memory. The establishment of this connection often arises when they encounter objects in a certain television program or in a certain news report, or any objects on an Internet platform which arouse their sympathy. Their blurred memories gradually become clear, and rural scenarios and lifestyles come back to life. Feelings which they have accumulated in the minds, in an instant, resonate with descriptions of content appearing in the media. Accordingly, they recall hidden memories of rural life and rural culture once again.

A young woman from Hunan whom we interviewed in Shanghai experienced the following deep feelings. Quite a few persons referred to their home dialect as *patois* (rustic language).

When they first came to the city, they distinctly avoided speaking their dialect in the presence of outsiders. On the one hand, they feared that their "*patois*" was incompatible with the language of urbanites. On the other hand, they feared that their dialect would reveal their identity as rural migrants. They fail to gain acceptance from urbanites. However, when the Internet publishes content on rural village dialects and customary practices which are connected with their language and customs back home, their native culture which seems to have been lost is brought back to them by the media. Customary practices back home such as speaking the "local dialect", which they once viewed as obstructions to adaptation to city life, now have a new status in their minds and hearts.

> My mobile phone [iPhone 4s] was a gift from my boyfriend. In my free time, I play on my phone, and log on to Weibo. I like to look at funny things. In the past when I saw a video in which Hunan dialect was spoken, it was humorous, and more importantly, it warmed my heart. In the past, I was immature. I felt that Shanghai dialect was quite fashionable. Now I realize that local dialects are found among people in every locale. There is nothing wrong with our Hunan dialect. Sometimes on the street when I hear someone speaking something which sounds like Hunan dialect, I will feel somewhat close to them.
>
> (Xiao Wang, female, from Hunan)

When language cultures clash, the differences between one's local dialect and other dialects will be continuously accentuated. Language represents a value system. In a group, the greater the cultural similarities, the greater the degree to which language identity is acknowledged within the group (Huang & Liu, 2008). Language identity also undergoes a complex transformation, from refusing to identify with one's dialect from home to multiple identification with both urban language and one's local dialect. And the appearance of local dialects in the media forms a pulling force which draws the new generation of rural migrant workers back to the native localities where they once lived.

Under the effect of such combined forces, the new generation of rural migrant workers has formed a core circle centred on two languages. As expressed in the words of Xiao Wang in the preceding text, who said that she was "continuously learning to speak Shanghai dialect". From her perspective, achieving language synchronicity with urbanites was a key component of ridding herself of her identity as a rural migrant worker. However, she currently believes that "Shanghainese and Hunanese are both dialects". From this statement we can understand that both enjoy equal status as dialects representing their respective regional cultures.

Actually, Xiao Wang already identifies with the Shanghai dialect, which is spoken in the region where she lives. On the other hand, the dialect spoken in Hunan at her home village, is also a core dialect which gives her a strong sense of intimacy and belonging. For Xiao Wang, the appearance of content in the media creates a "field" in which to experience her home culture and awakens her memory of culture in her home village. From this we can see that media has exerted a definite effect in restoring memories from home.

Xiao Wang is a single young man born in 1990, from Xuzhou in Jiangsu. He has lived in the city for six years and currently works at an exceptionally large factory. He is already the foreman of a small workshop, has several apprentices working under him, and earns good wages. After leaving Xuzhou, he has worked at the factory in Zhenjiang for six years until the present, during which he has undergone a number of transformations.

> I first saw computers when I came here, along with ZTE mobile phones,[3] the ones with the large screens. I had to use them, since everyone else was using them. At the time, I had no understanding of what people were talking about, but now I understand these things. I buy all my clothes and everything online. It's very convenient. Moreover, I am too busy at the factory and often work the night shift, so I have no time to go out.
>
> (Xiao Wang, male, from Xuzhou, Jiangsu)

During Qingming Festival,[4] Xiao Wang posted his feelings online: basically, how he really missed his deceased mother after returning home and standing beside the graves. During our conversations we learned that he grew up in a single-parent family, and that his mother had died of cancer several years ago.

Right after my mother died, I felt deeply hurt, and just listened to songs all the time without talking to anyone. Every time I read about such an event (the death of a parent) online, I feel extremely sad, because it reminds me of my mother. Now every time when Qing Ming Festival comes around, other people may go out to have fun, but I will always return home to pay my respects at her grave, no matter what. This has become an established practice in my life.

During our conversations we unexpectedly discovered that he loved to watch television shows. He said,

> Because conditions in the dormitory are not bad, we have an old model television set. I really enjoy watching television. Mostly I watch CCTV and Hunan TV. The TV shows I usually watch is "If You Are the One" and Hunan TV's "Happy Camp". I do not remember the others. I remember I once watched a television show about a poor family living in the mountains and a wealthy family, who swapped children (the wealthy child going to live with the poor

family and the poor child going to live with the wealthy family). I felt there was a great difference between the two families. There are many wealthy people, while there are even more persons who are less fortunate than I am.

Xiao Wang seems to have adjusted to the local way of life. Nonetheless, special experiences in life, and certain empathetic experiences often evoke memories which have been tightly locked in his mind. News events and television programs let him connect them with his own experiences back home, while also causing him to develop a renewed identity with his rural culture back home.

In fact, the connection between urban culture and rural culture primarily originates from the subjective consciousness of the new generation of rural migrant workers. The media plays a definite role in promoting the formation of this type of subjective consciousness. This is especially true with respect to content presentation. Television, as traditional media, presents such content through film and television dramas, special programs, etc. We Media platforms such as Weibo, use rich, colourful language, images, videos, and audio recordings to produce diversified content.

As such, the new generation of rural migrant workers is pulled by urban culture and is also drawn by culture from back home. With the gradual deepening of their urbanization, they are influenced by media content. After completing the resocialization of their identity, they are again drawn back into their original rural society. To a large extent, this changes the way they live in an urban environment. The awakening of memories of home does not have a negative impact on them. On the contrary, it redefines how the new generation of rural migrant workers adapt to and integrate into urban life.

3.3 The Recalling of Rural Memory: The Reconstruction of Migrant Workers' Collective Memory

People often believe that rural identity is traditional while urban identity is modern. Urban society is fraught with change, intense market competition, and risk. Rural migrant workers who leave home to work rarely have specific plans for the future. When they encounter dangers or difficulties in the city, the rural village is their last retreat. Nonetheless, the new generation of rural migrant workers thinks differently than their parents' generation. Many uncertain factors in the city and their inability to adjust cause them to "miss home", and think about retreating back to the village. However, most young people feel that "If I am not successful in the city, I can't show my face back home". Most members of the new generation of rural migrant workers, as fledgling adults, leave home to work in the city. After living in the city for several years, they gradually feel that they have adapted to the city and belong to the city. At this time, the rural homes which they have forgotten reappear in their living environment after their use of media, and in their interpersonal communications.

Xiao Lu, female, 21 years old, has lived in the city for two years and comes from a rural village in Jiangxi province. She currently works as a manicurist at

Haidilao in Nanjing. She has gone through many changes in the city, from missing home, to wanting to return home to work, to finding her present stable job in Nanjing and adapting to the city. For Xiao Lu, the reappearance of her home village was brought about by the special scenery of the locality. This type of scenery was sought after by urbanites, and its images were widely circulated on the Internet, which caused her to recall the beauty of her village back home.

> When I first came to Nanjing, people here only had a rough idea about Jiangxi. Actually, when I told people I was from Pingxiang, people did not know in what province it was located. They only knew that Jingdezhen[5] and Wuyuan[6] were in Jiangxi. In fact, I had never visited them before. I read on the Internet that in Wuyuan a lot of cole flowers blossomed in spring, and that many tourists visited the place. I felt that urbanites really had nothing better to do, cole flowers can be found everywhere! Why did they go to the trouble to run over there just to see cole flowers? The pictures on the Internet are very pretty, but our farmland back home also has such scenery. I do not feel there is anything special about it. When people say that Jiangxi is beautiful, I also feel quite happy.
>
> (Xiao Lu, female, from Jiangxi)

For the new generation of rural migrant workers, such outstanding local scenery has even become a medium for recalling one's native home. Their understanding of outstanding scenery back home in part comes from their own subjective intent and in part comes from passive acceptance (of other's opinions or portrayals in the media). The media contains many representations of rural life. However, certain media content not only enables urbanites to gain a better appreciation of such life but also awakens memories of home in the new generation of rural migrant workers living in the city.

From their worry and apprehension when initially coming to the city, to their urgency and resignation as recipients of information, members of the new generation of rural migrant workers have striven in their efforts and gone through trials during the process of urbanization. They also have "indulged in life's pleasures and forgotten their roots" as they adapt to the city. And ultimately the ideal adaptation to the city should be a combination of "rustic back home" and "modern living" to form dual cognition. During their reconstruction of rural culture, mediated emotional ties cause them to awaken from their urban environment, to establish a space which includes both urban characteristics and rural memory. Rural memory is a type of collective memory, which gives meaning to individual memory. In other words, individual memory is reliant on society. Under certain circumstances, the atmosphere constructed in a conversation between two people is a condition for creating collective memory, while the media satisfies conditions for the recreation of collective memory, thus becoming an important tool in negotiating dialogue.

At the same time, content carried by the media functions in another important way as a carrier which awakens memories of home to create a field in which memories of home can survive.

In reality, individual memory and collective memory among the new generation of rural migrant workers are reciprocally constructed. Collective memory is a reconstruction of history. History is passed down through a person's mental recollection and can also be transmitted through media. In the eyes of members of the new generation of rural migrant workers who have lived in the city for a certain length of time, the media is a tool for awakening their collective memory, to construct a perception of life back home.

This memory represents the inner world of the new generation of rural migrant workers. In the rural village, identifying with their local culture gives their lives a sense of belonging, while in the city, their identification with urban culture also enables them to have their own place in the city. Influenced by the urban living environment, daily use of mass media, and the ubiquity of interpersonal communication, the new generation of rural migrant workers finally establishes its identification with urban culture.

However, at the same time, with the reconstruction of memories of home, they have discovered a middle ground, a space founded on both rural and urban culture. In this social cultural space, the new generation of rural migrant workers is not only undergoing a process of continuous modernization to form an identification with the city but is also being drawn back into rural culture by the media, hence forming a new cultural space.

In summary of the preceding, the media environment enables the rebirth of memories of home among the new generation of rural migrant workers. Under the impact of the media, memories of home are continuously restored, to gradually become an indispensable component of adaptation to urban life. Even though their down-home rustic elements once made them feel low self-esteem, the new generation of rural migrant workers has actively integrated into city life by modernizing themselves. During this process, their memories of home have been continuously lost, which has caused them to fall into a dilemma. However, even as they were losing their memories of home, such memories were continuously being reawakened by the media, to form a situation in which balance was continually being broken and achieved. The new generation of rural migrant workers has a strong aptitude for learning, and proactively accepts new things. As such, they actively use the media and enthusiastically join the ranks of interpersonal communications.

More specifically, they use media as a tool for communication, to construct the culture of home in their emotional ties to folks back home. They also involve themselves extensively in new media, which enriches their self-perception and thus awakens their memories of home. Naturally, the process of reconstructing home memory will be affected by multiple factors. Media factors are significant in building this process of reconstruction. The media directly or indirectly creates a cultural community in which differences exist. Rural culture and urban culture are not immutable. On the contrary, they are continuously interacting, negotiating, and adjusting with one another, potentially resulting in the creation of a new culture.

4. Balanced Identity: The Road to Urban Adaptation From a Cultural Perspective

The term "rustic/native/rural" seems to have placed farmers in an isolated place from the city. For rural migrant workers who enter the city to work, especially the new generation of rural migrant workers, "getting rid of their rural identity" is something which they continuously strive to achieve in their integration into city life. Even if they "enjoy a good life" when they leave home to work outside, members of the new generation of rural migrant workers who seem to have obtained remarkable economic returns are also challenged by the aforementioned dilemma. Returning to their homes in the villages, they have many relatives and friends. During such important holidays as Qing Ming, Spring Festival, and so on, their home in the village is their "base area" (Xiong, 2013).

After freeing itself from the constraints of rural economic returns, the new generation of rural migrant workers begins to develop independently in the city. As we have observed in the present study, the impact of modern factors such as urban concepts of consumerism, career development, and culture, along with the influence of the urban media environment, have caused various modes of change, dilemmas arising from change, and the outcome of change for the new generation of rural migrant workers. As a matter of fact, we should also focus on memories of home as a deep-rooted social background, which, in fact, is also a type of cultural space that has positive significance for adaptation to and the inclusion of an urban environment for the new generation of rural migrant workers. Rural identity does not exist as an obstruction to integrating into city life.

On the contrary, during the continuous tug of war between rural culture and urban culture, the new generation of rural migrant workers has formed a multifaceted cultural identity, enabling them to better adapt to life in the city, while obtaining a strong sense of belonging. The significance of this research involves "rectifying the meaning" of rural culture.

While undergoing a rupture in its transmission, rural culture has also served as a bridge to span this break. Both in method and in content, all of these serve to guide the new generation of rural migrant workers on the road to urbanization. During this process, the road to urbanization also undergoes a transformation. Our research shows the road to urbanization involves a fusion of urban and rural culture. With respect to rural memory (memories of home), communication bridges the cultural gap, while guiding the new generation of rural migrant workers to mentally form a dual identity. At the same time, this destroys the principle of complete assimilation which previously had been fundamental on the road to urbanization. Based on the new principle of "seeking common ground while retaining differences", a cultural community has been established while maintaining the continuity of certain aspects of migrant workers' original culture. In the ongoing collision between urban and rural culture, these two can create a type of dual cultural space, thus achieving a cultural balance.

4.1 Dual Identity: The Possibility and Feasibility of Infusing Rural Memories With Urban Culture

In a broader Chinese social environment, the entry of tens of thousands of rural migrant workers into the city has naturally produced cultural diversity. And the phenomenon behind such cultural diversity is indeed the dual identity formed at an early stage in the minds of the new generation of rural migrant workers. When urbanites believe that only their way of life is civilized, healthy, modern, and correct, cultural prejudice has not been eliminated. Moreover, from the perspective of the new generation of rural migrant workers, when they still persist in chasing after urban civilization while covering up their rural culture, a real cultural community fails to be established. Actually, a genuine cultural community is a differentiated community, in which communication abolishes cultural centralism, that is, the cultural hegemony of urban culture upheld in people's minds.

This enables people to accept different cultures with an open mind. Specifically, media portrayal of rural social ecological environments, living customs, and other cultural attributes, involves an intuitive transmission of information to city dwellers, and constitutes a means of communication which awakens memory among the new generation of rural migrant workers. It may be said that rural memory, that is, memories of home, play an important role in coalescing with urban culture.

The dual identity which we propose is founded on how the new generation of rural migrant workers internalizes rural identity and urban identity in their dual identification with rural culture and urban culture. A differentiated community can only come into being when founded on this dual identity. Within this are communication factors which indirectly guide a series of processes to promote adaptation to an urban environment through their impact on rural memory. Dual identity specifically means that identity is a type of cognition and description of oneself, including multiple dimensions from economic to cultural. The new generation of rural migrant workers differ from traditional rural migrant workers in their objective for working in the city. The new generation of rural migrant workers does not merely want to satisfy its material needs. Survival rationale and development rationale consistently guide the orientation of their behaviour. Starting as "outsiders" in the city, they suffer economic discrimination, identity discrimination, and cultural discrimination. As they become "new citizens" they must achieve economic adaptation, personal identity, and cultural identity. From retaining memories of home (rural memory) to the rupture of rural memory and the reappearance of rural memory, the process involved is not linear but intermeshed. For the new generation of rural migrant workers, their inner cultural space passes through a process of struggle, abandonment, amnesia, recovery, and fusion. In such processes the media acts as both a messenger and a tool, on the one hand resolving the identity crisis and on the other hand reshaping personal identity.

Over the long term, the clash between rural memory and urban culture results in the formation of a dual identity in the minds of the new generation of rural migrant workers. This type of identity facilitates integration into urban life. From an economic perspective, they adapt to the consumerism of urban life and distance themselves from the economic rules of rural society which dictate reliance on the land and farming to obtain income. From a social perspective, the new generation of rural migrant workers, during the process of urbanization, gradually comes to possess an awareness of its own autonomy with respect to planning careers, views on marriage and love, civic awareness, and so on. Psychologically, they have developed a new understanding of self-identity. Even if they have embraced concepts frequently held by urbanites on freedom in romantic relationships, late marriage, and delayed childbirth, they follow the rules of rural society in carrying out ceremonial traditions. In addition, the new generation of rural migrant workers must strive to adapt to the local dialect and learn to speak *Putonghua* well. However, when contacting their family members, they must switch to using their own dialect. Naturally, they also roam around night spots such as clubs and drinking spots, frequenting such consumer venues as Internet cafes, KTV, bars, and restaurants. Moreover, during key holidays and festivals they will return home to take part in certain special ceremonial activities. The preceding phenomena are not contradictory but are merely a means by which the new generation of rural migrant workers balances between urban and rural life.

The two identities of "villager" and "new citizen" enable the new generation of rural migrant workers to assume a dual identity. On the one hand, they actively experience various new things in the city, while accepting the urban cultural order. On the other hand, they stay in touch with their family members living in rural society, while also obeying the moral culture and rules of rural society. In summary, the rational cognition of this dual identity creates this type of ecological balance in their lives. The formation of this balance is the foundation of cultural space and a type of community.

In the tradition of Western thought, Aristotle believes that people live in a community. However, with the affordances of the media growing day by day, contact among people and among groups, and the links which bond their communications are no longer subject to restrictions of traditional blood ties and regional affiliations. Throughout human history, the community has been a stable mass of people united by certain bonds in their communal life, including clans and tribes formed through blood ties, families formed through marriage and along blood lines, and nationalities formed by bonds of language, culture, and so on. And the new generation of rural migrant workers in the city possesses geographical connections identical to their fellow urbanites, living in the same physical space, and always strives to live in the same spiritual community as urbanites.

The cultural space in this venue is built on social, individual, group, and organizational interaction, relying on the combination of a certain mode and social standard to form a community in which lives are interconnected. Its members possess shared values, lifestyles, mutual benefits, and needs, along with a strong awareness of identity (Zhang, 2010).

Urban living and communication exchanges have given birth to a modern urban cultural space belonging to the new generation of rural migrant workers. This type of cultural space is not completely identical to the urban cultural space but is a common system in which heterogeneity is permitted to exist. With the rapid development of society, people's thoughts and ideas begin to be impacted by various forces, while the original meaning of the community is gradually lost. Hence, recognition of identity is a major factor in the generation of a community. The issues resolved by such recognition are, in fact, self-identity, sense of belonging, and sense of meaning.

When the new generation of rural migrant workers believes that it is impossible to maintain its rural identity in the city, and actively strives to embark on a course of modernization, their rural roots and the city fail to truly merge. On the contrary, the increasing distance between the rural environment and the urban environment results in a rupture of communication. They enter deeper into the urban communications environment and strive to become a member of the urban community. They completely break away from rural society and separate themselves from rural culture, even to the extent of believing that their native homes are places to which they will never return. However, it is communication which makes such a return a possibility. Returning to one's native place does not mean returning to live in rural society but means allowing rural culture to become re-established in an urban environment. The community of the new generation of rural migrant workers is not a cultural space founded on urban civilization but is a community which incorporates differences. Such differences originate from different rural cultures at various locations throughout China. Communication constructs a community which possesses differences. The new generation of rural migrant workers absorbs cultural characteristics from society to further generate a collective consensus. Utilizing the mechanism of communication, they obtain symbolic signs of urban and rural life. Based on the aforementioned methods, channels and tools of communications cause their rural culture to reappear.

In summary, with respect to the new generation of migrant workers, the journey from the rupture to continuance of communication is a process of evolution on the road to urban adaptation and social inclusion. Rupture of communication can form a cultural gap which may also be bridged by the media. From the perspective of rural culture, dynamic construction by the media has cast a new cultural space. Accordingly, memories of home (rural memory) are also a type of cultural space. From a macro perspective, it is communication which has enabled the recovery of rural memory and has enabled urban culture to move from a position of opposition to one of fusion, to bridge the gap between urban and rural culture. The road to urbanization thus undergoes further changes to form a type of differentiated community. In this continually deepening process of communication, rural memory possesses significant social value, while the meaning of urban integration moves from an urban bias towards a state of balance.

4.2 A New Form of Cultural Inclusion: The Question of Balance in the New Generation of Rural Migrant Workers' Adaptation to the City

The urbanization of rural migrant workers has been a significant problem during China's period of social transformation. Rural migrant workers' adaptation to city life has always been an issue of great concern to academia. Whether external factors of urban environment, national policy, and social class, or internal factors involving the subjective experience of the new generation of rural migrant workers, all of these should receive our full attention.

And the arrival of rural migrant workers in the city necessarily involves adaptation to urban life. In the context of China's national situation, from the most idealized perspective, the new generation of rural migrant workers must satisfy several conditions to adapt to urban life. Firstly, they must have relatively stable jobs in the city, jobs which can give them a good economic income, and enable them, as rural migrant workers, to interact with local people. In addition, when interacting with local people, they must accept and form values which are identical to those of local people.

Simply stated, the new generation of rural migrant workers' assimilation into city life includes three aspects: economic, social, and cultural. Of course, these three aspects of adaptation to urban life do not exist independently. These three aspects form a certain relationship in which they progress interactively. More specifically, economic adaptation is based on a urban foundation, obtaining a relatively high income, satisfying one's needs in the areas of materials and services, and catering to the trend of consumerism in the city. Social adaptation is a further requirement of living in the city and covers a broad scope. Accordingly, it is also an embodiment of the breadth (and extent) of assimilation into city life. Cultural adaptation may be said to be a spiritual or mental adaptation intimately related to the new generation of rural migrant workers' identification with urban life. Economic adaptation and social adaptation naturally can further advance cultural identity.

Hence, adaptation to urban life is a process which includes adaptation to external factors and adaptation to psychological factors. From the preceding text we can understand that the new generation of rural migrant workers' adaptation to the city involves adaptation at the economic, social, and cultural level. Their urban adaptation includes two aspects: one aspect involves adaptation to urban culture, while the other aspect involves the reconstitution of rural culture.

The extent of urban culture starts from nonexistence to become something tangible, evolving from the superficial to the profound, while memories of home frequently undergo contradictions. When rural identity amnesia occurs, the new generation of rural migrant workers are faced with a cultural vacuum. When their memories of home resurface, an important change will also occur in the position occupied by urban culture, to achieve an ideal balance.

In *The Polish Peasant in Europe and America*, the American sociologist William Isaac Thomas and the Polish sociologist Florian Znaniecki investigate Polish immigrants who came to the United States during the last years of the 19th century and the early years of the 20th century, to provide an understanding of the mental state of such immigrants. The process of modernization undergone by Polish farmers immigrating to the United States in fact holds great meaning as a reference with respect to the modernization undergone by China's rural population. Traditionally, Poland has been a country with elements of both Eastern and Western culture. Nonetheless, its mainstream culture is primarily Western.

The process under which Polish farmers immigrated to the United States was not merely one in which American culture was accepted; it was also a process of renewed Westernization. When Polish farmers came to live in the United States, there was two-way, interactive cultural transmission between both parties. At the same time, these Polish farmers made their own culture a part of American society (Thomas & Znaniecki, 2000). Many researchers on immigration have defined this as "dual identity", a type of balance in cultural inclusion. However, one fact which does not completely tally with research on Polish immigrants is that the new generation of Chinese rural migrant workers has not completely migrated to the city. Instead, they continue to travel back and forth between the village and the city. In a traditional sense, cultural inclusion among the new generation of rural migrant workers should be a type of adaptation in which rural migrant workers assimilate local culture and accommodate urban culture, making every effort to appear to be a member of the city.

However, this research proposes a new form of cultural inclusion, in which the new generation of rural migrant workers, in their cultural adaptation to the city, undergo a process which they themselves determine, whereby they define their adaptation to the city. This new form of cultural inclusion is a process in which balance is maintained, in which the two ends being balanced consist of memories of home and urban culture. When these two types of culture blend with each other, balance is achieved in urban adaptation. In this situation, the new generation of rural migrant workers will not feel pressure due to self-consciousness about their rural identity and will not feel low self-esteem for failing to assimilate into urban life. Achieving balance is not something which once it occurs undergoes no further change. Rather, it is a process of dynamic change. Cultural adaptation among the new generation of rural migrant workers inevitably involves finding a new balance among contradictions. The new generation of rural migrant workers obtains a wealth of information in their use of the media and interpersonal communications. The re-emergence of memories of home is merely one element among a multitude of information (sources). However, it is an element which cannot be overlooked.

The media on the one hand deconstructs the spaces occupied by urban culture and rural culture, and on the other hand reconstructs the two cultures. These two seem to be mutually opposed but ultimately merge with one another. The inclusion of migrant workers into urban life involves those workers obtaining a sense of belonging. This sense of belonging is not achieved in the context of cultural hegemony in a unilateral convergence with urban life: it is a reciprocal combination of urban culture and rural culture. This facilitates the creation of a dual cultural identity by the new generation of rural migrant workers to further form a new cultural space and find a balance between the city and their rural origins.

Notes

1 Translator's note: standard Mandarin.
2 Translator's note: Fei Xiaotong (1910–2005) was one of the foremost Chinese sociologists and anthropologists, noted for his studies of China's rural society and ethnic groups.

3 Translator's note: *ZTE* is a *Chinese* multinational telecommunications equipment and systems company headquartered in Shenzhen, Guangdong.
4 Translator's note: a uniquely Chinese event when the Chinese visit the graves of their ancestors, also known as Tomb Sweeping Day in English.
5 Translator's note: a city in southern Jiangxi province. Having produced porcelain for nearly 2000 years, Jingdezhen houses one of the world's most impressive collections of Chinese ceramic art and artifacts.
6 Translator's note: a county in Jiangxi province that is famous for the cole flower scenery.

References

Ding, W., & Tian, Q. (2009). The mobile home: A case study of new media usage and migrant workers' social relationship. *Journalism & Communication, 1,* 61–70+109.
Hu, X. (2008). Self-identity dilemma of the new generation of migrant workers in social memory. *China Youth Study, 9,* 42–46.
Huang, Y., & Liu, X. (2008). Linguistic identity and cultural psychology. *Journal of Ocean University of China (Social Sciences), 6,* 78–81.
Li, Q., & Li, L. (2014). Peasant workers' modernity and urban adaptation from the perspective of cultural inclusion. *Nankai Journal (Philosophy Literature and Social Science Edition), 3,* 129–139.
Liu, Y. (2009). The power of national identity: On the reconstruction of collective memory by mass media. *Journal of East China Normal University (Humanities and Social Sciences), 6,* 77–81.
Thomas, W. I., & Znaniecki, F. (2000). *The Polish peasant in Europe and America* (Y. Zhang, Trans.). Translin Publishing House.
Wang, G. (2010). Transplantation, structure and evacuation: The practical logic of the new generation of migrant workers to Chinese traditional culture. *The Journal of Humanities, 3,* 171–176.
Wang, H., & Sun, Z. (2015). Localism, modernity and group interaction: Migrant workers' hometown identity and its influence factors. *Shandong Social Sciences, 2,* 21–27.
Xiong, F. (2013). Local colour: Core mechanism and theoretical dialogue. *Journal of Anhui University (Philosophy and Social Sciences Edition), 2,* 139–144.
Yan, H. (2009). Collective memory and cultural memory. *China Book Review, 3,* 10–14.
Zhang, Z. (2010). Definition, notion and evolving – Literature review of community. *Science of Science and Management of S.& T., 10,* 14–20.

References

Allen, P. B. (2011). *Personality theories* (X. Du, Trans.). Shanghai Education Publishing House (Original work published 1994).

Baldwin, E. (2004). *Introducing cultural studies*. Higher Education Press.

Bao, L. (2005). An exploration of the time perspective of the life course theory. *Sociological Studies*, *20*(4), 120–133.

Bao, Y. (Ed.). (1997). *Cultural capital and social alchemy – An interview with Bourdieu*. Shanghai People's Publishing House.

Beck, U. (2004). *Risk society* (B. He, Trans.). Yilin Press.

Bi, Y. (2004). On the Bourdieu's theory of "field-habitus". *Academic Exploration*, *1*, 32–35.

Bourdieu, P., & Wacquant, L. (1998). *An invitation of reflexive sociology*. Central Compilation and Translation Bureau.

Cao, J. (2009). Communication technology and gender: A case study on the use of cellphone by migrant domestic women in Shanghai. *Journalism & Communication*, *16*(1), 71–77+109.

Cao, Y., & Liu, H. (2004). Urban migrant workers' cognition of self-image in mass media – A case study of Nanjing. In *China communication forum conference proceedings* (pp. 83–91).

Chang, J. (2015). Nostalgia with a pioneering stance: A study of the identity of Chinese internet culture producers. *Journal of International Communication*, *37*(5), 106–124.

Chen, F. (2007). From isolation to adaptation: The culture transition of migrant workers in Chinese cities. *Journal of East China University of Science and Technology (Social Science Edition)*, *3*, 84–87.

Chen, H. (2004). Research on the relation between mass media and social marginal groups: A case analysis of news on wage arrears for migrant workers. *Journalistic University*, *4*, 6–10.

Chen, Q. (2010). *Spatial mobility and rational choice – The action logic of migrant workers' migration in the context of financial crisis*, Master Dissertation. Northwest University.

Chen, S. (2003). Empowerment: A new perspective of the theoretical and practical approach for social work. *Sociological Studies*, *5*, 70–83.

Chen, X. (2002). *Qualitative research in social sciences*. Educational Science Publishing House.

Chen, X. (2004). Review and criticism: Review of the theory of media function. *Journal of Southwest Minzu University (Humanities & Social Sciences)*, *11*, 368–372.

Cheng, C. (2012). College students' social network, knowledge and status attainment: An empirical analysis based on investigation of college students in western China. *Youth Studies*, *4*, 22–34+94–95.

Conger, J., & Kanungo, R. (1900). The empowerment process: Integrating theory and practice. *The Academy of Management Review, 13*, 3 (Cited in Ding, W. (2009). New media and empowerment: A practical social research. *Chinese Journal of Journalism & Communication, 10*, 76–81).

Cooley, C. H. (1989). *On self and social organization* (F. Bao & Y. Wang, Trans.). Huaxia Publishing House (Original work published 1902).

Crane, D. (Ed.). (2006). *The sociology of culture: Emerging theoretical perspectives*. Nanjing University Press.

Cui, C., & Chen, H. (2007). A survey of social capital theory. *Journal of Tongling University, 4*, 25–30.

Ding, W. (2009). New media and empowerment: A practical social research. *Chinese Journal of Journalism & Communication, 10*, 76–81.

Ding, W. (2011). New media empowerment: Theoretical construction and case analysis – A case study of online self-organization of rare blood groups in China. *Open Times, 1*, 124–145.

Ding, W. (2014). *Mobile homelands – Community communication and identity practices of the "you county cab driver village"*. Social Sciences Academic Press (China).

Ding, W., & Tian, Q. (2009). The mobile home: A case study of new media usage and migrant workers' social relationship. *Journalism & Communication, 1*, 61–70+109.

Duan, J. (2004). The division of social classes and the manipulation and use of media in China. *Journal of Xiamen University (Social Science Edition), 1*, 44–51.

Fan, P. (2010). From communication technology to productive tool: A sociological research on the use of mobile phone by Chinese mid-and-low income classes. *Journalism & Communication, 1*, 82–88+112.

Fang, X. (2001). An investigation and analysis on the use of mass media in rural areas of Jiangsu province. *Journalism & Communication Review, 1*, 125–132+267+274–275.

Fang, Y. (2012). An analysis of medialized interpersonal relationship. *Journal of International Communication, 34*(7), 52–57.

Featherstone, M. (2000). *Consuming culture and postmodernism*. Yilin Press.

Feng, J. (2011). From strong ties to weak ties: A sociological analysis on the transformation of migrant workers' social network. *Journal of Southwest Agricultural University, 9*(12), 79–93.

Fiske, J. (2001). *Understanding popular culture*. Nanjing University Press.

Fiske, J. (2011). *Understanding popular culture*. Central Compilation and Translation Bureau.

Fiske, S. T. (2004). Social beings: A core motives approach to social psychology. *John Wiley and Sons*, 398–400.

Fu, P. (2006). Urban adaptability of young migrant workers: A perspective of sociology of practice. *Society, 2*.

Fu, P., & Jiang, L. (2007). Limitations and breakthroughs in studies of migrant workers' integration into city life. *The World of Survey and Research, 6*, 14–17.

Gao, M., & Zheng, X. (2013). City imagination and identity identification of rural residents: Evidence from Jiangsu. *Chongqing Social Sciences, 4*, 43–49.

Geoffrey, G. (2000). *Leisure in your life*. Yunnan People's Publishing House.

Giddens, A. (1988). *Modernity and self-identity* (X. Zhao & W. Fang, Trans.). Shanghai Sanlian Bookstore.

Gong, L. (2007). The different fields of view between Bourdieu and Marx on practice ideology. *Journal of Henan University (Social Science), 3*, 76–80.

Gu, X. (2001). Initial exploration on the structure of vocational value. *Exploration of Psychology*, *21*(1), 58–63.

Guan, J. (2011). *Portray, the media image of the mutation, and perspective – Analysis of media image of migrant workers on sina.com during the prosperity of network media*, MA Thesis. Southwest University.

Guan, L. (2014). Deconstruction and reconstruction of traditional interpersonal interaction patterns in the media environment. *Journalism Research Herald*, *5*(13), 55–56.

Guo, J. (2008). *Emotion sociology: Theory, history and reality*. Shanghai Sanlian Bookstore.

Guo, L., & Zhang, X. (2016). Modernity conflict and bridging between urban and rural cultures from the perspective of migrant workers. *Gansu Social Sciences*, *1*, 165–168.

Guo, X., & Chu, H. (2004). Rural to urban: An empirical study of social distance between migrant workers and urban residents. *Jianghai Academic Journal*, *3*, 91–98.

Hamilton, A., Jay, J., & Madison, J. (2009). *The federalist papers* (F. Cheng, H. Zai, & X. Shu, Trans.). The Commercial Press (Original work published 1788).

He, X. (2007). Changes in Chinese farmers' values and their impact on rural governance: A survey of Dagu Village in Liaoning province. *Study & Exploration*, *5*, 12–14.

He, X. (2011). A female migrant worker's life of working in the city for 30 years: A perspective based on life course theory research. *China Youth Study*, *5*, 37–41.

Hsu, L. K. (2001). *Under the ancestors' shadow* (F. Wang & L. Xu, Trans.). Taipei Nantian Bookstore.

Hu, J. (2001). Mass media and leisure cultural life of urban youth – A questionnaire of 592 urban young people. *Research of Youth*, *1*, 6–10.

Hu, X. (2008). Self-identity dilemma of the new generation of migrant workers in social memory. *China Youth Study*, *9*, 42–46.

Huang, D. (2009). Demonizing and reproduction of power relations: A content analysis on news coverage of migrant workers. *Northwest Population Journal*, *3*, 35–40.

Huang, H., Ma, Q., & Liu, D. (2008). Migrant workers' adaptation to cities and its influence on their social cognition. *Journal of Southwest University*, *34*(6), 148–152.

Huang, Y., & Liu, X. (2008). Linguistic identity and cultural psychology. *Journal of Ocean University of China (Social Sciences)*, *6*, 78–81.

Inkeles, A., & Smith, D. (1992). *Becoming modern: Individual change in six developing countries*. China Renmin University Press.

Jiang, L. (2003). Urbanity & the adaptability of rural-to-migrant workers. *Social Science Research*, *5*.

Jiang, L. (2007). Cross-cultural communication: Culture shock and how to deal with it. *Sino-US English Teaching*, *3*, 61–65.

Jing, E., & Yang, L. (2008). *An analysis of the problems of metropolis image constructed by mass media*. Communication Studies and China: Fudan University Forum.

Knowles, M. (1989). *Andragogy in action* (Y. Lin, Trans.). People's Publishing House.

Levinson, P. (2004). *Cellphone, the story of the world's most mobile medium and how it has transformed everything*. China Renmin University Press.

Li, H. (2003). Strength of relationships & virtual community: A new perspective on rural migrant workers' research. In P. Li (Ed.), *An economical & sociological study of Chinese migrant workers*. Social Sciences Academic Press.

Li, H. (2009). *Rural communication and urban-rural integration: An empirical study of Beijing natives and rural migrant workers*. Social Sciences Academic Press.

Li, H., & Qiao, T. (2005). Stigmatization and labelling: The media image of migrant workers. *21st Century*, *7*.

Li, J. (2002). Multiple separation of labor market in China and its impact on labor supply and demand. *Chinese Journal of Population Science, 2*, 1–7.

Li, J. (2003). Urban and rural psychology and life world – From Simmel to Schutz. *The Journal of Humanities, 4*, 149–156.

Li, P. (1996). The social network and social status of migrant workers in China. *Sociological Research, 4*, 42–52.

Li, Q. (1995). Emotions of rural-to-urban workers and social conflicts. *Sociological Research, 4*, 63–67.

Li, Q. (2004). *Rural-to-urban migrant workers and social stratification in China.* Social Sciences Academic Press.

Li, Q., Deng, J., & Xiao, Z. (1999). Social change and personal development: A paradigm and methodology for life course research. *Sociological Study, 6*, 1–18.

Li, Q., & Li, L. (2014). Peasant workers' modernity and urban adaptation from the perspective of cultural inclusion. *Nankai Journal (Philosophy Literature and Social Science Edition), 3*, 129–139.

Li, Y. (2005). News media and "the underprivileged" in western communication studies: A literature review. *Journalism & Communication, 2*, 48–55.

Li, Y. (2006a). On mental capital. *Wuhan University Journal (Philosophy & Social Sciences), 59*(6), 741–746.

Li, Y. (2006b). Portraying a heterogenous group of people: A narrative analysis of news coverage on "PIL" in China's urban newspapers. *Journalism & Communication, 13*(2), 2–14.

Liang, Y., & Wang, S. (2007). Migrant workers' access to public health information. *China National Conditions and Strength, 3*, 43–44.

Lin, N. (2004). *A theory of social structure and action.* Shanghai People's Publishing House.

Lippmann, W. (2002). *Public opinions.* Shanghai People's Publishing House.

List, F. (1983). *The national system of political economy* (W. Chen, Trans.). The Commercial Press (Original work published 1841).

Littlejohn, S. (1999). *Theories of human communication.* China Social Sciences Press.

Liu, N. (2008). *Study on leisure lift style of rural labors in urban architecture industry – Based on investigation of rural labors in Wuhan architecture industry,* MA Thesis. Huazhong Agricultural University.

Liu, Y. (2009). The power of national identity: On the reconstruction of collective memory by mass media. *Journal of East China Normal University (Humanities and Social Sciences), 6*, 77–81.

Ma, H. (1998). On leisure theory in the field of cultural spirit. *Qilu Journal, 3*, 98–106.

Ma, H. (2003). The evolution of leisure, historical cultural and philosophical perspectives. *Studies in Dialectics of Nature, 1*, 55–65.

Ma, H. (2005). Culture, cultural capital and leisure: More reflections on recreational issues. *Studies in Dialectics of Nature, 10*, 68–73.

Ma, J. (2006). *Bar factory: A study of urban culture in southern China.* Jiangsu People's Publishing House.

Ma, S. (2012). Investigation and reflection on the leisure life of the new generation of migrant workers – An empirical study based on 186 new generation of migrant workers in Beijing. *The Border Economy and Culture, 12*, 164–166.

McLuhan, M. (2000). *Understanding media: The extensions of man* (D. He, Trans.). The Commercial Press (Original published in 1964).

Ministry of Culture of People's Republic of China. (2011). *Opinions on further strengthening the cultural work of migrant workers*. www.mcprc.gov.cn/xxfbnew2011/xwzx/lmsj/201112/t20111203_213449.html

Pamela, J. (Eds.). (2003). *Communication yearbook 27*. Routledge.

Pan, Z. (2007a). Social exclusion and predicament of future development: An empirical study of migrant workers in China. *Zhejiang Social Science, 2*, 96–103.

Pan, Z. (2007b). Social classification and group symbolic boundaries – The case of migrant workers' social classification. *Society, 4*, 48–67+206.

Poster, M. (2000). *The second media age*. Nanjing University Press.

Qin, M. (2005). A study on the construction of emigration identity. *Zhejiang Social Sciences, 1*, 88–94.

Qiu, L. (2013). *The world factory in the information age: New working-class network society*. Guangxi Normal University Press.

Qu, J. (2001). Strength of relationships in real life: The life trajectory of rural migrants in Chinese cities. In L. Ke & Hanlin Li (Eds.), *Off-farm migrants in large Chinese cities*. Central Compilation & Translation Press.

Ren, Y. (2012). Localized social capital and social integration of migrants in urban China. *Comparative Economic & Social Systems, 36*(5), 47–57.

Rosaldo, R. (1994). Others of invention: Ethnicity and its discontents. *Voice Literary Supplement, 82*.

Scott, J. (2007). *Weapons of the weak: Everyday forms of peasant resistance*. Yilin Press.

Shen, Y. (2003). Obligatory relationship: Beyond the emotional or instrumental relationship. *Chinese Journal of Sociology, 9*, 21–25.

Shi, B. (2010). An analysis of the social distance between the new generation of migrant workers and urban residents. *South China Population, 25*(1), 47–56.

Singerhoff, L. (2009). *Why we need rituals: The meaning, power and support of the heart* (Y. Liu, Trans.). China Renmin University Press.

Soja, E. (2008). Postmetropolis. In M. Wang, et al. (Eds.), *The city culture studies, a reader*. Peking University Press.

Sun, L. (2000). Process-event analysis and the state-farmer relations in contemporary China. In *Tsinghua sociology review* (Special ed.). Lujiang Publishing House.

Sun, L. (2003a). *Cleavage: The Chinese society since 1990s*. Social Sciences Academic Press.

Sun, L. (2003b). The new dual structure between urban and rural areas and the flow of migrant workers. In P. Li (Ed.), *An economical & sociological study of Chinese migrant workers*. Social Sciences Academic Press.

Tang, X. (2005). *Mass media and rural-to-urban migrant workers*, PhD. Thesis. Nanjing Normal University.

Tao, J. (2003). Media exposure of rural migrant workers: A case study of Xuhui District in Shanghai. *Journalistic University, 4*.

Tao, J. (2004). A study on the influence of mass media on migrant workers' perceptions. *Journalism & Communication, 11*(2), 10–15.

Tao, J. (2010). A study of migrant workers' interpersonal communication behaviors and influencing factors. *Journalism & Communication, 19*(5), 97–104+112.

Tao, J., & Xu, H. (2012). Personal modernity and interpersonal communication of the new generation of migrant workers – An empirical study based on survey data in Shanghai. *Journalistic University, 1*, 80–86+108.

Tarde, G. (2008). *Laws of imitation* (D. He, Trans.). China Renmin University Press (Original work published 1890).

Thomas, W. I., & Znaniecki, F. (2000). *The Polish peasant in Europe and America* (Y. Zhang, Trans.). Translin Publishing House (Original work published 1918–1921).

Tian, Q. (2012). The use of new media and the modernization construction of migrant workers: The case of taxi drivers from Hunan Youxian in Shenzhen. *Modern Communication, 34*(12), 28–32.

Tong, Z. (2011). Career development and work adaption: Urban practice of the new generation of migrant workers. *China Youth Study, 1*, 10–14+41.

Wacquant, L. (1989). Towards a reflexive sociology: A workshop with Pierre Bourdieu. *Sociological Theory, 7*.

Wan, L. (2012). Research on social interaction of online learning community based on QQ group. *E-Education Research, 33*(9), 54–58+68.

Wan, M., et al. (2006). The outlet and modernization of Chinese farmers – Reading Polish peasants in Europe and America. *Hubei Social Sciences, 1*, 102–104.

Wan, T. (2010). Housing levels and housing consumption of the new generation of migrant workers – A comparative analysis based on intergenerational perspective. *China Youth Study, 5*, 47–51.

Wang, C. (2001). The social recognition and integration of a new generation of rural migrants in China. *Sociological Research, 3*.

Wang, C. (2003). Social mobility and the change of social status of migrant workers. *Journal of Jiangsu Administration Institute, 4*, 51–56.

Wang, C. (2006). Watch out for rural migrant workers' "belief in fatalism". *Chinese Cadres Tribune, 5*, 1.

Wang, C. (2011). Analysis on the media image representation of migrant workers in films – A case study of the films with the theme of migrant workers in China from 2001 to 2010. *Southeast Communication, 8*, 49–51.

Wang, F. (2007). The relationship between mass media & migrant workers: A case study of People's Daily's coverage of rural migrant workers. *Research on Development, 1*, 45–48.

Wang, G. (2010). Transplantation, structure and evacuation: The practical logic of the new generation of migrant workers to Chinese traditional culture. *The Journal of Humanities, 3*, 171–176.

Wang, H., & Sun, Z. (2015). Localism, modernity and group interaction: Migrant workers' hometown identity and its influence factors. *Shandong Social Sciences, 2*, 21–27.

Wang, K. (Ed.). (1988). *Sociology dictionary*. Shandong People's Press.

Wang, X. (2004). Mass media and the urbanization of rural migrants. *Journal of Wuhan University of Technology (Social Science Edition), 4*, 467–470.

Wang, Y. (1995). Review of lifestyle research. *Sociological Studies, 4*, 41–48.

Wang, Y. (2011). A sociological interpretation of knowledge of spiritual capital. *Academimc Forum, 34*(2), 169–173.

Wang, Y., & Zhang, D. (2004). Re-socialization of migrant workers in the urbanization process. *Journal of China Agricultural University (Social Sciences Edition), 1*, 9–13.

Wei, S. (2004). Mass media and the discourse power of farmers: The case of rural migrant workers' suicidal jumping from high-rise Building. *Journalism & Communication, 2*, 16–20.

Wen, Y. (2011). *Research on the status of information contact and urban integration of the migrant workers in two different residential models*, Doctoral Dissertation. Central South University.

Xie, J. (2008). Empowerment in communication studies. *Chinese Journal of Journalism & Communication, 4*, 33–37.

Xin, B. (2005). A new interpretation of modern people's way of life. *Theoretical Investigation, 5*, 46–48.

Xiong, F. (2013). Local colour: Core mechanism and theoretical dialogue. *Journal of Anhui University (Philosophy and Social Sciences Edition), 2*, 139–144.

Xu, B. (2007a). Social networks and interpersonal communication of migrant workers moving to cities. *Journal of East China University of Science and Technology (Social Science Edition), 22*(3), 92–96.

Xu, C. (2007b). The social mentality of the new generation of migrant workers in urban life. *Science of Social Psychology, 10*, 57–59.

Xu, C. (2007c). Will the new arrivals settle down? A study on the adaptability of a new generation of migrant workers in Chinese cities. *South China Population, 4*(22), 52–59.

Xu, C. (2010). Ways of migrating into the city and occupational mobility of migrant workers: Comparative analysis of two generations of migrant workers. *Youth Studies, 3*, 1–12+94.

Xu, X. (2008). On media prejudice and discrimination in news coverage of rural migrant workers. *Journal of International Communication, 2*, 40–43.

Xu, X. (2009). Media projection of a special group – A study on the image of migrant workers in media representation. *Journal of International Communication, 10*, 42–45.

Xu, X., Ren, M., & Wu, M. (2009). The media representation of rural migrant workers: Realities and causes. *Modern Communication-Journal of Communication University of China, 4*, 39–41.

Yan, C. (2007). The transformation of the consumption mode of migrant workers in cities of the Yangtze River Delta – An investigation on the consumption of migrant workers in eight cities of Jiangsu province in the Yangtze River Delta. *Jiangsu Social Sciences, 3*, 224–230.

Yan, H. (2009). Collective memory and cultural memory. *China Book Review, 3*, 10–14.

Yang, D. (2005). Communication and the articulation of migrant workers' rights and interests. *Contemporary Communications, 6*, 3.

Yang, H. (2010). *The hidden world – Women's belonging and meaning of life in a water village in Southern Hunan*, Doctoral Dissertation. Huazhong University of Science and Technology.

Yang, S., & Xie, X. (2008). How does mass media guide the socialization of migrant workers? *Southeast Communication, 9*, 35–37.

Yang, Y. (2012). Internet media literacy of the new generation of migrant workers. *Journal of China Institute of Industrial Relations, 2*, 81–85.

Ye, J., & Wang, Y. (2009). The media "discourse" missing in the process of migrant workers entering the city of and its reconstruction. *Chongqing Social Sciences, 10*, 37–40.

Yin, X. (2014). Media constructed "city space": A discussion from the perspective of communication study. *Journal of Hangzhou Normal University (Social Sciences Edition), 36*(2), 118–124.

Yu, S., et al. (2011). Empirical study on information demand of migrant workers in Guangdong province. *Journal of South China Agricultural University (Social Science Edition), 3*, 67–71.

Yu, X., & Pan, Y. (2008). Consumer society and remarking the subjectivities of "new generation of female migrant workers". *Sociological Studies, 3*, 143–171+245.

Zeng, Z. (2003). The re-established social network of migrant workers and its internal flow of resources. *Sociological Research, 3*, 99–110.

Zhai, X. (2003). Research on Social mobility and relationship trust: Relationship intensity and job-seeking strategies of migrant workers. *Sociological Studies, 1*, 1–11.

Zhang, C. (2011). Modernity and marginalization: A discussion on the characteristics, problems and outlets of the new generation of migrant workers. *Academic Journal of Zhongzhou, 3,* 98–102.

Zhang, T. (2006). Public opinions in the context of a mediated society. *Modern Communication (Journal of Communication University of China), 5,* 12–15.

Zhang, Z. (2007). Social capital and employment of migrant workers. *Comparative Economic & Social Systems, 6,* 123–126.

Zhang, Z. (2010). Definition, notion and evolving – Literature review of community. *Science of Science and Management of S.& T., 10,* 14–20.

Zheng, X. (2011a). *Rural communication: An empirical analysis and strategy discussion based on the audience.* Zhejiang University Press.

Zheng, X. (2011b). On the new generation of peasant workers' adaptation to city life: From the perspective of communication. *Nanjing Journal of Social Sciences, 3,* 71–77.

Zhou, B., & Lv, S. (2011). An empirical study on the use and evaluation of new media of the new generation of migrant workers in Shanghai. *Journalistic University, 2,* 145–150.

Zhou, H. (2004). The media discourse of Chinese farmers and their access to mass media. *Press Circles, 3,* 46–47.

Zhou, M. (2004). The culture adaptability and personal identification of retained young migrant workers in Chinese cities. *Society, 5,* 4–11.

Zhou, X. (1998). The impact of migration and rural experience on the modality of off-farm workers in Chinese cities: A comparative study on two local communities in Beijing and Wenzhou City, Zhejiang Province. *Sociological Research, 5,* 14.

Zhu, L. (2002). On the adaptability of rural-to-urban migrant workers. *Jianghai Academic Journal, 6,* 82–88+206.

Zhu, L., Zhao, L., & Wu, J. (2010). Half-initiative pattern vs. constructive pattern: Social adaptation patterns of the new generation of the migrant workers. *Journal of Gansu Administration Institute, 4,* 4–10, 126.

Index

adaptive capital 171–172
alienation 134–135, 137–138, 143, 177, 193
assimilation 3–4, 134–135, 156, 199, 314, 318

blood relation 37, 139, 178, 305
Bourdieu, Pierre 250–251, 255–256, 275, 284, 321–322, 326

capital accumulation 198, 201, 281
career planning 99, 203, 218–220, 227
career quotient 220
collective power 221
communication channel 7, 23, 130, 139, 141, 227–228
communication studies i, v, 1, 4–7, 10, 14, 52, 78, 143, 202, 323–324, 326
consumer culture 258–259, 261, 267, 270, 280–284
consumerism 53, 106, 220, 305, 314, 316, 318
consumption vi, 2, 5, 7, 9, 30, 39, 52–53, 75, 76, 98, 119–122, 147, 243–244, 257–285, 326–327
consumption behaviour 98, 257–258, 260–261, 266, 271, 274, 276, 279–280, 282–284
continuing education v, 174, 181
Cooley, C.H. 78, 84, 322
cultivation 146, 162, 165, 275
cultural identity vi, 264, 266, 279, 283, 286, 296, 304, 314–315, 318–319
cultural inclusion 52, 317, 319–320, 324

disadvantaged 157, 159, 196, 199
discrimination 3, 5, 14, 33, 65, 75–76, 87, 89–90, 141, 157, 268, 281, 303, 315, 327
dual identity 82, 142, 314–316, 319

economic capital 201, 275
education i, ii, v, 2, 8–9, 11, 13, 16–18, 22, 41, 50, 54, 56–60, 62, 64–65, 89, 97, 101, 103, 111, 126, 137, 155–156, 158, 174, 176, 178, 181–183, 190, 199–200, 202, 213, 231, 236, 247, 263, 272, 274–277, 282, 284, 297, 306–307, 321, 326
emotional quotient 220
emotional solace 194
emotional ties 53, 86, 119, 293–295, 306, 308, 312–313
enhancement 81, 99, 155, 162, 165, 171, 223
entertainment 20, 61, 121, 124, 135, 140, 143, 146–149, 152–153, 157, 164, 172, 208, 210, 219, 231, 235, 237–238, 241–246, 248–249, 252–255, 259, 262, 267, 273, 275–278, 280

field i, 4, 7, 9, 12, 46, 78, 82, 88, 97–98, 124, 149, 161, 167, 179, 190, 204–205, 211–212, 223, 244, 247, 249–252, 254–256, 258, 264, 273–275, 278–279, 299, 303, 310, 312, 321–322, 324
field survey 12, 244, 252, 275
Fiske, J. 266, 271–272, 279, 285, 322

habitus 249–252, 255, 321
heterogeneous capital 139
household registration system 1, 53, 83, 199
hukou 283
hysteresis 155

identity awareness 268, 279, 281, 284
identity construction v, 53, 79, 303
identity crisis 83, 296, 315
identity reconstruction 80
information barrier 155, 162, 171–172
information communication technology 75

information explosion 146
information literacy v, 146–147, 149, 152, 154–155, 157, 159, 162, 165, 170–172
information sharing 191–193
information tool 146, 159–162, 170–171, 198
insiders 193, 226
intelligence quotient 221
Internet, the 4, 7, 12, 42–44, 46, 48, 50, 54, 60–62, 75–79, 95, 99–102, 108, 111, 114, 119, 122, 127–128, 130–133, 136–137, 147, 155–157, 159, 162–164, 169–171, 178–179, 181, 187–188, 190–192, 194–196, 200, 205, 211–212, 219, 228, 238, 243, 245, 248, 253, 257, 261–262, 265, 271, 275–278, 280, 282, 305, 308–309, 312
interpersonal communication v, 20, 26, 38–39, 49–50, 72, 79–83, 102–107, 110–112, 115–119, 125–126, 129–130, 132–145, 147, 150–152, 154, 172, 182–183, 186, 188–189, 195, 204–205, 208–210, 212, 218, 221, 223, 225, 227–228, 296–297, 311, 313, 319, 325, 327
interview i, 11–13, 24, 45, 55, 62, 68, 70, 72, 87, 89, 108, 110, 120, 124–125, 127, 129, 133, 148, 152–153, 155, 168–169, 179, 184–185, 189, 204, 209, 212, 235, 242–243, 258, 260, 284, 289–290, 295, 299, 303, 309, 321
involution 138, 142–143

job acquisition 212, 218
job-seeking 178, 182, 197, 211, 230, 327

kinship 37, 149–150, 159, 192, 199, 204, 206, 211, 228, 295

latent capital 200–201
left behind 18, 21, 57, 92, 133, 216, 296
leisure activities 13, 19, 48, 153, 232–234, 237–238, 241–247, 252–253
leisure life vi, 120, 124, 231, 234, 237, 239, 241–244, 246, 248–258, 324
life experience 6–8, 10–11, 36, 49–51, 70–71, 79, 89, 92, 95, 119, 144, 159, 164, 168–169, 177, 181, 186, 201, 203, 213, 216, 231, 237, 242, 252, 255, 283
life spaces 12
living condition 2, 5, 17, 33, 37, 39, 101, 106, 125, 146–149, 159, 231, 289
looking-glass self v, 53–84

marginalized 65, 68, 75, 116, 122–123, 178, 197, 267, 272, 281–283, 292, 296, 302–303
mass media 4–9, 13–17, 20, 26, 40–42, 48–50, 52, 60, 68–69, 74–75, 78–79, 83, 86, 96–99, 101, 105–106, 112, 115–117, 146, 163, 165, 170, 175, 179, 181, 190, 192–193, 198–199, 205–208, 210–211, 225, 228–229, 237, 243–244, 246, 256–258, 261, 267, 271, 273–275, 280, 282–285, 303, 305, 313, 320–328
material symbol 76
McLuhan, M. 47, 52, 324
media empowerment 140, 196–198, 201, 229, 252, 254, 322
media environment 5, 7–9, 12, 60, 75, 79–80, 82, 116, 141, 143–147, 154–155, 163, 199, 201, 242–243, 246, 251–252, 268, 275–276, 313–314, 323
media support vi, 203–230
mediatization 144
migrant worker i, v, vi, 1–21, 23, 26–43, 45–60, 62–206, 208–223, 224–239, 241–264, 266–296, 298–306, 308–328
mirror image v, 16–52, 78
mobile phone 7, 21, 40, 43–44, 48, 50, 61, 69, 75–76, 99, 101, 113, 115, 122, 127–128, 130–133, 136–138, 147, 152–153, 155, 159, 162, 170, 202, 245, 256, 306–307, 309–310, 322
mobility dilemma 175
modernization i, 6–7, 9, 33, 47, 101, 105, 110, 118, 138, 174, 183, 207–208, 226, 241, 294, 303–304, 313, 317–318, 326
modernize 70, 138, 176, 258, 264, 272, 280, 283–284, 303

new citizens 258, 261–264, 268, 279–284, 315
new generation of migrant workers i, v, 1–2, 4, 7, 10–11, 13–14, 52, 72, 74, 76, 78, 80, 82, 84–85, 90, 95, 106, 112, 116–120, 122, 125, 128, 130, 132, 134, 135, 138–140, 142–143, 146–147, 149–161, 163–172, 174, 176–181, 184–186, 191–193, 196–197, 199, 201, 203, 208–209, 211, 217–218, 223, 225–231, 235, 244–245, 256, 283, 317, 320, 323–328
new media i, ii, iii, 12, 42–44, 46, 48, 50, 52, 54, 60, 75–78, 83, 99–102, 105–106, 112, 115–116, 118–119, 127–128, 130–136, 138–146, 152, 155, 159,

169–170, 179, 187–188, 191–193, 196–197, 200, 202, 205–208, 210–211, 218–220, 227–229, 242, 305, 313, 320, 322, 326, 328

occupational attainment 211
off-farm worker 1, 7, 10–11, 15, 203, 285, 328
organizational communication 186, 204, 222, 227–228
outsiders 13, 31, 34, 41, 46, 63, 72–74, 88–89, 107, 120, 155, 157, 159, 226, 272, 300, 309, 315

para-social interaction 141
peer relationship 192
planning for life v, 85–118
platform 62, 76–77, 83, 100, 130–136, 143, 145–147, 149, 154, 160–161, 165, 167, 171, 187, 189, 191–193, 195, 197, 200–201, 208, 211, 219–220, 227, 238, 261, 270–272, 308–309, 311
power structure 197
prejudice 15, 34–35, 49, 78, 82, 145, 156–158, 268, 271, 315, 327
primary relationship network 131, 140, 178, 208, 210–211, 226, 228
professional adaptation vi, 203–204, 208–210, 215, 218, 222, 225–228
professional consciousness 218, 226
public opinion 7, 47, 159, 230, 268, 271–272, 279, 285, 294, 324, 328

qualitative research 10–11, 13, 321

radio 17, 48, 60–61, 78, 146–148, 152, 154–155, 205, 243, 245, 276
renqing 126, 141
rural conservatism 157
rural identity 74, 93, 203, 206, 286–287, 291–296, 299–300, 302, 304, 311, 314–315, 317–319
rural memory 204, 304–305, 311–312, 314–315, 317
rural self 78–79
rural-urban migration i, ii, iii, 5, 146–147, 149–150, 152, 155, 163–165, 168, 170–171

self-actualization 125, 252–255, 273, 283
self-development 100, 104–105, 111, 174–175, 179, 184, 189, 192, 200–201, 242, 246, 248–249, 254–255, 272–273

self-efficacy 196–197, 201, 223, 225, 244–245, 253
self-esteem 158, 179, 236, 307, 313, 319
self-generated capital 196, 198, 201
self-identity 54–55, 62–63, 69, 72, 74, 76, 78–79, 81–82, 95, 196, 198, 202, 218, 225, 281, 286, 296, 300–304, 316–317, 320, 322–323
self-learning 172, 179, 186, 188, 192, 194, 196, 198, 200, 219
self-presentation 140
self-realization 198
sense of belonging 53, 67, 92, 119, 124, 125, 200–201, 229, 262, 290, 293, 295, 303, 313–314, 317, 319
smartphone 43, 45, 60, 75, 96, 101, 151–154, 159, 208, 226, 241, 246, 258, 267
social capital 4, 10, 48, 70, 86, 101, 104, 135–136, 139–142, 171–172, 193, 198–202, 219, 228, 252–253, 275, 296, 322, 325, 328
social inclusion i, 13, 98, 105, 112, 115–116, 119–120, 132, 139–140, 142–146, 168, 171, 174, 193–194, 196, 203, 229, 286, 290, 298, 302, 317
socialization 3–5, 7, 9, 14–15, 54, 63, 82, 89, 99, 101, 105, 127, 140, 225, 311, 326–327
social networks 10, 90, 101, 104, 118–119, 141–142, 150, 194, 198, 200–201, 212, 218, 225–226, 229, 249, 268, 295, 305, 327
social order 266, 274, 279, 294
social power 199
social relationship 10, 39, 70, 105, 111, 139–140, 199, 229, 242, 248–249, 274, 288, 320, 322
social resources 43, 139–140, 174, 197–199, 228–229, 253, 274–275, 278
social security 87, 120, 198, 272
social welfare 2
stereotypes 7, 68, 76–77, 122, 271–274, 278
stigma 14, 123, 268, 271, 273, 279, 284–285, 303, 323

Taobao 101, 111, 122, 133, 136–137, 187, 220, 238, 261, 267, 270
television 4, 17–19, 24–25, 38, 40–42, 44, 48–50, 56–57, 60–62, 69, 71, 78, 87, 95–98, 101, 108–111, 114, 122, 124, 131, 133, 145–148, 153–154, 168, 175, 196, 205, 211, 237, 244, 258, 305, 308–311

Tencent QQ 13, 152
thirdspace 280
traditional mindset 155, 163, 165, 170

urban adaptation 52, 98, 119–120, 130,
    139–140, 143–144, 146, 171, 177, 193,
    196, 198, 203, 211, 286–287, 290, 298,
    302, 304, 314, 317–320, 324
urban-rural dichotomy 200, 268
urban self 78

virtual social networks 218
virtual space 100, 102, 105, 132, 134, 136,
    140, 142–145, 193, 195

WeChat 13, 45, 77, 99, 114, 131–132, 149,
    151–153, 188, 192, 208, 238, 248–249,
    305
Weibo 13, 44, 131, 133–134, 153–154,
    188–189, 191, 208, 238, 305,
    309, 311